fRENCH LEAVE 3

Richard Binns

CHILTERN
HOUSE

During the last two years more than a thousand letters have arrived at Chiltern House from *French Leave* readers; I estimate that they contained well over three thousand references to the various establishments recommended in the previous edition. Not surprisingly, those informative letters have considerably influenced the content of *French Leave 3*.

Some of you have suggested that I discuss, as frankly as possible, our mutual eating-out disasters in France. One reader wrote: 'We can only afford one outing each holiday to any of the *best* restaurants. Tell us what's good and bad about them before we decide where we spend our hard-earned francs.'

I agree – it's an excellent suggestion. You will see that I have accepted the challenge; there's a sharper cutting edge to this third edition. I am not influenced by reputations; I take chefs' skills as I find them – on their plates. Of course, some of our mutual 'unfortunate' visits may have been on chefs' off-days; though some aspects of their operations that I criticise have nothing to do with one bad day's work. None of us are infallible: chefs, readers or this author. But I have tried to apply consistent, experienced judgement to all my comments; I hope that this new approach will help *French Leave 3* readers to assess just what their francs will buy for them before they visit any of the *best* restaurants. (There are 15 bottles of Champagne to be won; see the foot of page 4.)

An important caveat: President Mitterrand's new exchange controls have forced the French to holiday at home. This means that two-thirds of them will rush to the popular coastal areas in the period from mid July to mid August. If you want to do the same be sure to book rooms as early as possible or, better still, use *French Leave 3* and enjoy inland France instead.

Cover photographs taken by the author. Front cover: top left – Lake Annecy at Duingt (Savoie); top right – *hors d'œuvre* at the France, Fayence (Côte d'Azur); centre, middle row – abbey park at the Cirque de Consolation (Jura); bottom left – Raguenès-Plage (Brittany); other pictures taken at Grasse and Cannes.

Back cover: centre, top row – Abbaye de Royaumont (Ile de France); bottom left – château at La Rochepot (Burgundy); bottom right – Mont Blanc in the early morning, Chamonix (Savoie); other pictures taken at Grasse and Cannes.

All photographs in *French Leave* were taken by the author other than the one facing page 225 – the work of Frank Clancy. The watercolours facing pages 97 and 128 were painted by John Stanton and Denis Pannett – both artists are neighbours of the author. Both paintings are reproduced with their permission.

My thanks to Pierre Couppé – a *French Leave* reader who lives in France – for his many helpful suggestions and his constructive comments and advice.

Published by Chiltern House Publishers Limited, Chiltern House, Amersham Road, Amersham, Bucks HP6 5PE

ISBN 0 9507224 6 4
Editing assistance Jane Watson. Christine Starmer

Maps by H. Plews Gregory. Illustrations by Richard Binns

Cover design by Frank Clancy, Clan Creative Ltd., 4 Montagu Row, London W1

Typeset by Art Photoset Limited, 64 London End, Beaconsfield, Bucks

Printed in Great Britain by Butler & Tanner Limited, Frome, Somerset

Entente Cordiale – Dead or Alive?

Since I started my do-it-yourself publishing enterprise I have received over a thousand letters and press reviews from every corner of the globe. One alarming aspect has emerged from some of that correspondence and press comment: all of you seem to love France and accept the proposal that 'Everyone has two countries – his own and France'; but some of you dislike the French a great deal – finding them unacceptably hostile.

The letters and reviews make sad reading: 'on the whole the English like France but not the French' . . . 'haughty superiority' . . . 'the French don't deserve France' . . . 'supercilious' . . . 'unfriendly and bloody-minded' . . . 'thoroughly bad-tempered – as only the French know how to be.'

The French can be enigmatic and contrary, that's for certain; they were voted by North American travel writers to be a nation of people as unfriendly as Russians and Iranians. I myself have had a few thoroughly bad experiences – and, more than once, witnessed some unpleasant treatment being meted out on unsuspecting, innocent visitors. However, I've come across a far, far greater number of exceptional examples of kindness, helpfulness and friendliness and in no way whatsoever can I condone the cruel hostility one seems to encounter these days in the press; I suspect it has become the fashion to knock the French as often and as hard as possible. Much of the criticism is sheer hypocrisy. Are Anglo-Saxons that perfect? Hardly.

The French are a proud, strongly nationalistic race; we should try to copy that patriotism – not deplore it. We should try, too, to emulate their exceptional industry and the great respect they have for the 'family'; and we could also study their turbulent history – no wonder they are suspicious of others.

It would be tragic if France drifted further apart from Britain and her oldest Allies across the Atlantic in North America. Certainly the French themselves could try to tone down what often can be arrogant and unfriendly behaviour; be a little less serious at times and to develop a stronger sense of humour; find out a good deal more about their neighbours; and be less selfish and ruthless in pursuing their own interests.

But I believe even more strongly that **visitors to France should meet the French more than half-way**; they should make an effort to understand some of the language and they should try to seek out and meet more French people – rather than just following the crowded tourist tracks to the same endless ancient monuments. Always begin any conversation – whatever the situation – with a smiling *Bonjour*; the French put a high value on that common courtesy. Visitors should also see more of provincial France where the real heart of the country still beats strongly; and to avoid the cities whose inhabitants are no more nasty than those found in any other metropolitan jungle. Theodore Zeldin, in his book *The French*, wrote: "French people often feel that they are misunderstood by foreigners, that they are insufficiently appreciated, unloved.' They are right; but we must share the blame equally with them for that.

Maurice Buckmaster, the head of the French section of the Special Operations Executive (SOE) during 1941-45, has urged that we all breathe new life into the Edwardian *Entente Cordiale* – signed in 1904. In 1984 it is incumbent on all of us to do just that – whether we live across the Channel or on the other side of the Atlantic. We must all work harder to improve the harmony between our countries; a family relationship that currently appears to be in a bad state of health and a great deal less cordial than it ought to be. (See page 126.)

The chefs' chef Three years ago, when I published the first
French Leave, I made an unequivocal observation about one
genius of a chef: today, that opinion remains unchanged;

*as a cuisinier and restaurateur (not necessarily the same
thing), Frédy Girardet – a Swiss – stands head and shoulders
above his famous contemporaries in France or elsewhere.*

Can Frédy's restaurant be called the best in the world? Can he be
called the best 'French' chef in the world? Impossible claims –
how can one person make such judgements. But what can be said
is that an ever-growing number of professional critics and
sceptics, each of whom knows a varying number of the world's
greatest restaurants and chefs, all come to one conclusion;

each of them knows of none better.

With few exceptions other famous chefs who have tested his
skills agree with this proposal and more of them make the
pilgrimage to Crissier than to any of the three-star shrines. The
reason why I am so critical of Bocuse and Vergé is because I
compare them with Girardet. As a Swiss Frédy wins no Michelin
stars – but, as Allan Hall said: 'He is the 'King' of chefs and
deserves to wear a crown.' (See page 146 – and photo, page 32.)

A 'team' of favourite French chefs The alphabetical list below
is an idiosyncratic selection – a 'rugby team' of my XV favourite
chefs: Girardet is not included – he would be the manager; two
are ladies; three are three-star chefs; seven are some of the young
chefs who make a nonsense of the 'star' system (Costa is chosen
mischievously as the 'joker in the pack'); and Choisy is the
epitome of so many unpretentious French *cuisiniers* providing
superb value for money. (Page numbers in brackets.)

Blanc, Georges (189)	Mme Gardillou (116)	Meneau (75)
Chabran (205)	Giraud (158)	Mme Menneveau (73)
Choisy (98)	Guérard (287)	Pic (209)
Costa (156)	Kéréver (57)	Rayé (271)
Delbé (231)	Lallement (85)	Turin (39)

Dozens of other chefs are also particularly recommended; see
pages 6 and 12 for an explanation of the symbol Ⓡ

A 'team' of favourite young chefs In addition to the seven in the
first list, I also recommend a further XV.

Arrambide (291)	Clément (171)	Paul (188)
Bajade (261)	Fanton (242)	Philippe (36)
Barnabet (77)	Germain (229)	Robin (260)
Bourhis (61)	Guichaoua (87)	Thuriès (157)
Bras (119)	Mazère (117)	Trama (121)

There are many more within this edition of *French Leave*.

A 'team' of favourite cuisinières Support the lady chefs of
France – it's amazingly difficult for them to succeed. Two were
included in my favourite 'team' of XV. Here are XIII others.

Barral (120), Beauvalot (230), Benoît (243), Bex (119), Bodinaud (240),
Castaing (202), Cayron (120), Crouzier (168), Garnier (145), Gouin
(272), Gracia (290), Guillou (57), Venturino (103).

My favourite 'cuisine' region My vote goes to the Southwest
(page 284). The most disappointing? Normandy (page 212).

Brickbats Which were my most disappointing restaurant meals
during the last two years? There were many: a few were bad
enough not to warrant inclusion; others are explained within
these pages. XV of the latter were particularly unhappy visits – a
'rugby team' of the *best* restaurants where the chefs failed to
score! See if you can identify them. Send your list – one per
reader – to me at 4 Amersham Road, Amersham, Bucks, England
by 31st March, 1984. 15 bottles of Champagne to the first 15
correct entries opened on April 1st – an appropriate date!

So you want to be a do-it-yourself publisher?

Many of you will not know how I came to be a do-it-yourself publisher. Some of you do know the story and have suggested that it should form a small part of this third edition of *French Leave*. For those of you who are interested, here are a few facts about the author and his long-suffering, loyal family.

I am 46 and was married in 1960: my wife, Anne, and our two children – Andrew (21) and Sally Anne (19) – have shared with me many of my numerous visits to France during the last three decades; though, sadly, these days I make most of my 'research' trips on my own – Anne stays at home to look after the shop!

Chiltern House is in fact our home in Amersham – it gave its name to our do-it-yourself publishing venture; everything functions from our home. We get tremendous satisfaction from the planning, the research, the writing, the typing, the design of each page, the line drawings, the drafting of maps, the taking of photographs, the compilation of glossaries and indexes, the typesetting, the proof-reading (the most exasperating job of all – any errors are mine), the marketing, the distribution, and the book-keeping – just about everything. The only thing we don't possess is a printing press. Four friends have been associated with various aspects of the venture: Jane Watson, Christine Starmer, Frank Clancy and H. Plews Gregory (Greg).

It proved to be a fateful day indeed in June 1980 when we decided to gamble everything and to borrow heavily against our home to bring out the first edition of *French Leave*. Why did we do it? A derisory contract from a major publisher was on offer; although I had no experience of publishing, I knew the world of business inside out and I felt sure I could do better on my own.

The whole family supported that tough decision with great courage. They all felt the bigger gamble had been taken five years earlier when I resigned from a successful career with an American computer company to become self-employed; offering my business experience to companies in the role of a data-processing adviser, management training consultant and computer broker. From 1955 to 1975 I had trained first as an accountant and then worked for 15 years in the world of computers – in systems, sales and management; a strange mix of experience for a do-it-yourself publisher but, in reality, a good combination of qualifications. Some of you have asked if I am an overweight gourmet? I'm not – it's the financial risks that keep both the pounds and hair at bay! *Nouvelle cuisine* helps, too.

My present-day attachment for France all started with a teenage interest in maps and motor rallying. Subsequently as a navigator I won many of the best-known British events in the period 1960 to 1965; and as an organiser I was the winner of the first British Rally of the Year award in 1962. Like one of my readers in Alderney, I, too, consider myself a 'Francophiliac Mapoholic'. Why not join the club? The only qualifications are an appetite for both maps and cuisine, a lack of fear about ever getting lost, and a desire to explore dead-end roads.

My family and I laughed long and hard when all our four previous books made the U.K. bestsellers' lists (unbelievably without one second's help from TV); but much greater delight has come from the vast number of letters we have received. I count myself fortunate that I have encouraged so many of my readers to seek out and enjoy the best of France.

So you want to do-it-yourself? Well, it can be done: on the debit side you could lose a lot; on the credit side is the excitement and fun that comes from doing everything from soup to nuts – and, in my case, eating and drinking a great deal more in between.

Abbreviations

menus	range of cost of fixed-price menus (*prix-fixe*)
alc	minimum cost of three courses from à la carte menu (only shown where no fixed-price menus available)
rooms	number of bedrooms and price band range (inclusive price for the room). Establishments are obliged by law to offer bedrooms without demanding that clients dine in their restaurants
cards	accepted: AE – American Express; DC – Diners Club; Visa – as shown. (Always check with establishments)
closed	annual and weekly dates of closing (a **caveat**; check ahead)
post	local post code, village or town name, *département*
phone	area code (in brackets) and telephone number (see page 320)
Mich	Michelin yellow map number on which recommendation is located (see page 320 for general advice on maps and guides)

Price Bands

A	40 to 80 Francs	**C**	150 to 250 Francs
B	80 to 150 Francs	**D**	Over 250 Francs

D2, D3, D4: multiply **D** by figure indicated. All price bands include service charges and taxes; wine is not included in meal price bands, nor are breakfasts included in room price bands.

Maps & Text

Villages and towns in which recommended restaurants and hotels are located are shown in one of three ways on each regional map and in each regional text: within the regional text the villages and towns are listed alphabetically – in one of **three categories**, explained below. Examples:

Category 1: Name of village/town   Name of hotel
        CAMBO-LES-BAINS   **Errobia**

These are **base hotels** – always *sans restaurant* (no restaurant) and always in a quiet or secluded location.

Category 2: Name of village/town   Name of restaurant with rooms/hotel
        ARGELES-GAZOST   **Thermal**

These are recommendations where, for me, **cuisine takes second place**. Cooking will be of an adequate standard; often very good though not up to category three levels. Other factors count as much in making the recommendation: a value-for-money stop; perhaps the site; attractive surrounding countryside; its usefulness as a 'base' (ignoring its restaurant when I suggest you do so). **Do not expect great things from the chef.**

Category 3: Name of village/town   Name of restaurant/hotel
        PLAISANCE   **La Ripa Alta**

These are recommendations where **cuisine takes pride of place**; they include both the simplest and the greatest of establishments.

Some recommendations are special favourites of mine: either they offer particularly good cuisine or they have some other attractive feature. Their entries are highlighted with this symbol – Ⓡ

Some establishments offer their clients particularly good value for money: the term **good value** is used to highlight these recommendations.

Most of the wine villages and wine-producing areas referred to in the regional texts are shown in coloured print or by coloured shading on each regional map. Examples: ● *Madiran*   *Jurançon*

Regional maps also show cheese-producing areas. Example: **Iraty**

Places of special interest – towns, villages, rivers and other scenic attractions – referred to in each regional text (in **bold** print) are shown on the maps as follows: ● **Pau**   ● **Azur**   **Adour**   **Pyrénées**   **Landes**

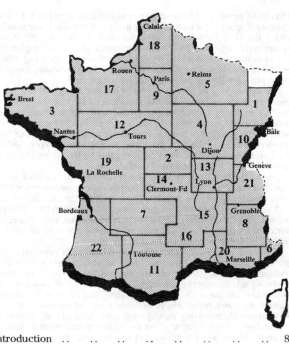

Introduction

This third edition of *French Leave* is the fifth new book I have published since that eventful day in June 1980 when my family and I decided to become do-it-yourself publishers. What an amazing three years it has been – my life has changed completely. I have never worked so hard yet I have never enjoyed any other period of my life so much; I know that most of you would happily swop places with me without much prompting.

The one aspect of this new way of life that has given me most pleasure is the volume of correspondence I have received from readers in every corner of the globe; many letters have come from seasoned, experienced Francophiles – one or two of whom have been visiting France for 40 years or more. Every writer has received a reply from me; the views and opinions expressed in the letters have contributed considerably to the many changes made in this third edition of *French Leave*.

During the last three years my own attitudes and outlook have changed significantly; you could hardly expect otherwise, when you consider that I now spend many months of the year in France and spend the rest of the year assembling material, writing, publishing and distributing the various books that have emerged during that time. These changes of outlook are easy to spot – you'll find some of them in the first few pages.

The most important change in my thinking has been an ever-growing admiration for the vast majority of French hoteliers and restaurateurs and, above all, the country's supremely talented chefs – particularly the younger ones and the few *cuisinières* (who take on the men so successfully). I have been fortunate enough to meet many chefs in their working environment: to accompany them on buying expeditions; to hear of their financial headaches; to see them at work for 18 hours at a stretch; and to listen to the views of their wives (and husbands in a few cases). The chapter called *A day in the life of a chef and his wife* is my own way of bringing to your notice facets of their lives which you, the reader, may never have considered before.

Life has been very tough for hotel and restaurant owners in France during the last two years: high inflation; price freezes; increased indirect taxation and social security levies; these have been just a few of their problems. One cruel setback was the introduction, in 1982, of a punitive 30 per cent tax imposed on all business entertaining. To top it all, the French eat out less now – higher personal taxes see to that.

Other preferences and pet hates have hardened. Generally speaking I would far rather visit the restaurants of young chefs working hard to establish reputations for themselves. I still enjoy the simpler places where straightforward, unchanging dishes are presented with honesty and I treasure any value-for-money discoveries – at all levels, from the simplest to the greatest. I dislike pretentiousness in any form more than anything else – sadly, it appears too often: in presentation of food; in the manner and approach of owners and staff; and in the fixtures and fittings found in establishments.

One vitally important resolution of mine has been protected at all costs; I pay my way without one penny of help from **any** other source. I have turned down offers of sponsorship, advertisements in these pages, free travel arrangements or cars provided free of charge; in fact anything that prejudices my freedom to give my true opinions. Recommendations made in this book represent my personal choice; as do deletions and criticism. No one pays to be included in *French Leave*.

Put simply, I represent you, the reader. Like you, I pay my own bills; it certainly sharpens your wits and objectivity when you are not backed by expense accounts paid by employers. For the record the majority of my visits are made 'incognito'. To my readers, however, I am anything but 'incognito'.

I make no claim to special qualifications for assessing chefs' talents, other than my experience of French cuisine over a period of 30 years. During the last three years I have visited hundreds of restaurants: simple and humble, expensive and great – in every corner of France. Therein lies the secret – consistency of judgement. I can compare each great chef against his peers in other French regions; I may relish a simple place at midday and feel utterly miserable that evening in a luxury restaurant.

Consistency of judgement is perhaps the main shortcoming of all the famous guides. Accolades awarded to an individual chef can vary considerably from one guide to another – that perhaps is inevitable, as we are all fallible. But it is amazing how wide the regional discrepancies are within any one guide. The feature I like most about the Gault Millau guide is that it awards *toques* for the **cooking** skills of a chef; no attention is paid to fixtures and fittings, service, toilets and the like.

By far the most important conclusion that has emerged for me during the last few years is that there is an ever-increasing band of young chefs whose cooking skills match most of the great three-star names. Of course their amenities cannot and do not match the luxurious places – but what arrives on your plate certainly can and does. There must be a score or more of these young chefs who I would choose to visit rather than the majority of the famous *cuisiniers*. I get thoroughly bored by the lack of imagination shown by many of those household names; if only more Americans would follow the example of their Anglo-Saxon cousins and give them a miss – that might then wake them out of their complacent stupor. They have the talent; but like fat cats with big bank accounts some have become lazy and are resting on their laurels. I know dozens of you agree with me.

To show you how I have responded to your views and my own changing outlook, here are some of the more famous establishments that have been dropped from this edition: **Pyramide** at Vienne; **Auberge du Père Bise** at Talloires; **Chapon Fin** at Thoissey and **Les Santons** at Grimaud. Others like the Bon Laboureur et Château at Chenonceaux and the St-Barnabé at Murbach have been omitted; no wonder these two lost their Michelin stars last year – your letters gave early-warning clues. Others, too, have fallen by the wayside; over five per cent of the entries in the last edition. Whenever I get a very serious complaint I make an 'incognito' visit. In some cases I write and point out the complaint made; owners do take notice – the lack of further comment bears witness to that.

I ask only one favour of any establishment recommended in this book – that they look after you to the best of their ability. You visit them out of choice and because of my recommendation so make certain the owners know you have *French Leave*. Ask owners to give you any help you need; and use the phrases listed on pages 28 and 29 – full of ideas for you.

I have received scores of compliments about you, my readers, from hoteliers and restaurateurs recommended in previous editions of *French Leave*. They consider you their best clients.

Thank your for your support. I hope that this much improved and greatly extended third edition of *French Leave* helps you to enjoy the best of France and that – last but not least – it makes it easier for you to get to know the French themselves.

If only . . .

(The observations that follow represent my own opinions plus the many and varied views of numerous readers.)

• more of my North American readers would visit the restaurants of younger, up-and-coming chefs rather than exclusively giving their custom to the great *cuisiniers*. Some of the least enjoyable meals that I ate in 1982/83 – out of hundreds – were at the so-called *best* restaurants; some of the finest were created by unknown, young, talented masters.

• Michelin would continue the shake-out of their starred restaurants that they started in 1983. In my opinion there are still many that do not deserve to retain past accolades.

• all English-speaking visitors would use menu-decoders. I've seen people (not *French Leave* readers) eating pike *quenelles* and also hot *chèvre* cheese in pastry thinking they were chicken and fish respectively! Chefs frequently ask: "Why do so many visitors order *salade* and *entrecôte*?" It's the same reason.

• more people would determine carefully – before ordering – the prices of *apéritifs* and liqueurs.

• more chefs would introduce themselves to diners. Some like Pic and Chapel are quiet, introverted folk – though Guérard is hardly a shy type; but there is no excuse for any of them if some can do it. Of course, some arch-truants may not be there to present themselves in the flesh anyway.

• Auberon Waugh and Arthur Eperon would publish the detailed information I have asked them for; please see the entries for La Napoule (page 102) and Vonnas (page 189).

• more care was given to the welcome and attention of clients at the prestigious, expensive places. As one reader wrote: 'It is no use to be welcomed by a junior committee of staff and to be ignored by senior members.'

• some top chefs would limit their restaurant seating to a maximum of 60 or so diners. Standards certainly do slip badly when 100 or more clients are being served at any one time.

• some restaurants would stop weighing their tables down with advertising rubbish – of all types. If you see it, why not ask for it to be removed – they'll soon get the message.

• more *menus dégustations* were offered (really small portions of several specialities). I'm not hoodwinked by Chapel's jibe that *menu dégustation* means 'menu disgusting': is it because it requires great organisation in the kitchen to provide them?

• some restaurants would offer more half-bottles of wine. If young Alain Rayé at Albertville can provide a choice of over 50, why cannot Bocuse, for one, list even 10?

• more French chefs would remember the most important words of advice that exist in any cooking – *faites simple*. They should try to emulate the best aspects of Japanese cooking – many *nouveaux* chefs have already done so.

• more of the *nouveaux* masters would stop turning vegetables into baby-food purées; some offerings are inedible.

• more chefs would remember that small portions are what most people want. Mercifully, the French on the whole comprehend the health benefits that accrue from frugality.

• more restaurants would follow the example of one or two adventurous places and offer dishes on their à la carte menus at half price – for half portions; or let clients share them.

• more British and North American visitors to France would stop assuming that value for money means quantity.

• some restaurateurs, who also provide bedrooms, would remember that their responsibilities extend to ensuring that baths, showers and toilets work; that things like paper cups in bedrooms, broken toilets and stale toilet smells lingering in corridors will not do. (Even multi-starred places are guilty.)

• some establishments would stop serving those minute, foil-wrapped mouthfuls of butter. The smallest of places don't do it – so there are no excuses for some luxury hotels stooping to such penny-pinching meanness. When hotels in dairy regions like Normandy and the Jura provide them – together with 'Longlife' milk – their owners should be sent to the guillotine!

• hotels would try to improve the quality of bread offered at breakfasts. Far too often it is stale – far too often there is no variety. Breakfasts seem to be too much trouble for some.

• some restaurants, too, would improve their appalling bread offerings. Bocuse, Vergé and even the Troisgros brothers have a lot to learn from people like Girardet and Alain Rayé.

• restaurants would stop treating bread and coffee like gold. Be like Oliver Twist – pester them for further helpings.

• chefs would ensure that waiters don't serve *le grand dessert* as a sickening jumble of mixed-up tastes – more akin to the pig trough. Though often it's the greedy client who is at fault.

• some restaurants would stop serving such awful *petits fours* (it's just as true for appetisers); six-year-olds could do better. 'After-Eight' mints would be preferable – the French love 'em.

• more visitors to France would react by walking out when the worst two 'cons' are pulled on them: the first is the habit of offering only an à la carte menu at the start of a meal; the second is the shameful lie when one is told that cheaper rooms are full – but the most expensive rooms are free. (A variant of the latter is to make a family occupy two rooms when a large family room remains unoccupied.)

• some establishments (particularly a few pretentious, luxury places) would stop using plastic flowers. If cost is a problem they should try gathering wild flowers or use dried varieties. I suspect it's sheer laziness on the part of owners.

• more places would stop setting themselves up as 'boutiques' selling dresses, pictures, pottery, tapestries, toys, T-shirts, perfumes, antiques, etc., etc. I've seen them all.

• more owners and staff would ignore the TV set during meals. Their priority should be their clients – not the 'goggle-box'.

• my North American readers would write direct to places and book – not through agents. Use my model letters – and avoid the ludicrous 'rip-offs' that I have heard about from some of you.

• an ever-growing number of French hotel and restaurant owners would adopt the motto of a U.K. hotel group: 'Bigger Smile – Better Value'. They should pay considerable attention to the service that their staffs provide – supercilious, slovenly and insolent service should be stamped out; many readers complain about this. As one said: 'Staff have an incredible habit of disappearing when any work is in the offing – such as helping with luggage or providing a drink between meals.'

• more people would take great care to agree *pension* terms before accepting rooms.

• all establishments would remember that they are now obliged by law to offer bedrooms without demanding that clients dine in their restaurants – high season or not.

• some Anglo-Saxons would take more notice of the skills of *cuisiniers* rather than the efforts of decorators. And why is it that some U.K. guides on France concentrate more on wallpapers and furnishings than the pleasures of the table? One example: of 70 words used to describe Marc Meneau's home at St-Père (Burgundy) not one referred to his cooking talents.

How to use French Leave

In this third edition I have made some important changes in the way I classify my hotel and restaurant recommendations. They are now listed under one of **three categories**: refer to the key on page 6 for an explanation of how the three classifications are shown in each regional text and on each regional map.

The **first** category is for **base hotels**. These have been a success with readers – so much so that I have researched hard to discover many more. There are over 100 listed in this new edition: all of them are *sans restaurant* and have quiet or secluded sites. Use them either for a stay of several days – to explore a region; or for one night – when you want to eat at a nearby restaurant (without bedrooms) or one that does have them but where room charges are excessive.

The **second** category of recommendation is where, for me, **cuisine takes second place** (all of them have bedrooms). At these establishments cooking will be of an adequate standard; often very good though not up to category three levels. Other factors count as much in making the recommendation – for example: a value-for-money stop; the site; nearby attractive countryside; its usefulness as a 'base' (ignoring its restaurant when I suggest you do so); and so on. One important tip (this applies to category three as well): avoid agreeing terms for an overnight stay where a fixed price is quoted for a meal, bed and breakfast – the set meal you get usually offers little or no choice.

The **third** category is where **cuisine takes pride of place**; recommendations range from the simplest to the greatest of places and at all price levels. Many of the restaurants have hotel facilities. Remember that *pension* meals and low-price menus do not always provide 'gastronomic experiences'. For most entries some specialities are listed – remember they do vary from season to season and from year to year.

In each category some recommendations – both simple and expensive – are particular favourites of mine: they offer either especially good cuisine or they have some other attractive feature; their entries are highlighted with this symbol – ⓡ

Some recommendations offer their clients particularly good value-for-money cooking or amenities – ideal for readers with small budgets. The term **good value** highlights these places.

A list of general **caveats**: in France a *garden*, a *park*, a *lounge* or a *living room* has many versions and do not always expect the British or American equivalents; always try to check annual and weekly closing dates – changes can and do occur; just a few establishments listed in this guide do not have bedrooms with baths or showers – these are clearly indicated; and please do remember that *simple* means what it says. Do not expect miracles – sadly, too many people expect too much, too often.

Some general guidance on **prices**: all price bands include service charges and taxes; wine is not included in meal price bands; breakfasts are not included in room price bands – nor is it compulsory to have them or in that case pay for them; room price bands indicate the price for the bedroom, not per person.

Other **tips**: for good value choose a fixed-price menu; have no qualms about sharing dishes; cheapest menus are not always available on Sundays or public holidays; try always to book ahead; take a portable cold-box – to keep picnic purchases fresh; inspect rooms before accepting them; to pay deposits, buy foreign currency cheques from banks – but check their fees first; most petrol (gasoline) stations are modern and have toilet facilities; an easy way to start a conversation with French people is to offer to take a picture of them using their own cameras.

In the first edition of *French Leave* I wrote that 'the next decade will be a better time than ever to explore France.' Three years into that decade have proved my words to be true. The country has everything: real value-for-money hotels and restaurants – to suit any budget; seductive scenery; a rich heritage of historical treasures; a vast range of beaches and coastlines; majestic mountains; lovely lakes; superb rivers; vast tracts of forests and woods; and, to top it all, an immense larder of culinary delights.

How can you ensure you enjoy your share of all those appealing and alluring pleasures? In the three years since I started to give all my time to researching and writing about this richly endowed nation, I have come to realise, more than ever, that maps are the essential key to opening the door to any country. A good large-scale map will repay its small outlay a thousand times over. Immerse yourself in maps – pore over them; every hour spent studying them will be time wisely spent. If you are going to spend, say, 6,000 or more francs on a French holiday, then put aside 60 francs (just one per cent) to buy large-scale maps of the regions you are going to explore; you'll not regret it.

Remember *French Leave* is for the motorist and recall, too, that I deliberately do not direct you into the centres of large towns and cities, where noise, traffic, navigation and parking are a nightmare. Make intelligent use of your car. Capitalise on the autoroute system to get from one region to another – quickly and safely. But, to get the best from any region, head your car up the quiet lanes to discover the uncrowded sights. My three books – *French Leave, France à la Carte* and *Hidden France* – all help you to find those hidden corners.

How does *French Leave* help? There are various ways to explore each region. You may already have your own base: a hotel, a flat, a villa, a *gîte*, a caravan or a tent. If not, the three categories of recommendations within this guide will help you select the best hotels and restaurants – at all price levels.

Method One Use a base hotel whenever you can: all of them are *sans restaurant* (no restaurant); all of them have quiet or secluded sites. You have the freedom to eat wherever you wish – be it lunch or dinner, both, or not at all – and at every price level. You should also get a good night's sleep at all of them.

Method Two The second way of seeing a region would be to stay at an establishment with hotel facilities, moving on from spot to spot every day or two. Each entry in the guide shows where bedrooms are available. Establishments are obliged by law to offer bedrooms without demanding that you dine in their restaurants. In some cases – in my second, new category – I suggest you give the restaurant a miss anyway.

Method Three You can permutate base hotels and other establishments from region to region, staying a varying number of days at each – remembering that the law now forbids establishments to demand that you dine in their restaurants; you are free to eat anywhere. If you choose *pension* terms – agree them beforehand.

How else does *French Leave* help? May I implore you to use the *Glossary of Menu Terms* (much extended); may I urge you to refer to the lists of specialities (easily spotted as they're in the second colour) and cheeses detailed in each region and may I remind you to make use of the *Index of Wines* and the extended *Index of Cheeses* – both in France and at home. Finally, may I suggest you read *So you think you know that road sign?* – it's full of surprises. The *General Notes* on page 320 contain useful advice to help you enjoy the best of France, too.

A day in the life of a chef and his wife

Jean was half-awakened by the shrill rattle of the alarm clock – it was 5 a.m. He raised one eyelid, then closed it; momentarily he slipped again into the enveloping arms of half-conscious sleep – the sudden realisation that it was Tuesday brought him sharply to his wide-awake senses.

How he hated Tuesday – the start of his six-day week after the blessed relief of a lazy Monday. He slid gently out of bed – Jacqueline was oblivious to the noisy alarm. Quietly he tiptoed past the rooms of his young children. A cold shower took two minutes of his time, he dressed quickly and skipped shaving – he had to arrive at the market by 6.00, 70 kilometres away.

The Renault 18 Estate moved silently and swiftly along the deserted, misty roads – it was May and just getting light. Jean had plenty of time to reflect on his lot in life. At 34 he had already made a name for himself; Gault Millau, with an enthusiastic recommendation, had given him a flying start three years earlier, a year after he and Jacqueline had bought the old auberge. Two months ago the first Michelin star had shone above the auberge – it had been a proud day for them. At last those 12 years of working at Roanne, Crissier and London had paid off.

The market was busy and crowded. Juggernauts had already arrived from all parts of France: they had brought fish and shellfish from both the Atlantic and Mediterranean ports; fresh spring vegetables and fruit from Provence; cheeses, butter and cream from Normandy; and poultry, *grenouilles*, *cailles* and *pigeons* from Bresse. Jean moved rapidly around the market – apparently relaxed, but missing nothing, and with the time to exchange greetings with his important suppliers; they, too, were proud to share in his success. His final purchases were armfuls of flowers; Jacqueline prided herself on her displays.

By 7 a.m. he had left the market and already he had a working outline of what that day's menus would be. On the drive back to the auberge he clarified his thoughts; he changed his three fixed-price menus and his à la carte menu every day. A master stroke had been the purchase of a small word processor a year earlier: within its memory it already had stored the menu descriptions of many scores of his specialities; he could manually add any new creation of his in a few seconds. Each day, after giving his 'toy' some simple instructions, it would whistle out as many copies of his menus as he required – rapidly, neatly and with a professional print-like presentation. It made the art of being a skilled *nouvelle cuisine* chef so much easier – though he prided himself that his menus always included a few regional favourites.

At 8.00 he arrived back at the auberge; Jacqueline and the youngsters were up and about and for twenty minutes they shared an animated breakfast. Then she whisked them away to school, to return as quickly as she could to ensure that their 16 bedrooms were all spic and span before the first guests of the week arrived, later that day; Tuesday was the only day each week when there were no guests requiring breakfast.

A second, more leisurely shower left Jean refreshed and ready for the battle of the week ahead. His first job was to ensure that his three kitchen staff were hard at work. He gave them a quick idea of what the menus would be and he saw to it that they made a start on as much of the preparatory work as possible. Jean was a particularly skilled *pâtissier* and took great care in the preparation of his appetisers, superb desserts and delectable *petits fours*. To complicate matters Jean baked his own bread – offering six varieties to his clients at both lunch and dinner.

By mid morning he was free to play with his word processor

'toy'. Occasionally it would break down – then all hell would let loose. This Tuesday it went well. For the first time that day he remembered that a *cuisinière* colleague – on her day off – was paying him a visit for lunch. She was 10 years older than Jean and was now known throughout France as one of the few top lady chefs. He admired her greatly; she had brought up two children – they were now in their teens – and she had a husband who supported her efforts with fantastic enthusiasm. Jean shook his head in awe at the energy she managed to find each day; the same was true – to a lesser extent – of Jacqueline.

He decided on the spur of the moment that he would use his visitor as a guinea pig for a new speciality he had perfected. Each year Jean spent his annual holiday in February visiting the legendary chefs; in Burgundy he had relished a new cheese course offered by Marc Meneau and called a *feuilleté de fromage chaud sur salade*. Jean had experimented for months to create his own version; he would prepare that especially today and see what reception it would receive from his visitor and her husband.

At 11.30 Jean and Jacqueline joined the kitchen staff and their four young waiters for their own hurried lunch. It gave him the chance to encourage and – without them knowing it – influence his staff, in myriad ways; the couple placed great emphasis on all of them being friendly, knowledgeable and watchful. By midday they were ready for their clients.

Jacqueline supervised the ordering of the *apéritifs*, dishes and wines. Most of the specialities were prepared at the last minute, the most severe test of discipline being the critical timing needed to prepare and present the seven courses making up the *menu dégustation*. The restaurant could seat 50 people; often, more than half of Jean's clients would order the *dégustation* menu – all sitting down at different starting times.

Relentlessly the minute kitchen got noisier, more chaotic and hotter; occasionally tempers flared briefly. Periodically each of the kitchen staff needed to retire outside for a few seconds to gasp in some cool air. As the pressure eased Jean visited the dining room to have just a brief chat with his clients: today he gave a warm welcome to his special guest.

At 4.00 Jean was welcoming his bank manager – he needed to ask for a further loan of 200,000 francs. He had not had the good fortune to inherit a family hotel free of debt; everything the couple possessed had to be paid for and already they had long-term debts of over a million francs. Now they needed to extend the kitchen and continue the task of renovating their bedrooms (their plans included the task of adding a bathroom to each one). With the French economy floundering and with sky-high interest rates, Jean felt he was walking on a bed of razor blades at times; interest charges were one of his biggest overheads.

An hour later he had his loan. Then his wine merchant arrived. Jean's magnificent wine cellar – with more than 10,000 bottles – was a huge drain on his capital, but he considered it an absolutely vital investment. He spent another 50,000 francs on wine.

That evening the whole hectic cycle was repeated – with the added complication of welcoming overnight guests. At 7.00 Jean snatched a few brief minutes with his children before they went up to their rooms; then followed another few hours of energy-sapping effort. After their guests retired, Jacqueline, too, went up to bed. 11.30 saw Jean with his staff deciding what tomorrow's purchases would be.

A few minutes before midnight Jean slipped quietly into bed – as silently as he had risen from it, 19 hours earlier.

Enjoying the best of French cuisine

Interestingly, 60 years ago, Curnonsky – the French gastronome and writer – identified the four quite different types of French cuisine: *la haute cuisine*; *la cuisine Bourgeoise*; *la cuisine Régionale*; and *la cuisine Improvisée*. He also emphasised that good cooking resulted when 'ingredients taste of what they are.'

Six decades later, and allowing myself some licence, I could say that nothing has changed. Certainly the term *la cuisine Improvisée* was coined long before *la nouvelle cuisine* became so fashionable, though the latter's emphasis on natural-tasting ingredients – and improvisation – represents two of its most important aspects. Curnonsky would relish present trends.

It is my hope that the notes that follow will interest the most experienced Francophiles and those of you who have yet to make your first trip to France. I must stress that they are very much my own personal points of view.

Nouvelle Cuisine

What is it? Six years ago Frédy Girardet, in conversation with Craig Claiborne, said this: "*La nouvelle cuisine* is nothing more than good taste. It is to prepare dishes to preserve their natural flavours and with the simplest of sauces."

Thankfully *nouvelle cuisine* has established itself strongly during the last two decades. Today, its most enthusiastic promotors are Henri Gault and Christian Millau, who are the two individuals who coined the phrase – though for many years now they have regretted that they did not call it *cuisine libre* (free). Girardet calls it *la cuisine spontanée* (spontaneous).

It is utterly different from classical cuisine (*la haute cuisine*); for far too long chefs blindly attached themselves to the rules of the old ways, established over many generations and culminating in the work and writings of Escoffier at the turn of the century. Ironically though, it was Escoffier himself who wrote the two priceless words that epitomise what *nouvelle cuisine* is all about – *faites simple*. Escoffier was a creative genius and he established many of the vital principles of good cooking that are still valid today. Most chefs acknowledge this.

Sadly, *nouvelle cuisine* is misunderstood by many visitors to France. For years dire predictions have been made for its early demise. But it is flourishing strongly and, despite some chefs who get it a bad name from time to time, it is likely to become increasingly established.

Why has this happened? I wrote three years ago that Fernand Point was the first to see that times were changing. As far back as 1925 he had realised that his customers had smaller appetites and were concerned about their health and their diets. His menus changed from day to day and depended entirely on what he had bought in the markets; he began the move towards lightness and simplicity, away from the heavy sauces and huge helpings of the past. He trained many of today's great masters: Bocuse, Outhier, Chapel, Vergé and the Troisgros brothers amongst them.

Simplicity is the key. In its purest, simplest form, *nouvelle cuisine* allows the basic ingredients to count most; the emphasis is on highlighting one natural flavour at a time. Mercifully portions border on the frugal – though this can be torture for those with old-fashioned appetites. Fast cooking is everything – whether it be fish, veal, *foie de canard* or vegetables: steaming, together with poaching and baking, are vital methods of preparation, slow cooking and dishes requiring vast lists of ingredients are not. Flour is all but banned; paper-thin *feuilletés* appear everywhere – no wonder, as they require so little flour.

Sauces, as developed for classical cuisine, are a thing of the past; old chefs would not acknowledge the modern-day, light reductions as sauces at all. These are no more than the concentrated juices of the food released during cooking. Butter, cream and wine are still used – but not to any great excess.

Are mistakes made? Of course they are: far too many superb vegetables are puréed into a sort of baby-food mush – often they all taste the same; helpings can still be too large – particularly the pig trough-like *grand dessert*; vegetables have been duplicated from one course to another at even the most famous restaurants; and combinations of food can sometimes be nauseating. Witness, as examples, the following: Chapel with what was literally a mixed grill of various parts of a lamb – truly awful; Vergé's *loup* and *endive* (the latter was inedible); Mathy's (Belfort) mixture of duck's liver, raspberry vinegar, strawberries, sliced apple and a cut-out bit of toast shaped like a duck!

Apart from in the great restaurants, kitchen staffs are small – often no more than three or four individuals. Machines, therefore, are essential in the kitchens of *nouvelle cuisine* practitioners: food processors; micro-wave ovens; ice cream and sorbet makers, and dry steam ovens. In the hands of skilled chefs the results are never slapdash; they go to considerable pains to get perfection, and presentation of the dishes is done by the *cuisiniers* in the kitchen – it's not left to a careless waiter to destroy their efforts in the dining room. You should never finish a meal feeling bloated – you can fulfil Brillat-Savarin's most famous bit of advice, universally ignored, to leave the table with an appetite. Consequently, what would otherwise appear to be a daunting obstacle, is now a pleasure – a *menu dégustation*; five to eight courses made up of very small helpings of the chef's specialities. It requires great discipline and organisation in the kitchen to prepare and present a well-balanced *menu dégustation* for clients; many of the great chefs fight shy of this – offering all sorts of excuses for not doing it.

Many people confuse nouvelle cuisine with cuisine minceur (slimming cuisine); one writer even thinks that Guérard won his third star for his *minceur* menus. *Nouvelle cuisine* is hardly calorie free: *cuisine minceur* requires the use of practically no butter, little cream, fat, oil or egg yolks and certainly no flour or sugar; only Guérard can make it reasonably interesting.

Finally, let me explain, in an unusual way, what the greatest benefit of all is – the complete freedom it has given chefs to be creative and brilliantly inventive. If you study really old editions of Michelin, it will soon become crystal clear that the classical cuisine of those days meant repetitive specialities in every town in France. Now look at today's guide. Hundreds of specialities are listed – endless variations based on dozens of basic products; indeed many of the menu decoder books on the market are a waste of money as they cannot help you to translate the menu descriptions. Some of the descriptions are amazing – often extending to 24 words to describe a dish (Chapel and Vergé are the worst culprits). Others cheat by using culinary terms to describe concoctions for which they were never intended; I have seen *saucisson* and *andouillette* used for fish dishes.

The very simplicity of *nouvelle cuisine* is its greatest pitfall; originality is not enough – talent and technique are just as important. Some chefs are incapable of rising to the test; it would be best if they did more to promote real regional cuisine rather than giving *nouvelle cuisine* a bad name or, worse still, sticking to the easy life of cooking *cuisine Bourgeoise* dishes.

17

Regional Cuisine

In 1980 I wrote that 'there has been a considerable move to preserve and encourage regional specialities.' Three years later, after spending many, many months of each year in France, driving tens of thousands of miles, and eating at hundreds of restaurants, I have to conclude that the evidence I found on my travels all adds up to a different conclusion; times have changed.

Regional cuisine in provincial restaurants – using old regional specialities – is withering away in most areas of France. Gault Millau are too optimistic about its strength; even Jean Didier (ex-editor of the now defunct Kléber Guide) was woefully short of the mark in suggesting that regional cuisine was making a strong comeback. I know of only one writer who agrees with me – Anne Willan of La Varenne Cookery School in Paris. (Her superb book – *French Regional Cooking* – is the epitome of what a book 'packager' – Marshall Editions Ltd. – can do.) The endless books on French regional cooking (and glossaries) list speciality after speciality but you'll not see them in many provincial restaurants – if at all. I feel that French chefs (particularly those who find *nouvelle cuisine* difficult and who run simpler restaurants) could do far more to research and promote regional specialities, rather than the repetitive, impersonal dishes that predominate in *cuisine Bourgeoise*. Thankfully, there are some chefs who make a superhuman effort to protect regional specialities.

If I had my way, the works of Elizabeth David, Anne Willan and Jane Grigson would be compulsory reading for chefs (with translators at hand). More often than not it's the *charcutier*, *pâtissier* and *boulanger* who keep local traditions alive.

What you will find though in all the French regions is the magnificent use that chefs make of local produce and raw materials – in each of the four different types of cuisine. In the next three pages it is this aspect of regional cooking that I emphasise; referring also to the specialities that you are likely to find in **restaurants** – not those in cookery books, many of which seem to have been taken from ancient reference books. Please also refer to the lists of specialities in each region (easily spotted as they are in the second colour).

Surprisingly, it is becoming more and more difficult for chefs, looking for the best quality and variety of produce, to obtain it locally; frequently they have to buy it from Rungis (the great Paris wholesale market near Orly Airport) – because the best local produce has been swallowed up by the buying methods of centralised distribution systems. An example is in the North – where the best fish, the best of local potatoes and other vegetables are to be discovered at Rungis, not in nearby markets.

In the notes that follow on the cuisine of each region, I examine first the French regions with Atlantic seaboards – starting in the north on the Belgium border and finishing at the Spanish frontier; then the regions that border Belgium, Germany, Switzerland, Italy and the Mediterranean; and, finally, the many differing regions making up the vast mass of inland France. As I consider each region in turn, please refer to the map on page 7; the identifying numbers I use with each regional heading correspond to those shown on that page.

In the following three pages I do not refer to the individual cheeses of each region, though there is a short introduction to cheeses on page 22. I would ask that you read, within the introduction to each region, the details listed on cheeses.

Equally, the same goes for the country's wines, liqueurs and brandies; please read the comprehensive notes detailed in each regional introduction and on pages 305, 306 and 307.

North (18) Fish takes pride of place – freshly landed at the ports of Boulogne, Calais and smaller ones like Le Crotoy. *Sole, turbot, maquereaux, barbue, lotte de mer, flétan, harengs, merlan, moules, crevettes* – all appear on menus. So do soups and stews – many with root vegetables: *waterzooï* – fish or chicken stew; *hochepot* – meat and vegetable *pot-au-feu*; *carbonnade* – beef stew with beer. Leeks are superb – enjoy *flamiche aux poireaux* (*quiche*-like pastry). Seek out the *hortillonages* (water-gardens) of Amiens and their young vegetables. Try *gaufres* – yeast waffles and *ficelles* – pancakes with various stuffings. Beer is excellent.

Normandy (17) Land of cream, apples and the pig. Vallée d'Auge gives its name to many dishes – including chicken, veal and fish; it means cream, apples or cider, or apple brandy (Calvados) have been added. Cider is superb. Pork products are everywhere: *andouilles* – smoked sausages, eaten cold; *andouillettes* – grilled sausage of pork and veal. Fish are superb: *sole à la Normande, à la Dieppoise, à la Fécampoise, à la Havraise* (the last three are ports); *plats de fruits de mer*; shrimps; oysters; *bulots* (whelks); mussels – and all the treasures from the seas. Enjoy tripe; *ficelles* – pancakes; cow's milk cheeses; butters – salty and sweet; salad produce and potatoes from Caux; exquisite apple tarts; *canard à la Rouennaise*; and fish stews.

Brittany (3) Fish and shellfish are commonplace: lobsters, *huîtres, langoustes*, crabs – of varying sorts, *moules*, prawns, shrimps, *coquilles St-Jacques*; to name just a few. Enjoy *cotriade* – a Breton fish stew with potatoes and onions; *galettes* – buckwheat flour pancakes with savoury fillings; *crêpes de froment* – wheat flour pancakes with sweet fillings; *far Breton* – a batter mixture with raisins; *gâteau Breton* – a mouthwatering concoction; *agneau de pre-salé* – from the salt marshes near Mont-St-Michel (fine omelettes are also made there); and *poulet blanc Breton*. It's also one of France's market-gardens: artichokes, cauliflowers, peas, beans, onions and strawberries.

Charente/Vendée (10) western half of Poitou-Charentes. La Rochelle is a great fishing port; consequently fish predominates – oysters are magnificent (see the entry at Bourcefranc). The port of La Cotinière, on the island of Oléron, is famous for its shrimps. Challans – in the Vendée – is world renowned for its ducks. Charentes is reputed for its butter, cabbage, goat's milk cheeses, Charentais melons, Cognac, mussels and salt-marsh lamb from the hidden fen country of the Marais Poitevin.

Southwest (22) One of the great larders of France – it can be divided into several distinct areas. From the countryside that lies in a semicircle to the north-west, west, south and south-east of Bordeaux comes: lamb from Pauillac; oysters (*gravettes*) from Arcachon; eels; beef (*entrecôte Bordelaise* is the best-known version); onions and shallots; *cèpes*; *alose* (shad); and *lamproie* – lamprey (eel-like fish). The Garonne Valley is one of the orchards of France: prunes from Agen; peaches; pears and dessert grapes. South of the Garonne is **Gascony**: famous for *foie gras* (both ducks and geese); *confit* (preserved meat from both these birds); jams and fruits; and its Armagnac. Try a *Floc* (see page 278)!

To the south and west of Gascony are **Béarn** and the **Landes**. From the latter come *palombes* and *ortolans*, ducks and chickens. Among traditional Béarn specialities are *garbue* – the most famous of vegetable soups; *poule au pot* – the chicken dish given its name by Henri IV; *tourin, ouliat* and *cousinette* (*cousinat*). See the Southwest specialities for further details.

West of Béarn is **Basque** country: tuna, anchovies and sardines are excellent; salmon (from Béarn also), Bayonne ham, *piperade,* *ttoro* (fish stew) and *gâteau Basque* (pastiza) – try them all.

Champagne-Ardenne (5) Ile de France (9) Many of the specialities listed earlier in the North appear in this region, which is renowned for its potatoes and turkeys. In the Ardenne you'll enjoy smoked hams – sold in nets; *sanglier; marcassin;* and red and white cabbages. West of Verdun, at Ste-Menehould, try *pieds de cochon* (pig's trotters); *petits gris* (snails); and the many differing sweets and sugared almonds (Verdun is famous for them). Troyes is famous for pork *andouillettes.* (See the next Alsace section for some of the Lorraine specialities.)

Regional specialities are all but non-existent in the Ile de France – though there are many restaurants in Paris serving the best dishes of all the French regions. Enjoy the *pâtés* and *terrines* and the offerings of the many *pâtissiers* and *charcutiers.*

Alsace (1) There is a strong German influence in much of the cooking; pork, game, goose and beer are common. *Foie gras* (fattened goose liver) is magnificent; so, too, are a range of fruits – used in tarts (*linzertorte* – raspberry or bilberry open-tart; *flammekuchen* – flamed open tart), jams, fruit liqueurs and *eaux-de-vie* (see Alsace wines). Stomach-filling *choucroute* and local sausages are on all menus; as are *kougelhopf, beckenoffe* and *lewerknepfle* (see regional specialities). Enjoy *tourte Alsacienne* – pork pie; drink beer with it.

Lorraine on the north-west borders is known for its *madeleines* (tiny sponge cakes), its *macarons*, its super *quiche Lorraine*, its fruit tarts, its omelettes and its *potée.*

Jura (10) This is dairy country – witness the cheeses in the regional introduction. Try *Jésus de Morteau* – a fat sausage smoked over pine and juniper; *brési* – wafer-thin slices of dried beef; and many local hams. *Morilles* and other fungi are common – so are freshly-caught trout and other freshwater fish.

Savoie (21) Hautes-Alpes (8) *Plat gratiné* applies to a wide variety of dishes – it always means 'cooked in breadcrumbs'; *gratins* of all sorts show how well milk, cream and cheese can be combined together. Relish *fondue* and *gougère*. Freshwater lake fish are magnificent – see the regional introduction for Savoie. Walnuts, chestnuts, all sorts of fruits and marvellous wild mushrooms are other delights.

Côte d'Azur (6) Provence (20) A head-spinning kaleidoscope of colours and textures fills the eyes: aubergines, peppers, tomatoes, cauliflowers, asparagus, beans, olives, garlic, artichokes, courgettes – the list is endless. Fruit, too, is just as appealing: melons from Cavaillon; strawberries from Monteux; cherries from Remoulins; glacé fruit from Apt; truffles from Valréas. Fish from the Mediterranean are an extra bonus: *bar* and *loup de mer, daurade,* superb *St-Pierre,* monkfish and mullet – these are the best. Lamb from the foothills of the Alps near Sisteron; herbs of every type from the *département* of Var; honey and olive oil; *ratatouille;* sardines; *saucisson d'Arles; bouillabaisse* (see page 93) and *bourride; soupe de poissons* and *soupe au pistou;* what memories are stirred as I write!

Languedoc-Roussillon (11) Cévennes (16) The same products – and dishes – listed in the previous section are available here. Also oysters and mussels from the lagoons (particularly Bouzigues – Thau lagoon; see map page 244). Excellent, too, are a variety of shellfish. Apricots and pumpkins flourish. *Brandade de morue* (salt cod) appears frequently – as do *confit d'oie* (and *canard*), *cassoulet* and *saucisses de Toulouse.*

Loire (12) This long strip of country – on either side of the Loire – is made up of several areas: the river itself in its last stretch before the Atlantic, east of Nantes; Anjou-Touraine – between Angers and Orléans; and the *étang*-filled forests of the Sologne. The river and its many tributaries provide *alose*, *sandre*, *anguille*, carp, perch, pike, salmon and *friture*. A tasty *beurre blanc* is the usual accompaniment for fish. *Charcuterie* is marvellous: *rillettes*, *rillons*, *andouillettes*, *saucissons*, *jarretons* – and other delights. Cultivated mushrooms come from the limestone caves near Saumur and wild mushrooms are plentiful in the many forests. The whole area is a vast orchard.

The **Sologne** is famous for its asparagus, frogs, game, freshwater lake and river fish and wildfowl. You'll be offered, too, many a *pâté*, fruit tarts (it's the home of *tarte Tatin*) and pies.

Burgundy (4) Refer to the often seen regional specialities. Many dishes are wine based: *coq au Chambertin* and *poulet au Meursault* are examples. Enjoy hams, freshwater fish, vegetables, *escargots*, mustard and gingerbread from Dijon and blackcurrants (used for *cassis* – the term for both the fruit and the liqueur made from them).

Lyonnais (13) The culinary heart and stomach of France – there is a variety of superb produce on hand: Bresse chickens (*chapons* – capons – are unforgettable treats); *grenouilles* and game from Les Dombes; Charolais cattle from the hills north of Chauffailles; freshwater fish from the rivers and pools (pike *quenelles* appear everywhere); *charcuterie* from Lyon – particularly sausages called *rosette* and *saucisson en brioche*; *cervelas* (saveloy); chocolate and *pâtisseries* from Lyon.

Auvergne (14) **Ardèche** (15) Both areas that keep alive old specialities. Refer to the regional lists but here are the best of them: *potée Auvergnate* – a stew of cabbage, vegetables, pork and sausage; *friand Sanflorin* – pork meat and herbs in pastry; *aligot* – a purée of potatoes, cheese, garlic and butter; *pounti* – a small egg-based savoury soufflé with bacon or prunes; and delectable *charcuterie* – hams, *saucisson*, *saucisses sèches* (dried sausages), *pâtés* and so on. The quality and variety of cheeses are magnificent. Cabbages, potatoes, bacon and cheese feature on menus. The area around Le Puy is famous for its lentils and Verveine du Velay – yellow and green liqueurs made from over 30 mountain plants. Fine chestnuts are found in the hills of the Ardèche (relish *marrons glacés*).

Berry-Bourbonnais (2) **Poitou** (19) – eastern half of Poitou Charentes. The flat terrain of Berry-Bourbonnais is dull country – the granary of France. It's known, too, for its beef, deer, wild boar, rabbits, hares, pheasants and partridge.

Much of Poitou lies in the deserted countryside of Limousin (as do the western edges of the Auvergne). Apart from the specialities listed look out for *mique* – a stew of dumplings; *farcidure* – a dumpling, either poached or sautéed; and *clafoutis* – pancake batter, poured over fruit (usually black cherries) and baked. Limousin is reputed for its *cèpes* – fine, delicate flap mushrooms; and also for its reddish-coloured breed of cattle.

Dordogne (7) A land of truffles, geese, ducks, walnuts, *cèpes*, chestnuts and fruit of all types. *Foie gras* of both goose and duck is obligatory on menus; as are *confits* of both birds (preserved in their own fat) and *magrets* (boned duck-breast meat), which have become popular in the last decade throughout France. *Pâtés* incorporating either poultry or game – and truffles – are common. If you see *miques* (yeast dumplings) or *merveilles* (hot, sugar-covered pastry fritters) on menus – order them. In the south – in the Garonne and Lot Valleys – it's a land of orchards: plums, prunes, figs, peaches, pears and cherries.

21

Classical Cuisine

Henri Gault once claimed that classical cuisine was based on recipes and techniques developed in order to conserve food without the help of refrigeration and to mask food that had already gone bad. *Nouvelle cuisine* requires fresh produce – menus are consequently short and revolve around the chef's purchases each day at the market. Compare that approach with old menus which offered clients scores, if not hundreds, of dishes. How fresh could that produce have been?

Classical French cuisine – *la grande cuisine* – started 450 years ago when Catherine de Medici came to France to become Queen; she brought with her a dozen or so Italian chefs from Florence. Just over 250 years later the developing art came to a standstill with the storming of the Bastille. In 1800 *la grande cuisine* re-emerged and Antonin Carême takes most of the credit for establishing it as the greatest cuisine of its time; in his day ice was not used to keep food fresh – raw materials were either smoked, salted or preserved in vinegar. At the start of the 20th century Escoffier – with the advantage of being able to use refrigeration – took classical cuisine to its supreme peak.

And there it remained; the basic repertoire of hundreds of sauces and garnishes hardly changed – it all became a rigid set of rules, which required faithful copying and little else. Raw materials were obliterated by an excess of butter, cream, alcohol, *foie gras*, truffles, onions, mushrooms, cheese and anything else that could disguise natural tastes.

I hope I do not appear, like Henri Gault, to be too cynical; that would be unfair because over the years my wife and I have enjoyed many of the great classical dishes – and still do. But we do admit, without any hesitation, that simplicity and freshness – in any form of cooking – attracts us far more.

Cuisine Bourgeoise

This is the simple cooking that the majority of French chefs offer to visitors; to their credit it is invariably done well, using good produce, either from the locality or elsewhere in France. More often than not it represents value for money. The repertoire sometimes appears to revolve around the same 20 to 30 dishes – wherever you are in France: *terrine, jambon, truite, escalope, côte de veau, entrecôte, gigot, côte d'agneau, poulet*, and so on. Rarely do you see a *navarin* or a *blanquette*; these are costly to prepare and must be thrown away – if not ordered. Often the more enjoyable alternative is to picnic; then you have the chance to try the appetising alternatives of the *pâtissier, boulanger* and *charcutier*. Take a portable cold box – ideal for keeping picnic things cool.

Cheeses

Within each region I have listed most of its cheeses; the well-known ones can be found throughout the country. They are made from the milk of cows (*vaches*), goats (*chèvres*) or ewes (*brebis*). Try all types and don't be prejudiced about them. In any restaurant follow a good French custom of selecting small portions of several varieties (ask for *une bouchée* – a mouthful – or *une petite tranche* – a small slice). Make waiters identify every cheese. Soft cheeses should be soft and creamy (not runny) and if they smell of ammonia, they are off! Blue cheese that is crumbling and falling apart is unacceptable. The right season for the best cheese will depend on two things: when the cows are put out to pasture and how long it takes to make the cheese. Wherever possible, I indicate the best season.

Jean-Anthelme Brillat-Savarin (1755–1826) Born at Belley (see *Savoie*), he was the greatest of all French gastronomes. He was a lawyer by profession, a linguist, an inventor and violinist; and a do-it-yourself publisher. His book *La Physiologie du gout* (published by Penguin as *The Philosopher in the Kitchen*) had a profound influence on gastronomic thinking.

Antonin Carême (1784–1833) By the end of the 18th century– during the French Revolution – *la grande cuisine* had ground to a halt. Carême, more than any other chef – through his writings and his genius for creating sauces – took it to new levels of excellence. The father of classical cuisine, he developed it to its extravagant excesses. He came from the poorest of families – one of 25 children. The first 'superstar' chef.

Auguste Escoffier (1847–1935) He became known as 'the King of chefs and the chef of kings'. Born at Villeneuve-Loubet (near Nice), he worked for over 40 years in various kitchens – mainly in London; he was one of the founders of the Savoy Hotel. Through his writings and his creative talent he had a great influence on classical cuisine; all modern masters admit that they owe much to the sound principles laid down by Escoffier.

Les Mères Who would argue that the Lyonnais has more first-class chefs than any other region in France? This priceless legacy was conceived over 200 years ago by a series of talented, skilled women: La Mère Guy started it all; La Mère Fillioux was the most famous. During this century others have continued the traditions: La Mère Blanc (Vonnas); La Mère Brazier (30 years ago one of France's few three-star chefs); La Mère Bourgeois (Priay); and La Mère Barattéro (Lamastre).

Fernand Point (1899–1956) He was the father of *nouvelle cuisine* and was the first to see, over 50 years ago, that eating habits were changing. He built his menus each day around his purchases at the market; he began the move towards lightness and simplicity. Another contribution to the new ways was his training of Bocuse, Vergé, the Troisgros brothers and others.

Alexandre Dumaine A simple man who won for himself a world-wide reputation. He retired in 1963 after working 50 years in kitchens; 30 of them at his Hôtel de la Côte-d'Or in Saulieu (Burgundy). A great chef who used local produce: trout from the Cure; hams from the Morvan; local cheeses; and the best Burgundian wines. He, too, trained many famous chefs of today.

Paul Bocuse Now in his middle fifties, he's the modern-day 'Emperor of chefs' and without any doubt is the best-known *cuisinier* in the world. Won his first Michelin star in 1961 – his third in 1965; a record. Said to have been the greatest advocate of *nouvelle cuisine*, though that hardly applies today. The family auberge, near Lyon, started life in 1765 – Paul Bocuse represents the seventh generation to carry on the tradition.

Michel Guérard Almost 50, he is the greatest innovator of all the new masters. The inventor of *cuisine minceur* (see *Nouvelle Cuisine*), his rejuvenation, as a chef and as a man, came ten years ago when he married Christine Barthélémy and moved to her family's thermal resort hotel at Eugénie-les-Bains. No other chef works in such an inspiring spot; France's best hotel.

Frédy Girardet Frédy is 47 and towers head and shoulders above the other modern greats. A brilliant Swiss chef, a talented restaurateur (which cannot be said of all chefs), an inspiring leader and a loyal family man; he stays at home in his kitchens and, despite not having the guarantee to fame and fortune that a three-star Michelin rating brings, he is considered by other chefs, critics and sceptics to be the world's greatest 'French' chef.

Main wine-growing areas of France

Your appreciation and enjoyment of French wines will be greatly enhanced if you understand some basic bits of knowledge.

Grape types and soil

One wine will differ from another because it has been made from a different variety of grape. Through hundreds of years of selection and development, each region has its own best single or group of grape varieties. Red Burgundy is made of one grape type, the Pinot Noir. The best white Burgundy is made from the Chardonnay grape (the second rank Burgundy white grape is the Aligoté). Red Bordeaux can come from a variety of grape types: amongst them the Cabernet Sauvignon grape, the Cabernet Franc grape, the Merlot and the Malbec. Cabernets give wine which matures later; Merlot is ideal for quick-developing wine. Blending allows wines to be produced which provide either characteristic: clearly, when long-lasting potential is wanted (particularly for the great Médoc wines), the Cabernet vines predominate; in Saint Emilion the Merlot is widely used.

You should recognise some of the important grape types: the two kinds of Cabernet, Gamay and Pinot Noir (red wine grapes); Riesling, Sauvignon Blanc, Sémillon, Chardonnay, Gewürztraminer (Traminer) and Muscat (six white wine grapes). I refer to these ten, plus several others, throughout the regions.

In some regions you will see a few wines described by their grape type name – *varietal* wines: Gamay (the Beaujolais grape) will appear in the Loire, in Savoie, in the Ardèche and elsewhere; Chardonnay will appear in the Lyonnais, in Champagne country and in obscure wine areas like Poitou. All the wines of Alsace take their names from the grape type used.

Bear in mind that apart from the differing grape vines, the type of soil in which they are grown plays the major part in determining the quality and status of French wines (climate plays another important part). That is why in Burgundy there are so many differing AC classifications – soil can vary from one acre to the next. That is also the reason why the Gamay wines, so delightful in Beaujolais, are never quite matched in other parts of France where the Gamay vine has been planted.

24

The main classifications

In every region I list the local wines. Most of them are AC (*Appellation d'Origine Contrôlée*) or VDQS (*Vin Délimité de Qualité Supérieure*) wines; these classifications are shown clearly on bottle labels – the AC is always known as *Appellation Contrôlée* – and they mean that the authenticity of each wine is guaranteed by the French Government and, in addition, the AC or VDQS identifies each wine to its precise birthplace. There are many hundreds of wines with the AC and VDQS guarantee and all but one or two of them are mentioned within the pages of this book. To win these classifications each wine must match its pedigree: specific area, specific grape type or types, maximum yield per acre, minimum alcohol content and so on. Liken the AC wines to the First and Second Division Football League clubs (they can vary from the very best of the First Division to the worst teams of the Second Division): the VDQS wines are the Third Division ones – and, believe me, a few of these Third Division wines, on their home grounds, are perfectly capable of beating some of their big brothers!

Identifying the wines of France

I have tried to make it as simple as possible for you to identify all the wines of France. You may be in a restaurant in France (**or anywhere else in the world**) with a wine list in your hand, or, you may be back home, wanting perhaps to locate a specific wine before buying it. **Use the index at the back of the guide** – this lists hundreds of wine names (see page 308). It includes all the AC and VDQS wines of France, together with most of the more common *Vins de Pays* (explained later). It also includes most of the important village names which, themselves, take the AC or VDQS classification of the region (this is particularly true in the south). Throughout France you can often be confused by this method of description – reference to many of the starred restaurants in the Michelin guide will illustrate what I mean: do you know **Bruley**, **Bué**, **Mareuil** or **Taradeau** wines?

In the regional texts on wines all these hundreds of varieties have been shown in **bold print**, so, whenever you see a label name on a wine list, it will be easy for you to quickly identify it and to find its birthplace on the regional map.

How does the Appellation Contrôlée system work?

Let us consider Beaujolais wines as a way of explaining the AC system; the same logic applies in the other wine-making areas of France. Beaujolais is the area north of Lyon and south of Mâcon on the west side of the River Saône (see map on page 174). From the hills in that area come lovely, fresh, light red wines, all made from the Gamay grape. If you see a bottle with an **Appellation Beaujolais Contrôlée** label, the wine could have originated in any part of the Beaujolais area. It will be a *generic* wine, both cheaper and of a lesser quality than the following wines.

If the label states **AC Beaujolais Villages**, the wine will have been made in any one of the thirty or more villages in the north of the Beaujolais region which have not yet earned their own AC status. It will be a superior wine to the previous one.

If the words say **AC Brouilly**, the wine will have come from the *commune* of Brouilly itself (one of the eight Beaujolais villages that have their own AC classification); if the wine has originated from the hillsides of Mont Brouilly, the label would say **AC Côte de Brouilly**, the ninth individual AC of the area. Often the best vineyards are on the *côtes* (sides). Finally, if the label has the addition of **Château Thivin** to the words **AC Côte de Brouilly**, this will be wine from the best estate on the Mont.

Generally speaking, the larger the geographic area described on the label, the cheaper and less superior the wine will be.

VDQS wines

There are plenty of other good wines in France without the AC classification which are just as appealing and enjoyable – and less expensive. The main category below AC is VDQS, made by producers who are working hard to earn their own AC status. Examples are **Minervois** and **Corbières**, red wines originating from Languedoc-Roussillon.

Vins de Pays and Vins de Table

Below the VDQS classification are *Vins de Pays* (liken them to the Fourth Division of football clubs) scattered throughout the country. These meet strict French Government controls; the labels specify precisely from which *département* or, in some cases, from which tiny area they come and the wines must be made from the grape varieties designated by Government order. They must meet minimum alcohol levels (not less than 10 per cent in the South, 9 or 9.5 per cent elsewhere). There are some one hundred possible *Vins de Pays* classifications throughout France – over half of them in the *départements* of Aude, Hérault, Gard and Pyrénées-Orientales (Languedoc-Roussillon). You may never see some of them. I have tried to identify and locate the most common ones; I have a lot of tasting to do . . . why not help me? *Vins de Table* is the lowest category of all – your non-league wines or your supermarket plonk. Some of them, bottled by the best producers – like Listel – are really good; but most are tasteless rubbish. Many of these wines, grown in the vast vineyards of the Midi, are blended with imported Italian wine (France buys vast quantities of it).

What to order

Whatever the restaurant, always order local or regional wines: if you explore each region in the way this guide suggests, it will follow, without fail, that you will gain some basic idea of where the main wine-producing areas are situated, the villages within them, and the varying types of wine coming from the local vineyards. It is not imperative to order a wallet-busting bottle of the best Burgundy or Bordeaux *Grand* or *Premier Cru* vintages when you eat at the great restaurants. Alsace, Savoie, Lyonnais, Provence, the Southwest and the Côte d'Azur have their own marvellous local wines and the best of these are on the wine lists of all the great restaurants in each of those regions. It is significant that, during the last decade, many restaurants have been doing far more to promote the unknown, local wines; with the high prices being asked world-wide for Burgundy and Bordeaux vintages this had to happen. This guide will equip you to profit from your knowledge. Don't take wines too seriously – enjoy them, as my wife and I have enjoyed many scores of the local wines recommended in this book.

At the best restaurants take the advice of the *sommelier*. Look for their small lapel badge (a bunch of grapes); they have worked and studied hard to acquire their knowledge of wines. With the aid of *French Leave* there is no need to feel intimidated by them.

Essential terms you should understand are: **Brut** very dry; **Sec** dry (*Champagne* – medium sweet); **Demi-sec** medium sweet; **Doux** or **Moelleux** sweet; **Mousseux** sparkling; **Crémant** a little less sparkle; **Pétillant** a slight sparkle; **Perlant** (**perlé**) a few bubbles; **Cru** growth, as in *first growth* – meaning vineyard status; **Blanc de Blancs** any white wine made from white grapes, rather than white and black. For other useful and interesting information see pages 305, 306 and 307. *Santé!*

Michelin

Since 1900 Michelin have been the guardians of hotel and restaurant standards in France. Unlike Gault Millau they have never set out to change the status quo of French cuisine. Their annual 'Red Guide' is a miracle of organisation; and in what it sets out to do it has no equal. Its superb maps are masterpieces and no other guide manages to pack so much into 1200 pages.

Michelin rely a great deal on the opinions of readers; they only have a dozen or so full-time inspectors in France. They are conservative to the point of being irritating and their awards are, in my opinion, often frustratingly inconsistent from region to region. They take their time awarding accolades and they take their time removing them; I believe major surgery should be applied to many of their starred restaurants – at all levels. Unlike Gault Millau, who award *toques* for cuisine skill alone, Michelin take into account other aspects as well: kitchens, toilets, service, fixtures and fittings, wines and so on.

Many of you have complained about the difficulty you have in translating the Michelin symbols; but without that shorthand it would lose much of its appeal. Annual sales of all 'Red Guides' exceed one milion copies and over two million 'Green Guides' are sold each year – plus all their maps. With sales like that no wonder the France 'Red Guide' is such value for money.

Gault Millau

Henri Gault and Christian Millau have changed the face of French cuisine during the last 14 years – and all but killed off classical cuisine. Former journalists, for some their approach is refreshing, witty and irreverent; for others it is cynical, full of cruel barbs and can be nauseatingly gushing at times. They appear not to be put off by reputations: some chefs they seem to dislike intensely – others are established firm favourites who can do no wrong.

Henri Gault told Richard Kann, a journalist, that he considers Michelin to be "The Bible – but just the Old Testament, we preach the New Testament – The Gospel."

GM award *toques* (a chef's hat) – from one to four; and points – from 10 to 19, out of 20. (Please *The Good Hotel Guide* – get it right in your 1984 edition!) Their system is superior to Michelin's. For example they give their top rating of four *toques* to a dozen or so chefs; Michelin give their top rating of three stars to 18 chefs – far too many. GM wax lyrical about up-and-coming chefs long before Michelin do; with few exceptions they get their crystal-ball gazing right – as Michelin, invariably, promote the same people a year or two later. Conversely GM can go over the top with some of their favourites. Their guide has no town maps – you need the Red Michelin to use it. An extremely serious flaw of the first English edition of the France Guide is that it has no general area maps of any description.

GM have fought shy from awarding the ultimate 20 points; most people would agree that Girardet (a Swiss) should be the first chef to win that supreme accolade. But can two Frenchmen ever bring themselves to sacrifice that honour to a Swiss?

Both writers are in their early fifties. In recent years they have spent much of their time researching and publishing similar guides in the U.S., U.K. and Europe.

Le Bottin Gourmand

An excellent, expensive newcomer in 1983 – edited by Jean Didier (ex Kléber). I think this one could become the best of all the guides – when its comments have a touch of constructive criticism in them. Organised by *départements*. Good maps.

To reserve bedrooms – options on right (in brackets)

1	Would you please reserve a room	(2 rooms, etc.,)
2	with a double bed	(with 2 single beds) (one room with) (each room)
3	and bathroom/WC	(and shower/WC) (and shower)
4	for one night	(2 nights, etc.,)
5	*(indicate day, date, month)*	
6		(We would like *pension* (half-*pension*) terms for our stay)
7	Please confirm the reservation as soon as possible and please indicate the cost of the rooms	(your *pension* terms for each person)
8	An International Reply Coupon is enclosed	
9	Yours faithfully	
1	**Pouvez-vous, s'il vous plaît, me réserver une chambre**	**(2 chambres, etc.,)**
2	**avec un lit à 2 places**	**(avec 2 lits à une place) (une chambre avec) (chaque chambre)**
3	**avec salle de bains/WC**	**(et douche/WC) (et douche)**
4	**pour une nuit**	**(2 nuits, etc.,)**
5	**le** *(indicate day, date, month)*	
6		**(Nous voudrions pension complète (demi-pension) pour notre séjour)**
7	**Veuillez confirmer la réservation dès que possible, et indiquer le tarif des chambres**	**(le tarif de pension par personne)**
8	**Ci-joint un coupon-réponse international**	
9	**Je vous prie, Monsieur, d'accepter l'expression de mes salutations distinguées**	

To reserve tables – options in brackets)

Would you please reserve a table for __ persons for lunch (dinner) on *(indicate day, date, month)*. We will arrive at the restaurant at *(use 24 hour clock)* hours. (We would like a table on the terrace.) Please confirm the reservation. An International Reply Coupon is enclosed. Yours faithfully

Pouvez-vous me réserver une table pour __ personnes pour déjeuner (dîner) le. Nous arriverons au restaurant à heures. (Nous aimerions une table sur la terrasse.) Veuillez confirmer la réservation. Ci-joint un coupon-réponse international. Je vous prie, Monsieur, d'accepter l'expression de mes salutations distinguées

Useful Phrases – General

Can I have **Puis-je avoir;** Can we have **Pouvons-nous avoir;**
an (extra) pillow **(encore) un oreiller;** a blanket **une couverture;** a towel **une serviette;** some soap **du savon;** heating **le chauffage;** a laundry service **une blanchisserie;** some hot (cold) milk **du lait chaud (froid);**
a knife **un couteau;** a fork **une fourchette;** a spoon **une cuiller;** a bottle of . . . **une bouteille de** . . . a half-bottle of . . . **une demi-bouteille de** . . . the wine list . . . **la carte des vins** . . .
an ashtray **un cendrier;** a glass **un verre;** a plate **une assiette;**
Fill the tank up (petrol). **Faites le plein**
Check the oil, please. **Vérifiez l'huile, s'il vous plaît**
May I park here? **Puis-je me garer ici?**
Get a doctor. **Appelez un médecin**

Useful Phrases – at the hotel

Can I have **Puis-je avoir**; Can we have **Pouvons-nous avoir**;
I would like **Je voudrais**; We would like **Nous voudrions**;
May I have some ... **Pourrais-je avoir ...** ;
May I see the room? **Puis-je voir la chambre?**
No, I don't like it. **Non, elle ne me plaît pas**
What's the price ... ? **Quel est le prix ... ?**
Do you have anything ... ? **Avez-vous quelque chose ... ?**
   better **de mieux**; bigger **de plus grand**;
   quieter **de plus tranquille**; cheaper **de moins cher**;
Haven't you anything cheaper please? **N'avez-vous rien de moins cher, s'il vous plaît?**
Fine – I'll take it. **D'accord – je la prends**
What is the price for full board (half-board)? **Quel est le prix pour la pension complète (demi-pension)?**
I would like a quiet room, please. **Je voudrais une chambre tranquille, s'il vous plaît**
Can we have breakfast in our room? **Pouvons-nous prendre le petit déjeuner dans la chambre?**
Please telephone this hotel/restaurant and reserve a room/a table for me. **Pouvez-vous, s'il vous plaît, téléphoner à cet hôtel/ce restaurant et me réserver une chambre/une table**
Would you recommend the best local *pâtissier/charcutier/ boulanger*? **Pouvez-vous me recommander le meilleur pâtissier/charcutier/boulanger du coin?**

Useful Phrases – in the restaurant

Can I have **Puis-je avoir**; Can we have **Pouvons-nous avoir**;
I would like **Je voudrais**; We would like **Nous voudrions**;
Could we please have ... **Pouvons-nous avoir ... s'il vous plaît**
We would like to have a look at the fixed-price menu, please.
Nous voudrions voir le menu à prix-fixe, s'il vous plaît
What's this? **Qu'est-ce que c'est que ça?**
Would you please recommend your regional specialities?
Pourriez-vous nous recommander les spécialités de la région, s.v.p?
We would like to share this speciality between us, please. **Nous aimerions partager cette spécialité entre nous, s'il vous plaît**
May we change this speciality for another one? **Est-ce que nous pouvons changer cette spécialité pour une autre?**
Which local wines would you recommend that we try? **Quels vins du pays nous recommanderiez-vous d'essayer?**
Please do not serve us big portions. **Ne nous servez pas de trop grosses portions, s'il vous plaît**
That is not what I ordered. I asked for ... **Ce n'est pas ce que j'ai commandé. J'ai demandé ...**
rare **saignant**; medium-done **à point**; well-done **bien cuit**;
Could you bring another plate, please? **Pourriez-vous apporter une autre assiette, s'il vous plaît?**
Would you please identify your local cheeses? **Pouvez-vous nous donner les noms de vos fromages du coin, s.v.p?**
May we have decaffeinated coffee, please? **Pouvons-nous avoir du café décaféiné, s'il vous plaît?**
May we please see your kitchens after our meal? **Serait-il possible de visiter les cuisines après le repas, s.v.p?**
May we please see your wine cellar after our meal? **Serait-il possible de visiter la cave après le repas, s'il vous plaît?**
Would you give us the address of your wine merchant? **Pourriez-vous nous donner l'adresse de votre marchand de vins?**
Would you give us the name of your cheese supplier? **Pourriez-vous nous donner le nom de votre fournisseur en fromages?**

ALSACE

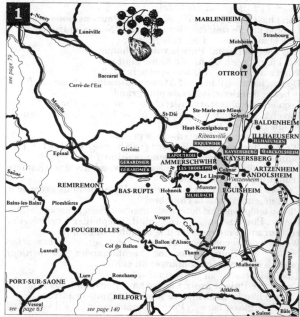

This region is ignored by so many visitors to France, especially those from the British Isles and North America. It is bordered on one side by the **Rhine** and on the other by the dark and mysterious forests of the **Vosges** mountains, which are particularly worth exploring. On the eastern slopes of the Vosges lie the thriving vineyards of Alsace and the picturesque wine villages. Most of them have un-French sounding names; driving from north to south on the Route des Vins d'Alsace you will find some of them: **Ribeauvillé**, **Riquewihr**, **Kaysersberg**, **Ammerschwihr**, **Witzenheim** and **Eguisheim**.

What are the sights and countryside a traveller should try to incorporate into a stay of several days? Apart from the wine villages, be sure to visit the Château de **Haut-Kœnigsbourg**, restored in 1900 by Kaiser Wilhelm II. You should, without fail, see **Colmar**, one of the many French towns where the narrow central streets have been closed to traffic and converted for pedestrian-only use. As a consequence you can wander at your leisure through the old town – full of timber houses from the 16th century – down to the River Lauch and the Quartier de la Krutenau. Visit the Musée d'Unterlinden with its lovely treasures; see the Maison Pfister, claimed to be the most beautiful house in the world.

Mulhouse, further south, is a modern city. On its southern borders are a fine zoo and botanical gardens, and on its western edge is the French Railway Museum, an essential halt for all railway enthusiasts. For vintage car fans there is the greatest show of Bugatti cars housed under one roof to be found anywhere in the world; thankfully, the Schlumpf collection can now be viewed again – you'll find it in the Avenue de Colmar. It's a not-to-be-missed treasure house.

It will be the Vosges that will give you the best chance to get away from the crowds. Drive the **Route des Crêtes**, which runs along the ridge of peaks, from **Cernay** in the south to **Ste-Marie-aux-Mines** in the north. Stop at the First World War Memorial at Vieil Armand (north of Cernay) and also drive to the top of the **Hohneck**; a remarkable panorama awaits you there.

Enjoy the many lakes: the tiny Lac Blanc; Lac Noir; the larger Lac de Gérardmer; and Lac de Longemer. Explore **Gérardmer** and **Epinal** on the western edges of the Vosges. Historical **Belfort** should also be included in your travels; the famous Lion of Belfort was sculptured by Bartholdi, who cast the Statue of Liberty. North-west of Belfort, on the N19, is world-famous **Ronchamp**; the modern church with its concave roof, was designed by the controversial Le Corbusier.

Other recommended drives are the roads west from **Les Trois-Epis**, via the Col du Wettstein and the Cimetière des Chasseurs up to the Col du Bonhomme; it is a particularly quiet drive through the dense pine forests. Spare time for the unusual site of **Le Linge**; apart from the museum there telling the story of this First World War battlefield, it's graphically illustrated by the remnants left on the neighbouring hillside. The trenches and rusty barbed wire are still there – a grisly reminder of how scores of lives were lost to gain a yard at a time. Navigate the narrow forest lanes south of both Lac de Longemer and Lac de Gérardmer; see the tiny Lac de Retournemer. From Giromagny drive up to the summit of the **Col du Ballon** – Tour de France cycling country and superb views.

One interesting aspect of eating out in Alsace now is the differing value for money you get on either side of the Vosges. On the east side, restaurants – even in midweek, in winter – are full to the rafters with Germans; the owners have it too easy. Not so on the western side; life is tough there and it's reflected in their efforts to provide real value.

Further afield, but easily reached by autoroutes, is the northern edge of the Jura, well worth a day's drive (see my entry for Goumois – page 148). Across the Rhine is the Black Forest. To the south, an hour away, is **Bâle**, and the best zoo in the world. Beyond is Switzerland: I have made a day trip to Lucerne quite easily from Colmar in the past, now even simpler with autoroutes opened-up all the way.

There are many quiet valleys, forest tracks and small hidden villages for you to discover for yourselves. I promise they will give you a lot of pleasure, a lot of surprises, and a lot of contentment.

Michelin *yellow* maps: 242.87.62.66. Green Guide: Vosges
IGN *série verte* map: 31. *série rouge* map: 104
Airports: Strasbourg. Bâle/Mulhouse
Distances from: Paris–Colmar 444 km Calais–Colmar 640 km

Cheeses Cow's milk

Carré-de-l'Est soft, edible, white rind, made in a small square; milder than Camembert. Bland taste. Available all year

Gérardmer same cheese as Gérômé, alternative name

Gérômé soft, gold-coloured cheese, a little more solid than Munster, often covered with fennel or caraway. Made as a thick disk. Spicy taste and at its best in summer and autumn. Good with full-bodied red wines

Munster soft, gold-coloured, stronger taste than Gérômé, made as a small disk. Munster *Laitier* (made by commercial dairies) available all year. *Fermier* (made by farms) at its best in summer and autumn. Try them with **Traminer** wines. **Munster au cumin** (with caraway seeds)

Regional Specialities

Beckenoffe a stew, or hotpot, of potatoes, lamb, beef, pork and onions, cooked in a local wine

Choucroute garnie sauerkraut with peppercorns, boiled ham, pork, Strasbourg sausages and boiled potatoes. Try it with a beer (*bière*)

Chou farci stuffed cabbage

Foie gras goose liver

Kougelhopf a round *brioche* with raisins and almonds

Krapfen fritters stuffed with jam

Lewerknepfle (Leber Knödel) liver dumpling (pork liver dumpling)

Matelote Alsacienne in Alsace made with stewed eels (in the past from the River Ill) – sometimes with freshwater fish

Pflutters Alsacienne potato puffs

Potage Lorraine potato, leek and onion soup

Schifela shoulder of pork with turnips

Tarte (aux mirabelles) golden plum tart. Also with other fruits

Tarte à l'oignon Alsacienne onion and cream tart

Wines best years 59 61 66 71 73 75 76 79 82

Until recently there was a single Appellation Contrôlée (AC) for the region, **AC Alsace** (or **Vin d'Alsace**). A few years ago an additional AC was announced, **AC Alsace Grand Cru**; these being the wines from the best vineyards.

The wines of Alsace take their names from the type of grapevine; followed by the village or winegrower's name.

    AC Alsace – Traminer d'Ammerschwihr (village name)

    AC Alsace Grand Cru – Riesling Hugel (producer's name)

Some restaurants will identify the best wines to their precise birthplace by indicating vineyard names – examples: **Kaefferkopf** (south of Ammerschwihr); **Schoenenbourg** (near Riquewihr); **Schlossberg** (east of Kaysersberg).

Almost all the wines are white but some are pink or light red. They are dry, fresh and fruity – a few are ideal dessert wines.

The grape types are:

    Riesling for dry white wine

    Gewürztraminer (**Traminer**, for short) dry white wine, with a spicy scent and flavour

    Sylvaner a light, tart, workhorse grape for white wine

    Pinot Blanc or **Klevner** related to the Chardonnay grape, but not as good; a fresh, aromatic white wine

    Muscat dry, white wine and with a perfume fit for your handkerchief!

    Tokay dAlsace for spicy, full-bodied white wine – known also as the **Pinot Gris** grape type. Needs ageing

    Pinot Noir for rosés and light red, full-bodied wines

    Chasselas an inferior white grape with no flavour. Now rarely seen in Alsace, being replaced by the Pinot Blanc

Wines with the **AC Vin d'Alsace-Edelzwicker** label are the most basic of Alsace wines, made from a mixture of grape types, usually Sylvaner and Pinot Blanc; they are fruity and light whites. Rarely seen is a white **Crémant d'Alsace** (it represents about one per cent of Alsace production). Alsace wines are sold in distinctive green bottles, called *flûtes*.

Don't miss any of the Alsace brandies – called *eaux-de-vie*. These are colourless liqueurs distilled from fermented fruit juices: *kirsch* – cherry; *framboise* – raspberry; *prunelle* – sloe; *mirabelle* – golden plum; *quetsche* – purple plum; and *myrtille* – bilberry (blueberry). Look out for brightly-coloured fruit liqueurs; these are macerated – hence their lovely colours.

Frédy and Muriel Girardet – Crissier (Jura)

The lake at Gérardmer (Alsace)

Le Linge – west of Les Trois-Epis (Alsace)

The château at Meillant (Berry-Bourbonnais)

Base Hotels

GERARDMER   Echo de Ramberchamp

Very simple hotel
Quiet/Gardens/Good value

Two kilometres west of the town – on the southern shore of the
lake. A modern, chalet-type hotel with a backdrop of wooded
hills. Close to the town swimming pool. Ideal for keep-fit fans.
No restaurant *rooms* 16 **A-B**
Closed Mid Nov-Xmas. 10 Jan-end Feb. Mon (except July-Aug).
post Ramberchamp. 88400 Gérardmer. Vosges.
phone (29) 63.02.27 *Mich* 242 Colmar 54 km

ILLHAEUSERN   La Clairière

Very comfortable hotel
Secluded/Tennis/Lift

A modern building in an isolated site west of the village.
No restaurant *rooms* 24 **C**
Closed Jan-5 Mar. Mon (Nov-Jan).
post Illhaeusern. 68150 Ribeauvillé. H.-Rhin.
phone (89) 71.80.80 *Mich* 242 Colmar 17 km

KAYSERSBERG   Remparts

Comfortable hotel
Quiet/Gardens   ®

One of my favourite French base hotels. Madame Keller speaks
excellent English and will look after you well. Ask her to
introduce you to the Faller family – small wine producers making
wines of superb quality. 200 metres from the modern hotel is the
house where Albert Schweitzer was born.
No restaurant *rooms* 27 **B-C** *cards* AE
closed Open all the year.
post 68240 Kaysersberg. H.-Rhin.
phone (89) 47.12.12 *Mich* 242 Colmar 11 km

MARCKOLSHEIM   St-Martin

Comfortable hotel
Quiet/Gardens/Good value

On the D10 – west of the village. In May, there is a grand display of
lilacs – of all colours – in the garden next door.
No restaurant *rooms* 18 **B**
closed Mid-end Jan. Wed.
post 67390 Marckolsheim. B.-Rhin.
phone (88) 92.51.55 *Mich* 242 Colmar 22 km

RIQUEWIHR   Riquewihr

Very comfortable hotel
Quiet/Lift

Newly built, east of village – facing Schoenenbourg vineyards.
No restaurant *rooms* 49 **B-C** *cards* AE DC Visa
closed Open all the year.
post 68340 Riquewihr. H.-Rhin.
phone (89) 47.83.13 *Mich* 242 Colmar 13 km

GERARDMER
Gd. Hôtel Bragard/rest. Gd Cerf

Luxury hotel
Quiet/Gardens/Swimming pool/Lift

In the last edition of *French Leave* I complained about the huge size of the menu; a reader wrote to say it helped those with poor sight. It was no surprise to find that the Michelin star has gone up in smoke; cooking is basic and, as some of you have confirmed, service is abysmal. Meals are not compulsory – use it as a 'base' and enjoy the many facilities.
menus **B-C** *rooms* 62 **C-D2** *cards* AE DC Visa
closed Mid Oct-20 Dec. Mar. Apl.
post 88400 Gérardmer. Vosges.
phone (29) 63.06.31 *Mich* 242 Colmar 52 km

LAPOUTROIE
du Faudé

Comfortable hotel
Fairly quiet/Gardens/Swimming pool/Good value

An attractive *Logis de France* – in the village itself and well clear of the N145 bypass to the east. Bedrooms are in a modern annexe. Typical Alsace specialities with good regional wines and cheeses. Locals recommend the Hôtel Les Alisiers for good eating, too – secluded site 3 km to the south.
menus **A-C** *rooms* 25 **B** *cards* Visa
closed Mid Nov-2 Dec. 1-15 Mar. Thurs midday (summer).
Wed evg. Thurs (winter).
post 68650 Lapoutroie. H.-Rhin.
phone (89) 47.50.35 *Mich* 242 Colmar 19 km

MUHLBACH
Perle des Vosges

Comfortable hotel
Quiet/Gardens

Another *Logis de France* and in a super site; high above the village with extensive views south to the Ballon peaks. It would make a good 'base', though do give the restaurant at least one try. **Munster** cheeses come from the valley below the hotel.
menus **A-C** *rooms* 25 **A-C**
closed Jan. Rest: Wed (out of season).
post Muhlbach. 68380 Metzeral. H.-Rhin.
phone (89) 77.61.34 *Mich* 242 Colmar 24 km

LES TROIS-EPIS
Croix d'Or

Simple hotel
Quiet/Good value ®

A *Logis de France* and just outside the village – nearly 2000 feet above sea-level and yet only 12 km from Colmar. Views of the Vosges forests and peaks to the south-west. Though meals are not obligatory, do try the basic, good-value menus; one highlight being *La Table Hans em Schnokeloch* – a vast buffet-style *hors d'œuvre*. Visit nearby Le Linge.
menus **A-B** *rooms* 12 **B-C**
closed Jan. Wed.
post 68410 Les Trois-Epis. H.-Rhin.
phone (89) 49.83.55 *Mich* 242 Colmar 12 km

34

AMMERSCHWIHR   Aux Armes de France

Very comfortable restaurant with rooms/Michelin★★

Elizabeth David, please – keep away from the modern-day Aux
Armes de France; preserve the memories we both have of
happier days some 20 years ago when you first wrote about it in
French Provincial Cooking. My last visit was a miserable affair;
even in midweek on a cold winter's evening it was packed to the
rafters – and run more like a production-line German brasserie.
The car park had given a clue before I even climbed the stairs to
the dining rooms – rows of cars from across the Rhine, all with
German number plates. Pierre Gaertner, now joined by his son,
Philippe, is hardly likely to go bankrupt with such support. The
influence of Philippe means that many dishes are modern – but
father continues to offer classic Fernand Point specialities (he
was a student of the great man); typical is a *gratin de queues
d'écrevisses*. Superb wines – but big helpings, ultra-fast service
and a beer-cellar atmosphere make this one place I would miss –
although some may love it. Awarded two stars 30 years ago; but
not worthy of them today.
menus **C** *rooms* 8 **C** *cards* AE DC Visa
closed Jan. Wed evg (Oct-June). Thurs.
post 68770 Ammerschwihr. H.-Rhin.
phone (89) 47.10.12 *Mich* 242 Colmar 7 km

ANDOLSHEIM   Soleil

Comfortable hotel/Michelin★
Quiet/Gardens

Owned for decades by the Mergenthaler family – now joined by
son-in-law Henri Bost, a *Maître Cuisinier de France.* Le Soleil
continues to offer regional cuisine – *foie gras frais* being
particularly good; a classical dish which still finds a place on the
menu is *florentine de brochet*. Wines are an excellent feature of
eating out here. The hotel has been improved over the years and
mercifully these days the main N415 is a bypass to the north of
the village.
menus **B-C** *rooms* 17 **A-C** *cards* DC
closed Feb. 1st week July. Tues.
post Andolsheim. 68600 Neuf-Brisach. H.-Rhin.
phone (89) 71.40.53 *Mich* 242 Colmar 6 km

ARTZENHEIM   Auberge d'Artzenheim

Comfortable restaurant with rooms
Quiet/Gardens/Good value

Another of the many Alsace restaurants that provide typical
regional classics – but Edgard Husser, who spent some time at
the Auberge de l'Ill, at nearby Illhaeusern, has introduced many
lighter touches to the cooking. Good sweets – particularly
recommended are the various *sorbets*. Amongst the conventional
dishes worth trying are *foie gras chaud aux pommes* and *coq au
Riesling*. Attractive gardens are a welcome and much
appreciated bonus; a Michelin star may come soon.
menus **A-C** *rooms* 10 **B-C** *cards* AE DC
closed Mid Feb-mid Mar. Rest: Mon evg and Tues.
post Artzenheim. 68320 Muntzenheim. H.-Rhin.
phone (89) 71.60.51 *Mich* 242 Colmar 16 km

BALDENHEIM Couronne

Comfortable restaurant/Michelin★
Good value

I was delighted to see this ever-improving restaurant win its first Michelin star in 1982 – a just reward for Angèle Trébis and her talented son-in-law, Daniel Rubiné. A mixture of traditional cuisine married to some lighter treats – like *feuilleté de grenouilles au Riesling*. An old favourite of ours – on the D209 north-west entrance to the village.
menus **A-C** *cards* AE DC
closed Mid-end July. 1-15 Jan. Sun evg. Mon.
post Baldenheim. 67600 Sélestat. B.-Rhin.
phone (88) 85.32.22 *Mich* 242 Colmar 30 km

BAS-RUPTS Host. Bas-Rupts

Very comfortable restaurant with rooms/Michelin★
Fairly quiet/Tennis ®

A great many of you have been utterly delighted by the cooking of handsome, talented Michel Philippe – a *Maître Cuisinier de France*. Michel is one of four brilliant chefs who weave their magic on the western side of the Vosges; here they have to try much harder as the easy German tourist business doesn't cross the ridge of high hills. A *nouveau* master, Michel has improved his cooking and the facilities out of all recognition since my wife and I first visited the restaurant many years ago. My last visit was on the day after my miserable experience in Ammerschwihr; every single aspect of the meal was better here. *Foie gras d'oie cuit à la vapeur en feuille de chou* was one highlight – as was a **Léon Beyer** 1979 Riesling. Menus represent value for money. You'll get a warm welcome and Michel will ensure you enjoy his *Logis de France* and *Relais du Silence*.
menus **A-C** *rooms* 20 **C-D** *cards* AE DC Visa
closed Open all the year.
post Bas-Rupts. 88400 Gérardmer. Vosges.
phone (29) 63.09.25 *Mich* 242 Colmar 56 km

BELFORT Host. du Château Servin

Very comfortable restaurant with rooms/Michelin★★
Quiet/Gardens/Lift

Dominique Mathy, the young chef here, is the darling of both Michelin and Gault Millau. He's a talented *nouveau cuisinier* – that's for sure; witness his *petite nage de langouste 'René Servin' au beurre de basilic* (named after the owner's late husband) and his *farandole des douceurs* – mouthwatering sweets. But one offering demonstrated perfectly why even the best chefs can get *nouvelle cuisine* a bad name; a mixture of duck's liver, raspberry vinegar, strawberries, sliced apple and a cut-out bit of toast shaped like a duck – ugh! It tasted even worse that it sounds. Lucie Servin looks after you well at this ugly house in a quiet, side street – but it is very expensive. Don't miss the delectable white wine – **Kaefferkopf** (see wine notes).
alc **C-D** *rooms* 10 **C-D** *cards* AE DC
closed 10 July-10 Aug. Mid Feb-mid Mar. Fri.
post 9 rue Gén.-Négrier, 90000 Belfort. Ter.-de-Belfort.
phone (84) 21.41.85 *Mich* 242 Colmar 74 km

EGUISHEIM   Le Caveau
Comfortable restaurant/Michelin★

Nothing ever changes here in the first-floor *cave* – Roger
Vonderscher, the owner, sees to that; it's Alsace cuisine in an
Alsace-style dining room. Before your meal walk the narrow
lanes, past houses with flower-laden balconies; you will need a
big hole in your stomach to put away *tarte à l'oignon, grenouilles
au Riesling* and a gargantuan *choucroute* – all washed down by
the memorable Léon Beyer **Eguisheim** wines.
menus **B-C** *cards* DC
closed Last week June. Mid Jan-end Feb. Wed evg. Thurs.
post Eguisheim. 68420 Herrlisheim. H.-Rhin.
phone (89) 41.08.89 *Mich* 242 Colmar 7 km

FOUGEROLLES   Au Père Rota
Comfortable restaurant/Michelin★
Good value   ®

Bravo Jean-Pierre and Chantal Kuentz, owners of this old
favourite of ours, on winning your first Michelin star in 1982. The
young couple have brought fame again to Joseph Rota's old
auberge, in a town surrounded by orchards, whose harvests are
used to distill *eaux-de-vie* – particularly *kirsch*. Jean-Pierre is the
second of the talented *nouveaux* chefs working wonders in the
west of the region: *foie et aiguillette de canard tiède en salade,
suprême de pigeonneau en croûte au porto blanc* and *sorbet au
kirsch* are three of his specialities. The attractive menu cover
was painted by Chantal's father.
menus **B-C** *cards* AE DC Visa
closed 1-15 July. Mid Nov-mid Dec. 21-28 Feb. Sun evg. Mon.
post 70220 Fougerolles. H.-Saône.
phone (84) 49.12.11 *Mich* 242 Colmar 107 km

ILLHAEUSERN   Auberge de l'Ill
Luxury restaurant/Michelin★★★
Gardens   ®

During the 20 years we have known this exquisite place, we have
seen it change out of all recognition as the Haeberlin brothers
grew more and more famous. Today it's so much bigger and, to be
honest, it really is too busy; as one reader said 'it's always full of
Germans.' Nevertheless, Jean-Pierre still welcomes you warmly
and brother Paul, aided by his son Marc, continues to concoct
treasures in his kitchens. It still has the lowest prices of all the
three-star restaurants in France – they make U.K. ones seem like
blackmail. On my last visit two dishes – and a 1977 **Clos Ste-
Hune Riesling** – were perfection: *la salade de rouget et
langoustines au beurre de coriandre* – a picture and a shame to
touch it; and *le feuilleté de pigeonneau de Bresse aux choux et
aux truffes* – one word 'wow' was all I wrote in my notes. Wines
and sweets are superb – *petits fours* are certainly not so. And
please, Jean-Pierre, don't put all your English-speaking guests
together in one corner of your dining rooms!
alc **C-D** *cards* DC
closed 1st week July. Feb. Mon evg. Tues.
post Illhaeusern. 68150 Ribeauvillé. H.-Rhin.
phone (89) 71.83.23 *Mich* 242 Colmar 17 km

KAYSERSBERG   Chambard

Very comfortable restaurant with rooms/Michelin★
Quiet/Lift

President Mitterrand's punitive tax on business entertaining –
imposed in 1982 – has made little impression in eastern Alsace.
With so many Germans filling the restaurants, their owners could
not care less about the tax – or, in my opinion, about their clients.
What a change for the worse has taken place at Pierre Irrmann's
restaurant. It was a thoroughly pathetic show when I was there
last: a badly-balanced menu; no appetisers with the *apéritif*;
amateurish, appalling *petits fours*; and an *assiette des sorbets*
which was an utter disgrace; overall a very poor performance.
Since my visit Gault Millau have chopped one *toque* from the
rating here; what about the star, Michelin? One dining room is
very comfortable – the other more like a shed, where smoke
hangs around for far too long. A new hotel section has 18
excellent rooms in a quiet setting.

menus **B-C** *rooms* 18 **D** *cards* DC
closed 1-21 Mar. Rest: Sun evg. Mon.
post 68240 Kaysersberg. H.-Rhin.
phone (89) 47.10.17 *Mich* 242 Colmar 11 km

MARLENHEIM   Host. du Cerf

Comfortable hotel/Michelin★
Gardens

Two readers persuaded me to add the Cerf to the Alsace entries;
they had been impressed by the fine welcome they had received,
by the excellent cooking and the overall impression that nothing
was too much trouble for the owners. I agree with all those
sentiments – and the cuisine is first class. Robert Husser, ably
assisted by his son, Michel, trained by Senderens and Paul
Haeberlin, are *nouvelle cuisine* fans; menus change day by day –
but amongst the many specialities you may find delights like
minute de saumon au basilic and *foie d'oie frais aux choux* –
both marvellous dishes.

menus **B-D** *rooms* 17 **B-C** *cards* AE DC Visa
closed Mon. Tues (except evgs Easter-mid Nov).
post 67520 Marlenheim. B.-Rhin.
phone (88) 87.73.73 *Mich* 242 Colmar 65 km

OTTROTT-LE-HAUT   Beau Site

Comfortable hotel/Michelin★
Good value

A Strasbourg reader pointed me in the direction of the three
Schreiber brothers – André, Martin and Christian (who runs the
kitchens); the three of them are steadily improving their hotel's
reputation. I was not greatly impressed – my preference would
be to visit some of the other Alsace chefs first. But I did enjoy the
noisettes de chevreuil and the red **Ottrott** wine. The hotel lies in
the shadow of Mont Ste-Odile – with its mountain-top convent
and its mysterious wall.

menus **B-C** *rooms* 14 **B-C** *cards* AE DC
closed 25 June-7 July. Jan. Rest: Sun evg. Mon.
post Ottrott-le-Haut. 67530 Ottrott. B.-Rhin.
phone (88) 95.80.61 *Mich* 242 Colmar 49 km

PORT-SUR-SAONE   Château de Vauchoux

Very comfortable restaurant/Michelin★
Quiet/Gardens/Swimming pool/Tennis   Ⓡ

What a stunning performance Jean-Michel Turin produced on my
first visit to his delightful restaurant. Just a few hundred metres
from the infant River Saône, it forms part of a château with
extensive grounds. This is a case where Michelin – with its
legendary symbols shorthand – tell you nothing. Instead, it was
the other three chefs of the talented western Alsace team of four,
who insisted I seek out this 38 years old chef and his attractive
wife, Franceline. At least one of them thinks Turin is the equal of
Paul Haeberlin. He could be right; it was a magical show – full of
innovations. What was so surprising to me, after all my travels
during the last 36 months, was that his appetisers, desserts and
presentation of dishes all contained new touches I had not seen
before.

The couple started off here eight years ago – and yet again
Jean-Michel is the perfect example of how a chef, nearing forty,
so often gets 'fired' by some inner motivation and jumps from
being a competent *cuisinier* to a brilliant one. I just hope he can
keep it up. Amongst the memorable dishes I enjoyed were *le filet
de bar à la vapeur sauce aux filaments de safran* and a selection
of mouthwatering desserts – an orange *terrine*, two excellent
sorbets and *une marquise chocolat amer* were three examples of
his light touch.

The restaurant has no bedrooms; the Turins suggest dinner
clients should use the Hôtel Lion in nearby Vesoul. After your
meal – and when Jean-Michel has finished his work in the
kitchens – ask him to show you his cellar; I'll not describe it in
detail – but you'll be fascinated by it. Make every effort to visit the
Turins – a rewarding port of call!

menus **B-D** *cards* Visa
closed 1st week July. Feb. Mon. Tues.
post Vauchoux. 70170 Port-sur-Saone. H.-Saône.
phone (84) 91.53.55 *Mich* 242 Colmar 150 km

REMIREMONT   Les Abbesses

Comfortable restaurant/Michelin★   Ⓡ

Jean Claude Aiguier is the fourth member of the *cuisine libre*
team of chefs who work wonders in the western Vosges hills.
Gault Millau and Le Bottin Gourmand rate him the best of the
four; he is a talented, creative chef but he would be the first to
admit that both Philippe and Turin are his equal. It's a simple,
happy place – very much a family affair; Francine, his wife,
welcomes you and takes care of you. Specialities change from
day to day – depending on what is available at the market:
highlights include *foie gras cru au poivre, sandre soufflé au
Crémant d'Alsace* (sparkling wine) and some marvellous local
cheeses and desserts.

I can't recommend the restaurant enough – it offers real value.
I was delighted to introduce a young Englishman to the Aiguiers
– what an exacting training he got in their kitchens.

menus **C** *cards* AE Visa
closed Mid-end June. Mid-end Nov. Wed evg (Sept-Apl). Sun evg.
Mon.
post 93 rue Gén.-de-Gaulle, 88200 Remiremont. Vosges.
phone (29) 62.02.96 *Mich* 242 Colmar 80 km

BERRY-BOURBONNAIS

I must be very frank and admit that my preference is for countryside where a mountain aspect fills the eye with pleasure – wherever that may be. Like the Loire Valley, I ignored the pleasures of this heartland of France for too long.

Most of the north-western quarter of this region is flat, unexciting country – the plentiful wheat-fields of France. Further south are gentle, rolling hills; but everywhere meadows are green, the cattle graze contentedly and the poultry are plump. It is no wonder the country folk love their land and the generous harvests it provides. This is the true heart and soul of France; it is here you sense the basic strengths of the country lie, despite all the upheavals over the centuries.

Surprise yourself by allowing two to three days to explore the quiet, delightful lanes that abound everywhere. The **Indre** Valley is to the west, together with **La Châtre**, nearby **Nohant** (Georges Sand's home) and **Culan**, with its medieval fortress – Joan of Arc stayed there. All the countryside here is at its best in glorious June, when the golden broom shines forth brilliantly. **Lignières** – 20 kilometres east of **Ambrault** – is famous for its château, rebuilt in the 17th-century, and because Calvin, in his student days at Bourges, held meetings in the village.

The most renowned of the Berry châteaux is at **Meillant**. **Bourges** is an intriguing place – its proudest possession is its cathedral; it is one of the finest in France and it took 130 years to build. The town is full of historical treasures.

My bases allow you to do many things. To the north-east is the majestic **Loire** – **Nevers** and **La Charité**, both on its eastern bank, are fascinating towns – and further afield the hills of

40

southern Burgundy beckon. The spa towns of **Bourbon-Lancy**, **Bourbon-l'Archambault** and **St-Honoré-les-Bains** are rewarding diversions; but one essential *déviation* you must make is to the **Forêt de Tronçais** – privately owned and one of the finest oak forests in Europe. Its future will be as interesting as its past; careful regeneration since the war, and thinning-out in the decades to come, will ensure that some magnificent specimens will be growing there by the end of the century. A second essential detour, via lovely **Moulins**, is to the ancient Priory St-Pierre at **Souvigny** – with its intriguing, 12th-century *calendrier*. The last detour you should make is to **Paray-le-Monial**, an old Burgundian town full of riches.

Michelin *yellow* maps: 238.68.69.73. Green Guides: Dordogne (English). Auvergne

IGN *série verte* maps: 35.36.42.43. *série rouge* maps: 108.111

Airport: Clermont-Ferrand

Distances from: Paris–Moulins 293 km Calais–Moulins 587 km

Cheeses Cow's milk

Chambérat is a fruity-tasting cheese – made as a flat, pressed disk. Ideal with **St-Pourçain** wines

Goat's milk

Chevrotin du Bourbonnais a truncated cone and creamy tasting. Best in summer and autumn. Also known as **Conne**

Crézancy-Sancerre small ball – similar taste to Chavignol (see Loire cheeses). **Santranges** is a related, similar cheese

Graçay is a nutty, soft cheese – made as a dark blue-coloured cone

Also see the cheeses listed in the Loire – page 162

Regional Specialities

Bignons small fritters

Bouquettes aux pommes de terre grated potato, mixed with flour, egg white and fried in small, thick pieces

Brayaude (gigot) lamb cooked in white wine, onions and herbs

Chargouère (Chergouère) pastry turnover of plums or prunes

Cousinat (Cousina) chestnut soup (*salée* – salted) with cream, butter and prunes – served with bread

Gargouillau a *clafoutis* of pears

Gouéron a cake of goat cheese and eggs

Gouerre (Gouère) a cake of potato purée, flour, eggs and *fromage blanc*, cooked in an oven as a *tourtière*

Lièvre à la Duchambais hare cooked slowly in a sauce of cream, chopped-up shallots, vinegar and pepper

Milliard (Millat – Milla) a *clafoutis* of cherries

Pâté de pommes de terre a tart of sliced potatoes, butter, bacon and chopped-up onions, baked in an oven. Cream is added to the hot centre

Poirat pear tart

Pompe aux grattons a cake, in the shape of a crown, made of a mixture of small pieces of pork, flour, eggs and butter

Sanciau thick sweet or savoury pancake – made from buckwheat flour

Truffiat grated potato, mixed with flour, eggs and butter and baked

Wines

A small area but interestingly enough some fine wines originate from its borders. **Châteaumeillant** VDQS reds, made from the Gamay grape, are good; **Vins de St-Pourçain-sur-Sioule** are enjoyable Gamay reds and particularly fine Loire-type whites; **Reuilly** and **Quincy**, small wine-making areas to the west of Bourges, have excellent local reputations for their dry white wines – made from the Sauvignon Blanc grape.

ST-PIERRE-LE-MOUTIER   Vieux Puits

Simple hotel
Quiet/Good value

A truly modest, inexpensive place; it has the merit of being well
away form the N7 – on the western side of that busy highway and
very close to the village church.
No restaurant *rooms* 11 **B**
closed Open all the year.
post 58240 St-Pierre-le-Moutier. Nièvre.
phone (86) 68.41.96 *Mich* 238 Moulins 31 km

SANCOINS   Parc

Comfortable hotel
Quiet/Gardens/Good value   ®

An ideal 'base'; an old house in a quiet side street and with the
benefit of a garden, dominated by fir trees. The Parc is well
placed for you to enjoy much of the area: the Forêt de Tronçais;
Meillant; and the Priory at Souvigny. The Hôtel Le Tronçais at
Tronçais has been praised by readers.
No restaurant *rooms* 12 **B**
closed Open all the year.
post rue M.-Adoux, 18600 Sancoins. Cher.
phone (48) 74.56.60 *Mich* 238 Moulins 47 km

Recommendations where cuisine takes second place

AMBRAULT   Commerce

Comfortable restaurant with rooms
Gardens/Good value   ®

An old favourite of ours; the *Logis de France* is just to the north
of Nohant – once the home of Georges Sand. We always enjoyed
inexpensive, copious, fresh fare here – though one reader has
suggested that tinned salmon and food from the freezer was set
before her. That's rare in France and don't let it put you off
visiting the Commerce.
menus **A-B** *rooms* 10 **A-B**
closed 21-28 Mar. Mid Sept-mid Oct. 1-8 Jan. Sun evg. Mon.
post Ambrault. 36120 Ardentes. Indre.
phone (54) 49.01.07 *Mich* 238 Moulins 110 km

SAIL-LES-BAINS   Grand Hôtel

Comfortable hotel
Secluded/Gardens/Tennis/Lift

Don't be fooled by the impressive name; it's an oasis of charm to
the north of the N7 as it heads towards Lyon and the south.
There's a very short season here – the hotel being part of a tiny
spa, the thermal baths lying just below it. Simple cooking. Ideally
placed to explore both the Monts de ſa Madeleine and the
Beaujolais hills.
menus **A-B** *rooms* 32 **B-C**
closed Oct-mid May.
post Sail-les-Bains. 42310 La Pacaudière. Loire.
phone (77) 64.30.81 *Mich* 73 Moulins 74 km

Recommendations where cuisine takes pride of place

BANNEGON   Auberge Moulin de Chaméron

Comfortable restaurant with rooms
Secluded/Terrace/Gardens/Swimming pool   Ⓡ

I cannot recommend this glorious spot enough to you. A tiny
moulin set in lovely country – comfortable bedrooms are in a
separate modern annexe. A bonus is that Jacques Candoré
speaks fluent English – he spent many years in England; Annie,
his wife, acquired her command of the language in California.
Excellent cuisine – *œufs en meurette à la Berrichonne* is an
example. Don't bypass this *Relais du Silence*.
menus **B-C** *rooms* 10 **B-C** *cards* Visa
closed Nov-mid Mar. Thurs (except June-mid Sept).
post Bannegon. 18210 Charenton-du-Cher. Cher.
phone (48) 60.75.80 *Mich* 238 Moulins 65 km

BOURBON-L'ARCHAMBAULT   Acacias

Simple hotel/Michelin★
Gardens

Bourbon-l'Archambault is a small, cool spa town. The Dubost's
restaurant is one of two one-star places here; old Henri Dubost,
once a chef to the Presidents of the Republic, provides
unexciting classical cuisine – much of it built around the beef of
the local Charolais cattle. Support the local wines – the reds from
Sancerre and **St-Pourçain** whites.
menus **A-C** *rooms* 25 **A-B**
closed Feb. Mar. Rest: Mon evg.
post 03160 Bourbon-l'Archambault. Allier.
phone (70) 67.06.24 *Mich* 238 Moulins 23 km

DIGOIN   Gare

Comfortable hotel/Michelin★★
Gardens/Good value   Ⓡ

Jean-Pierre Billoux and the Troisgros brothers at Roanne
(further upstream on the Loire) have much in common: their
hotels are adjacent to stations (two decades ago the now world-
famous Troisgros Restaurant was also called the Hôtel de la
Gare); and their restaurants are well away from the main
autoroutes that take so much traffic south from Paris. Jean-
Pierre is a young man and I still compare his present efforts with
those of his famous neighbours when I first visited them 16 years
ago. He has the skill to go on and become one of the great French
chefs – though, in my opinion, his brilliant talent seems to have
reached a plateau these days. Much inspired in his early days by
the legendary Alexandre Dumaine, he continues to provide
clients with creative, modern cuisine – at remarkable value-for-
money prices: *terrine de pigeonneau à l'ail, côte de bœuf à
l'estragon* (still the best of its kind in France) and excellent
desserts are all examples of his talent.
   The hotel has been modernised by Jean-Pierre and his wife,
Marie-Françoise; but bedrooms overlooking the main road are
noisy and how I hate the hideous pillars in their dining room.
menus **B-C** *rooms* 14 **B-C** *cards* AE DC Visa
closed 19-28 June. Jan. Wed (except July-mid Sept).
post 71160 Digoin. Sâone-et-Loire.
phone (85) 53.03.04 *Mich* 69 Moulins 59 km

MAGNY-COURS   La Renaissance

Very comfortable restaurant with rooms/Michelin★★
Quiet   ®

I enjoyed a magnificent meal on my last visit to this fine
restaurant, south of Nevers. Jean-Claude Dray and his wife watch
over you with great care – and what arrives on your plate is quite
splendid. Attention to detail matters a great deal to this talented
nouveau master – you see it in his delectable and creative *crème
de langoustines*, his *escalope de turbot au concassé de baies
roses* and above all in his range of mouthwatering desserts. Be
sure, too, to try *tapinaude Morvandelle* – a local *gratin
Dauphinois* – and Jean-Claude's version of *fromages rôtis* – a
crottin de Chavignol served hot on toast and accompanied with
a salad, lightly flavoured with a tasty dressing. This is certainly
one restaurant you should not bypass on the busy N7, which,
thankfully, is to the east of the village.
menus **C-D** *rooms* 10 **C** *cards* AE DC
closed 1-15 June. Feb. Sun evg. Mon.
post 58470 Magny-Cours. Nièvre.
phone (86) 58.10.40 *Mich* 238 Moulins 42 km

MOLLES   Relais Fleuri

Comfortable restaurant with rooms
Quiet/Terrace/Gardens/Good value

A small, pretty *Logis de France* run by two sisters – Suzanne
Barichard and Jeanne Lassalle. Their restaurant is just north of
the village, on the D62. It has a sound local reputation for basic
classical cuisine with dishes like *terrine de canard*, *ris de veau
au porto*, *tournedos à la moutarde*, *gratin de fruits de mer* and
pâtisserie maison.
menus **A-C** *rooms* 10 **A-C**
closed Mid Nov-Dec. Wed.
post Molles. 03300 Cusset. Allier.
phone (70) 41.80.01 *Mich* 73 Moulins 65 km

MOULINS   Paris

Luxury hotel/Michelin★★
Lift

Is the Paris for you? Some of you seek – and can afford – luxury
hotels. It could be that this one is for you – though I doubt it.
These days there's no sign of the Laustrial family 'influence'. You
feel that most in the restaurant; despite many waiters buzzing
about, several ordered items (like advertised appetisers and hot
milk with coffee) failed to appear. Cuisine is characterless
classical; regional specialities must be ordered days in advance.
My acid test in places like this is to ask for an inexpensive 'local'
wine (in this case a white **St-Pourçain**) and see what happens.
The look on the *sommelier's* face was the predictable sign of
what inevitably occurred; the wine remained in its ice bucket
until the middle of the second course before I was asked to taste
it! Two stars? No, second rate.
menus **B-C** *rooms* 29 **B-D2** *cards* AE DC Visa
closed Jan. Sun evg and Mon midday (Sept-mid July).
post 21 rue Paris, 03000 Moulins. Allier.
phone (70) 44.00.58 *Mich* 238

POUILLY-SUR-LOIRE   Espérance

Very comfortable restaurant with rooms/Michelin★
Terrace/Gardens

Jacques Raveau makes great use of the renowned products that come from his local *pays*: the Loire figures strongly in many fish dishes – *filets de sandre, matelote, friture* and *mousseline de brochet* are just four examples; the local wines feature in delights like *coq au vin blanc Pouillysoise* and *aiguillette de canard au Sancerre rouge;* and the first-class *chèvre* cheeses from **Chavignol** make a good end to any meal here – served hot on toast. Jacques is a long-established chef and enjoys the reputation of being Pouilly's best *cuisinier*.

menus **B-C** *rooms* 4 C *cards* AE DC Visa

closed Dec (except Xmas). Jan. Sun evg and Mon (out of season).

post 58150 Pouilly-sur-Loire. Nièvre.

phone (86) 39.10.68 *Mich* 238 Moulins 91 km

POUILLY-SUR-LOIRE   Le Relais Fleuri

Comfortable hotel
Fairly quiet/Terrace/Gardens/Good value

The Astruc's hotel is to the south of the village – itself, thankfully, bypassed by the N7. If you want an out of doors lunch with extensive views of the Loire and the hills to the west, this is the place for you. A *Logis de France* where cuisine is completely conventional and of a modest standard; enjoy *truite meunière, truite aux amandes, poulet au Pouilly, cuisses de grenouilles, filets de perche à l'oseille* and *canard rôti* – accompanied by **Pouilly-Fumé** and **Sancerre** wines.

menus **A-C** *rooms* 9 B *cards* Visa

closed 1-15 Oct. Jan. Feb. Wed evg and Thurs (out of season).

post 58150 Pouilly-sur-Loire. Nièvre.

phone (86) 39.12.99 *Mich* 238 Moulins 91 km

ST-POURCAIN-SUR-SIOULE   Chêne Vert

Comfortable hotel/Michelin★

I was persuaded by several readers – including Robin and Judith Yapp (see below) – to visit this long-established and fine family hotel. The Giraudons marry good old-fashioned skills to equally appealing old-fashioned ideas of just what service and comfort should be. I can't say you will get excited about the cuisine – what you will find are classical dishes prepared and presented with care and honesty: the famous *poulet au fromage* (in which **Gruyère** and **Fourme d'Ambert** cheeses feature), *saumon au fenouil, canard Duchambais* and a good *chariot de pâtisseries maison*. Whatever you eat be sure to drink with your food the local wines of **St-Pourçain** – particularly the excellent whites. Be certain to explore the Sioule Gorges – upstream on the river towards its source high in the Auvergne.

I also recommend Robin and Judith's *Vineyards and Vignerons* – a fine, unusual book available from Yapp Brothers, Wine Merchants, The Old Brewery, Mere, Wiltshire.

menus **A-C** *rooms* 35 A-C *cards* AE DC Visa

closed Jan. 1-15 Oct. Tues (Oct-Apl).

post 03500 St-Pourçain-sur-Sioule. Allier.

phone (70) 45.40.65 *Mich* 69 Moulins 31 km

BRITTANY

I have often said in my books that France is so fortunate in having such widely-differing, seductive scenery. Here in Brittany is one of the corners of France which could not be more dissimilar from the other three – namely, the Southwest, Alsace and the Côte d'Azur.

How can I say it is even one region, in the way I have tried to analyse most of the others, when it has a coastline hundreds of kilometres long. What I have decided to do is to split this region into three areas – my base hotels being centred near **St-Malo** on the north coast, at several points in inland Brittany and at various places along the southern coast. Even so I have not included the southern-most tip of the region (around **La Baule** and **St-Nazaire**), an area which could be an alternative holiday spot for any visitor to this part of France.

My northern recommendations cover the coast from **Brest** to **Avranches** in the east. My southern bases allow you to explore from Brest to **Vannes** and provide the chance to get inland – to the **Montagnes Noires** and to a Regional Park with its woods and its gorse, broom and heather moorlands.

Let us look at the north first. You can base yourself close to St-

see page 210

see page 232

see page 150

Malo; its magnificent ramparts, surrounding the old town, will thrill visitors of all ages. My wife and I ignored **Le Mont-St-Michel** for 20 years or so, prejudiced as we were about tourist traps. How stupid we were; it is an enthralling sight and it is worth climbing every step to its summit. The bay is badly silted-up now and the huge, racing tides are much rarer these days.

Dinan and **Dinard** are special favourites of ours. Dinan is the loveliest of Breton towns and, like so many others in France, is a jewel. Dinard is an attractive place, with safe beaches and a good Maritime Museum and Aquarium. In addition it has a large sea-water swimming pool; both our children learned, in a matter of days, how to swim in that supporting water. The nearby **Rance** is a hard-working, rewarding river; literally, as a drive to the tidal power station east of Dinard will prove. Boat trips on the Rance, from either Dinan or St-Malo, are especially interesting.

The coast itself can provide many happy days: **Cancale** and the attractive D201 road to St-Malo, **St-Briac**, **St-Cast**, **Sables d'Or** and the Baie de **Saint-Brieuc**; all of them give endless pleasure to children and adults alike.

From St-Malo you can make a day's run into Normandy's *little*

47

Switzerland, south of Falaise and down to **Bagnoles-de-l'Orne**, itself a delightful spa town set in wooded country. Or you can explore parts of the western edge of the Cotentin Peninsula: **Jullouville**, **Granville** and Coutainville – all are popular.

Alternative bases are provided at several points in the quiet inland parts of Brittany. You could spend weeks exploring the countless coves and bays of Finistère. The hinterland, warmed by the Gulf Stream, is one of France's market-gardens – famous for its early spring vegetables. Many quiet pleasures lie inland: **Huelgoat** and its surrounding countryside; **St-Thégonnec** and **Guimiliau**, each with their *enclos paroissiaux* (parish enclosures) – scores of remarkable 400 years old sculptures – and worthy of the two stars Michelin give them.

Nothing could be nicer for a Brittany holiday than linking together all three sections. If you do this, then you can cross the **Argoat**, the wooded land of inland Brittany. Make the journey travelling via **Josselin** and its famous, picturesque castle (the town is on the canal built by Napoléon from Brest to **Nantes**) and **Pontivy**, a thriving market town.

What are the places to visit from the southern bases? Well, I am assuming, as I do with the Côte d'Azur and Provence, that you will want to do something more than just swim, fish, sail or perhaps ride. This is the coast the British know so well. It is a playground for children; consequently, it is impossibly crowded in July and August – bear this in mind when you follow through any of my suggestions. Every house and every building seems to be a freshly whitewashed one; it certainly is one of the smartest of French regions.

Try to see some of the fishing ports: **Audierne** and **Douarnenez** in the north-west; **Concarneau** further down the coast. Douarnenez (a preserved, medieval town) can be combined with an outing to one of the nicest of all Breton beaches at **St-Anne-la-Palud** with its secluded Hôtel La Plage. Drive up to the nearby **Ménez-Hom** (extensive, panoramic views) and then wander through the lanes to the south of the River **Aulne** (a Regional Nature Park). Nearby **Locronan** is a specially attractive treasure; every visitor should spend an hour or so exploring it. Another fine view awaits those who drive to the top of the Montagne de Locronan.

Carnac is at the centre of a vast area where megaliths are found; over 3000 of these granite pieces, of all sizes, shapes and patterns are scattered over the ground. Both **Vannes** (a fine, historical town) and the inland sea of the **Golfe du Morbihan** deserve your attention. The many boat trips available from Vannes are well worth your time; it is an exhilarating way of seeing this inland sea. The more adventurous will take the ferry from **Quiberon** to **Belle-Ile**; there is no more effective way of finding real peace and quiet. There are the towns of **Quimper** and **Quimperlé** to amble through and to the south of them lie dozens of tranquil lanes, which lead you to coves, rivers, beaches, headlands, beechwoods and pinewoods. There is so much you can see and do. Out of season it is one of the best parts of France, especially in May, June and September.

Michelin *yellow* maps: 230.58.59.63. Green Guide: Brittany (English)

IGN *série verte* maps: 13.14.15.16.24. *série rouge* map: 105

Airports: Nantes. Brest. Rennes. Quimper

Distances	Paris–St Malo	372 km	Calais–St Malo	502 km
from:	Paris–Quimper	552 km	Calais–Quimper	717 km
	Paris–Lannion	511 km	Calais–Lannion	623 km

Cheeses Cow's milk

Campénéac a pressed, uncooked cheese. Strong smell and made in thick disks. Good all the year

Meilleraye de Bretagne at its best in summer. Light smell, ochre-yellow rind, made in large squares

Nantais dit Curé (Fromage du Curé) (Nantais) strong smell, supple, small square of cheese. Good all the year

Port-Salut is a semi-hard, mild cheese, good all the year. Port-Salut was the monastery where the cheese was originally made – at **Entrammes** (Mayenne); the name was sold to a dairy company, though a variety of the type is still produced there. St-Paulin is a related cheese

St-Gildas-des-Bois a triple-cream cheese with a mushroom smell – cylinder shape and available throughout the year

St-Paulin semi-hard, yellow, mild, smooth-textured with a washed, bright orange rind. Made commercially throughout northern France: in Brittany, the Loire Valley, Normandy and Champagne-Ardenne

Try any of these cheeses with the reds from the **Coteaux d'Ancenis** or the whites of **Muscadet** or **Gros Plant du Pays Nantais**.

Regional Specialities

Agneau de pré-salé leg of lamb, from animals pastured in the salt marshes and meadows of Brittany

Bardatte cabbage stuffed with hare – cooked in white wine – and served with chestnuts and roast quail

Beurre blanc sauce for fish dishes; made from the reduction of shallots, wine vinegar and the finest butter (sometimes with dry white wine)

Cotriade fish soup with potatoes, onions, garlic and butter

Crêpes Bretonnes the thinnest of pancakes with a variety of sweet fillings – often called **Crêpes de froment** (wheat flour)

Far Breton batter mixture with a raisin filling

Galette takes various forms: can be a biscuit, a cake or a pancake; the latter is usually stuffed with fillings like mushrooms, ham, cheese or seafood and is called a **Galette de blé noir** (buckwheat flour)

Gâteau Breton thick *galette* (sweet type), flavoured with rum

Gigot de pré-salé same as *agneau de pré-salé*

Palourdes farcies clams in the shell, with a *gratiné* filling

Poulet blanc Breton white Breton chicken. Spend the last few weeks of their lives running free in the meadows

Wines

Whites *best years* 71 74 75 76 78 79 80 81 82

Let me be charitable and allow this region to claim **Muscadet** wines, grown on the southern bank of the Loire, near Nantes. The white, very dry and inexpensive white wines are made from the Muscadet grape (hence their name) and are ideal to drink with fish. The AC wines are **Muscadet**, **Muscadet de Sèvre-et-Maine** and **Muscadet des Coteaux de la Loire**. A junior VDQS cousin is **Gros Plant du Pays Nantais**, made from the Folle Blanche grape. Enjoy, too, the marvellous Breton cider.

Reds

A good VDQS red comes from Ancenis (**Coteaux d'Ancenis**), made from the Gamay grape; the area is east of Nantes, on the northern bank of the Loire.

Vins de Pays

These are similar to the Muscadet whites and Ancenis reds: they will be classified by *département* – **Maine-et-Loire** and **Loire-Atlantique** or **Vin de Pays des Marches de Bretagne**. Vast amounts are made – lots of it is tasteless rubbish; much of the latter makes its way, sadly, to the U.K.

BENODET   Menez-Frost

Very comfortable hotel
Quiet/Gardens/Swimming pool/Tennis

Centrally situated, the Menez-Frost is a mixture of several
buildings – old and new – in a quiet site away from traffic. The
countryside in this part of Brittany is called Cornouaille (the
French translation for Cornwall is *Cornouailles*). Be sure to
make a boat trip on the River Odet – upstream to Quimper. Note
that the impressive Pont de Cornouaille that crosses the Odet at
Bénodet is a toll bridge.

No restaurant *rooms* 52 **C-D2**
closed Oct-Easter.
post 29118 Bénodet. Finistère.
phone (98) 91.03.09 *Mich* 230 Quimper 16 km

BRANDERION   L'Hermine

Comfortable hotel
Quiet

A modern building with an unusually-shaped roof – only nine
bedrooms are available. You will find L'Hermine to the west of
the village on the main road to Hennebont; it makes a good 'base'
if you want dinner at the nearby Château de Locguénolé without
the punitive cost of sleeping there.

No restaurant *rooms* 9 **C**
closed Jan-mid Mar.
post Brandérion. 56700 Hennebont. Morbihan.
phone (97) 36.22.98 *Mich* 230 Quimper 79 km

ERQUY   Eden

Very simple hotel
Quiet/Gardens/Good value

I cannot stress enough that this is a simple place, a few minutes
walk from the fine sandy beach. From the rear of the Eden there
are views over the bay. It's hard to find; locate the *mairie* – and
then drive up the road behind it.

No restaurant *rooms* 17 **A-B**
closed Oct-Mar.
post rue Castelnau, 22430 Erquy. Côtes-du-Nord.
phone (96) 72.32.58 *Mich* 230 St-Malo 48 km

HUELGOAT   An Triskell

Simple hotel
Quiet/Gardens/Good value   ®

Another good-value 'base' – this one is in the heart of inland
Brittany, in an area called the Argoat (in Breton that means
wooded country). It's a simple, whitewashed building, on the D14
to the south of the town. The woods surrounding Huelgoat are a
paradise for walkers – the streams provide fishing for those of
you who want sport of a less strenuous kind.

No restaurant *rooms* 11 **B**
closed Mid Nov-mid Dec.
post route Pleyben, 29218 Huelgoat. Finistère.
phone (98) 99.71.85 *Mich* 230 Lannion 73 km

MORLAIX
Menez

Comfortable hotel
Secluded/Gardens/Good value   ®

An absolutely splendid base hotel – six kilometres north-east of Morlaix at St-Antoine-Plouezoch. The Menez is a stone building; it has immaculate gardens and extensive views to the south-west. It makes an ideal overnight stop if you want to eat at the Relais de Bon Voyage at nearby Plounérin; or, alternatively, if you want peace and quiet and a chance to explore the coast from Roscoff to Lannion.
No restaurant *rooms* 10 **B-C**
closed Sept-mid Oct. Sun evg and Mon (out of season).
post St-Antoine-Plouezoch. 29252 Plouezoch. Finistère.
phone (98) 67.28.25 *Mich* 230 Lannion 35 km

PARAME
Chateaubriand

Comfortable hotel
Quiet

A small place, well to the east of St-Malo. Apart from the bonus of overlooking the sea it provides the chance for you to enjoy the inexpensive restaurants in both St-Malo and Cancale – the latter is famous for its oysters.
No restaurant *rooms* 21 **B-C**
closed Mid Nov-Jan. Mar.
post 8 bd. Hébert, Paramé. 35400 St-Malo. Ille-et-Vilaine.
phone (99) 56.01.19 *Mich* 230 St-Malo 4 km

PARAME/ST-MALO
Alba

Comfortable hotel
Quiet

Another small base hotel but this one is nearer St-Malo itself. It overlooks the sea; the *digue* (promenade) that lies between the hotel and the beach fortunately carries no traffic – a big bonus if children's safety is an important factor.
No restaurant *rooms* 22 **B-C** *cards* Visa
closed Open all the year.
post sur digue, 35400 St-Malo. Ille-et-Vilaine.
phone (99) 56.07.18 *Mich* 230 St-Malo 2 km

PLOMODIERN
Ferme de Porz-Morvan

Simple hotel
Secluded/Gardens/Tennis   ®

A restored 150 years old farm with eight modern, but rather small bedrooms. It has a variety of plus features to its credit: tennis for the active sportsman; a small garden facing south where the inactive can do their bit by just sunbathing; a series of inexpensive restaurants in nearby Châteaulin and Le Faou; and there are many fine sandy beaches close at hand lining the shores of the Baie de Douarnenez.
No restaurant *rooms* 8 **B-C** *cards* Visa
closed Nov-Easter.
post 29127 Plomodiern. Finistère.
phone (98) 81.53.23 *Mich* 230 Quimper 32 km

POULDREUZIC
Moulin de Brénizenec

Comfortable hotel
Quiet/Gardens

An old, stone-built mill converted into a charming 'base' with the bonus of extremely attractive gardens and a pool.
No restaurant *rooms* 10 **C**
closed Mid Sept-Easter.
post route d'Audierne, 29134 Pouldreuzic. Finistère.
phone (98) 58.30.33 *Mich* 230 Quimper 25 km

QUIMPER
Sapinière

Simple hotel
Fairly quiet (rooms at rear)/**Tennis/Good value**

Not an attractively-sited 'base' – but it is inexpensive. Four kilometres south of Quimper on the Bénodet road.
No restaurant *rooms* 40 **B** *cards* AE DC Visa
closed Mid Sept-mid Oct.
post route Bénodet, 2900 Quimper. Finistère.
phone (98) 90.39.63 *Mich* 230 Quimper 4 km

QUIMPERLE
La Châtaigneraie

Very comfortable hotel
Secluded/Gardens

A small, stone-built, 'extrovert' hotel in a wooded park; it's to the south of Quimperlé on the eastern side of the River Laïta and just west of a village called Guidel.
No restaurant *rooms* 10 **D** *cards* DC Visa
closed Open all the year.
post 56520 Guidel. Morbihan.
phone (97) 65.99.93 *Mich* 230 Quimper 58 km

RAGUENES-PLAGE
Men Du

Comfortable hotel
Secluded/Gardens ®

A magnificent, isolated site with sea views from all the bedrooms. You'll not find a nicer 'base' in Brittany.
No restaurant *rooms* 14 **C**
closed Oct-Easter
post Raguenès-Plage. 29139 Nevez. Finistère.
phone (98) 06.84.22 *Mich* 230 Quimper 39 km

VANNES
Les Chèvrefeuilles

Comfortable hotel
Secluded/Gardens/Good value

A super spot; its name – honeysuckle – does it justice. An attractively-designed, modern building set in pretty gardens. On the D19, west of Vannes, on the way to Ste-Anne-d'Auray.
No restaurant *rooms* 10 **B-C**
closed Xmas. Weekends (Oct-Apl).
post 56000 Vannes. Morbihan.
phone (97) 63.14.77 *Mich* 230 Quimper 115 km

Recommendations where cuisine takes second place

DOL-DE-BRETAGNE
Bretagne

Simple hotel
Good value

The Bretagne is a whitewashed *Logis de France*, tucked away in a corner of a square near the 13th-century Cathedral of St-Samson. Catherine Morel-Haelling and her husband, Patrick, maintain the long-established Morel family traditions of first-rate service. Another, more comfortable *Logis*, is the Logis Bresche Arthur (owned by Christian Faveau); both the Dol establishments offer real value-for-money meals.

menus **A** *rooms* 30 **A-B**
closed Mid Sept-mid Oct. Rest: Sat (Oct-Mar).
post place Châteaubriand, 35120 Dol-de-Bretagne. I.-et.-V.
phone (99) 48.02.03 *Mich* 230 St-Malo 24 km

LE FAOU
Vieille Renommée

Comfortable hotel
Lift

Don't be persuaded by others to visit only *Logis de France* hotels; if you did that you would miss many fine places throughout France. The Vieille Renommée is a modern building and both it, and its near neighbour, the Relais de la Place, provide value-for-money cuisine – basic stuff with things like *moules marinière*, *langoustine mayonnaise, faux-filet* and oysters. Both hotels are strongly recommended.

menus **A-C** *rooms* 38 **B-C** *cards* Visa
closed 1-15 Sept. Mid Oct-mid Nov. Feb. Mon.
post place Mairie, 29142 Le Faou. Finistère.
phone (98) 81.90.31 *Mich* 230 Quimper 41

FOUESNANT
Armorique

Comfortable hotel
Quiet(annexe)/**Gardens**

It's the modern annexe at the rear that has the comfortable rooms with fully-fitted bathrooms; the older auberge section has more basic bedrooms. In May the gardens are a riot of colour with camellias in full bloom. Cooking is of a high standard and there's a choice of several low cost menus; Jacques Morvan ensures you get honest value for money.

menus **A-B** *rooms* 25 **B-C**
closed Mid Sept-Mar. Mon (except July-Aug).
post 29170 Fouesnant. Finistère.
phone (98) 56.00.19 *Mich* 230 Quimper 15 km

LANNION
Campanile

Simple hotel
Quiet/Gardens

A useful 'base' – north of the town behind the Rallye supermarket. Modern, small bedrooms. Ignore the grill.

menus **A-B** *rooms* 27 **C** *cards* Visa
closed Open all the year.
post 22300 Lannion. Côtes-du-Nord.
phone (96) 37.70.18 *Mich* 230

PORT LAUNAY   Au Bon Accueil

Comfortable hotel
Lift

Another whitewashed, modern hotel, overlooking the Aulne, and downstream from Châteaulin. The Aulne is a famous salmon river; Mme Le Guillou, the hotel owner, ensures you can try *saumon* in the season – also *sole*, *langouste* and *homard*.
menus A-C *rooms* 59 B-C *cards* AE DC Visa
closed Jan. Rest: Mon (mid Sept-Apl).
post Port Launay. 29150 Châteaulin. Finistère.
phone (98) 86.15.77 *Mich* 230 Quimper 29 km

QUIMPERLE   Hermitage

Comfortable hotel
Secluded/Gardens/Swimming pool   Ⓡ

How welcome that new French law is here – the one that lets you eat wherever you wish; thankfully, you don't have to use the Hermitage's very average restaurant. The hotel section is a series of four buildings in the most enchanting of settings and is surrounded by trees; the *parc* extends to several acres and falls away from the hotel into a wooded, small valley. Two km south of the handsome town.
menus A-C *rooms* 26 C-D
closed Nov-Mar. Rest: Mid Dec-mid Jan. Mon (out of season).
post 29130 Quimperlé. Finistère.
phone (98) 96.04.66 *Mich* 230 Quimper 46 km

ROTHENEUF   Centre

Very simple hotel
Gardens/Good value

This small, whitewashed, unpretentious hotel gave my children a lot of pleasure when they were younger; your letters confirm that is just as true today for the family with hungry youngsters to feed. Menus are based mainly on fresh fish from the ports of Cancale and St-Malo.
menus A *rooms* 23 A-B
closed Mid-end Oct. Mid Dec-Jan. Mon (Oct-Easter).
post Rothéneuf. 35400 St-Malo. Ille-et-Vilaine.
phone (99) 56.96.16 *Mich* 230 St-Malo 6 km

TREBEURDEN   Ti al-Lannec

Comfortable hotel
Secluded/Gardens   Ⓡ

A *Logis de France* and a *Relais du Silence*. Dominated by huge fir trees at the front, it has an added bonus of providing splendid views of the rocky coast 50 metres below you. Cooking is of a better than average standard with delights like *soupe de poissons* and *tarte chaude aux pommes*. The Ti al-Lannec also makes an excellent 'base' hotel.
menus B-C *rooms* 23 C-D *cards* AE
closed Mid Nov-mid Mar. Rest: Mon midday (out of season).
post 22560 Trébeurden. Côtes-du-Nord.
phone (96) 23.57.26 *Mich* 230 Lannion 9 km

AUDIERNE
Le Goyen

Comfortable hotel/Michelin★
Terrace/Lift

Adolphe Bosser is a talented chef – much admired and praised by Gault Millau for his *nouvelle cuisine*. Undoubted highlights on my recent visit were his various pastry specialities: a *ragoût fine de langouste et noix de St-Jacques en millefeuille*; and his fine desserts based on *millefeuilles* with differing fruits, depending on the season. I would not dispute the claim that Le Goyen has probably one of the best restaurants in Finistère. The hotel is a much modernised, old building overlooking the busy port – some rooms have balconies but many are unfortunately small. Under no circumstances must you miss the views from the Pointe du Raz; the bird sanctuary at the Réserve du Cap Sizun; and the 65 metres high lighthouse at Eckmühl.

menus **B-D** *rooms* 34 **C-D**
closed Nov-Mar. Mon (out of season).
post 29113 Audierne. Finistère.
phone (98) 70.08.88 *Mich* 230 Quimper 35 km

CHATEAULIN
Auberge Ducs de Lin

Comfortable restaurant with rooms
Quiet/Gardens

A small place to the south of the town on the Quimper road. The attractive views below you of Châteaulin and the River Aulne will remind you that it is a famous salmon river; that noble fish appears on the menus in many forms – grilled, poached or smoked. Other treasures from the seas appear on the same menus: *huîtres*, *homard*, *crabe* and *sole*. In addition to these delights Louis Le Meur is a first-rate *pâtissier*. Six nice, but expensive bedrooms are available.

menus **A-C** *rooms* 6 **C**
closed Mar. Mid Sept mid Oct. Mon.
post 29150 Châteaulin. Finistère.
phone (98) 86.04.20 *Mich* 230 Quimper 29 km

DINAN
Caravelle

Comfortable restaurant with rooms/Michelin★
Ⓡ

Jean-Claude Marmion is an inventive *cuisinier* – working wonders in a first-floor kitchen above his restaurant; he's much admired by Gault Millau and certainly I'll confirm he is one of the best chefs in Brittany. Seek him out in this ravishing, favourite Breton town of ours – with its arcaded, old streets and the fine views from the bridge across the Rance. The town is loved by painters; Jean-Claude is an artist in his own right. Examples of his imaginative touch and eye are 'pictures' such as *filet de St-Pierre en maillot vert à la crème de poivrons rouges* and *paupiette de bar fourrée aux langoustines au citron vert.* Portions are too big, though mercifully, this chef is not a purée fan. Christiane Marmion looks after you well. Bedrooms are very basic indeed.

alc **C** *rooms* 11 **A-B** *cards* AE DC
closed Oct. Wed (out of season).
post 14 place Duclos, 22100 Dinan. Côtes-du-Nord.
phone (96) 39.00.11 *Mich* 230 St-Malo 29 km

DINAN   D'Avaugour

Comfortable hotel
Gardens/Lift

What a strange – perhaps unique – record Georges Quinton holds according to *French Leave* readers; there have been several letters of complaint concerning poor service and Oliver Twist-sized portions. On the other hand I've received an equal number of glowing compliments – some of you rating the hotel as the best you came across on your northern Brittany holidays. Personally I would not now rate Georges Quinton's cuisine as the best in this part of Brittany – but nevertheless it is creative and good. The hotel is an appealing place with the huge Place Du-Guesclin at the front and the ramparts of Dinan, surrounded by gardens, at the rear. Cooking highlights were *St-Jacques à la nage* and *huîtres chaudes au curry*.

menus **A-C** *rooms* 27 **C-D** *cards* AE DC Visa
closed Mon (out of season).
post 1 place Champs-Clos, 22100 Dinan. Côtes-du-Nord.
phone (96) 39.07.49 *Mich* 230 St-Malo 29 km

LA GOUESNIERE   Gare

Very comfortable hotel/Michelin★
Gardens

This is probably the only Michelin-starred restaurant where the guide gives credit to two chefs – Roger Tirel, the son of the owner, and his brother-in-law, Jean-Luc Guérin. The two of them, and their wives, run a busy dining room: serious diners paying top prices, budget-conscious eaters and noisy groups of package-tour Brits are all shoe-horned in together. I predicted the first star – and I'll predict no further success unless the owners work out a better way of organising their restaurant. (Perhaps they are content to stay the way they are but they could at least reorganise the dining rooms.) Some bedrooms are tiny. The hotel, easily missed, is opposite a railway goods yard surrounded by cauliflower fields.

menus **A-C** *rooms* 58 **A-C**
closed Mid Dec-mid Jan. Rest: Sun evg (Oct-Mar).
post La Gouesnière. 35350 St-Méloir-des-Ondes. I.-et-V.
phone (99) 58.10.46 *Mich* 230 St-Malo 12 km

HENNEBONT   Château de Locguénolé

Very comfortable hotel/Michelin★★
Secluded/Gardens/Swimming pool

An ugly monstrosity of a château – yet here is one of Brittany's most enchanting hotel settings; encircled by handsome woods and, to the west, the estuary of the River Blavet. Madame de la Sablière is the fortunate owner of this successful business; additional good fortune comes with the creative genius of Michel Gaudin – a talented chef and a master of light, *nouvelle cuisine* creations. The hotel is furnished with fine pieces of furniture and several majestic tapestries.

menus **C-D** *rooms* 38 **D-D2** *cards* AE DC Visa
closed Dec-Feb. Rest: Mon (except evgs in season).
post 56700 Hennebont. Morbihan.
phone (97) 76.29.04 *Mich* 230 Quimper 72 km

LIFFRE   Hôtellerie Lion d'Or

Luxury restaurant/Michelin★★
Gardens   ®

Michel Kéréver and his charming wife, Nelly, continue to beguile
visitors to their alluring, luxury restaurant with its small but
pretty garden. If, one day, Brittany is to have its first three-star
restaurant, it will be Michel who will win that coveted honour; his
cuisine is expensive, of course, but nevertheless represents
remarkable value for money. Our last visit was a prodigious tour
de force; his *menu dégustation* was one of the best we have had
in France – full of glittering jewels. An *effiloché de St-Jacques au
caviar*, a *cassolette de langoustines au curry* and a *blanc de
barbue* were exceptional highlights. Michel has opened a much
simpler, smaller dining room, called Le Jardin, next door to the
main restaurant; good-value, basic specialities and much lighter
on the pocket. If you want to stay overnight use La Reposée in
Liffré or Le Germinal at Cesson-Sévigné, well clear of and to the
east of Rennes (quiet/lift).
menus **C-D** (Le Jardin **B**) *cards* AE DC Visa
closed Mid July-mid Aug. Mon. Tues midday.
post 35340 Liffré. Ille-et-Vilaine.
phone (99) 68.31.09 *Mich* 230 St-Malo 73 km

LOCMARIA   Auberge de la Truite

Comfortable restaurant with rooms/Michelin★
Gardens

Don't expect miracles at Mme Le Guillou's restaurant in a
verdant setting. Classical dishes served in a Breton-furnished
house; trees surround it and fill the nearby countryside. The trout
come from the Aulne behind the hotel; *homard* from the Brittany
ports. Try the *gâteau Breton*.
menus **B-D** (evgs-*alc*) *rooms* 6 **A-B**
closed Mid Nov-mid Dec. Sun evg and Mon (except July-Aug).
post Locmaria-Berrière-Gare. 29218 Huelgoat. Finistère.
phone (98) 99.73.05 *Mich* 230 Lannion 73 km

MOELAN-SUR-MER   Les Moulins du Duc

Very comfortable restaurant with rooms/Michelin★
Secluded/Gardens/Swimming pool

Without any shadow of doubt this must be one of the most
delectable settings of any hotel or restaurant in France; indeed, if
you were writing a fictional description of the ideal site it would
probably fail to match the setting here. It's an old, 16th-century
mill on the River Belon (famed for oysters); there's a pool,
cascades and extensive gardens adding extra interest. Bedrooms
are in separate cottages – plagued by ants and noisy 'mini-bar'
fridges. Les Moulins is a 'managed' establishment – you are
unlikely to have contact with the owners, the Quistreberts. A
Japanese, Shigeo Torigai, is the chef: his *nouvelle cuisine* is
much better than average but spoilt by absurd purées; we had
one made with sweetcorn – yuk!
menus **B-D** *rooms* 22 **D** *cards* AE DC Visa
closed Nov-Mar.
post 29116 Moëlan-sur-Mer. Finistère.
phone (98) 96.60.73 *Mich* 230 Quimper 45 km

LE MONT-SAINT-MICHEL

Mère Poulard

Very comfortable hotel/Michelin★
Quiet

Chefs come and go at this world-famous institution – but Bernard
Heyraud manages to maintain high standards in all aspects of his
operation. The Mont is a unique and breathtaking curiosity –
don't miss it. Combine your visit with a meal here; inevitably it
will mean trying the foamy *omelette* made famous by the
legendary Annette Poulard who died 50 years ago. It is the
simplest of dishes cooked with great showmanship in long-
handled pans – fresh eggs, butter and a frenzied, but skilled *tour
de main*. Another not-to-be-missed, appetising speciality is
agneau de pré-salé – lamb, from animals pastured in the vast salt
marshes that surround the Mont. *Homard* and *langouste beurre
blanc* feature strongly – usually grilled and, on the dessert front, a
fairly ordinary *omelette flambée Mère Poulard*. All conventional
stuff in a far from conventional setting.

menus **B-D** *rooms* 27 (only ½ *pension* **D-D2**) *cards* AE DC
closed Oct-Mar.
post 50116 Le Mont-St-Michel. Manche.
phone (33) 60.14.01 *Mich* 230 St-Malo 52 km

MUR-DE-BRETAGNE

Auberge Grand'Maison

Comfortable restaurant with rooms

Jacques and Brigitte Guillo have a well-deserved reputation at
their family Auberge for remarkable, value-for-money, skilled
cuisine; an 'oasis of pleasure' (what awful green paint is used for
the exterior decoration) in what is otherwise a gastronomic
desert in central Brittany. Relish offerings like *turbot mariné à
l'huile de basilic, blanc de St-Pierre au vert, huîtres chaudes* and
a *gratin de fraises*. Jacques recently lost his Michelin red 'R'
rating – but Gault Millau continue to sing his praises. Don't miss
the nearby Lac de Guerlédan and the Forêt de Quénécan in the
hills to the south of the lake.

menus **B-C** *rooms* 15 **B-C**
closed Mid-end June. Mid Sept-end Oct. Sun evg/Mon (except
July-Aug).
post 22530 Mur-de-Bretagne. Côtes-du-Nord.
phone (96) 28.51.10 *Mich* 230 Lannion 76 km

PLEUVEN

Le Gribil

Simple restaurant
Good value

Ⓡ

Many of you have commented very favourably about this tiny,
simple restaurant tucked away in a hidden corner of Cornouaille.
Le Gribil is a few kilometres north-east of Bénodet, away from
the main road and opposite the village church. Nothing
imaginative or inspired about the cooking of Yves Le Coz – just
unpretentious fare based mainly on fresh fish: *daurade aux
algues, turbot, homard* and *belons*; often accompanied with
classic sauces – *au beurre blanc* or *à l'oseille*.

menus **A-B**
closed Sun evg. Mon.
post Pleuven. 29170 Fouesnant. Finistère.
phone (98) 91.62.71 *Mich* 230 Quimper 13 km

PLOUMANACH   Rochers

Very comfortable restaurant with rooms/Michelin★

Ploumanach is a tiny port just west of Perros-Guirec and on the
highly scenic Corniche Bretonne that runs along the granite
coast to Trébeurden. The modern restaurant here is called Chez
Justine – after its owner; it overlooks the bay of Ste-Anne –
unusual in that you cannot identify just where the sea enters the
inland bay. Above average cooking with a few enterprising
offerings: *galette de moules au sabayon, feuilleté de fruits de
mer* and *charlotte aux fraises*. Don't miss the nearby Rochers
(rocks) – an interesting site.
menus **B-D** *rooms* 15 **C** *cards* AE
closed Oct-Mar.
post Ploumanach. 22700 Perros-Guirec. Côtes-du-Nord.
phone (96) 23.23.02 *Mich* 230 Lannion 15 km

PLOUNERIN   Relais de Bon Voyage

Comfortable restaurant/Michelin★   ®

Within three months of strongly recommending Patrick Fer's
small restaurant in the last edition of *French Leave,* I received no
less than three serious letters of complaint. I, in turn, wrote a very
strong letter to Patrick pointing out, constructively, several areas
where changes were needed. A dramatically fast improvement
materialised – and not a single complaint has been received
since; I hope I did not hurt his feelings too much. Patrick is a
brave – but agonisingly timid – individual who has established a
sound reputation for himself at his tiny, unattractive restaurant
on the south side of the busy N12. Cuisine is a mixture of modern
and classical dishes: a series of salads based on *langoustines,
saumon* and other fish; *terrine de rouget au vin de Graves* is a
particularly delightful, light speciality; and many excellent fresh
fish offerings from the local ports – *bar* and *St-Pierre* are just two
examples.
menus **B-C** *cards* AE DC
closed Mid Jan-mid Feb. Wed.
post 22910 Plounérin. Côtes-du-Nord.
phone (96) 38.61.04 *Mich* 230 Lannion 23 km

PONT-AVEN   Moulin Rosmadec

Very comfortable restaurant/Michelin★

Monsieur Sébilleau's famous restaurant is getting expensive. He
is cashing in on its glorious site and he knows full well that he has
to exercise little imagination in the dishes he prepares; tourists
will turn up whatever he does. A pity because the converted mill,
one of the score or so built during the last two or three centuries
along the River Aven, has an enchanting setting. Pont-Aven has
had a long association with many painters, including Gauguin;
artists are still attracted to it today. What pictures will fill your
eyes on your plates here? *Sole au Champagne, langoustines à la
nage, canette au poivre, homard grillé* and other grilled fish
dishes.
menus **B-C**
closed Mid Oct-mid Nov. Feb. Wed.
post 29123 Pont-Aven. Finistère.
phone (98) 06.00.22 *Mich* 230 Quimper 37 km

QUESTEMBERT   Bretagne

Very comfortable restaurant with rooms/Michelin★
Gardens   ®

At the start of 1982 Gault Millau and Michelin, unwittingly, managed to publish their guides with two totally contrasting verdicts on the cooking of Georges Paineau. Michelin gave him the guillotine by chopping off his second star; GM awarded his restaurant three *toques* – one of few in France. In my opinion, GM were right; here you find audacious invention, super, light dishes and a refined, highly personalised style of cooking. I was impressed by some of Georges' offerings: *les suprêmes de pigeonneaux en papillotes aux jeunes légumes* and *fromages de chèvres fermiers en salade* were two; but very unimpressed by some baby-food mush, masquerading under the pretentious name of *l'œuf de grenouille au sabayon de persil*, and his exorbitantly-priced wines. The expensive bedrooms are ultra-modern – complementing his cooking.

alc **C-D** *rooms* 5 **D** *cards* AE DC Visa
closed Jan-mid Mar. Sun evg. Mon.
post rue St-Michel, 56230 Questembert. Morbihan.
phone (97) 26.11.12 *Mich* 230 Quimper 142 km

RAGUENES-PLAGE   Chez Pierre

Comfortable hotel
Quiet/Gardens/Good value   ®

A modernised *Logis de France* – in a quiet setting a few hundred metres from a quiet coast and beach. Cuisine is simple, copious and good value – based primarily on fish: *turbot au Champagne*, *barbue à l'oseille* and *filets de sole aux morilles* are examples. Chez Pierre has a Gault Millau *toque* and a Michelin 'R'.

I have two unusual stories to tell you – one about Chez Pierre and another about my favourite 'base'. In late 1982 I was admonished by a reader for attracting 'the wrong kind of clientèle' to Chez Pierre. Within a few weeks of receiving the letter, *The Good Hotel Guide 1983* was published. Imagine my surprise when the same reader was one of the named contributors recommending the hotel in this fine guide. At about the same time the *Holiday Which? Guide to France* – another fine book – was published saying: 'It's sought out by discriminating English.' What were my reader's motives? Consider her letter's final plea: 'Please don't spoil all of these small hotels for us.'

The second 'tale' concerns my favourite 'base' in France – Le Bosquet at Pégomas (Côte d'Azur); I've known it for two decades. In 1980 I was perhaps one of the first in the U.K. to recommend it, writing: 'I absolutely loathe making it public.' From your letters I know how much pleasure Simone and Jean-Pierre Bernardi have given you. The same *GHG*, in making its recommendation, quoted a couple who said: 'No matter that the Binnses and the Eperons have got here first.' It's possible that the couple took my tip in the first place. I would appreciate them explaining just what they meant – particularly when you consider that Eperon has never recommended it!

menus **A-B** *rooms* 21 **B-C**
closed Mid Sept – May (open Easter). Rest: Wed.
post Raguenès-Plage. 29139 Nevez. Finistère.
phone (98) 06.81.06 *Mich* 230 Quimper 39 km

ROSPORDEN   Arvor

Comfortable hotel
Good value

The Carrets continue to offer sound value-for-money cuisine at
their long-established family hotel. No complaints have been
received about the safe-as-houses, conventional cooking.
menus **A-C** *rooms* 34 **B-C** *cards* Visa
closed Jan. Fri evg, Sat, Sun evg (except mid June-mid Sept).
post place Gare, 29140 Rosporden. Finistère.
phone (98) 59.20.32 *Mich* 230 Quimper 22 km

ROSPORDEN   Gare

Comfortable hotel
Lift/Good value   ®

On the night of May 26/27 1982, a tragic disaster hit young Marcel
Bourhis and his pretty wife, Maryvonne; the Gare was completely
destroyed by fire. The rebuilt building is now a modern, purpose-
built hotel. Before the fire I received many letters of praise for
this talented, budding genius of a chef. I implore you, support the
unlucky couple. Let's hope it will not be long before their first
star arrives.
menus **A-C** *rooms* 25 **C** *cards* Visa
closed Sun evg and Mon (mid Sept-mid June).
post place Gare, 29140 Rosporden. Finistère.
phone (98) 59.23.89 *Mich* 230 Quimper 22 km

STE-ANNE-LA-PALUD   Plage

Very comfortable hotel/Michelin★
Secluded/Gardens/Swimming pool/Lift   ®

This expensive, beguiling hotel continues to charm everyone
who visits it – in a secluded setting, alongside a beach and
protected by a headland. Mme Le Coz continues, too, to delight
her clients, and her chef, Jean-Pierre Le Gloanec, has found a
new creative touch; his fish dishes are ultra light. Two of his
sweets are excellent: *crêpes farcies Morgane* and *duo de soufflés
au fromage blanc et citron*. Please: if you visit the Plage don't
order *salade* and *entrecôte*!
menus **B-C** (evgs – *alc*) *rooms* 30 **D** *cards* AE DC Visa
closed Oct-Mar.
post Ste-Anne-la-Palud. 29127 Plomodiern. Finistère.
phone (98) 92.50.12 *Mich* 230 Quimper 25 km

LE VAL-ANDRE   Cotriade

Comfortable restaurant/Michelin★

Jean-Jacques Le Saout and his wife, Marie-Thérèse, spent years
at the Lutèce, New York. His classical cooking has a light touch:
saumon mariné, feuilleté de barbue and *turbotin au coulis de
homard* are a few of the fish delights. Book ahead at his first-floor
restaurant – with lovely sea views.
menus **B-C** *cards* DC
closed Mid Dec-mid Jan. June. Mon evg. Tues.
post Port de Piégu. 22370 Pléneuf-Val-André. Côtes-du-Nord.
phone (96) 72.20.26 *Mich* 230 St-Malo 54 km

BURGUNDY

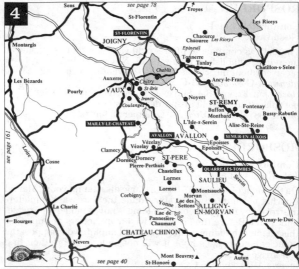

see page 78

see page 161

see page 40

Autoroutes bring big benefits in many ways but they also create their own problems. I must have driven many tens of thousands of kilometres through the back roads of France and I have no reservations in recommending every reader to do just the same. Equally, there are times when I will suggest you get to a chosen region as soon as you can and then explore it quietly and at your own pace. Autoroutes make it easy for you to reach far-flung regions quickly – and safely – particularly if you only have a few days' holiday available. The snag is they can also take you past many of the regions you ought to be enjoying; Burgundy is most certainly one of those regions.

Probably 95 per cent of travellers in France have never ambled through the lanes of Burgundy – little do they realise how much they have missed. You could tour the region several times and still not exhaust all the possibilities.

I would be the first to encourage you to visit the two Burgundian towns known throughout the world, **Dijon** and **Beaune**. But I would not encourage you, the independent tourist, to either sleep or eat in them, as I myself was doing 15 to 20 years ago; there are far better ways of having your cake and eating it. Dijon has a fine museum, the Beaux Arts, and to see it you must make for the lovely inner-city area surrounding the Place de la Libération. When you are there make a special point of walking through the nearby pedestrian-only Rue des Forges.

Beaune, in population terms, is one-eighth the size of Dijon. The Hospices de Beaune and Hôtel-Dieu, together with the Musée du Vin de Bourgogne, are the highlights, but any ramble through the whole inner-town, and the ramparts surrounding it, is well worthwhile. Not far from Beaune is the Château de La Rochepot, with its lovely, multicoloured, tile roof. Towns like **Sens** and **Auxerre** have fine cathedrals; these will lure you if your interests are history and architecture. However, my philosophy is to get away into the hidden attractions of the countryside.

After exploring **Avallon**, you can make one of the many drives in France that demonstrate dramatically what I mean by discovering hidden France. I have rarely seen reference to it, particularly the first part of the excursion. From Avallon follow the **Serein** Valley, from **L'Isle-s-Serein**, through the sleepy old towns of **Noyers**, Annay, Poilly and Chemilly to **Chablis**. Then go east to **Tonnerre** and find time to make a detour to the Château de **Tanlay** and its intricate links with the Coligny brothers and memories of the Religious Wars in the 16th century. Further up the valley towards **Montbard** is **Ancy-le-Franc**, a Renaissance château with magnificent rooms and other treasures. Six kilometres before Montbard is **Buffon** and the Forges de Buffon. The Taylor-Whitehead family will welcome you and show you this intriguing ancient monument (1 June–30 September: afternoons only). Another example of a quiet drive through deserted country is the Yonne Valley south from **Irancy**, through the picturesque towns of **Clamecy**, **Dornecy** and **Corbigny**.

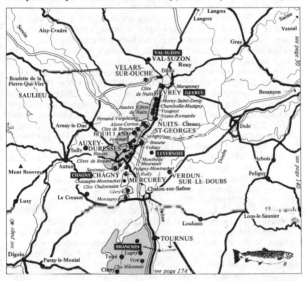

Clamecy is full of old treasures – a rewarding spot if you stop and give it some of your time. The cheese called Dornecy is made in the area between these towns.

It is essential you spend time in the Regional Nature Park of Morvan, from **Autun** in the south to Avallon in the north. It is calm, green countryside studded with lakes and woods – but it is totally ignored by most visitors to France. Don't make the same mistake. Start from Autun in the south (detour via **Sully** with its marvellous château and park); take in the extensive views from **Mont Beuvray**, between Autun and **St-Honoré**. Then strike north to **Château-Chinon** from where you will enjoy more panoramic views, both from the town and the hill above it. To the north are two lakes; **Lac des Settons** and **Lac de Pannesière-Chaumard** – drive the lanes encircling them. Then lose yourself in the maze of minor roads that fan out to the north – on either side of the River **Cure** – but don't on any account miss **Chastellux-s-Cure** and **Pierre-Perthuis**. A pilgrimage to **Vézelay** is imperative – *France à la Carte* tells you about its history. Wander through the Cousin Valley to the south of

63

Avallon. Drive across to the ancient Abbey of **Fontenay**, near Montbard; marvellously restored, it is a superb example of the Cistercian abbeys built 900 years ago. On your way there go via the old fort-like château at **Époisses** and take time out to see the fortified hill-town of **Semur-en-Auxois**. North-east of Semur is the Roman citadel of **Alise-Sainte-Reine** and a kilometre or two away to the north is the best of all the châteaux of Burgundy – **Bussy-Rabutin**; a delightful, small building with lovely gardens.

Autun, an old Roman town, once called the *sister of Rome* by Julius Caesar, is another exhilarating place to make an excursion to; its 800 years old Cathedral of Saint-Lazare is a special highlight. **Taizé**, west of **Tournus** and north of **Cluny** (see Lyonnais, page 174), has a community within it, founded by Brother Roger in 1940. It has attracted thousands of people, of all nationalities – particularly youngsters – in their search for some meaning and inspiration in their lives.

All travellers in France, spending some time in Burgundy, and whether or not they are interested in wine, should explore the two great and important wine-producing areas. The first is the smaller one of Chablis (north of Avallon), including both the village and its surrounding hills and valleys.

The second much bigger and more important area stretches from Dijon down to Mâcon in the south. The Côte d'Or is the general name given to the area from Dijon to **Chagny**; all the great wines come from here. The Route des Grands Crus starts from **Marsannay** in the north, near Dijon, and takes you, in the space of just a few kilometres, through names of tiny villages known throughout the world: **Gevrey-Chambertin**, **Morey-Saint Denis**, **Chambolle-Musigny**, **Vougeot** and **Vosne-Romanée**. This section, between Dijon and Beaune, is called the Côte de Nuits – this the home of most of the great red wines.

South of Beaune is the Côte de Beaune, and again, a host of ordinary but famous villages: **Pommard**, **Volnay**, **Auxey-Duresses** and **Meursault** – most of the great whites come from this area. Beyond Chagny is the Côte Chalonnaise with **Rully**, **Mercurey**, **Givry**, Buxy and **Montagny**. Further south still is the Côte Mâconnais with hamlets like Fuissé (see the Lyonnais region). Many of the cheaper Burgundy wines come from the *côtes* (sides) south of Chagny. All the lanes, hills, fields and villages of these four famous *côtes* are worth seeing; leave your car behind as much as you can and roam them on foot. The area produces some wine beyond the reach of most of us; thankfully, there is much we can all afford (my restaurant recommendations will give you the chance to try them).

One final, isolated spot I would ask you to seek out in the heart of the Morvan Regional Park is just west of **Montsauche** – near Le Boulard. Follow the signs that say *Maquis Bernard* – the track gets rough but don't turn back – and soon you'll arrive at the most poignant cemetery I know in France. Hidden in the trees are the graves of 24 members of the French Resistance, side by side with those of two British airmen (they were shot down returning from a bombing raid on Dijon). What a price was paid by so many brave people to ensure our freedom; it's a heart-stirring place to remember our debt to the hundreds of thousands of soldiers and civilians who died during the last war.

Michelin *yellow* maps: 65.66.69.70. Green Guide: Bourgogne
IGN *série verte* maps: 28.29.36.37. *série rouge* map: 108
Airports: Paris. Lyon
Distances from: Paris–Avallon 224 km Calais–Avallon 518 km
                Paris–Beaune 315 km Calais–Beaune 609 km

Michel and Nelly Kéréver – Liffré (Brittany)

Noyers (Burgundy)

Buffon Forge (Burgundy)

Bénodet (Brittany)

Cheeses Cow's milk

Aisy-Cendré cured in **Marc** and stored in wood ashes. Firm, strong-smelling, fruity taste; good with full-bodied red wines

Boulette de La Pierre-Qui-Vire amusingly named – made at the abbey of the same name near St-Léger-Vauban. Small, firm ball – herb flavoured

Chaource to the west of Les Riceys. At its best in summer and autumn – a creamy cheese, made in cylinders; mushroom smell

Cîteaux thick disk, very rare and made by the monks at Cîteaux Monastery – once a rival of Cluny. Cîteaux is to the east of Nuits-St-Georges

Ducs from the area of Tonnere; a soft cylinder ideal with **St-Bris** whites

Epoisses soft, orange-dusted, made as a flat cylinder. At its best in the summer, autumn and winter and it goes well with full-bodied red wines

Langres small, cone-shaped and strong. Related to Epoisses – and is made north of Dijon. Try it with red Burgundies

Les Riceys from the borders of Champagne and Burgundy; a still **Rosé des Riceys** comes from the same area and is classified as a Champagne wine. Try it with this soft, fruity-tasting, small disk of cheese

Rouy related to Epoisses. Strong smell, soft and made as a square

St-Florentin related to Epoisses. Smooth, red-brown appearance with spicy taste. Season summer to winter

Goat's milk

Dornecy just west of Vézelay. Small, firm, upright cylinder

Lormes south of Avallon, related to both Dornecy and Vézelay

Montrachet soft, mild and creamy – made as a tall cylinder

Pourly slight nutty flavour, soft and made as a small cylinder

Vézelay a farm produced cheese, at its best in summer and autumn. Soft, and in the form of a cone, with a bluish rind

Regional Specialities

Bœuf Bourguignon braised beef simmered in wine-based sauce

Charolais (pièce de) steak from the excellent Charolais cattle

Garbure heavy soup, with mixture of pork, cabbage, beans and sausages

Gougère cheese pastry, based on Gruyère cheese

Jambon persillé parsley-flavoured ham, served cold in its jelly

Jambon en saupiquet, Jambon à la crème, Jambon à la Morvandelle ham with a piquant cream sauce, wine and wine vinegar

Matelote freshwater fish soup, usually based on a red wine sauce

Meurette red wine-based sauce with small onions. Accompanies fish or poached egg dishes

Pain d'épice spiced honeycake from Dijon

Pochouse (pouchouse) stew of freshwater fish and garlic, usually white wine based

Potée see *Garbure*

Wines

I have asked you to always try local wines; the only difficulty in this region is that some of the locals are the most famous and expensive in the world. Some *Grand Cru* wines, dating back to the best vintage years, could cost as much as you are paying for your whole holiday. The simple reason for this is that the Côte d'Or, where the best Burgundy wines come from, produces less than one-tenth of the AC wines of Bordeaux; yet, there is a complex patchwork of many dozens of Appellation Contrôlée classifications, every one of them listed here. All the famous Burgundies, those at the very top of the pyramid, both in quality and price, will have labels that identify them down to the *commune*, followed by the vineyard, *Domaine* or *Clos* itself, some no bigger than a pocket handkerchief. Most of them will have their own AC, whereas in Bordeaux, the famous châteaux share the AC for the local *commune* or region. In Burgundy, the term *Premier Cru* means the second rank vineyards – below the *Grand Cru* top level.

The best red Burgundy is usually less dry and is sweeter than a claret, warm and more full-bodied. The great white Burgundies, rich and dry, are far and away the best whites to drink with food, but most of them are priced out of reach of us all. The groups of AC classifications that follow have all been listed in **north** to **south** order; this will help you to locate and identify each village, and the estates within them, more readily.

Famous Reds *best years* 49 59 61 64 69 71 76 78 79 81 82
This first group are the great red wine *communes*, each with their own AC; in brackets are shown the individual Appellation Contrôlée estates within each village. These are the great wine-producing estates, the *Grand Cru* vineyards:

Gevrey-Chambertin	(**Mazis-Chambertin, Ruchottes-Chambertin, Chapelle-Chambertin, Griotte-Chambertin, Chambertin Clos de Bèze, Chambertin, Charmes-Chambertin, Latricières-Chambertin, Mazoyères-Chambertin**)
Morey-Saint Denis	(**Clos de la Roche, Clos Saint Denis, Clos de Tart**)
Chambolle-Musigny	(**Bonnes Mares, Musigny**)
Vougeot	(**Clos de Vougeot**)
Vosne-Romanée	(**Echézeaux, Grands Echézeaux, Richebourg, Romanée-Saint Vivant, Romanée, Romanée-Conti, La Tâche:** these are some of the world's best vineyards)
Nuits-Saint Georges	
Aloxe-Corton	(**Corton, Charlemagne**)
Pernand-Vergelesses	
Savigny-lès-Beaune	
Beaune	
Pommard	
Volnay	(**Volnay-Santenots;** not a *Grand Cru* and lying in Meursault)
Monthélie	
Auxey-Duresses	
Santenay	

Famous Whites *best years* 71 74 75 & 77 *(Chablis)* 78 79 81 82
The following are the famous white wine villages with AC classifications (estates with their own AC are shown in brackets):

Chablis	To the east of Auxerre; **Grand** and **Premier Cru** classifications
Aloxe-Corton	(**Corton-Charlemagne**)
Meursault	
Puligny-Montrachet	(**Chevalier-Montrachet, Bienvenues Bâtard-Montrachet, Montrachet, Bâtard-Montrachet, Criots-Bâtard-Montrachet**)
Chassagne-Montrachet	
Pouilly-Fuissé	Well to the south, near Mâcon

Rosés
Perhaps the best rosé in France comes from **Marsannay**, the village at the northern end of the Route des Grands Crus. It takes the **AC Bourgogne** with the addition of the words **Rosé Marsannay**. A host of general rosé wines have their own AC

classifications – all starting with the word **Bourgogne**: **Grand Ordinaire Rosé**; **Ordinaire Rosé**; **Rosé**; **Rosé Hautes Côtes de Beaune**; and **Rosé Hautes Côtes de Nuits**.

Less-Famous Wines

The ordinary traveller will have to be content with the wines carrying humbler labels, and thankfully, amongst the dozens of appellations, there are many really good, inexpensive wines like the following examples:

Reds

Bourgogne Ordinaire. **Bourgogne Grand Ordinaire** (made from the Gamay grape – the lowest Burgundy Appellation: *Clairet* – this term, if applied to any Burgundy wines, means they will be light red wines). **Bourgogne Passetoutgrains** (a mixture of Gamay – two-thirds – and Pinot Noir – one-third: slightly further up the quality scale). **Bourgogne** – made from Pinot Noir – is an even more highly thought of Appellation and is produced in much the greatest quantities amongst the reds of the area. **Bourgogne Marsannay** and **Bourgogne-Marsannay-la-Côte**. **Fixin**. **Bourgogne Hautes Côtes de Nuits**. **Côte de Nuits (Vins Fins)**. **Côte de Nuits-Villages**. **Bourgogne Hautes Côtes de Beaune**. **Ladoix**. **Chorey-lès-Beaune**. **Côte de Beaune**. **Côte de Beaune-Villages**. **Blagny**. **Dezize-lès-Maranges**. **Sampigny-lès-Maranges**. **Cheilly-lès-Maranges**. **Mercurey**. **Givry**. **Mâcon (rouge)**. **Mâcon Supérieur**.

Whites

Petit Chablis. **Bourgogne**. **Bourgogne Aligoté** (the second rank grape type, but the most common general white Burgundy). **Auxey-Duresses**. **Saint Romain**. **Saint Aubin**. **Rully-Montagny** (the wines of **Buxy** take the AC for Montagny). **Mâcon (blanc)**. **Mâcon-Villages**. **Pinot Chardonnay-Mâcon** (an example of a *varietal* wine). **Pouilly-Loché**. **Pouilly-Vinzelles** (these last two villages, just east of Fuissé, are cheaper alternatives to Pouilly-Fuissé; they do not have the right to that famous name). **Saint Véran** (see page 174: several villages straddling Pouilly-Fuissé and including Saint Vérand – note the different spelling – have the right to this AC; again, a similar wine to its famous namesake). Many restaurants in the area describe Mâconnais wines by village names: noteworthy are **Viré** and **Lugny**.

Many of the villages in the lists produce both red and white wines. Remember also that many of the well-known *communes* in the first two lists will have vineyards in them that have the right to claim the AC for the village, but, nevertheless, do not have the reputation of some of their famous neighbours; many of those villages will have excellent wines at much lower price levels.

Other wines

If you are based at Avallon, or anywhere in the north of the region, look out for the red **Irancy**, the light **Rosé Irancy** and the crisp, dry, white wine called **Sauvignon de St-Bris**, made in two tiny villages on the eastern bank of the Yonne. Other local villages are **Chitry** and **Coulanges** – their names are often seen on wine lists. Look out, too, for a **Crémant de Bourgogne** or a **Bourgogne mousseux**. Try the **Marc de Bourgogne**, pure spirit, distilled from grapes after the final pressing. Dijon is where Cassis is produced; that rich syrup made from blackcurrants, and, when added to white wine (particularly good with Aligoté) it becomes **Kir**, named after Canon Kir, a mayor of Dijon and a hero of the *Résistance*. With Crémant de Bourgogne – called **Royal Kir**. Relish, too, Liqueur de Poires William.

AVALLON   Moulin des Templiers

Comfortable hotel
Secluded/Gardens   ®

This is certainly one of my favourite base hotels in France; it's
one of two in Burgundy that echo perfectly what I consider to be
the ideal qualifications for a 'base'. For a start it is *sans
restaurant* – this allows you to eat wherever you wish or not at
all for that matter. The handsomely restored old *moulin*, owned
by Madame Hilmoine, has another important ingredient of any
'base' – either a quiet or a secluded setting; in this case it's an
isolated spot, alongside one of the prettiest small rivers in
Burgundy, the tree-lined Cousin. The third desirable qualification
is met, too: a whole host of good restaurants are nearby – from
Vaux in the north, down to Saulieu in the south. Close at hand of
course are some other fine restaurants including, in my opinion,
at St-Père, one of the best in France. At Pontaubert, just a few
hundred metres away, is a small *Logis de France* called Les
Fleurs; two readers have praised its simple, honest cuisine – but
I've not had the chance to try it yet. Finally, the Moulin des
Templiers gets a 100 per cent rating when it comes to considering
the last qualification – things to see and enjoy in the
neighbourhood; there's endless variety to choose from here.
You'll love the Moulin.
No restaurant *rooms* 14 **B-C**
closed Nov-mid Mar.
post 89200 Avallon. Yonne.
phone (86) 34.10.80 *Mich* 65 Avallon 4 km

AVALLON   Vauban

Comfortable hotel
Fairly quiet/Gardens/Lift

A new 'base' in Avallon; the Manoir has been dropped as its
owners have allowed it to become a decrepit place. The Vauban
is much quieter than you think – despite being on the N6. It's an
old building, completely modernised, and all but one or two of
the bedrooms are at the rear of the hotel – overlooking a park; all
bedrooms are extremely well fitted out. I suggest you ask for *une
chambre tranquille* when you reserve rooms. The Vauban is
ideally placed for you to enjoy Jean Breton's cooking up the road
at the nearby Restaurant Morvan.
No restaurant *rooms* 26 **B-C**
closed Mid-end Nov.
post 53 rue Paris, 89200 Avallon. Yonne.
phone (86) 34.36.99 *Mich* 65

CHAGNY   Poste

Simple hotel
Fairly quiet

The Poste is 100 metres or so away from the world-famous
Lameloise Restaurant. Here you will save francs if you don't
mind a simple place to rest your head for the night.
No restaurant *rooms* 11 **C**
closed Dec-Feb. Sun (out of season).
post 17 rue Poste, 71150 Chagny. Saône-et-Loire.
phone (85) 87.08.27 *Mich* 69 Beaune 15 km

GEVREY-CHAMBERTIN   Grands Crus
Comfortable hotel
Quiet/Gardens   ®

This is the second base hotel in Burgundy that I consider among
the very best in France. The Grands Crus is a small, modern hotel
– built a few years ago, it has some of the prettiest window boxes
you'll see anywhere. The owners have real green fingers (or do
they belong to Madame Mortet?), as the show of magnificent
geraniums will confirm; the care taken in planting a variety of
shrubs, plants and bushes when the hotel was first built is now
producing real benefits – as the whole site has the look of a long-
established building and garden. The hotel is to the north of the
village and lies on the Route des Grands Crus; across the road are
some of the famous *commune* vineyards. The owners are also
very fortunate in having possibly the most attractive manageress
you'll meet in France – Geneviève Méry; she speaks English well
and looks after you admirably. She was very surprised by one
group of *French Leave* readers from the United States who took
my advice on base hotels just a bit too literally; amongst their
evening restaurant visits was one to Paul Bocuse in Lyon – 180
kilometres away. It did not help matters when they got lost on
their way back – it meant a long wait-up for poor Geneviève.
Another group even drove to Bordeaux and back in a single day!
If you prefer a simpler, less expensive meal than the high cost of
eating out at La Rôtisserie, try Les Millésimes, just around the
corner from the hotel; this latter restaurant, recommended by
many of you, is closed on Tuesdays.
No restaurant *rooms* 24 **C**
closed Mid Dec-mid Feb. Sun (mid Nov-end Feb).
post 21220 Gevrey-Chambertin. Côte-d'Or.
phone (80) 34.34.15 *Mich* 66 Beaune 27 km

LEVERNOIS   Parc
Simple hotel
Quiet/Gardens/Good value

This simple place has proved very popular with *French Leave*
readers – the hotel is a clever conversion of some old farm
buildings. To find it, leave the A6 (Beaune exit) and follow signs
towards Verdun-sur-le-Doubs (D970). Be certain to book ahead –
particularly in the high season.
No restaurant *rooms* **B**
closed Mid Nov-mid Dec. 25 Feb-mid Mar.
post Levernois. 21200 Beaune. Côte-d'Or.
phone (80) 22.22.51 *Mich* 69 Beaune 5 km

VAL-SUZON   Le Chalet de la Fontaine aux Geais
Comfortable hotel
Secluded

Le Chalet is easily missed as you pass through the village on the
N71; it's in an attractive wooded setting behind the Host. Val-
Suzon – see the entry listed in category three.
No restaurant *rooms* 10 **B-C**
closed Mid Nov-mid Mar. Wed.
post Val-Suzon. 21121 Fontaine-lès-Dijon. Côte-d'Or.
phone (80) 31.61.19 *Mich* 66 Beaune 55 km

Recommendations where cuisine takes second place

MAILLY-LE-CHATEAU
Le Castel

Comfortable hotel
Quiet/Gardens
®

The perfect example of what I had in mind when I decided on three separate categories in this edition of *French Leave*; a *Relais du Silence* resting quietly in the shadow of a 13th-century church. Good cooking. Enjoy the river views of the Yonne from the terrace on the edge of the village. M. Breerette speaks English.

menus **A-B** *rooms* 12 **B-C**
closed Mid-end Nov. Jan-mid Feb. Tues evg/Wed (Oct-Mar).
post 89590 Mailly-le-Château. Yonne.
phone (86) 40.43.06 *Mich* 65 Avallon 30 km

QUARRE-LES-TOMBES
Nord et Poste

Simple hotel
Good value
®

Hidden France readers have fallen in love with this Burgundian auberge – in the heart of the Morvan Regional Park. You'll enjoy Burgundy specialities – like *saupiquet* and *jambon du Morvan* – and many lighter, newer dishes, such as *terrine aux 3 poissons*. The Rostains look after you well. Be certain to seek out the views from the Rocher de la Pérouse.

menus **A-B** *rooms* 35 **B-C**
closed Open all the year.
post 89630 Quarré-les-Tombes. Yonne.
phone (86) 32.24.55 *Mich* 65 Avallon 19 km

ST-FLORENTIN
Moulin des Pommerats

Comfortable hotel
Secluded/Gardens

A delightful *Logis de France* – north of St-Florentin at Venizy. Apart from the delectable setting of the Moulin, what can be guaranteed is a warm welcome from the owner, Paul Reumaux D'Equainville – a marvellous individual who speaks fluent English. He's a proud ex-RAF flyer – a member of the 345 French Squadron, based in England during World War II.

menus **A-C** *rooms* 12 **C-D** *cards* AE DC Visa
closed Mid-end Feb. Sun evg and Mon (out of season).
post Venizy. 89210 Brienon sur Armençon. Yonne.
phone (86) 35.08.04 *Mich* 61 Avallon 87 km

SEMUR-EN-AUXOIS
Lac

Comfortable hotel
Quiet/Terrace/Good value

This entry should perhaps be in category three – cooking is of a high standard. You will enjoy Burgundian specialities like *jambon persillé, escargots* and *truite de Fontenay* (the trout farm is near the famous abbey). The modern, lakeside hotel is south of the medieval town of Semur.

menus **A-B** *rooms* 23 **A-C** *cards* Visa
closed Mid Dec -Jan. Mon (except July-Aug). Rest: Sun evg.
post 21140 Semur-en-Auxois. Côte-d'Or.
phone (80) 97.11.11 *Mich* 65 Avallon 45 km

Recommendations where cuisine takes pride of place

ALLIGNY-EN-MORVAN   Auberge du Morvan

Very simple restaurant with rooms
Good value

One of the most humble restaurants you'll find in *French Leave 3*;
like the Morvan Regional Park, which surrounds the Auberge, it
gives simple, rustic satisfaction. Relish Morvan delights like
jambon en saupiquet and *potée du Morvan*.
menus **A-C** *rooms* 5 **B**
closed Mid Nov-mid Dec. Jan. Rest: Thurs. Evgs in winter.
post Alligny-en-Morvan. 58230 Montsauche. Nièvre.
phone (86) 76.13.90 *Mich* 65 Avallon 50 km

AUXEY-DURESSES   La Crémaillère

Comfortable restaurant

I was taken to task last year because I described this place as
'simple – but a smarter than usual village restaurant.' O.K. then –
it's comfortable. Enjoy regional dishes like *coq au vin*, *estouffade
à la Bourgogne* and *jambon persillé*. You are surrounded by
vineyards; try the wines at the restaurant's *caveau*.
menus **A-B**
closed Feb-mid Mar. Mon (except July-Aug). Tues.
post Auxey-Duresses. 21190 Meursault. Côte-d'Or.
phone (80) 21.22.60 *Mich* 69 Beaune 8 km

AVALLON   Hostellerie de la Poste

Luxury hotel/Michelin★★
Quiet/Terrace/Gardens

In the last edition of *French Leave* I recalled how, in 1963, my
wife and I visited the famous Hostellerie de la Poste and had our
first meal at a three-star restaurant. We made many sacrifices to
have that chance – but how disappointed we were. The following
year the Poste lost its third star. In earlier editions I did not
recommend it; however, two or three of you wrote and suggested
I should try it again.
  I did – and, to be blunt, I'm utterly flabbergasted that this over
rated restaurant should still have two Michelin stars. (To put my
criticism to the test first try the nearby Espérance at St-Père –
Marc Meneau's superb home.) The debits are many: a small,
uncomfortable dining room; cooking which is a mixture of both
classical and poor *nouvelle cuisine* – both a *bisque de homard*
and a *filet de chevreuil poivrade et ses purées* must have had the
contents of a pepper-pot dropped in them; some tasteless purées;
miserable desserts; and such wretchedly expensive wines. I had
a magnificent 1979 **Pommard** but that pepper-pot ruined it. Two
Americans, at a nearby table, made this telling comment: "This is
a place where you feel you could do better at home." They had
made the mistake – as so many tourists do – of booking meal and
room at a fixed price. The consequence of that is that you eat
what you are given; a chicken dish put before them was pathetic.
Please, my American friends – give it a miss; perhaps Napoléon
and Mrs Simpson had no choice!
alc **C-D** *rooms* 30 **D-D2** *cards* AE DC Visa
closed Dec.
post 89200 Avallon. Yonne.
phone (86) 34.06.12 *Mich* 65

AVALLON   Morvan

Very comfortable restaurant/Michelin★
Terrace/Gardens   ®

Jean Breton – a *Maître Cuisinier de France* – does what he sets
out to do marvellously well; a straightforward set of specialities
prepared in an unpretentious manner and served in an equally
unpretentious setting. Don't expect imaginative creations –
you'll find dishes like *boudins aux fruits de mer*, *délice de
volaille au Noilly*, *escalope de veau fourrée* and a host of old-
fashioned choices. But his many *terrines* are magnificent –
particularly the famous *Le Rougeot* (smoked wild duck); he
'bottles' a whole range of these delights and you can buy them
before you leave the Morvan – they travel well!
menus **B** *cards* AE DC Visa
closed Feb. Thurs. Evgs (out of season but except Sat).
post 7 route Paris, 89200 Avallon. Yonne.
phone (86) 34.18.20 *Mich* 65

BOUILLAND   Host. du Vieux Moulin

Very comfortable restaurant with rooms
Secluded

A new young chef has taken over the reins at this ravishing spot
at the head of the Rhoin Valley – a bit of Jura-like country. Jean-
Pierre Silva is not yet 30 – some of his training was at the Auberge
Mourrachonne at Mouans-Sartoux (see Côte d'Azur). Doesn't it
show as his style is light, modern and enjoyable: *bavarois de
truite de mer à la crème d'herbes fraîches* is one example; relish,
too, his *petits choux farcis* – in which he uses different fish and
fungi, depending on the season.
menus **B-C** *rooms* 8 **C** *cards* AE DC Visa
closed Mid Dec-Jan. Wed.
post Bouilland. 21420 Savigny-lès-Beaune. Côte-d'Or.
phone (80) 21.51.16 *Mich* 66 Beaune 16 km

CHAGNY   Lameloise

Very comfortable hotel/Michelin★★★

I wrote in the last edition of *French Leave* what a constant source
of delight it had been for me to watch, over two decades, the
progress of a family and the continually improving standards of
cuisine that have emerged at Lameloise. Old Jean Lameloise and
his son, Jacques, have converted their Burgundian home into a
comfortable hotel; their fixed-price menus, considering the
standard of their cooking, represent value for money – but not
the à la carte menus. What a lack-lustre performance they
managed on my last visit. Every dish was of a mediocre quality:
this applied equally to the *foie gras frais*, the *blanc de turbot*, the
ris de veau and the desserts. The restaurant was packed solid –
including a huge party of Japanese visitors in a private dining
room; it's always the same when 100 guests or more are dining –
standards slip badly. Three-star quality? Hardly. Lameloise 'T-
shirts' are on sale. What next?
alc **C** *rooms* 25 **C-D** *cards* Visa
closed 24 Apl-4 May. Mid Nov-mid Dec. Wed. Thurs midday.
post 71150 Chagny. Saône-et-Loire.
phone (85) 87.08.85 *Mich* 69 Beaune 15 km

CHATEAU-CHINON   Au Vieux Morvan

Simple hotel
Good value

Many of you have written praising this modest hotel – though one reader complained, justifiably, of having to pay 25 francs for the use of a shower! The town is 2000 feet above sea-level and is at the southern end of the Morvan Regional Park; you get extensive views from the hotel, the town and the viewpoint called Le Calvaire above it. Menus concentrate on regional fare – at modest cost and with generous portions: *terrine de campagne*, *andouillette au Pouilly* and *jambon au Madère* are examples of the sort of pleasures you will enjoy. Michelin – why have you dropped the red 'R' recommendation?
menus A-B *rooms* 23 A-C
closed Mid Nov-Dec.
post 58120 Château-Chinon. Nièvre.
phone (86) 85.05.01 *Mich* 69 Avallon 62 km

GEVREY-CHAMBERTIN La Rôtisserie du Chambertin

Very comfortable restaurant/Michelin★   ®

Here at Gevrey-Chambertin, Céline Menneveau takes on the male chefs of France – and shows most of them how it should be done. In male-orientated France – particularly in professional kitchens – that is no mean task, believe me. Over the years Céline has become one of the best chefs in the country; what stresses and pressures she must have had to undergo to achieve her present status – I admire her greatly. She has yet to win the second Michelin star that she so richly deserves – but Gault Millau are one step ahead of their rivals and have already honoured her with the rare accolade – for a *cuisinière* – of three *toques*. Bravo Gault Millau!

The air-conditioned restaurant is in old wine cellars; the descent to the dining rooms is in itself full of interest. You pass rooms with papier mâché and wax figures, dressed authentically, carrying out various tasks associated with wine making; each scene is full of detail, matched by clever lighting and taped background Burgundian drinking songs. Céline's husband, Pierre, who speaks fluent English, is a loyal and enthusiastic supporter of his wife's superb talent.

She is full of inspired ideas. I remember one supreme delight: some raw salmon with a mousse of smoked haddock and caviar – what exquisite perfection; Pierre ensures you try all these different-tasting ingredients together – rather than one at a time. Another memorable dish was *les ravioli aux truffes* – with a magical sauce of tarragon, mushrooms, lemon and cream. Anne and I finished our meal here with some of the most beguiling *petits fours* we have had in France – no less than nine different varieties. At the end of your meal, accompanied no doubt by a bottle or two from the Menneveau wine cellars, ask to see the minute, modern kitchen where Céline weaves her magic. Over the years Bocuse has had some very tough things to say about lady chefs – 'unimaginative' was one description. Céline, as much as any other, proves him wrong.
alc C
closed 23 July-22 Aug. Feb. Sun evg. Mon.
post 21220 Gevrey-Chambertin. Côte-d'Or.
phone (80) 34.33.20 *Mich* 66 Beaune 27 km

JOIGNY
A la Côte St-Jacques

Luxury restaurant with rooms/Michelin★★
Swimming pool

My last visit to Michel Lorrain's lavishly fitted-out 18th-century restaurant left me with mixed impressions. First the positive reactions: excellent, modern, creative cooking – epitomised by *agneau de lait des Alpilles aux petits légumes* without, for once, those *purées* of mashed-up vegetables filling the plate; a magnificent selection of cheeses – served with a huge basket of walnuts; and the chance to order many specialities in small quantities for just about half the normal price. Some negative aspects grated however: far too many plastic flowers for a luxury-rated, swish restaurant; an *aiguillette de caneton aux figues fraîches* – unbelievably sweet; a boutique selling dresses; and wines at sky-high prices – including the local ones.
menus **C-D** *rooms* 18 **C-D** *cards* AE DC Visa
closed Jan. Mon evg and Tues (except July-Aug-Sept).
post 14 fg. Paris, 89300 Joigny. Yonne.
phone (86) 62.09.70 *Mich* 65 Avallon 87 km

JOIGNY
Modern' H Frères Godard

Very comfortable hotel/Michelin★
Swimming pool

An old family favourite of ours; though these days it really has been changed and improved out of all recognition from a couple of decades ago – with a corresponding hike in prices. Jean-Claude Godard runs the Joigny hotel (brother Charles looks after the newly-acquired Paris et Poste in Sens) – his style of cuisine is changing rapidly, too. Many of his father's famous dishes are still on the menus but so are a host of less heavy alternatives – thank heavens for that.
menus **B-C** *rooms* 22 **C-D** *cards* AE DE Visa
closed Mid Nov-mid Dec.
post av. Robert-Petit, 89300 Joigny. Yonne.
phone (86) 62.16.28 *Mich* 65 Avallon 87 km

MERCUREY
Hôtellerie du Val d'Or

Comfortable restaurant with rooms/Michelin★
Gardens/Good value ®

I've received a veritable deluge of letters in praise of this fine Burgundian restaurant: Jean-Claude Cogny, his family and his highly competent staff should be justly proud of the shower of compliments they have caused to be rained down on me. His specialities – both classical and regional treasures – are priced at levels which make the ones at the Joigny establishments above look like highway robbery. A 90 francs menu included three fine dishes – particularly good being the *terrine chaude de lotte aux moules* and an excellent dessert. A warm, welcoming dining room, full of flowers – made even more glowing with a **Mercurey** Chante Fluté white, a lovely local wine.
menus **A-C** *rooms* 12 **B-C** *cards* Visa
closed 1-15 Sept. Mid Dec-mid Jan. Mon. Tues midday (mid Mar-mid Nov). Sun evg (mid Nov-mid Mar).
post Mercurey. 71640 Givry. Saône-et-Loire.
phone (85) 47.13.70 *Mich* 69 Beaune.27 km

NUITS-ST-GEORGES   Côte d'Or

Comfortable restaurant/Michelin★

You will not find a more conscientious, diligent chef than Jean Crotet – a dark, quiet man who has worked immensely hard in establishing a top-class name for himself in Burgundy. Jean follows the classical cuisine road and he does it very successfully indeed. Undoubtedly for me the highlight of any meal here would be Jean's own *foie gras de canard Côte d'Or*; it's exceptional by any standards – and it's no wonder that he has the reputation for serving perhaps the best *foie gras* in Burgundy. Other highlights were a *panaché du pêcheur au beurre blanc*, a *magret de canard aigre-doux* (as good as any you would get in Gascony itself) and some delectable *sorbets maison*. There are some magnificent vintages on the restaurant's wine list; Jean calls them *vins du pays* – which is a bit of an understatement to put it mildly.

menus **B-C** *cards* AE DC Visa
closed Aug. 19 Dec-4 Jan. Sun evg. Wed.
post 21700 Nuits-St-Georges. Côte-d'Or.
phone (80) 61.06.10 *Mich* 66 Beaune 17 km

ST-PERE   Espérance

Very comfortable restaurant with rooms/Michelin★★
Gardens   ®

For me there are no doubts now – Marc Meneau is currently one of the very best chefs in France. For a decade I have thrilled at the progress Marc has made in developing his formidable cooking skills – I sensed as long ago as 1974 that here was a three-star chef of the future. (Michelin are dragging their heels, making absolutely sure.) Gault Millau have already rated him one of the best – he was their 'chef of the year' in 1983.

Marc was born in the village, close to his present auberge and was trained in Charleville-Mezières. Françoise, his wife, is a local girl, too; together they took over the family restaurant business in 1968 and six years later they bought their present house. Just turned 40, Marc has a rare talent and is an inspired chef – the master of *faites simple*. The road to a third star is not an easy one – it's frightening to hear him talk of the expensive investments they have made in improving the fabric of the place: the superbly done glass dining room extension; the bedrooms in the old building that are being modernised, one by one; and the *moulin* that acts as an annexe. After one visit in 1982 – following the receipt of three letters from *French Leave* readers who complained about service and prices – it was clear that I had to make constructive observations about some aspects of the operation. To do this with a favourite chef was not easy – but it is a measure of the man that he accepted the complaints without quibbling and has put matters right.

Menus change from day to day. Amongst many memorable delights that I can recall, *langoustines rôties au beurre léger*, fingers of Bresse chicken breasts with a curry sauce, and a superb hot *feuilleté de fromages* (using Roquefort, Reblochon, Emmenthal and a local *chèvre*), stand out as highlights. Marc certainly lives by those two vital words – *faites simple*.

menus **B** (lunch only-not Sun)-D *rooms* 19 D *cards* Visa
closed Jan. Tues (out of season). Wed midday.
post St-Père. 89450 Vézelay. Yonne.
phone (86) 33.20.45 *Mich* 65 Avallon 15 km

ST-RÉMY

St-Rémy

Very comfortable restaurant
Good value

Jean and Madeleine Clara's restaurant was recommended to me
by the Taylor-Whiteheads (their home is a *monument historique*
– a fascinating restored forge at Buffon, just a mile or two away).
St-Rémy is four kilometres from Montbard, on the N5 towards
Paris; the restaurant has the main Paris railway line behind it and
across the road is the Canal de Bourgogne. It will be a range of
Burgundian specialities that will entice you here: *œufs en
meurette, escargots* and *saupiquet Montbardois à la façon de M.
Belin* (the great chef at the Hôtel de la Gare in Montbard – he died
a few years ago).
menus **A-B** *cards* DC Visa
closed 10-30 Sept. Jan. Mon. Evgs (except Sat).
post St-Rémy. 21500 Montbard. Côte-d'Or.
phone (80) 92.13.44 *Mich* 65 Avallon 44 km

SAULIEU

Côte d'Or

Very comfortable restaurant with rooms/Michelin★★

Gault Millau are great fans of Bernard Loiseau – they rate him
among the top 20 or so French chefs. He must believe what they
say about him because his prices have been jacked-up to three-
star levels – as high as those at Blanc, Lameloise and Chapel. I
revisited Loiseau last year to see if my earlier criticism had been
misplaced – but I'm still not happy. His cooking is ultra-modern,
ultra-light and ultra-*libre*. A *soupe de St-Jacques aux orties* was
tasteless; a *vinaigrette de saumon aux endives* was excellent; so
was a *tarte chaude et légère aux pommes* – a paper-thin miracle
of lightness. His *petits fours* were a joke.

   The Côte d'Or is a soulless place, lacking in atmosphere. It was
the home of the legendary Dumaine (see *Pen Pictures*); in his day
he provided the personality that compensated for the morgue-
like feel of the place. Neither Loiseau, nor his new wife, Chantal,
appeared once during the evening; with only five clients that
wouldn't have been asking a lot. What a fundamental error to
make – especially at the dull Côte d'Or.
alc **C-D** *rooms* 17 **C-D** *cards* AE DC Visa
closed Mid Nov-mid Dec. Tues (Nov-Apl).
post 21210 Saulieu. Côte-d'Or.
phone (80) 64.07.66 *Mich* 65 Avallon 39 km

VAL-SUZON

Host. Val-Suzon

Comfortable restaurant with rooms
Quiet/Gardens

I first used this country auberge over two decades ago when the
Ballot family had established it as a one-star restaurant; these
days the old, rustic building – in a green, attractive setting – is as
pleasant as ever. A young chef, Yves Perreau, is in the kitchens –
his specialities include things like *escargots* and *gratin de
queues d'écrevisses.*
menus **B-C** *rooms* 8 **B-C** *cards* AE DC
closed Jan. Wed. Thurs midday.
post Val-Suzon. 21121 Fontaine-lès-Dijon. Côte-d'Or.
phone (80) 31.60.15 *Mich* 66 Beaune 55 km

VAUX   La Petite Auberge

Comfortable restaurant/Michelin★   ®

Jean-Luc and Marie Barnabet have won the hearts of many
French Leave readers; I fell in love with their tiny Auberge – in a
tranquil setting alongside the tree-lined River Yonne – many
years ago. Like so many young couples starting off with their own
restaurant, they have had to work like slaves to make their mark;
Marie recently had her first baby and that has increased the
pressures on her. Jean-Luc is progressing rapidly; in 1983 he won
his second *toque* from Gault Millau – an excellent sign of
improving cooking skills. He does much to promote local wines:
witness the reds from **Epineuil** – near Tonnerre; and the **Clos de
la Chaînette** vintage from a pocket-sized vineyard in the shadow
of the cathedral at Auxerre – Alexandre Dumas considered this
one of the greatest of red wines. There are no signs that the
Barnabets are going to re-open their bedrooms; so, in the
meantime, use Les Clairions in Auxerre (quiet, modern and with
the advantage of a lift).
menus **B-C**
closed 1-15 July. Feb. Sun evg. Mon. Public holidays.
post Vaux. 89290 Champs-sur-Yonne. Yonne.
phone (86) 53.80.08 *Mich* 65 Avallon 46 km

VELARS-SUR-OUCHE   Auberge Gourmande

Comfortable restaurant/Michelin★
Good value

A flower-bedecked Auberge, close to the Canal de Bourgogne.
The Michelin star is awarded to the Barbiers for doing basic
things really well. They will offer you a range of inexpensive
delights like *terrines, coq au vin, soupe de langoustines* and
turbot grillé – unexciting but good value.
menus **A-B** *cards* DC
closed Sun evg. Mon.
post Velars-sur-Ouche. 21370 Plombières-lès-Dijon. Côte-d'Or.
phone (80) 33.62.51 *Mich* 66 Beaune 44 km

VERDUN-SUR-LE-DOUBS   Host. Bourguignonne

Very comfortable restaurant with rooms
Quiet (annexe)/**Gardens**

Young Dominique Lauriot and his wife, Evelyne, will give you a
warm welcome at their Normandy-styled auberge – set in its own
grounds to the south-east of the town. Slowly but surely the
present generation of Lauriots are restoring the reputation that
the father enjoyed just after the war when a Michelin star shone
overhead. I did say in the last edition of *French Leave* that the
star ought to return soon; I think I was premature as there are
several aspects of the cuisine that need improving – certainly
Gault Millau seem generous in awarding them two *toques*.
Cooking is a mixture of Burgundy, Lyonnais and *nouvelle
cuisine*: *brochet du Doubs aux écrevisses de Saône* and *pochouse
Verdunoise* are good.
menus **B-C** *rooms* 14 **C** *cards* AE DC Visa
closed 15-30 Sept. 18 Dec-Feb. Mon evg (out of season). Tues.
post 71350 Verdun-sur-le-Doubs. Saône-et-Loire.
phone (91) 91.51.45 *Mich* 70 Beaune 22 km

CHAMPAGNE-ARDENNE

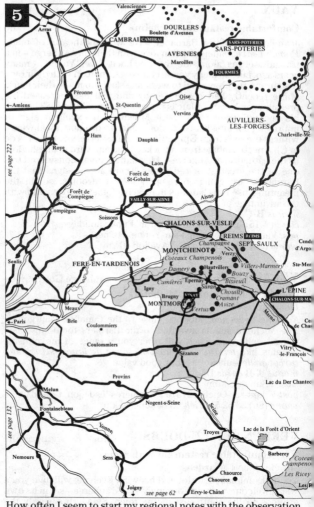

How often I seem to start my regional notes with the observation that so many travellers in France miss the special pleasures of that particular region; Champagne-Ardenne is no exception. I have split this region into three divisions: **Avesnes** and the countryside and the forests of the **Ardennes** to the east; the area between **Reims** and **Troyes**; and the quiet, wooded hills and valleys of Lorraine, contained in a triangle from **Verdun** to **Metz** to **Nancy** – the **Regional Nature Park of Lorraine**.

The country surrounding Avesnes is quiet, attractive, wooded and non-industrial (that sort of activity being far to the north-west). Due east from Avesnes are the forests of the Ardennes, on either side of the River **Meuse** and River **Semoy**. The Meuse is worth following down from Namur, through **Dinant** (both in Belgium) and on to **Charleville-Mézières**. Don't miss the latter –

78

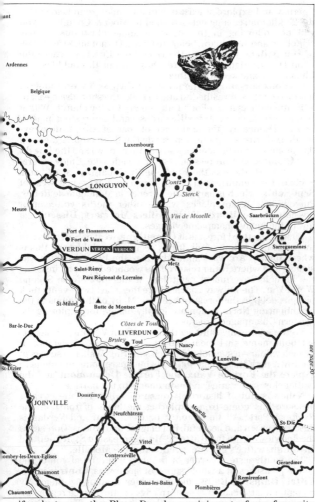

Ardennes

Belgique

Luxembourg

LONGUYON

Contz

Sierck

Meuse

Vin de Moselle

Saarbrücken

Fort de Douaumont

Fort de Vaux

VERDUN ▪VERDUN▪ ▪VERDUN▪

Metz

Sarreguemines

Saint-Rémy

Parc Régional de Lorraine

St-Mihiel

▲ Butte de Montsec

Côtes de Toul

LIVERDUN ●

Bruley ● Toul

Nancy

Bar-le-Duc

Lunéville

St-Dizier

Domrémy

JOINVILLE

Neufchâteau

Moselle

St-Dié

ombey-les-Deux-Eglises

Vittel

Contrexéville

Epinal

Gérardmer

Chaumont

Bains-les-Bains

Plombières

Remiremont

Chaumont

see page 30

if only to see the Place Ducale, reminiscent of my favourite square in Paris – the Place des Vosges (few tourists to the capital see it; built by Henry IV, it has a fascinating history, worth investigating). No wonder – as two architect brothers designed each of them.

Further south is Champagne country. **Laon** was once the capital of France and it sits on top of a high hill, with panoramic views of the surrounding country. Reims and **Epernay** should have top priority for a visit; primarily to see the cathedral at Reims which took 300 years to complete and is the most sacred building in France. All the kings of France were crowned there. Another good reason for a visit to either town is for you to tour any one of the hospitable cellars of the Champagne firms within them. Visit the Musée du Champagne et de la Préhistoire in

79

Epernay and explore at least one of the underground *caves* (try the 25 kilometres long cellar owned by Moët & Chandon – you will be following in the steps of some illustrious people, Napoléon and Wellington being just two). Do not miss the Abbey of **Hautvillers**, just across the river from Epernay, where the blind Dom Pérignon discovered how to put the bubbles into Champagne and keep them there.

Châlons-sur-Marne is far too easy to bypass. Take a couple of hours to explore its cathedral and to make the short drive east to **L'Epine** with its marvellous 15th-century Gothic church. Within striking distance of **Joinville** are several interesting places: Troyes, **Domrémy** (the birthplace of Joan of Arc), **Colombey-les-deux-Eglises** (where Général-de-Gaulle lived and died – a fine monument in his memory stands there now) and the **Lac du Der Chantecoq**, Europe's largest man-made lake. Enjoy several forests. First, there is the **Forêt de St-Gobain**, west of Laon. Second, the centuries-old beech forest of **Verzy**, just west of **Sept-Saulx**, which is part of the Forêt de la Montagne de Reims. Surrounding it are places whose other merits you cannot possibly ignore: **Bouzy**, Verzy, **Villers-Marmery**, **Bisseuil** – a few of the many Champagne villages.

Finally, the third forest is at **Compiègne**, west of **Soissons** and the most interesting of all. It has seen so much history: this is where Joan of Arc was captured; where the 1918 Armistice was signed; and where Hitler restored his wounded pride by insisting the French Government capitulate at the start of the Second World War. The railway coach where these last two events took place is deep in the forest of beeches. Many of the hotels in the neighbouring North region are ideally placed for exploring the western Champagne-Ardenne.

To the east is my third section, based on Verdun – a unique, symbolic name that means so much to France. A symbol of French valour – a symbol of French suffering. Walk the streets of the town with their many interests but spare some moments to explore the **Fort de Vaux**, the **Fort de Douaumont** and the battlefields, cemeteries and monuments to the north-east.

Nancy is full of historical treasures – but, for me, greater pleasure has come from exploring the lanes of the Lorraine Regional Park. All the country between **Toul** and Verdun is deserted, green and peaceful; full of lakes and woods. Don't miss the fine views from the **Butte de Montsec**, east of **St Mihiel**, and **Liverdun**, with its fine site, overlooking the **Moselle**.

The south-eastern corner of the map will remind you of the gentle pleasures of a whole series of spa towns: **Contrexéville**, **Vittel**, **Bains-les-Bains** and **Plombières** amongst them. My recommendations on the western edges of the Alsace region are ideally sited to allow you to explore these spas. The southern boundaries include a range of worthwhile diversions – the Burgundy bases at Avallon are close to them all. Troyes is the most obvious with its cathedral and many fine churches. Deserted alternatives are the cheese and wine villages of **Chaource** and **Les Riceys** and both the **Lac** and **Forêt d'Orient**. Michelin *yellow* maps: 241.53.56.57.61.62. Green Guides: Nord de la France. Vosges

IGN *série verte* maps: 4.5.9.10.11.22.23. *série rouge* maps: 101.103.104

Airports: Paris. Lille. Strasbourg

Distances from:	Paris–Avesnes	203 km	Calais–Avesnes	204 km
	Paris–Reims	143 km	Calais–Reims	287 km
	Paris–Verdun	263 km	Calais–Verdun	410 km

Cheeses Cow's milk

Barberey from the area between Chaource and Les Riceys. A soft, musty-smelling, small cylinder. Best in summer and autumn

Boulette d'Avesnes soft, pear-shaped and pungent bouquet. Sharp and strong – try it with **Genièvre** (see the North region)

Brie soft, white rind, the size of a long-playing record. Try with **Bouzy**

Caprice des Dieux soft and mild, packed in oval-shaped boxes

Cendré d'Argonne from north of Châlons-s-Marne; soft, ash coated

Cendré de Champagne (Cendré des Riceys) mainly from Châlons-s-Marne – Vitry area. Flat disk and coated with ashes

Chaource at its best in summer and autumn; a creamy cheese, made in cylinders and with a mushroom smell. From the borders of Burgundy

Chaumont related to Epoisses and Langres cheeses (see Burgundy). Cone-shaped, soft cheese with strong smell

Coulommiers like Brie, but a smaller, 45 rpm disc. At its best in summer, autumn and winter

Dauphin from the Avesnes area. Soft, seasoned, crescent-shaped, heart or loaf. Is related to Boulette d'Avesnes

Ervy-le-Châtel truncated cone – firm with a mushroom smell

Igny made by monks at the Igny Monastery – a pressed flat disk

Maroilles soft, slightly salty and gold. Appears in many regional dishes

Les Riceys from the area south of Troyes. Home also of a good Rosé des Riceys wine. Best seasons, summer and autumn. Flat disk, no strong smell and fruity taste. Try the local wine with it

Saint Rémy a spicy-tasting, strong-smelling, reddish-coloured square

Regional Specialities

Flamiche aux Maroilles see *Tarte aux Maroilles*

Flamiche aux poireaux puff-pastry tart with cream and leeks

Goyère see *Tarte aux Maroilles*

Hochepot a *pot-au-feu* of the North (see *Pepperpot*)

Pepperpot stew of mutton, pork, beer and vegetables

Rabotte (Rabote) whole apple wrapped in pastry and baked

Sanguette black pudding, made with rabbit's blood

Tarte aux Maroilles a tart based on the local cheese

Waterzooï a cross between soup and stew, usually of fish or chicken

Wines best years 64 66 69 70 71 73 75 76

Champagne is the only area in France where the AC classification does not have to be shown on the labels of bottles.

A **Crémant de Cramant** (*crémant* means about half the normal bubbles) is a delicious alternative to Champagne. There are many non-sparkling wines from the Champagne area worth looking out for; the broadest classification is **Coteaux Champenois**. Whites from **Cramant**, **Villers-Marmery**, **Avize** and **Chouilly** and a **Rosé des Riceys** (with its own AC – see map) are good. You may also see a **Chardonnay** (the Champagne area white grape), usually carrying a merchant's name (**Saran** – made by Moët & Chandon is one). Other good wines are the reds: a delicate **Bisseuil**; a light **Bouzy**; and those from **Vertus**, **Damery** and **Cumières** (all made from the other important Champagne grape – Pinot Noir). Refer also to the Montchenot entry. The term **ratafia** describes a mixture of brandy and unfermented Champagne.

To the north-east of the region – in Lorraine country – are two VDQS areas: **Côtes de Toul** (the village name **Bruley** is often used on local lists) and **Vin de Moselle** (from the Metz area – wines made in **Contz** and **Sierck**, both spas, appear on menus); wines of all shades are made in both areas but the dry **Vin Gris** (a pale pink) is the most common.

Base Hotels

CAMBRAI

Beatus

Very comfortable hotel
Quiet

A modern, two-storey building well back from the main N44 Paris road that heads south out of the town.
No restaurant *rooms* 26 **C** *cards* AE DC Visa
closed Open all the year.
post route Paris, 59400 Cambrai. Nord.
phone (27) 81.45.70 *Mich* 53 Avesnes 54 km

CHALONS-SUR-MARNE

Pasteur

Comfortable hotel
Quiet/Good value

Châlons is a fairly big town – but don't be put off; the Pasteur is easy to find, has a quiet site and no parking worries.
No restaurant *rooms* 28 **A-B** *cards* Visa
closed Open all the year.
post 46 rue Pasteur, 51000 Châlons-sur-Marne. Marne.
phone (26) 68.10.00 *Mich* 241 Reims 45 km

FOURMIES

Ibis

Simple hotel
Secluded

One of the Ibis chain of modern hotels; this one is in an isolated site at the Etang des Moines – south-east of Fourmies.
No restaurant *rooms* 31 **C** *cards* Visa
closed Open all the year.
post l'Etang des Moines. 59610 Fourmies. Nord.
phone (27) 60.21.54 *Mich* 241 Avesnes 16 km

SARS-POTERIES

Auberge Fleurie

Comfortable hotel
Quiet/Gardens/Good value   ®

The Auberge is a small, attractive hotel – an excellent conversion of old farm buildings. It is run as a separate business from the famous restaurant that sits alongside the main road in front of it. Ideal 'base' for the nearby restaurants.
No restaurant *rooms* 11 **B-C**
closed Mid-end Aug. Feb. Sun evg. Mon.
post 59216 Sars-Poteries. Nord.
phone (27) 61.62.72 *Mich* 241 Avesnes 9 km

VERDUN

Montaulbain

Simple hotel
Fairly quiet/Good value

Don't expect miracles here; it's modest, quiet and inexpensive – behind the Monoprix in the Rue Mazel.
No restaurant *rooms* 10 **B**
closed Open all the year.
post 4 rue Vieille-Prison, 55100 Verdun. Meuse.
phone (29) 86.00.47 *Mich* 241

REIMS
Novotel

Very comfortable hotel
Fairly quiet/Swimming pool

Like any Novotel I recommend, I intend you to use this one as a
'base' hotel – ignoring the grill. It's well clear of Reims – at the
point where the Paris autoroute passes underneath the Soissons
road. Ask for a quiet room (at the rear). You'll find this 'base' ideal
for the restaurants in Reims, Châlons-sur-Vesle and Montchenot.
Parking is easy. (See page 320.)
Ignore restaurant *rooms* 125 **D** *cards* AE DC Visa
closed Open all the year.
post 51100 Reims. Marne.
phone (26) 08.11.61 *Mich* 241

VAILLY-SUR-AISNE
Cheval d'Or

Very simple hotel (no showers or baths)
Good value

A mixed record for this humble place in the attractive Aisne
Valley. One or two of you wrote to say what good value it offers –
another letter complained about a 'rip-off' with wines. We have
known it for 25 years – and it has always provided simple fare at
low cost; don't expect miracles.
menus **A-B** *rooms* 20 **A** *cards* Visa
closed Feb.
post 02370 Vailly-sur-Aisne. Aisne.
phone (23) 54.70.56 *Mich* 56 Reims 49 km

VERDUN
Bellevue

Very comfortable hotel
Gardens/Terrace/Lift

The restaurant of this ugly-looking hotel has now closed; I have
not listed the Bellevue as a 'base' as it does not have a quiet site. If
you require meals use the Coq Hardi (see category three) – both
hotels are owned by the Leloup family. Across the road from the
Bellevue is *le jardin botanique* – an attractive corner of this
poignant town.
No restaurant *rooms* 72 **B-D** *cards* AE DC Visa
closed Feb.
post rond-point De-Lattre-de-Tassigny, 55100 Verdun. Meuse.
phone (29) 84.39.41 *Mich* 241

VINAY
La Briqueterie

Very comfortable hotel
Quiet/Gardens ®

Readers of my previous editions will not be surprised to hear that
this lovely, modern hotel, set in pretty gardens is still dropping
'bricks'; French law now allows hotel clients to eat wherever
they wish – so stick to the rules La Briqueterie! Meals are of a
reasonable standard – and expensive.
menus **C** *rooms* 42 **D** *cards* AE DC Visa
closed Xmas
post Vinay. 51200 Epernay. Marne.
phone (26) 54.11.22 *Mich* 241 Reims 33 km

AUVILLERS-LES-FORGES
Host. Lenoir

Very comfortable restaurant with rooms/Michelin★★
Quiet/Gardens/Lift

Jean Lenoir soldiers on – consistently supported by Michelin with a two-star rating; charity indeed. A mixed bag of comments have come from readers: some of you have enjoyed the quiet site of this long-established, family-owned Hostellerie in the hamlet of Auvillers, which is well away from the main N43 from Cambrai to Charleville-Mézières; some of you have admired his light hand applied to old classics and his own inventions; one or two of you have not been happy with Jean's cooking – 'nothing like it used to be' was a representative comment. Lenoir was trained at Namur, in Belgium – he is unique in that none of the other top French chefs have this background; not surprisingly Belgians flock here in great numbers – particularly at weekends. Typical specialities are: *escalope de foie d'oie au vinaigre de cidre, noisette d'agneau aux morilles, mousse de grives au foie gras* and a wide choice of sweets.

menus **B-C** *rooms* 21 **B-D** *cards* AE DC
closed Jan-mid Feb. Fri.
post Auvillers-les-Forges. 08260 Maubert-Fontaine. Ardennes.
phone (24) 54.30.11 *Mich* 241 Avesnes 56 km

AVESNES-SUR-HELPE
Crémaillère

Comfortable restaurant/Michelin★

Prior to 1983 Gault Millau used to get very excited about this Avesnes restaurant – thank heavens sense now prevails as they have demoted it to the more basic rating of one *toque*. If a Michelin star can be won with cuisine as ordinary as this – well, any of us can do it. A *St-Pierre Orientale* (with saffron) was not a success; nor were a wretched peach *feuilleté* dessert and pathetic *petits fours* – burnt and sickly. I can only imagine the crowded place thrives because of the Belgian trade; if you have an appetite you may like it, too. A dish worth trying is *Le Bouriboui* – duck with 1000 spices!

menus **B-C** *cards* AE Visa
closed 1-15 July. Jan. Mon evg. Tues.
post 59440 Avesnes-sur-Helpe. Nord.
phone (27) 61.02.30 *Mich* 241

CAMBRAI
Château de la Motte Fénelon

Very comfortable restaurant with rooms
Quiet/Gardens/Swimming pool/Tennis/Lift

This far better than average restaurant has a very unusual setting in the north-east corner of Cambrai – a series of buildings in a large wooded park. A big bonus for this part of France is that the swimming pool is an indoor one. Cooking, too, is excellent – with many welcome light touches: enjoy dishes like *navarin de grosses langoustines au Sauternes, rillettes de saumon rose* and *fricassée de ris et rognons de veau à la menthe.* Arguably Cambrai's only bright corner.

menus **B-C** *rooms* **C** *cards* AE DC Visa
closed Aug. Sun evg.
post square du Château, 59400 Cambrai. Nord.
phone (27) 83.61.38 *Mich* 53 Avesnes 54 km

CHALONS-SUR-VESLE   Assiette Champenoise
Very comfortable restaurant/Michelin★   ®

Jean-Pierre Lallement is one of the great young chefs of France; just turned 30, he has a shining talent that is going to get brighter as the years go by. He and his wife, Marie-Colette, are a quiet couple. They have turned the ground floor of a cottage-type building into three delightful dining rooms – attractive furnishings, stylish table settings and clever use of lighting all combine to give it a rare charm. Jean-Pierre was trained by Guérard, Vergé and his local hero – Gérard Boyer. He has an artist's skill in the presentation of his specialities; his extraordinary *les noix de St-Jacques à la nage de légumes* is one example – it tasted as good as it looked. Other examples are the unusual appetisers served before the meal – combinations of tastes sure to make tastebuds start working. This young genius knows what must be done to reach the top – you see it in his commitment already to employing four first-class young waiters – worthy of a three-star restaurant.

alc **B-C** *cards* DC Visa
closed Feb. Sun evg. Wed.
post Châlons-sur-Vesle. 51140 Jonchery-sur-Vesle. Marne.
phone (26) 49.34.94 *Mich* 241 Reims 10 km

DOURLERS   Auberge du Châtelet
Comfortable restaurant/Michelin★
Gardens

All sorts of changes to report at Dourlers. Jeanne Drouin has sold her old property – the Auberge du Grand St-Pierre – to the Carlier family. The latter sadly 'lost' their restaurant at Sains-du-Nord as a result of a fire in late 1982. Now they continue to please their clients in the new Auberge du Châtelet. Pierre Carlier speaks English. The same classical specialities are the order of the day here, too: *andouillette de Troyes grillée, tarte aux Maroilles* and superb *chevreuil* (in season). Marvellous value-for-money-cooking in a nice setting.

menus **A-C** *cards* AE DC Visa
closed Mid Aug – mid Sept. 1–15 Jan. Sun evgs. Wed.
post 59228 Dourlers. Nord.
phone (27) 61.06.70 *Mich* 241 Avesnes 8 km

L'EPINE   Aux Armes de Champagne
Comfortable hotel/Michelin★
Gardens

A series of mixed comments about the Pérardel's hotel – five miles or so to the east of Châlons-sur-Marne. Some of you love it – using it regularly for overnight stops as you travel south or east; many of you have complained about noise and service – and, in one case, a dead fly in the soup! Monsieur Houard's cooking is uninspired stuff with the merit of some light touches: *escalope de foie gras chaud au ratafia et aux épinards* and *pigeon au vin rouge des coteaux* are typical.

menus **A-C** *rooms* 39 **B-C** *cards* DC Visa
closed Mid Jan-mid Feb.
post L'Epine. 51000 Châlons-sur-Marne. Marne.
phone (26) 68.10.43 *Mich* 241 Reims 53 km

FERE-EN-TARDENOIS   Host. du Château

Luxury hotel/Michelin★★
Secluded/Gardens/Tennis

This is one of the great French châteaux hotels; part
Renaissance, part 19th-century, it has magnificent bedrooms and
general rooms. The site, too, is equally stunning – much loved by
film and TV producers; the ancient ruins of a 13th-century castle
dominate the scene. The pleasures of the table are also renowned
– mercifully cooking is modern, light and creative; standards are
high, expensive and are backed up by impeccable service and
first-rate fittings – but give me Lallement, down the road, any day.
One 'blot' on the Blots' copybook (the owners) was the inability
to provide a cup of tea in the late afternoon! Visit the American
World War One cemetery at Fère where 6012 are buried; it's
superbly maintained – and is a poignant, salutary reminder of the
part our U.S. Allies played in both wars.
menus **C-D** *rooms* 19 **D-D2** *cards* Visa
closed Jan. Feb.
post 02130 Fère-en-Tardenois. Aisne.
phone (23) 82.21.13 *Mich* 56 Reims 45 km

JOINVILLE   Poste

Comfortable restaurant with rooms
Good value

No complaints from any readers about this modest, roadside
establishment (some bedrooms can be noisy); yet Jean-Claude
Fournier has lost both his Michelin star and Gault Millau *toque*
during the last two years. I think that's fair. You still get first-rate
value for money here – with Jean-Claude making big efforts to
introduce some lighter touches to his specialities: *coquille St-
Jacques aux petits légumes* illustrates this while *croûtes aux
morilles* is a tasty dish from the old days. Try the wines from the
nearby **Côtes de Toul**; particularly the **Gris de Toul** – a good
rosé. Visit the de-Gaulle memorial at nearby Colombey.
menus **A-C** *rooms* 11 **A-B** *cards* AE DC Visa
closed Jan-mid Feb. Thurs (out of season).
post 52300 Joinville. Haute-Marne.
phone (25) 96.12.63 *Mich* 241 Verdun 107 km

LIVERDUN   des Vannes et sa Résidence

Very comfortable restaurant with rooms/Michelin★
Quiet/Gardens

The main guides and I can agree on one thing; the Simunic family
certainly deserve to have lost both their second star and *toque*
number two. Various members of the family are involved in two
other restaurants in this splendid village – with its fabulous views
overlooking the Moselle; the Golf Val Fleuri and the Host. Gare.
Classical cuisine is the order of the day here but the highlight of
any visit is the wine cellar – one of the best. An annexe, 300 yards
away, has a few fine bedrooms set in a pretty garden. Can the
Simunic sons restore those accolades?
menus **C-D** *rooms* 11 **C-D** *cards* AE DC Visa
closed Feb. Mon. Tues midday.
post 54460 Liverdun. Meurthe-et-Moselle.
phone (8) 349.46.01 *Mich* 241 Verdun 104 km

LONGUYON
Lorraine et rest. Le Mas

Very comfortable restaurant with rooms
Good value

Gérard and Viviane Tisserant took a gamble in refurbishing their family home; Longuyon is an unattractive town with few tourists passing through. To make matters worse the recession has hit the town hard and unemployment is high in this corner of France. Few will be travelling this way, but if you do, give the couple your support. Gérard applies a light touch to essentially a classical list of specialities: *aiguillettes de canard aux mirabelles de Lorraine* and *langoustines en feuilleté à la julienne de morilles* are typical. Meals are good value – served in a rustic-styled dining room.

menus **B-C** *rooms* 15 **A-C** *cards* AE DC
closed Jan. Rest: Mon (except July-mid Sept).
post face Gare, 54260 Longuyon. Meurthe-et-Moselle.
phone (8) 239.50.07 *Mich* 241 Verdun 48 km

MONTCHENOT
Auberge du Grand Cerf

Comfortable restaurant with rooms
Gardens
®

Alain Guichaoua and his wife, Françoise, are the new owners of this modest restaurant on the road to Epernay. The tiny hamlet of Montchenot is on the northern slopes of the legendary Montagne de Reims. Of course, at any of my recommendations in the Champagne area, you should enjoy and relish the world's greatest sparkling wines from the endless vineyards you'll see on your way to Epernay and beyond; but also be sure to try the fine reds of **Bouzy** and the exquisite still white wines – my favourite is called **Saran**, made by Moët & Chandon at Epernay and named after their own château just east of that town. The non-vintage, blended Champagnes are always good value; but if you can afford a vintage wine (designated as such by the experts of Champagne – and made only in exceptionally good years) you will readily understand Joseph Krug's famous words: "For vintage Champagne I have to share the credit with God." Be certain, too, to visit the Moët cellars in Epernay – an unforgettable experience, full of interest.

Alain's restaurant has a largish dining room; there are a few simple bedrooms (your alarm clock is the cockerel next door) – a much better alternative is the Novotel at Reims (category two). The *Menu Gourmand*, composed of seven courses, each of really small portions, is the perfect way to put his skills to the test. Among some of the specialities that my wife and I enjoyed were: *blanc de turbot au beurre rouge* (Bouzy red) – a palette of unusual colours; amazingly delicious *aiguillettes de canard aux mangues* (a caramel sauce with mangoes); and an innovative, tasty cheese course called *feuillatine de Thiérache et salade* (using **Maroilles** cheese). I am certain Alain will be going on to great things in the future. I am indebted to Serena Sutcliffe, M.W., who gave me the tip to visit this budding genius. Gault Millau have already nosed him out – Michelin will soon follow suit with a star.

menus **B-C** *rooms* 10 **B-C** *cards* Visa
closed Mid-end Aug. Mid-end Dec. Tues evg. Wed.
post Montchenot. 51500 Rilly-la-Montagne. Marne.
phone (26) 97.60.07 *Mich* 241 Reims 11 km

MONTMORT   Cheval Blanc

Comfortable restaurant with rooms
Good value   ®

We seem to have had a perpetual shower raining down on us here
at Chiltern House during the last three years – a shower of letters
praising this fantastic little place where the only words they
seem to know are 'value for money'. Pierre Cousinat offers
nothing more than himself: honest, down to earth satisfaction –
and it reflects in his simple cuisine and in the way his smart,
whitewashed restaurant is run. Montmort is 18 km south of
Epernay and the Champagne vineyards.
menus A-C *rooms* 12 **A-B**
closed Feb. Fri.
post 51270 Montmort. Marne.
phone (26) 59.10.03 *Mich* 241 Reims 45 km

0033

REIMS   Boyer 'Les Crayères'

Luxury restaurant with rooms/Michelin★★★
Gardens   ®

My readers will know well enough by now that I think Michelin
give too many restaurants a three-star rating. However, the Boyer
home is one of about six restaurants in the provinces (I'm not
including Paris in this) that truly deserve that ultimate accolade.
These days it is Gérard Boyer, the son, who controls the kitchens;
not yet at his peak, he is improving continually and will get even
better in the years to come. Gérard and his attractive wife,
Elyane, are a friendly, handsome couple; the welcome you win
from them has been praised time after time in the many letters
that have arrived at Amersham from all over the world.

Gérard is a talented *créateur* and places great emphasis on
using the produce from the oceans; that is no mean objective in
Reims which is so far from the ports of Normandy and Brittany.
*Langoustines, homard, turbot, bar, St-Pierre, coquilles St-
Jacques* – all appear on his menus. One speciality that pays
homage to a chef he admires is *la petite escalope de foie gras de
Freddy Girardet* – an honourable attempt at that fine dish
created by Frédy but this version has much too sharp a taste to it
and the Swiss genius would never serve the *foie gras* sitting on a
mixed green and red salad. The Boyer desserts are the best in
France; light, mostly mousse-based, attractive and a delight to
both look at and eat. As you would expect, his range of
Champagnes is a tour de force – hardly surprising as he must be
an invaluable asset for all the producers; by listing all their
offerings he can't offend any of them!

By the time this third edition is published the Boyers will be in
their new home in the south-east corner of Reims. Thankfully,
with my rule of missing city centres, it is well away from the
central area; it's near to the Parc Pommery on the N44 and is
surrounded by the six *caves* of the famous Champagne
producers. The new luxury home has 16 bedrooms. I understand
the old restaurant (La Chaumière – its original name) on the Av.
Epernay will remain open – serving simpler, cheaper meals; it's
near the *Hippodrome*, on the western edges of Reims.
alc C *rooms* 16 **D-D2** *cards* AE DC Visa
closed Mid Dec-mid Jan. Sun evg. Mon.
post bd. Henry-Vasnier, 51100 Reims. Marne.
phone (26) 82.80.80 *Mich* 241

SARS-POTERIES   Auberge Fleurie

Very comfortable restaurant/Michelin★

An attractive Auberge; the décor of the small dining room is described as 18th-century English. The Lequy family (Alain is the present chef) lost the support of Gault Millau some years ago – the excessive use of cream in their cuisine must have eventually been too much for them. It's not quite so bad these days – though cream is immediately in evidence in the famous Lequy speciality, *crustacés à la crème*. Other alternatives are *plats de poissons, agneau de lait rôti* and *magret de canard aux oignons*. See the base hotels section for details of the super place run as a separate business enterprise.
alc **B-C** *cards* AE DC Visa
closed Mid-end Aug. Feb. Sun. Mon.
post 59216 Sars-Poteries. Nord.
phone (27) 61.62.48 *Mich* 241 Avesnes 9 km

SEPT-SAULX   Cheval Blanc

Comfortable hotel/Michelin★
Quiet/Gardens/Tennis

A delightful corner in what is otherwise a dull mass of country to the south-east of Reims; the infant Vesle is an additional bonus here as it provides a pleasing backdrop to the gardens – where you can play mini-golf and tennis. Many of you are loyal clients of the Cheval Blanc; the cooking is hardly risky or audacious but relies in the main on a host of classical dishes. Champagne figures in some choices – with *écrevisses* and *brochet* for example; and the reputed Bouzy red is used with a *filet de bar. Canard, agneau* and *gibier* (in the season) are the backbone of the menus. Some excellent wines are recommended including **Bouzy** and **Villiers-Marmery**; these villages are just a few miles away on the slopes between Reims and Epernay.
menus C *rooms* **B-C** *cards* AE DC Visa
closed Mid Jan-mid Feb.
post Sept-Saulx. 51400 Mourmelon-le-Grand. Marne.
phone (26) 61.60.27 *Mich* 241 Reims 25 km

VERDUN   Host. Coq Hardi

Very comfortable hotel/Michelin★
Lift

What an ugly-looking building this is – all brown and white mock-Tudor style; the interior is a bit much, too – someone went over the top with the decoration! The cuisine is anything but overdone; refreshing light touches add extra appeal to the few Lorraine specialities – *filet de bar aux quenelles de rouget* and *saumon de fontaine au curry* are two examples of a modern outlook. Wines are expensive – even unfashionable local half-bottles; desserts are much above average. Don't miss the marvellous *pâtisserie* – Aux Délices – in the nearby Rue Mazel (next door to the Monoprix); Maurice Wach should be proud of his shop. Buy some cakes and Verdun sugared almonds.
menus **B-C** *rooms* 42 **B-D** *cards* AE DC
closed Mid Dec-Jan. Rest: Wed.
post 8 avenue Victoire, 55100 Verdun. Meuse.
phone (29) 86.00.68 *Mich* 241

COTE D'AZUR

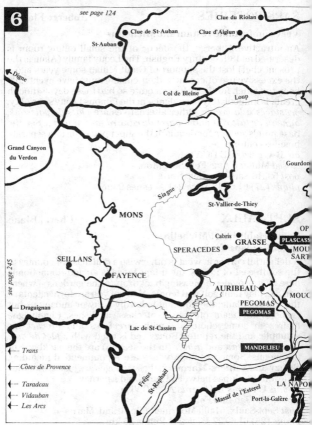

see page 124

6

Clue du Riolan •
Clue de St-Auban • Clue d'Aiglun •
St-Auban •

◄ *Digne*

Col de Bleine

Loup

Grand Canyon
du Verdon
◄

Gourdon

Siagne

St-Vallier-de-Thiey

MONS •

Cabris • **GRASSE**
SPERACEDES •
SEILLANS •
FAYENCE •

OP
PLASCASS
MOU
SART

see page 245

AURIBEAU •
PEGOMAS •
PEGOMAS

MOUC

◄ *Draguignan*

Lac de St-Cassien

◄ *Trans*

MANDELIEU

◄ *Côtes de Provence*

◄ *Taradeau*
◄ *Vidauban*
◄ *Les Arcs*

LA NAPO

Fréjus
St-Raphaël

Massif de l'Esterel
Port-la-Galère

Any words of mine will do very little justice to this area of France, renowned and loved throughout the world. But before I attempt to describe the region, I must stress that there is more to get excited about than just the narrow strip of coastal towns. **Cannes**, for me, is a marvellous resort – **Beaulieu**, a smaller place, is equally nice; all the remaining towns of the coast should be explored for their special attractions, but then left behind for other more attractive pleasures.

Where are these to be found? I often joke with my friends when I say I know from memory every lane in Wales (from my rallying days); I also make this claim about all the roads in the hills and mountains behind **Nice** and Cannes. With a car, you, too, will win the huge benefits that come from roaming through that hinterland. If you want to swim and sunbathe, the best beaches are between **La Napoule** and Cannes, assuming you use one of my base hotels in this area. You, being independent, can get to them easily in your car.

What next? Explore Cannes: the Croisette, the Rue Meynadier, the market, the port and the old town. Visit the flower market at Nice and walk the Promenade des Anglais. Make a trip to **Monaco** and see the Oceanographic Museum, the Palais and the

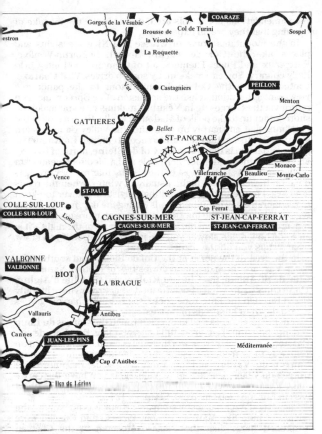

Jardin Exotique; across the harbour lies **Monte-Carlo** – take a promenade around its streets, its Casino and its lovely gardens. If you have the time, drive around the Grand Prix circuit. On your way to these towns include time for a detour to **Villefranche**, Beaulieu and **Cap Ferrat**. Drive the famous Corniche roads between Nice and **Menton** and gasp at the spectacular views. Drive the equally impressive coast road from La Napoule to St **Raphaël**, with the red, craggy mountains of the **Esterel** to the north. Then concentrate on the inland sights and have the minor roads to yourself.

Explore places like **Grasse** (especially on a hot day when the coast can be unbearable), **Mougins**, **Valbonne**, **Vallauris** (the potters' town made famous by Picasso), **Vence**, St-**Paul** and the perched hill-villages of **Auribeau**, **Cabris**, **Fayence**, **Gourdon** and many others. Fill your eyes with the sheets of colour that blanket walls, terraces and gardens: oleander, bougainvilia, veronica and hibiscus. It is magic country; very much one of my favourite parts of France.

Your car will take you through superb scenery. The roads in the gentler hills and valleys, south of Grasse, pass countless villas from the simple to the majestic. Many of my restaurant recommendations are in this area; do not make the mistake of thinking that they are all expensive.

In the mountains north of Grasse and Nice are sights and places like the **Col de Turini**, **Sospel**, St-Martin-Vésubie, Entrevaux and Puget-Théniers; all of them are in Monte-Carlo Rally country. You can make many superb drives. Visit **Coaraze**, continue on to the Col de Turini, detour to the panoramic viewpoint at L'Aution, relish the seclusion of Le Boréon and then return via the **Gorges de la Vésubie**, making sure you make the short detour up to the peak of Madone d'Utelle. Have a look at the hillclimbs that go sharply up from the **Var** Valley on its eastern side: the first to **Castagniers** and a second climb to **La Roquette**. An essential trip is the one to the **Col de Bleine**, north of Grasse; an alpine scene on the northern side and a Mediterranean vista on the southern slopes. Most of the spectacular motor rallying is done on these roads at night, usually in winter, when the roads are closed to the public. Competing rallyists are never too keen to reconnoitre any mountain roads during the day, for the simple reason they will see the long drops; it is much more preferable to remain ignorant of them during the dark hours of the night – it is amazing how much slower you are in a competition if you know what awaits you off the road!

In the area to the north of the Col de Bleine, and south of the River **Var**, are three dramatic curiosities of Mother Nature: the **Clue de St-Auban**; the **Clue du Riolan**; and the **Clue d'Aiglun**. These *clues* – rifts – have been formed where rivers have literally sliced through the limestone rocks; the resulting narrow gorges have a depth of hundreds of metres.

Other trips are ones that take you through the **Gorges du Loup** and up into the Tanneron hills surrounding the **Lac de St-Cassien**. Longer day trips worth doing (or you can fit them in on your way to or from the region) include the magnificent **Grand Canyon du Verdon** and, on a different scale, the impressive Gorges du Cians, leading up to Valberg. If you have the nerve, make a trip to the summit of the Col de la Bonette, the highest pass in Europe (2802 metres). See page 124.

The Côte d'Azur has inspired many artists; it is no wonder the talents of men like Matisse, Renoir, Picasso and Chagall were awakened here. Visit the Picasso Museum in the Château Grimaldi at **Antibes**, Renoir's old home at Les Collettes in **Cagnes-sur-Mer** (100 metres from a 'base' hotel) and the Chapelle du Rosaire at Vence (by Matisse).

One important caveat when eating out in the area, especially in the biggish towns: insist you see fixed-price menus; too many restaurants present just the à la carte menu.

Even a dozen trips to this lovely area will not do it justice because, apart from all the things to see, you will probably just want to relax beside a pool or on a beach; that is, when you are not enjoying an open-air lunch on a shady terrace. But do try to visit it outside the months of July/August, when it is impossibly crowded – particularly now that President Mitterrand, through exchange controls, has forced the French to stay at home. This advice is true for all coastal areas from mid July to mid August. Use *French Leave 3* and enjoy inland France instead.

Michelin *yellow* maps: 84.195 (a *green* map; scale 1 cm for 1 km).
Green Guide: French Riviera (English)
IGN *série verte* maps: 61.68. *série rouge* map: 115
Airports: Nice

Distances	Paris–Cannes	900 km	Calais–Cannes	1193 km
from:	Paris–Nice	933 km	Calais–Nice	1226 km

Cheeses Goat's milk

Banon a soft cheese made in a small disk, usually wrapped in chestnut leaves; sometimes *au poivre*, covered with black pepper

Poivre-d'Ane flavoured with rosemary or the herb savory (*sariette*). In this form same season as Banon. Aromatic taste and perfume

Ewe's milk

Brousse de la Vésubie from the Vésubie Valley; a very creamy, mild-flavoured cheese

Regional Specialities

Aïgo Bouido garlic and sage soup – with bread (or eggs & cheese)

Aïgo saou fish soup, without *rascasse*, served with *rouille*

Aïoli (ailloli) a mayonnaise sauce with garlic and olive oil

Anchoïade anchovy crusts

Berlingueto chopped spinach and hard-boiled eggs

Bouillabaisse a dish of Mediterranean fish (including *rascasse, St-Pierre, baudroie, congre, chapon de mer, langoustes, langoustines, tourteaux, favouilles, merlan,* and, believe it or not, many others!) and a soup, served separately, with *rouille, safran* and *aïoli*

Bourride a creamy fish soup (usually made with big white fish), thickened with *aïoli* and flavoured with crawfish

Brandade (de morue) à l'huile d'olive a mousse of salt cod with cream, olive oil and garlic

Capoum a large pink *rascasse* (scorpion fish)

Pain Bagna bread roll with olive oil, anchovy fillets, olives, onions, etc.

Pieds et paquets small parcels of mutton tripe, cooked with sheep trotters and white wine

Pissaladière Provençal bread dough with onions, anchovies, olives, etc.

Pistou (soupe au) vegetable soup bound with *pommade*

Pollo pépitoria Provençal chicken *fricassée* thickened with lemon-flavoured mayonnaise

Pommade a thick paste of garlic, basil, cheese and olive oil

Ratatouille aubergines, courgettes, onion, garlic, red peppers and tomatoes in olive oil

Rouille orange-coloured sauce with hot peppers, garlic and saffron

Salade Niçoise tomatoes, beans, potatoes, black olives, anchovy, lettuce and olive oil. Sometimes tuna fish

Tapénade a purée of stoned black olives, anchovy fillets, capers, tuna fish and olive oil

Tarte (Tourte) aux blettes open-crust pastry with filling of Swiss chard (not unlike Chinese cabbage) and pine nuts

Provençal earthenware dish

Wines

To the west of this region, and in the Var Valley, lie several wine-producing areas. The wines are fresh and fragrant – they have two per cent more alcohol than their northern cousins.

They are usually white or rosé; a few reds are produced, notably the excellent **Château Vignelaure** (see page 245) – a smooth, full-bodied wine. **Cassis, Bandol, Bellet** (near Nice), **Coteaux d'Aix-en-Provence, Côtes de Provence** are amongst the AC and VDQS classifications. Many of the latter wines carry village names on their bottle labels: **Pierrefeu, Cuers** and **La Londe** (all near Hyères); **Le Beausset** and **La Bégude** (near Aix-en-Provence); **Vidauban, Taradeau, Les Arcs** and **Trans** (south of Draguignan); **Gassin** – you may also see **Château Minuty**, a Gassin property, near St-Tropez. In Nice you may see **Château de Cremat** (the best Bellet wine); menus will list producers' names – like Listel or L'Estandon. See map page 245.

Base Hotels

CAGNES-SUR-MER   Hamotel

Very comfortable hotel
Quiet/Swimming pool/Tennis/Lift

On the D6 towards St-Paul; a modern building – part of a new,
purpose-built complex of attractive flats and villas.
No restaurant *rooms* 32 **C-D** *cards* AE DC Visa
closed Nov-mid Dec.
post 06270 Villeneuve-Loubet. Alpes-Maritimes.
phone (93) 20.86.60 *Mich* 84 Nice 17 km

CAGNES-SUR-MER   Les Collettes

Comfortable hotel
Quiet/Swimming pool/Tennis

Named after the Renoir Museum 100 metres away. Small,
modern building – some bedrooms have *cuisinettes*.
No restaurant *rooms* 13 **C-D**
closed Nov-mid Dec.
post avenue Collettes, 06800 Cagnes-sur-Mer. Alpes-Mar.
phone (93) 20.80.66 *Mich* 84 Nice 13 km

CAGNES-SUR-MER   Val Duchesse

Comfortable hotel
Fairly quiet/Swimming pool

In busy Cros-de-Cagnes – but away from main roads and close to
the sea. Some bedrooms have *cuisinettes*.
No restaurant *rooms* 18 **B-D**
closed Open all the year.
post 11 rue Paris, 06170 Cros-de-Cagnes. Alpes-Maritimes.
phone (93) 20.10.04 *Mich* 84 Nice 11 km

COARAZE   La Petite Auberge

Simple hotel
Quiet/Good value

Sadly Richard Delas died in 1981 – the restaurant had to close.
But now Yvette Delas runs her simple auberge *sans restaurant*.
Light fare available in the evenings if required.
No restaurant *rooms* 7 **C**
closed Oct-Mar.
post Coaraze. 06390 Contes. Alpes-Maritimes.
phone (93) 79.01.69 *Mich* 84 Nice 27 km

JUAN-LES-PINS   Mimosas

Comfortable hotel
Quiet/Gardens/Swimming pool

A nice spot with an attractive *parc*. The best *bouillabaisse* on the
Côte d'Azur? Judged by readers' recommendations it has to be at
Tétou; on the Golf-Juan beach – but it's expensive.
No restaurant *rooms* 37 **C-D**
closed Mid Oct-Mar.
post rue Pauline, 06160 Juan-les-Pins. Alpes-Maritimes.
phone (93) 61.04.16 *Mich* 84 Cannes 9 km

JUAN-LES-PINS — Welcome

Very comfortable hotel
Quiet/Gardens/Lift
If a lift is essential then this is an ideal 'base'. Close to the town centre, casino and beach – but quiet and with gardens.
No restaurant *rooms* 30 **C-D** *cards* AE DC Visa
closed Nov-Feb.
post 7 avenue Dr-Hochet, 06160 Juan-les-Pins. Alpes-Mar.
phone (93) 61.26.12 *Mich* 84 Cannes 9 km

MANDELIEU — Sant'Angelo

Simple hotel
Quiet/Gardens/Lift
A modern place, close to the beach and the lush greens of Cannes-Mandelieu Golf Club. Some rooms have *cuisinettes*.
No restaurant *rooms* 33 **C-D2**
closed Open all the year.
post 681 avenue Mer, 06210 Mandelieu. Alpes-Maritimes.
phone (93) 49.28.23 *Mich* 84 Cannes 8 km

PEGOMAS — Le Bosquet

Simple hotel
Secluded/Gardens/Swimming pool/Good value ®
There's no base hotel in France that we love more; the hard-working Bernardi family have known our children from toddlers to teenagers. It's popular; recently we were hoist by our own petard – we couldn't get in! Some *cuisinettes*. See page 60.
No restaurant *rooms* 24 **B-D**
closed Nov.
post 06580 Pegomas. Alpes-Maritimes.
phone (93) 42.22.87 *Mich* 84 Cannes 11 km

ST-JEAN-CAP-FERRAT — Clair Logis

Simple hotel
Secluded/Gardens ®
An ochre-coloured villa in a *parc* – with palm trees, firs and fig trees. A reader says the annexe is 'cramped'.
No restaurant *rooms* 15 **C**
closed Mid Nov-Jan.
post avenue Centrale, 06290 St-Jean-Cap-Ferrat. Alpes-Mar.
phone (93) 01.31.01 *Mich* 84 Nice 10 km

ST-PAUL — Le Hameau

Comfortable hotel
Quiet/Gardens ®
A series of villas in fragrant gardens – full of orange, lemon and apricot trees. Get written confirmation of bookings.
No restaurant *rooms* 14 **C-D**
closed Nov-Jan.
post route de la Colle, 06570 St-Paul. Alpes-Maritimes.
phone (93) 32.80.24 *Mich* 84 Nice 20 km

LA COLLE-SUR-LOUP
Marc Hély

Comfortable hotel
Secluded/Gardens

Much praised by some of you though one stinging letter of criticism was received from a *French Leave* reader; he complained about the owner's Jekyll and Hyde character. Use as a 'base'; evening meals are available for residents – but they're not recommended when so many good restaurants are nearby.
Ignore restaurant *rooms* 11 **C-D**
closed Nov-Jan (except Xmas-New Year).
post 06480 La Colle-sur-Loup. Alpes-Maritimes.
phone (93) 22.64.10 *Mich* 84 Nice 19 km

PEILLON
Auberge de la Madone

Comfortable hotel
Secluded/Terrace/Gardens   ®

What a delectable spot this is; the whitewashed *Logis* sits outside the perched village of Peillon. It's a long, tortuous climb up a mountain road to reach Peillon – but your efforts will be rewarded by the shaded terraces and the mass of fragrant roses and flowers. Good cuisine with dishes such as *crudités, gigot d'agneau* and *filet de bœuf.*
menus **B** *rooms* 17 **C-D**
closed Mid Oct-mid Dec. Wed (Sept-June).
post Peillon. 06440 L'Escarène. Alpes-Maritimes.
phone (93) 91.91.17 *Mich* 84 Nice 19 km

PLASCASSIER
Les Mouliniers

Simple hotel
Quiet/Terrace/Gardens/Good value

Only residents can have an evening meal here; if you want to enjoy a midday lunch on the terrace be certain to book ahead or you will be dumped in the dark dining room – which, on a sunny day, is torture. Extensive views from the terrace – overlooking the country south of Grasse. Sound Provençal cooking.
menus **A-B** *rooms* 10 (*pension* only **C**) *cards* Visa
closed Mid Oct-mid Nov. Rest: Wed.
post Plascassier. 06130 Grasse. Alpes-Maritimes.
phone (93) 60.10.37 *Mich* 84 Cannes 15 km

VALBONNE
Novotel

Very comfortable hotel
Secluded/Terrace/Gardens/Swimming pool/Tennis/Lift

An excellent Novotel – offering luxury to those who want a 'base' and don't mind paying for it. As with all Novotels ignore the grill. Surrounded by woods, it has an ideal location; not too far from the autoroute – it's just off the D35 Mougins-Antibes road. 1984 should see an Ibis hotel built nearby; similar facilities – but less expensive. (See page 320.)
Ignore restaurant *rooms* 97 **D** *cards* AE DC Visa
closed Open all the year.
post Sophia Antipolis. 06560 Valbonne. Alpes-Maritimes.
phone (93) 33.38.00 *Mich* 84 Cannes 12 km

Solange and Lucien Gardillou – Champagnac-de-Belair (Dordogne)

The fortress at Bonaguil (Dordogne)

The Massif de l'Esterel from Cap d'Antibes (Côte d'Azur)

John Stanton

Recommendations where cuisine takes pride of place

AURIBEAU   Nossi Bé

Simple restaurant with rooms
Terrace/Good value

Auribeau, a perched village, is an old favourite of ours; this
establishment was recommended by a reader who lives nearby.
An open-air meal on the terrace – with extensive views – is the
best way to enjoy Jean-Michel Retore's good cooking. *Soupe au
pistou, truite braisée au beurre de basilic* and *selle d'agneau
grillée à la menthe* are typical specialities.
menus **A-B** *rooms* 6 **B**
closed Mid Nov-mid Dec. Wed (Sept-May).
post Auribeau-sur-Siagne. 06130 Grasse. Alpes-Maritimes.
phone (93) 42.20.20 *Mich* 84 Cannes 15

BIOT   Café des Arcades

Simple restaurant with rooms
Good value

This is another recommendation from a *French Leave* reader
who wrote from the States and insisted I visit the Café. It's an
animated, small place; the house is a 16th-century delight – the
walls of the dining room are covered with paintings. Good
Provençal specialities like *colmar à l'Américaine, tourte de
blettes* and *sardines farcies*. If you are lucky enough to go on a
Sunday, relish *pistou* and tarte *Tropézienne*.
menus **B** *rooms* 10 **B-C**
closed Nov. Sun evg. Mon.
post 16 place des Arcades, 06410 Biot. Alpes-Maritimes.
phone (93) 65.01.04 *Mich* 84 Nice 22 km

LA BRAGUE   La Bonne Auberge

Luxury restaurant/Michelin★★★
Terrace/Gardens   ®

Though I have received many letters of complaint about the
other two three-star restaurants on the Côte d'Azur, only one
letter struck anything like a sour note about Jo Rostang's La
Bonne Auberge. My wife and I have relished his cooking for two
decades; prior to 1974 Jo Rostang had made his name at the
family auberge in Sassenage, near Grenoble. His son, Michel,
continued to run it until 1977, when it finally closed; he went on to
win fame and fortune (and two stars) when he opened his own
restaurant, Rostang, at the old Chez Denis establishment in Paris
(Craig Claiborne's readers will recall it).
    Of the three famous Côte d'Azur restaurants, I prefer this one –
though I am always amazed and saddened how clients are
packed in like *sardines farcies* at this otherwise pleasant
Provençal villa (incidentally it was famous 30 years ago when
Vincent Badouin had three stars). One positive aspect is that you
can be sure that Jo is on the premises; I'll be surprised if you don't
see him calling at your table during your meal. Jo, despite being
near retirement age, has changed his cooking over the last
decade to the modern, lighter ways of today.
menus **D** *cards* AE DC
closed Mid Nov-mid Dec. Mar. Mon.
post La Brague. 06600 Antibes. Alpes-Maritimes.
phone (93) 33.36.65 *Mich* 84 Cannes 15 km

CAGNES-SUR-MER

La Réserve

Very comfortable restaurant/Michelin★

®

Also known as Chez Loulou – the home of Loulou Bertho, a chef who is very much a man after my own heart; he is his own boss and free to do whatever he wants. You may even say that he, too, is mad – he closes during July and August, on Saturday evening, on Sunday and on *fêtes* days! What a man! What a chef, too. Nothing modern here. It's *poissons* that bring clients to his restaurant, clinging to the side of the hideous N98. Order *soupe de poissons, poissons grillés ou au four* or *crustacés (langoustes, homards)* and an excellent *tarte chaude*. If you want to be 'different' you can choose from several grills – but what a waste at this super fish restaurant.
alc C
closed July. Aug. Sat evg. Sun. *Fêtes*.
post 91 bd. Plage, 06170 Cros-de-Cagnes. Alpes-Maritimes.
phone (93) 31.00.17 *Mich* 84 Nice 11 km

LA COLLE-SUR-LOUP

La Belle Epoque

Very comfortable restaurant/Michelin★
Terrace/Gardens

Robert Compagnat has upset the local Gault Millau inspector; after some poisonous asides in their last but one guide they've now omitted him totally. Strange – as no complaints have arrived here; only compliments. The name describes accurately the atmosphere of this old-world restaurant, old-world cooking and old-world charm. A terrace seduces you at midday and clever exterior lighting captures your interest in the evening.
menus C *cards* AE DC Visa
closed Jan-mid Feb. Mon.
post 06480 La Colle-sur-Loup. Alpes-Maritimes.
phone (93) 20.10.92 *Mich* 84 Nice 17 km

FAYENCE

France

Simple restaurant
Terrace/Good value

®

If, like Anne and me, you've been an admirer of Elizabeth David's work for 20 years or more, you'll know of her love for Provence. If I had to suggest one corner of the south where you will grasp just what the magnetic lure of Provence means – it would be Fayence. Here at the France – where nothing changes – you will understand why Provençal cooking is so beguiling. For a start can there be anything nicer than a midday lunch on the shaded terrace – entertained by a noisy parakeet across the road? Begin with the *hors d'œuvre* (see front cover) – 16 alternatives usually grace the table; then choose a *tranche de gigot grillée aux herbes* or, perhaps, a *poulet sauté aux pignons*, or maybe a *coq au vin*. Would *écrevisses* be nicer or some *cuisses de grenouilles à la Provençale* or a simple *truite*? All this accompanied by a range of Provençal wines; Domaines Ott are the best. Don't miss Marcel Choisy's simple, honest cooking – but please book ahead!
menus A-B
closed Mid May-mid June. Mid Dec-mid Jan. Wed evg. Thurs.
post 83440 Fayence. Var.
phone (94) 76.00.14 *Mich* 84 Cannes 38 km

GATTIERES   Auberge de Gattières

Very comfortable restaurant
Gardens

You'll be well rewarded by the effort you make to seek out Daniel
Darbois and his attractive Provençal Auberge in the perched hill-
top village of Gattières, high above the Var Valley. Daniel's
training was classically based. You see this in his specialities:
écrevisses au pistou, filet de sole au cresson, suprême de canette
and *tournedos à l'échalote*. It's at places like this – in all parts of
France – that Gault Millau sometimes mislead their readers, by
stating that it's a restaurant that offers 'old regional recipes'. Oh
yes? Don't be put off by that comment – it's not made against
Daniel, who doesn't make the claim. You'll search without
success for 'old regional specialities' here I'm afraid. What he
does he does well. Out of season it is essential to book ahead for
evening meals.
menus **B-C**
closed June. Mid Nov-mid Dec. Wed.
post Gattières. 06510 Carros. Alpes-Maritimes.
phone (93) 08.60.05 *Mich* 84 Nice 24 km

GRASSE   Maître Boscq

Simple restaurant
Good value

Now here is a chef, Patrick Boscq, who really is making a
superhuman effort to give a kiss of life to old local recipes. His
minuscule bistro, hardly big enough to swing a kitten in, let alone
a cat, is 50 metres or so from the Place aux Aires (the site of an
open-air market – see front cover) in one of Grasse's steep alleys.
Book ahead for delicious *lou fassum* (cabbage stuffed with meat,
rice and herbs); *sou saussou* (cucumber salad); *oartagnade*
(fresh sardines marinated in tomatoes and herbs) and *fricot de
cacho-fuou* (cod with leeks). What weird names! Initiative like
this deserves support. See next entry for parking.
menus **A**
closed Sun. *Fêtes*. Mon (Oct-Feb).
post 13 rue Fontette, 06130 Grasse. Alpes-Maritimes.
phone (93) 36.45.76 *Mich* 84 Cannes 17 km

GRASSE   Chez Pierre

Comfortable restaurant
Good value

An old family haunt of ours – now finding favour with guides like
Gault Millau and L'Auto-Journal. Recommended, like the other
Grasse entry, for evening meals only – though this place has the
advantage of air-conditioning. Louis Dugert and his son, Jean-
Louis, have always been known locally for their value-for-money,
basic cuisine: *soupe de poissons, daube Provençale, loup en
croûte, foie de veau garni* and *tarte aux pommes* are the sort of
things you'll enjoy. Parking is easy – use the car park across the
road at the bus station.
menus **A-B**
closed June-mid July. Mon. sun evg (Oct-June).
post 3 avenue Thiers, 06130 Grasse. Alpes-Maritimes.
phone (93) 36.12.99 *Mich* 84 Cannes 17 km

MONS   Auberge Provençale

Simple restaurant
Good value

Highly recommended – and rightly so – by a reader who lives
near Amersham. Stunning views from the tiny restaurant literally
clinging by its nails to the side of the hill – follow signs for *table
d'orientation*. Good-value dishes: like *canard aux olives*, *gigot
aux herbes* and *tarte maison*.
menus **A** (lunch only except July-Aug)
closed Nov. Wed. (Also see line above.)
post Mons. 83440 Fayence. Var.
phone (94) 76.38.33 *Mich* 84 Cannes 52 km

MOUANS-SARTOUX   Auberge Mourrachonne

Luxury restaurant with rooms/Michelin★
Secluded/Terrace/Gardens/Swimming pool   ®

Two shocks await you at the magnificent Auberge. The first is the
'anything but typical' scene at the rear of the luxurious villa: it's a
bit of Normandy mixed with the Riviera; emerald-green pastures
combine with lovely trees – poplars, firs, blue cypresses and
many others of all hues. The second shock is the cost (the four
bedrooms are superb but their price will make a big hole in your
pocket). However, the cooking of Jean André (he wears the
spectacles) and Guy Tricon (with beard) is inspired. All sorts of
innovative and artistically presented dishes come from their
creative hands: *spaghettis de courgettes*, *assiette de poissons
crus* (a beautiful-looking speciality) with the thinnest and
smallest carrots, baby courgettes and cauliflower you will ever
see; and a *cassolette de crustacés* enticed us on our last visit. We
have known the place for years; the brave gamble the chefs took
to open up here has paid off.
menus **C-D** *rooms* 4 **D2** *cards* AE DC Visa
closed Dec-Feb. Sun evg (winter). Tues midday (summer). Mon.
post route Pégomas, 06370 Mouans-Sartoux. Alpes-Maritimes.
phone (93) 75.69.88 *Mich* 84 Cannes 13 km

MOUGINS   Feu Follet

Simple restaurant
Terrace/Good value   ®

What a breath of fresh air the Feu Follet has brought to Mougins.
André Surmain – the famous owner of the Relais across the road
– is the financier behind the enterprise; but it's his daughter
Micheline (who speaks fluent English) and her 25 years old
husband, Jean-Paul Battaglia (brother of the chef at the Auberge
Fleurie at Valbonne), who bring the real charm and spark of
pleasure to this good-value restaurant, sitting under an
enormous elm tree. You'll not be bankrupted here and you can
choose from a wide selection of treats: *terrine de poisson*,
biscuit de baudroie poché au basilic, *salade du marché*, *cuisse
d'agneau en croûte 'pèbre d'ai'*, *feuilleté Normand* – plus a host of
many inexpensive light wines.
menus **B**
closed Nov. Sun evg. Mon.
post place de la Mairie, 06250 Mougins. Alpes-Maritimes.
phone (93) 90.15.78 *Mich* 84 Cannes 7 km

MOUGINS

France

Comfortable restaurant with rooms
Terrace/Gardens/Swimming pool

These days Mougins appears for all the world like a film set; one reader called it a 'set from an opera' – so did Gault Millau. The France is the next door neighbour of the Relais à Mougins; and both of them sit opposite the *mairie* with its sentinels – two gorgeous, pencil-thin 'finger' trees. I have known the France for more than two decades – and particularly loved it in the days of Madame Donot who made such huge efforts to preserve and present Provençal specialities. Today, Bernard Lefèvre is the owner and he, too, successfully continues those traditions. There's a lovely terrace, shaded by two trees, where you can savour his regional cuisine: *daube Mouginoise, lapin à la Provençale, lotte à la Niçoise, poivrons aux anchois, tourte aux herbes, soupe de moules* and, for a change, a *tarte Tatin*. Be sure to explore Mougins.

menus B *rooms* 6 B-C *cards* DC Visa
closed Feb. Sun evg. Mon.
post 06250 Mougins. Alpes-Maritimes.
phone (93) 90.00.01 *Mich.* 84 Cannes 7 km

MOUGINS

Moulin de Mougins

Luxury restaurant with rooms/Michelin★★★
Quiet/Terrace/Gardens

Why is it that Roger Vergé and Paul Bocuse – more than any other French chefs – impose their names and faces so relentlessly on their clients? I find it particularly offensive when you consider that these are the two chefs who have capitalised most on their three-star fame – they have a variety of business interests far beyond their kitchen stoves; *le business* is truly big business! In the last edition of *French Leave* I criticised Vergé heavily; but not one of you has written to defend him.

When you open the envelope confirming your reservation, the first thing you will see is Vergé's face smiling at you from the letterhead; when you ask for the bill at the end of your meal it will be presented to you in a card holder, once again decorated with that same face, coupled with a final message from Denise and Roger, thanking you for your visit. In my case, on my various visits over the years, I have yet to see Vergé himself; in my opinion, it's sheer gall to personalise a 'thank you' *in absentia*. Have I been unlucky?

On my last visit his absence was all too obvious – consider the following: teeth-crunching bread rolls; wretched combinations like inedible chicory with *loup*; the same mushroom and tomato 'decoration' for successive dishes; ludicrously expensive sweets; menus with anything from 15 to 25 words used to describe dishes; piped music; no second cups of coffee; and so on. Vergé told *Fortune* magazine: "I spend more time in my office than my kitchen." Enough said – what can I add to that?

With those numerous other 'culinary' business interests both Vergé and Bocuse should decide what they really are – *cuisiniers* or entrepreneurs? Give me Girardet any day.

menus D *rooms* 3 D2 *cards* AE DC Visa
closed Mid Nov-Xmas. Mid Feb-Mar. Sun evg. Mon.
post 06250 Mougins. Alpes-Maritimes.
phone (93) 75.78.24 *Mich* 84 Cannes 5 km

101

MOUGINS   Relais à Mougins

Very comfortable restaurant/Michelin★
Terrace

André Surmain spent a good part of his working life in New York;
originally trained by Dumaine, he eventually made his name as
the owner of the Lutèce there. Success in that tough environment
inevitably means you develop a pretty blunt view of life and
business; André doesn't suffer fools gladly and he calls a spade a
spade. "The customer is not always right," is one of his telling
views of the restaurant trade. So perhaps I should not have been
surprised to receive some complaints – one being the most
scathing of all the letters I've had. In the latter case, after endless
waits between anything but adequate courses, my reader got up
and walked out – leaving open-mouthed staff behind him. No
wonder a star has been lost – hopefully that was an exceptional
event which will not be repeated. There have been other letters
from readers saying they enjoyed the mixture of classical and
modern cuisine; these kinder comments have come after the
arrival of a new, talented chef. Don't be intimidated by André:
accept the fact that you must take him as you find him; and then
you'll enjoy old-fashioned skills – with long waits – in animated
surroundings. Enjoy André's **Bugey** wines (see page 176).

menus C (lunch only) *alc* **C-D** *cards* Visa
closed Feb. Mar. Mon/Tues midday (except July-Aug). *Fêtes*.
post place de la Mairie, 06250 Mougins. Alpes-Maritimes.
phone (93) 90.03.47 *Mich* 84 Cannes 7 km

LA NAPOULE   L'Oasis

Luxury restaurant/Michelin★★★
Terrace

If, at times, you feel that I have been hard in my criticism of some
three-star chefs, do bear in mind my observations have been
made objectively – by comparing one with another, throughout
France. But my comments are nothing compared with the
statements expressed by two famous writers. Auberon Waugh
wrote: 'Three-star restaurants are just practical jokes played on a
gullible British and American market.' Mr Waugh – you should
give us the facts about all the 18 three-star shrines that caused
you to make such an important observation. Frederick Raphael
called L'Oasis and Vergé's Moulin de Mougins 'the mouth-
brothels of those to whom heaven itself will have to be on
American Express or they won't want to go.'

My wife and I have known L'Oasis since Louis Outhier started
it all as a *pension* two decades ago. We loved it once – but not
now; many of you have expressed displeasure at the mixed
performance of the place. I agree – it is a hotchpotch of good and
bad – mainly bad: piped music; 'a paltry selection of cheeses';
awful vegetables with tasteless purées and egg-custard based
dollops; stringy lamb; 'closely-packed tables'; and a surprisingly
small choice on the menus. Hardly compensating for this tale of
woe are a variety of desserts that look good (but have 'no soul' – a
reader said), and a staggering display, when I was there, of at
least 30 dozen pink roses on the tables.

menus D (Note Mr Raphael – no AE cards accepted here!)
closed Nov-Xmas. Mon evg. Tues.
post La Napoule-Plage. 06210 Mandelieu. Alpes-Maritimes.
phone (93) 49.95.52 *Mich* 84 Cannes 8 km

OPIO   Mas des Géraniums

Very simple hotel
Quiet/Terrace/Gardens/Good value   ®

Robert and Madame Fradois continue to charm clients at this
little jewel of an hotel – hidden among the olive groves lying
below the village of Opio. It's a bit more expensive these days;
but despite that, what could be nicer than some *hors d'œuvre*,
rouget, coquelet and a home-made *pâtisserie* – served at midday
in the pretty, shaded garden?
menus A-B *rooms* 7 A-B
closed Nov-Jan. Rest: Sun evg.
post Opio. 06650 Le Rouret. Alpes-Maritimes.
phone (93) 77.23.23 *Mich* 84 Cannes 20 km

PEGOMAS   L'Ecluse

Simple restaurant
Secluded/Terrace/Good value   ®

This isolated, unpretentious restaurant has won many friends
judged by the shoal of letters I've received; two readers wrote
their appreciative comments from the terrace alongside the
River Siagne. You'll be offered nothing more than *crudités*, lamb,
a trout or a grill, finishing off with some fruit, an ice-cream or
home-made cake. What could be better value? I'm glad I have
caused Monsieur Tognarelli to be so busy.
menus A-B
closed Sept-Apl.
post 06580 Pégomas. Alpes-Maritimes.
phone (93) 42.22.55 *Mich* 84 Cannes 11 km

PEGOMAS   Lou Pas de l'Aï

Simple restaurant

On the Route d'Or towards Tanneron (in February the hills are a
spectacular sight – a sea of mimosa). Grills and low-cost basic
dishes; appreciated by many of you.
menus A-B
closed Tues.
post 06580 Pégomas. Alpes-Maritimes.
phone (93) 42.22.76 *Mich* 84 Cannes 13 km

ST-JEAN-CAP-FERRAT   Les Hirondelles

Very comfortable restaurant/Michelin★
Terrace

A lovely, flower-filled, shady terrace is one of the prime pleasures
at this restaurant alongside the harbour at St-Jean. Another
pleasure is the excellent cooking of Madame Marie Venturino –
based almost exclusively on superb fresh fish: *daurade grillée
aux herbes de Provence, loup grillé au fenouil, rougets à la
Niçoise, bouillabaisse* and *bourride* are a few of the delights.
Sadly, it's expensive.
alc C *cards* DC
closed Mid Nov-end Jan. Sun. Mon.
post avenue J.-Mermoz, 06290 St-Jean-Cap-Ferrat. Alpes-Mar.
phone (93) 01.30.25 *Mich* 84 Nice 10 km

ST-JEAN-CAP-FERRAT   Petit Trianon

Very comfortable restaurant/Michelin★
Terrace/Gardens

During April last year I received a letter from a reader who was
annoyed that, on a visit to the restaurant earlier in the month, he
had found the terrace closed and in a 'dilapidated' state. Two
months later I called to see what he meant. The covered terrace
and the gardens at the rear were as lovely as ever! Take that as a
caveat for all southern recommendations; terraces are not
always open, nor maintained, during 'out-of-season' months.
Petit Trianon is in the heart of Cap Ferrat – so don't expect sea
views. Classical cuisine based primarily on fresh fish: *sole*,
rouget, loup, langouste and so on.
menus **B-C** *cards* AE DC
closed Nov. Dec. Wed evg. Thurs.
post bd. Gén.-de-Gaulle, 06290 St-Jean-Cap-Ferrat. Alpes-Mar.
phone (93) 01.31.68 *Mich* 84 Nice 10 km

ST-PANCRACE   Rôtisserie de St-Pancrace

Very comfortable restaurant/Michelin★
Terrace/Gardens

Things are looking up at this appealingly-situated restaurant,
high in the hills to the north of Nice; the setting and views are
themselves attractive enough to persuade you to desert noisy,
busy Nice. Classical cuisine with many lighter touches; the
introduction of a new chef to assist the Teillas family has brought
quick recognition from Gault Millau who now award the
restaurant two *toques*. Make the detour.
alc **C** *cards* Visa
closed Jan – mid Feb. Mon (Sept-Easter).
post St-Pancrace. 06100 Nice. Alpes-Maritimes.
phone (93) 84.43.69 *Mich* 84 Nice 8 km

SEILLANS   Clariond et H. de France

Comfortable hotel
Quiet/Terrace/Gardens/Swimming pool

The Clarionds are friendly hosts – ready to smile and ready to
help you in whatever way they can. They will look after you as
well as they look after their lovely home – it's a super example of
just how good a family-run French hotel can be. In summer
there's a chance to eat outdoors in a small square – sitting under
huge plane trees and alongside a fountain. In the evening there's
an airy, smart dining room – full of gorgeous flowers; Madame is
proud of her displays – and rightly so. Cuisine is simple and basic:
grills, cooked in an open fire are the best buy; *crudités* is a huge
basket of various raw, fresh vegetables; *salade Niçoise* is served
in a jumbo-sized claret glass; and desserts are generous. Some
trusted friends had a miserable visit last year: an overcooked
soufflé, poor-quality meat, strawberries straight out of the fridge
– too cold and tasteless – and highish prices. I hope that was a
solitary bad performance.
menus **B-C** *rooms* 26 **C-D**
closed Jan. Wed (out of season).
post Seillans. 83440 Fayance. Var.
phone (94) 76 96.10 *Mich* 84 Cannes 50 km

SPERACEDES   La Soleillade

Simple restaurant
Terrace/Good value

If it's an appetite you have then you will eat well at this good-value, simple restaurant. Michel Forest would be the last person on earth to claim that he was a budding great chef; for years he worked in circuses, including a spell with Bertram Mills. He is a dry-humoured, charming host with a cynical sense of humour. His cooking is a little more run of the mill: *canard aux olives, terrine de grive, tarte à l'orange* and *gâteau de Michel* are his current culinary tricks!

menus **A-B**
closed Nov. Wed.
post Spéracèdes. 06530 Peymeinade. Alpes-Maritimes.
phone (93) 66.11.15 *Mich* 84 Cannes 25 km

VALBONNE   Auberge Fleurie

Simple restaurant with rooms
Terrace/Gardens/Good value   ®

My wife and I originally discovered this young couple a decade ago at their first restaurant, the Relais Napoléon in nearby Mouans-Sartoux. Then they were just married – and young Jean-Pierre Battaglia was determined to capitalise on his training at L'Oasis. Today, he and Dominique, his wife, have three girls: Stéphanie, Corrine and Laura; what a strain it has been on Dominique, particularly during the last few tough years. Every penny they have has come from their own efforts. Jean-Pierre is a fine young chef; for the really exceptional skill that goes into his cooking you spend little indeed – on the coast you could pay double or treble and still not do as well. Consider one of his menus as an example: *scampis à la Provençale, St-Pierre à l'échalote, turbot au Champagne,* three superb cheeses in splendid condition and some marvellously light, mouthwatering sweets. The menu is a little over 100 francs; make every effort to support honest effort like that.

menus **A-B** *rooms* 10 **B-C**
closed Mid Dec-end Jan. Rest: Wed.
post Val de Cuberte. 06560 Valbonne. Alpes-Maritimes.
phone (93) 42.02.80 *Mich* 84 Cannes 12 km

VALBONNE   Le Bistro de Valbonne

Simple restaurant
Good value

I was led to this unassuming, simple place by American readers who spoke very highly of it. How right they were; Raymond Purgato owns a tiny bistro – lost in the middle of Valbonne, which is a criss-cross of narrow, dark streets. Once more I would say that his skilled efforts, though not particularly cheap, represent good value for money: enjoy *salade gourmande, moules farcies, magret de canard, papillote de turbot aux petits légumes* and fine *sorbets.*

menus **B**
closed Sun. Mon.
post 11 rue de la Fontaine, 06560 Valbonne. Alpes-Maritimes.
phone (93) 42.05.59 *Mich* 84 Cannes 13 km

DORDOGNE

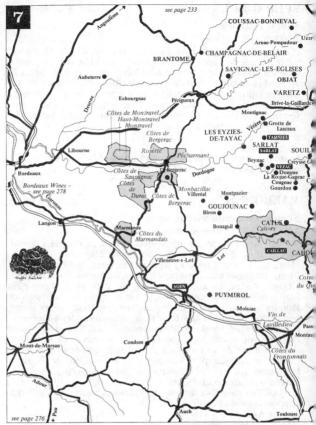

I plead guilty to taking the same liberty here as I do with the Lyonnais region. I am casting my net very wide; to reach places, sights and countryside lying beyond the technically correct description of the *Dordogne*.

I would suggest you base yourself at one of six hotels. Two of them are in the western part of the area, near **Sarlat**. From there you will be able to see all the river country, and you will be able to get to places like **Brantôme** to the north-west – a most attractive small town which I fell in love with over 20 years ago. Most recommendations are hotels in their own right – all make fine holiday hotels.

In the south you can explore the best parts of the **Lot** Valley, both west and east of the superb town of **Cahors**, set on a horseshoe bend of the river. All the Dordogne is still available to the north but in addition you can enjoy the sights of **St-Cirq-Lapopie**, **Cabrerets**, the **Grotte du Pech-Merle** and **Najac** in the **Aveyron** Valley.

Many visitors will choose to stay close to the River **Dordogne**; but they, too, can quite easily reach the countryside straddling the Lot and Aveyron. Most tourists to the famous northern river

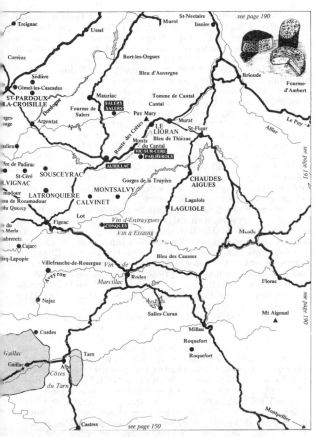

see page 190

see page 191

see page 190

see page 150

ignore everything south of **Gourdon** – a pity, as it is ideal country for a day trip, reached quickly and easily from the north. One trip alone will probably persuade you to plan a longer holiday there sometime in the future.

What, in more detail, are those sights I refer to earlier? At Cahors is the Pont Valentré, built in 1308 – said to be the most perfect fortified bridge in the world. Don't miss the fantastic ruined castle at **Bonaguil** – Hollywood has yet to better it; make sure you view it from the narrow lane on the hill to the south of the site. Also see the castle at **Biron**. Just north-west of Cahors is the Château de Mercuès; it used to be a famous and expensive hotel – drive up to the viewpoint at the entrance to its gates and enjoy the impressive view of the Lot Valley. At Pech-Merle are caves with the most amazing stone formations – shapes like saucers, plates and wheels; and, of course, some of the most famous wall paintings in the world. St-Cirq-Lapopie is built on top of a high cliff that falls vertically down to the Lot far below – it is one of France's most picturesque sites.

The Lot (from St-Cirq-Lapopie to **Cajarc**) and the Célé Valleys are almost lost valleys; you will want to lose yourselves, too, in these scenic treasure chests. Any visitors to the Dordogne who have missed these sights will have certainly also ignored delightful Najac and the Aveyron, going upstream to **Villefranche-de-Rouergue**. This is a stretch of river terrain where, if you want to see the best of it, you must use the minor tracks and lanes on both banks; navigate yourself down them – from time to time desert your car and use your feet.

A few kilometres further south from Najac is **Cordes** – a personal favourite of mine. This ancient, hill-top town was built in 1222; its fortifications, old houses and streets are full of interest. I have seen it twice during the last three years – after a gap of more than 10 years; I was so much more absorbed by the atmosphere of the place – perhaps because I had the chance to give it my complete attention rather than having to worry about our young children all those years ago. All the country south from the Aveyron is covered in more detail in the Languedoc-Roussillon region; put aside a few days sometime in the future to explore this hidden corner of France.

In the east you will have the pleasure of driving into the Massif Central countryside: **Montsalvy** and the treasures of **Conques** are to the south of **Aurillac** and to the east is the spectacular countryside surrounding **Murat**; **St-Flour** (named after its founder, one of the few sent out by Christ) and unique **Chaudes-Aigues** (it gets its hot water and central heating free from natural springs). One essential outing from Aurillac is the drive up the **Route des Crêtes** to the **Puy Mary**. For my wife and me the hills to the south-west of Aurillac are among the best in France. Why do so few people explore them?

But it is the area adjacent to Sarlat and between it and Aurillac that is the real Dordogne. Today it is very well known by a large number of visitors, particularly the British; 30 years ago it was quite undiscovered. **Corrèze** is still particularly unspoilt and its tiny and numerous lanes are as inviting as ever, lost amongst the finest trees in France. Be certain to detour to the isolated château at **Sédière** and the fantastic waterfalls at **Gimel-les-Cascades**.

It is idyllic country, another one of the rich pastoral gardens of France. The River Dordogne flows through its centre, and along or near its banks are a series of enticing villages and small towns: **Argentat**, with a perfect river setting; **Collonges-la-Rouge**, built of red sandstone; **Beaulieu**, full of ancient houses; **St-Céré**; **Souillac**; hidden **Creysse Gluges**; Sarlat, like Brantôme, full of treasures; **Beynac** and **La Roque-Gageac**, the two most picturesque of all the villages.

To the south of the river are several hill towns: marvellous **Domme**, **Gourdon** and, the most spectacular of all, **Rocamadour**. Poulenc rediscovered his Christian faith here in 1935 on a visit to the shrine of the Black Virgin (a statue of the Virgin Mary carved from black wood by Saint Amadour) and the profound experience he underwent is reflected in his *Litanies à la Vierge Noire* and his ensuing religious choral work. Nearby is the Gouffre de Padirac, where hundreds of metres underground you can travel for five kilometres in a punt on an icy, dark river – a fantastic world of stalagmites and stalactites.

We love the **Vézère** Valley and particularly the area between **Les Eyzies** and **Montignac**. The **Grotte de Lascaux** remains closed (a nearby facsimile is now open) but enjoy alternatives – the Grotte du grand Roc is one of them. Visit the **Cougnac** caves near Gourdon. The area is dotted with fine châteaux: among them the Château de la Treyne (they take paying guests), the Château de Fénélon and the Château Monbazillac.

This is yet another region of France where I implore you to get off the beaten track without fear of getting lost. It is superb country, especially so in May/June, when the endless varieties of trees are at their most beautiful, or in September/October, when the glorious autumn shades are at their best.

I knew 25 years ago that any countryside is best seen at sunrise – it was rallying that brought that point home to me. In the intervening years my wife and I have got up early on occasion (to our regret, not often enough) to see the awakening hedgerows, fields and woods during that hour or two when first light comes. We did this once one flawless, autumn morning in the eastern part of the Dordogne – it remains a vivid memory still today. I can recall a clear sky; dark in the west, pink in the east and mists shrouding the valleys below. A heavy dew carpeted fields, hedges and the verges, and a little later, as the sun rose, we stopped to see why many of the bushes were sparkling. We discovered spiders' webs, covered in dew, catching the rising sun – they were shimmering like magic lights. Most of the bushes at the spot we stopped at were laden down with blackberries; we must have collected two or three pounds of them in no time at all. That advice is just as valid today – get up early once in a while and ramble through the lanes during those still waking hours.

Michelin *yellow* maps: 235.239.75.76.79.80
Green Guides: Dordogne (English). Auvergne
IGN *série verte* maps: 48.49.57.58. *série rouge* maps: 110.111
Airports: Bordeaux. Toulouse
Distances from: Paris-Sarlat   537 km   Calais-Sarlat   831 km
                Paris-Aurillac 545 km   Calais-Aurillac 839 km

Cheeses Cow's milk

Many of the cheeses listed come from the Massif Central:

Auvergne (Bleu d') when made on farms at its best in summer and autumn. Strong smell, soft, made in the same way as Roquefort

Cantal from the Auvergne. Semi-hard, nutty flavour. Praised by Pliny; the best comes from Salers (**Fourme de Salers**). Also known as **Cantalon** and **Fourme de Rochefort**. *Fourme* is an old word describing how the cheeses were formed

Causses (Bleu des) a blue cheese with parsley-like veins, hence the term *persillé* – often used to describe a blue cheese. At its best in summer and autumn. **Bleu du Quercy** is a related cheese

Echourgnac pressed, uncooked, small disk – made by monks

Fourme-d'Ambert a summer and autumn season. A blue cheese from the Auvergne and in the shape of a tall cylinder

Laguiole related to Cantal. Big cylinders, penetrating bouquet

Murol a semi-hard cheese, like St-Nectaire. Made in small disks, mild with no special smell

Passe-l'An made as a huge wheel – a strong, hard cheese

St-Nectaire a purply-brown skin, made in larger disks than Murol. Semi-hard, mild cheese

Thiézac (Bleu de) at its best in summer and autumn. A blue cheese related to Bleu d'Auvergne

Tomme de Cantal a fresh, softish, cream-coloured, unfermented cheese; used in many Auvergne regional dishes

Goat's milk

Cabécou de Rocamadour gets its name from the patois for *little goat*. Very small size with nutty taste. At its best in summer and autumn

Ewe's milk

Roquefort the best blue cheese of all. Sharp and salty. See notes in Massif Central. Try it with a local red wine **Cahors** – or surprise yourself with an accompanying sweet **Sauternes**

Regional Specialities

Bourrioles d'Aurillac sweet pancakes, made from buckwheat flour
Cèpes fine, delicate mushrooms. Sometimes dried
Chou farci stuffed cabbage. Sometimes *aux marrons* – with chestnuts
Confit de canard (d'oie) preserved duck (goose)
Cou d'oie neck of goose
Foie de canard (gras) duck liver (goose)
Friands de Bergerac small potato cakes
Merveilles hot, sugar-covered pastry fritters
Mique stew or soup with dumplings
Pommes à la Sarladaise potatoes, truffles, ham or *foie gras*
Rillettes d'oie soft, potted goose
Sobronade soup with pork, ham, beans and vegetables
Tourin Bordelais (Ouillat) onion soup
Tourin Périgourdine vegetable soup
Truffes truffles; black and exotic tubers or fungi, as large as walnuts, they grow on the roots of certain oak and hazelnut trees
Truffes sous les cendres truffles, wrapped in paper (or bacon) and cooked in ashes

Wines

Reds
There are many good local wines made in the region itself. From **Bergerac** and the **Côtes de Bergerac** (circling the town, both north and south of the River Dordogne) come some fine wines; light-weight, claret-type reds. Similar wines are made in the **Pécharmant** area and the **Côtes de Duras** (south of Bergerac). **Sigoulès** and **Leparon** are Côtes de Bergerac wines.

Whites
Amongst the whites, look out for **Bergerac sec, Côtes de Bergerac**, **Côtes de Duras** and **Rosette** – all ideal for fish and entrées. Across the Dordogne from Bergerac is the *commune* of **Monbazillac**, where the famous, sweet, heady dessert wine is made; another sweet wine is **Côtes de Bergerac moëlleux**. From the **Côtes de Montravel**, **Montravel**, **Haut-Montravel** (three different areas) and the **Côtes de Saussignac** come medium-sweet whites; and a few dry whites.

Other Wines
Further south from the Dordogne itself are the wines of **Cahors** – full-bodied dark reds plus the white, **Blanc du Lot**. Gaillac makes reds, whites, rosés, plus the sparkling whites, **Gaillac mousseux** and **Gaillac perlé**; **Gaillac Premières Côtes** and **Gaillac doux** are medium-sweet whites. The town is on the Tarn (between Toulouse and Albi) and its wines have a pedigree going back to 920 A.D. Some good red and white VDQS wines are made in the Lot Valley, south of Montsalvy: **Vin d'Estaing** and **Vin d'Entraygues et du Fel**. North of Toulouse are the AC **Côtes du Frontonnais** (its main centre is **Villaudric**); good reds are made here. West of Cahors is the **Côtes du Marmandais** area and its reasonably good light reds and whites. Another light VDQS red comes from south of Cahors, called **Vin de Lavilledieu**.

All the wines of **Bordeaux**, detailed in my description of the Southwest (page 279), can be enjoyed here in the Dordogne. Many of the best are made on the banks of the River Dordogne, just before it flows into the Gironde.

Vins de Pays
Good examples flourish in this region. **Coteaux du Quercy** and **Côtes du Tarn** offer wines of all shades; *département* labels will say **Lot**, **Lot-et-Garonne** and **Tarn-et-Garonne**.

AGEN

Résidence Jacobins

Comfortable hotel
Quiet/Gardens ®

A beguiling, hidden corner of Agen where you'll be delighted by one of my favourite base hotels in France. Serge and Gisèle Bujan's *Logis* is in a quiet spot away from busy traffic. Both of them are charming, helpful hosts; a typical touch was a spray of lily of the valley that came on my breakfast tray – a national tradition in France on May 1st each year.

No restaurant *rooms* 15 **B-D**
closed Open all the year.
post 1 ter. place Jacobins, 47000 Agen. Lot-et-Garonne.
phone (53) 47.03.31 *Mich* 235 Sarlat 120 km

AURILLAC

La Thomasse

Very comfortable hotel
Quiet/Gardens

An attractive hotel on the western side of Aurillac; follow signs for the Parc des Sports. Gardens are a bonus; and considering the standard of comfort, the prices are not severe. Visit the Château St-Etienne – fine views of the Jordanne Valley and the Cantal peaks; and its Maison des Volcans – telling the story of the volcanic hills of Auvergne.

No restaurant *rooms* 21 **C** *cards* AE DC Visa
closed Open all the year.
post rue Dr.-Mallet, 15000 Aurillac. Cantal.
phone (71) 48.26.47 *Mich* 239

SALERS

Beffroi

Comfortable hotel
Quiet/Good value

A pleasant 'base' – in one of the tiny streets that lead off from the splendid Grande-Place. The town is a fascinating place with old streets and dark, handsome houses – made from the stone quarried from the basalt plateau on which Salers is perched. Don't miss the church and the fine views.

No restaurant *rooms* 10 **B**
closed Jan-mid Feb.
post 15410 Salers. Cantal.
phone (71) 40.70.11 *Mich* 239 Aurillac 49 km

SARLAT-LA-CANEDA

La Hoirie

Comfortable hotel
Secluded/Gardens ®

Most of you have been delighted by this pretty spot, south of Sarlat; but two readers complained that it is a bit 'primitive', a 'ramshackle place' and the gardens are 'badly kept'. Well, yes, the 'gardens' are not weeded – but the rooms and the owners are charming. I adore this unpretentious 'base'.

No restaurant *rooms* 13 **C-D**
closed Nov-Mar.
post 24200 Sarlat. Dordogne.
phone (53) 59.05.62 *Mich* 239 Sarlat 2 km

VEZAC   Oustal de Vézac

Comfortable hotel
Quiet

A modern, single storey building in an isolated position with magnificent views westwards towards the famous perched castle at Beynac. Be sure to visit the restored medieval château; from its hill-top setting you'll have some picturesque and spectacular views of the Dordogne.
No restaurant *rooms* 20 C *cards* AE Visa
closed Mid Nov-mid Mar.
post Vézac. 24220 St-Cyprien. Dordogne.
phone (53) 29.54.21 *Mich* 75 Sarlat 9 km

VIC-SUR-CERE   Auberge des Monts

Comfortable hotel
Secluded/Gardens

It's a short season at this isolated, modern hotel high above Vic-sur-Cère, at the summit of the Col de Curebourse. Fantastic views of the Cère Valley and the Cantal peaks to the north.
No restaurant *rooms* 27 C
closed Mid Sept-mid May.
post 15800 Vic-sur-Cère. Cantal.
phone (71) 47.51.71 *Mich* 239 Aurillac 27 km

Recommendations where cuisine takes second place

CAILLAC   Relais des Champs

Comfortable hotel
Secluded/Gardens/Swimming pool

You don't have to eat at the restaurant adjoining the Relais; though the cooking of Jean-Pierre Lemozit, a rugby fan, is regional and good. The rooms, modern enough, are minuscule; one reader reckons the bedrooms are smaller than the bathrooms! *Cuisinettes* available. There's glorious river country to both east and west – an added bonus to the facilities.
menus A-C *rooms* 22 B-D *cards* Visa
closed Mid Nov-mid Jan. Mon.
post Caillac. 46140 Luzech. Lot.
phone (65) 30.92.35 *Mich* 235 Sarlat 68 km

CONQUES   Ste-Foy

Comfortable hotel
Quiet

I wrote in *Hidden France*: 'an utter gem of a place, creeper-covered and nestling in the shadow of one of France's true jewels – the Eglise Ste-Foy.' I defy anyone not to be enchanted by the village and the glorious countryside lying in all directions. Only dinner provided at the hotel – good-value, basic cooking revolving around Auvergne specialities. Book ahead.
menus B *rooms* 20 B-D
closed Mid Oct-Mar.
post Conques. 12320 St-Cyprien-sur-Dourdou. Aveyron.
phone (65) 69.84.03 *Mich* 80 Aurillac 57 km

PAILHEROLS   Auberge des Montagnes

Simple hotel
Quiet/Terrace/Good value   ®

Don't ever be afraid of seeking out the more remote *Logis de France* that offer real value for money; this one is well and truly off the beaten track, 1000 metres above sea-level in the mountains to the south-east of Vic-sur-Cère. Cooking is modest but products are local and fresh – you'll relish the excellent Auvergne cheeses and offerings like *pounti* (see the Massif Central regional specialities). There is plenty of secluded countryside for your eyes to relish, too – it's virtually empty of both cars and people. Use your large-scale maps to find the isolated, medieval château at Messilhac (don't be put off by the roughish lane); the hamlet of Laussac – saved when the Truyère was flooded to make a long, man-made lake; the panoramic views from the hills above Carlat; and the ancient villages of Raulhac and Mur-de-Barrez. All those sites are to the south of Pailherols – to the north are the high Cantal peaks.
menus **A-B** *rooms* 11 **A-B**
closed Oct-Feb.
post Pailherols. 15800 Vic-sur-Cère. Cantal.
phone (71) 47.57.01 *Mich* 239 Aurillac 35 km

SALERS   Le Bailliage

Comfortable hotel
Quiet/Gardens/Good value

Both Charles Bancarel, at his modern Le Bailliage, and Madame Caby at her hotel, Les Remparts – its bonus is its view over the Maronne Valley – are well known for their good-value, basic cuisine. Both offer a variety of menus which rely heavily on regional specialities: things like *potée Auvergnate, tripoux, jambon de montagne, truffade* and *pounti* (see the Massif Central regional specialities). Don't be put off by the petrol pumps in front of Le Bailliage; just one of the enterprising ways in which Monsieur Bancarel has to earn his living. Be certain to try the renowned **Fourme de Salers** – one of the oldest of cheeses with a 2000 years old history.
menus **A-B** *rooms* 30 **B-C**
closed Nov-mid Dec.
post 15410 Salers. Cantal.
phone (71) 40.71.95 *Mich* 239 Aurillac 49 km

TAMNIES   Laborderie

Comfortable hotel
Secluded/Terrace/Gardens

Gabriel Laborderie owns an attractive, secluded hotel in a hill-top setting above the Beune Valley. An *étang* or two in the valley add extra interest with boating and fishing facilities. Conventional Périgord cooking with local specialities predominating: *foie gras en maison, omelette aux truffes, magret sauce Diane* and *confit de canard.*
menus **A-C** *rooms* 26 B-C
closed Mid Nov-mid Mar.
post Tamniès. 24620 Les-Eyzies-de-Tayac. Dordogne.
phone (53) 29.68.59 *Mich* 75 Sarlat 15 km

ALVIGNAC   Palladium

Comfortable hotel
Quiet/Terrace/Gardens/Swimming Pool

Alice Vayssouze owns one of the nicest hotels in the southern section of the Dordogne. Many 'features' translate into worthwhile 'benefits' for her clients: a country setting for the hotel building, part of which is modern and newly-built; a swimming pool and gardens; good-value cooking of an above average standard; and sights galore are near at hand to explore. Expect dishes such as *magret de canard, confit d'oie aux pommes, feuilleté aux cèpes* and other local products.
menus A-B *rooms* 27 C *cards* AE
closed Oct-Apl.
post Alvignac. 46500 Gramat. Lot.
phone (65) 33.60.23 *Mich* 239 Sarlat 63 km

BRANTOME   Moulin de l'Abbaye

Very comfortable restaurant with rooms/Michelin★
Secluded/Terrace/Gardens   ®

Within a stone's throw of the abbey church – set in one of the most picturesque spots in Périgord – young Régis and Cathy Bulot have transformed an old *moulin* into one of the region's best restaurants. They opened the doors of this, their summer house, in 1979; it has a short, five-month season – during the winter they run the Hôtel des Neiges at Courchevel. Though backed partly by finance from the Benoist family (Cathy's parents, and already well established in the hotel business), their story is a classic example of the sort of effort that has to be made by a young couple – in this case in their mid-thirties – to establish a successful restaurant business.

I have had the good fortune to see how the arithmetic of a year's trading works out here. I put on my accountant's hat and I was absorbed by the cost of overheads, borrowing money, taxes, social security payments, labour and produce expenses – and so on. But it is no wonder they have made a success of it; an example of their eye for detail is the handsomely-printed menu on hand-made paper. Cuisine is a mixture of regional and modern: *confit de canard aux cèpes* and *filets de rougets aux pâtes fraîches* are examples. See Bourdeilles and Aubeterre.
menus B-C *rooms* 8 D *cards* AE DC Visa
closed Oct-mid May. Rest: Mon.
post 24310 Brantôme. Dordogne.
phone (53) 05.80.22 *Mich* 75 Sarlat 84 km

CAHORS   La Taverne

Comfortable restaurant

Pierre Escorbiac has been succeeded by Patrick Lannes, who worked for Bocuse in his Rio de Janeiro and Osaka restaurants (that legend has fingers in many 'culinary' pies). His repertoire is a mixture of regional and classical with the odd lighter touch for those with less hearty appetites.
menus B-C *cards* AE DC Visa
closed Nov. Sun evg. Mon.
post 41 rue J.-B.-Delpech, 46000 Cahors. Lot.
phone (65) 35.28.66 *Mich* 235 Sarlat 72 km

CALES   Pagès

Simple hotel
Quiet/Terrace/Good value   ®

Several readers have spoken highly of this remarkable, value-for-money family enterprise – all the Pagès family are involved and their efforts work well. The best-liked features have been the quiet site; the comfortable, modernised rooms; and the excellent regional cuisine. Little things have been appreciated – like the slabs of butter at breakfast rather than, as one reader wrote, those 'revolting little plastic containers one gets practically everywhere in Europe.' An extensive range of local wines has been welcomed by one or two of you, too. Cuisine is regional with the inevitable *foie gras*, *cèpes de nos bois*, *sanglier*, *confits d'oie* and *de canard* appearing on the menus. What is also interesting is that some readers have commented on how impressed they were with the Grottes de Lacave (four kilometres to the north – alongside the River Dordogne) preferring them to the famous spectacular caves at Padirac. One of my own favourite value-for-money hotels in the Dordogne.
menus A-C *rooms* 15 B-C
closed Oct, Tues (out of season).
post Calès. 46350 Payrac. Lot.
phone (65) 37.95.87 *Mich* 239 Sarlat 52 km

CALVINET   Beauséjour

Simple hotel
Good value

One unhappy letter arrived last year expressing disappointment with this modest place. I think too much was expected of it; it seems appropriate to re-emphasise that 'simple' means what it says. Louis Bernard Puech strongly supports the cooking of his *pays* – there's nothing modern or new here: *pounti* from the Auvergne; *tripoux* from nearby Maurs; *omelette aux cèpes* and *civet de porc aux pruneaux*. The home-made sausages, hams and *charcuterie* that appear on the menus can be purchased from the shop linked to the hotel. Madame Puech and her son – trained by an old favourite of mine, Lucien Vanel at Toulouse – offer exceptional value, certain not to bankrupt you.
menus A-B *rooms* 19 A-B
closed Oct-Mar.
post 15340 Calvinet. Cantal.
phone (71) 49.91.68 *Mich* 239 Aurillac 39 km

CATUS   Gindreau

Comfortable restaurant
Terrace/Good value

Nothing could be nicer than lunch on the shaded terrace of Alexis Pelissou's restaurant; off the beaten track, it rewards the effort locating it – peace and quiet and fine views of the Vert Valley. Regional cuisine with dishes such as *pâté de lièvre*, *cassoulet* and *magret de canard*.
menus A-C
closed Nov. Feb. Tues evg/Wed (out of season). Mon (July-Aug).
post St-Médard-Catus. 46150. Lot.
phone (65) 36.22.27 *Mich* 235 Sarlat 50 km

CHAMPAGNAC-DE-BELAIR   Moulin du Roc

Very comfortable restaurant with rooms/Michelin★★
Secluded/Terrace/Gardens   ®

If you met Solange Gardillou socially you would never guess that
the slight, pretty woman was one of the best *cuisinières* in
France; indeed, one of the best chefs in the land – male or female.
So many of you have been delighted and charmed by the culinary
pleasures of the Moulin du Roc and you have also been bowled
over by its seductive, verdant setting – alongside the tree-lined
River Dronne. One of my American readers, David Shaw (writing
in the Los Angeles Times), reckoned that Solange's cooking is
better than at least half of the 18 Michelin three-star restaurants
in France. I agree David; no wonder she recently won her well-
deserved second star – something I predicted years ago. I predict
also that it will not be too long before she wins a third *toque* from
Gault Millau.

The usual husband and wife roles are reversed at this tiny
establishment; Lucien Gardillou, Solange's husband, looks after
you with painstaking care and is a fantastic supporter of his
wife's efforts. You may not even see Solange because she slaves
away in her kitchen – running it with just a handful of staff. They
opened their doors at this 17th-century walnut oil mill 15 years
ago; they've made a magnificent job of renovating it. Bedrooms
are very comfortable and each of them has a name rather than
the conventional number. The dining room (it needs more
lighting) seats few clients – so book ahead.

It was Bocuse who claimed that women make 'unimaginative'
chefs. Solange – together with Menneveau at Gevrey-Chambertin
and Nahmias in Paris – does more to prove him wrong than any of
the other *cuisinières* of France. Self-taught, her cooking is a
mixture of *cuisine libre* and regional classics – but presented in a
light, digestable form. Space prevents me from listing many
specialities – they change frequently but could include dishes
like *pigeon aux choux verts, langouste grillée au beurre rose* and
foie gras poêlé à la ciboulette. Accompanying this cuisine is
Lucien's cellar of more than 10,000 bottles – particularly good are
the Bordeaux varieties. Be certain to find your way, one day, to
the superb Moulin du Roc.

menus **B-C** *rooms* 8 **D** *cards* AE DC Visa
closed Nov-Mar. Rest: Tues.
post 24530 Champagnac-de-Belair. Dordogne.
phone (53) 54.80.36 *Mich* 75 Sarlat 90 km

CHAUDES-AIGUES   Aux Bouillons d'Or

Comfortable restaurant with rooms
Lift/Good value

Jean-Michel Cornut has already won accolades from Gault
Millau and Le Bottin Gourmand. No wonder, as his menus
represent first-class value – regional cooking with light touches.
Enjoy *filet de truite à la ciboulette, tourte au Cantal* and
marmite de trois poissons de rivière (*sandre, saumon* and
truite). A modernised building with five floors (note the lift). The
town has the hottest spa waters in Europe – 82 degrees C.

menus **A-C** *rooms* 12 **C**
closed Dec-Mar. Tues (mid Oct-Apl).
post 15110 Chaudes-Aigues. Cantal.
phone (71) 23.51.42 *Mich* 239 Aurillac 94 km

COUSSAC-BONNEVAL   Voyageurs

Comfortable restaurant with rooms
Quiet/Gardens/Good value

An enticing spot: a vine-covered restaurant, sitting in the shadow of the village château. Henri Robert is a loyal supporter of both Périgord and Limousin specialities: witness the *salade Limousine*, the *confit de canard aux châtaignes* and the many dishes that feature *cèpes*. Don't miss nearby Arnac-Pompadour – the horse centre of France.

menus **A-C** *rooms* 12 **A-B** *cards* Visa
closed Jan. Feb. Mon (out of season).
post Coussac-Bonneval. 87500 St-Yriex-la-Perche. Haute-Vienne.
phone (55) 75.20.24 *Mich* 239 Sarlat 118 km

LES EYZIES-DE-TAYAC   Centenaire

Very comfortable hotel/Michelin★★
Terrace/Gardens

My visit here last year was a delightful affair – quite different from the very unhappy meal I had in 1980. Young Roland Mazère – the talented chef – has improved dramatically quickly and now truly merits his second Michelin star. He is the son of Madame Lasserre, the owner; his sister, Geneviève, and her husband, Alain Scholly, share the responsibility of running this popular Dordogne hotel. Alain, who speaks English well, is a talented host – one of the best in France. Many of you have spoken highly of the annexe which is a kilometre or two away.

Roland is justly proud of his modern kitchen; his cooking is light and creative – putting the produce of Périgord to excellent use. Highlights of my last meal were a superb hot *foie de canard*, an original and tasty *raviole de langoustines en papillote*, a brilliantly innovative *croutade blanc de volaille aux cèpes* and first-class sweets which included a smooth *glace au lait d'amande*. A young, English-speaking waiter proved to be one of the best I've seen in France. Without any shadow of doubt Roland would be one of the main reserves for my favourite team of XV chefs. Bravo Roland! Bravo Alain!

menus **B-D** *rooms* 32 **B-D** *cards* AE DC Visa
closed Nov-Mar. Rest: Wed midday (out of season). Tues midday.
post 24620 Les Eyzies-de-Tayac. Dordogne.
phone (53) 06.97.18 *Mich* 75 Sarlat 21 km

LES EYZIES-DE-TAYAC   Centre

Comfortable hotel
Terrace/Good value

Gérard Brun and his wife took over this small hotel in the centre of the village, and near the river, a couple of years ago; they are keen to make a success of it and to see that the Centre continues to be known for value for money. Many of you reckon they are doing just that. Regional cuisine, married to Gérard's skills, make this the ideal place if you have a limited budget. The previous owner, the late Monsieur Garrigue, would be pleased.

menus **A-C** *rooms* 18 **C** *cards* Visa
closed Mid Nov-mid Feb.
post 24620 Les Eyzies-de-Tayac. Dordogne.
phone (53) 06.97.13 *Mich* 75 Sarlat 21 km

LES EYZIES-DE-TAYAC

Cro-Magnon

Very comfortable hotel/Michelin★
Terrace/Gardens/Swimming pool

®

My wife and I paid our first visit to this hotel – evocative of so much in the Dordogne – in the early days of our married life some 24 years ago. During the three or four years that followed we took both our young children – when they were still toddlers. Consequently, we have a very strong love for the Cro-Magnon and much of the neighbouring terrain. We have seen it in the spring and in the rewarding months of autumn. It's at its best then, when the leaves of the chestnut trees are turning into glowing shades of orange and flaming gold. The virginia creeper-covered Cro-Magnon becomes a red torch. If you're lucky and the sky is clear, which it always seems to be, then there's nothing nicer than a terrace lunch under the shadow of several chestnut trees or an after-lunch nap across the road in the cool gardens of the hotel's annexe. The Cro-Magnon has plenty of character and atmosphere – and, as we discovered all those years ago – it suits children, too.

The hotel was founded in the 19th-century by the discoverer of the celebrated Cro-Magnon skull. One unchanging aspect is that the Leysalles family still own and run it – you can be sure of a warm, friendly welcome. Jacques and Christiane Leysalles are the third generation – they remain as charming now as they were over two decades ago.

There have been one or two changes of chefs in recent years; the cuisine falls far short of the exceptional standards set by Roland Mazère down the road. It's all safe, conventional cooking with no frills; if you want modern, innovative brilliance you must go to the Centenaire. But if you put a premium on nice gardens, a swimming pool and a hotel full of character – then head for the Cro-Magnon.

menus **B-C** *rooms* 29 **C-D** *cards* AE DC Visa
closed Mid Oct-Mar.
post 24620 Les Eyzies-de-Tayac. Dordogne.
phone (53) 06.97.06 *Mich* 75 Sarlat 21 km

GOUJOUNAC

Host. de Goujounac

Simple restaurant
Good value

This must be one of the two or three most humble and unpretentious restaurants in *French Leave 3*. Jean-Pierre Costes and his mother offer their clients many regional treats – at bargain-basement prices: *foie gras, confit de canard, mique, cous farcis, rillettes* and many other old recipes.

Before any *déviation* here for lunch or dinner, put aside some hours to treat yourself to four man-made treasures: first the castle at Biron – with *donjon* (keep), Renaissance chapel and fine *place d'armes*; then the fortress at Bonaguil – an astonishing structure, best seen from the narrow lane on the wooded hillside to the south; and, finally, two of the best examples of the *bastides* – fortified towns built over 700 years ago – at Monpazier (English) and Villeréal (French).

menus **A-B**
closed Oct.
post Goujounac. 46250 Cazals. Lot.
phone (65) 36.68.67 *Mich* 235 Sarlat 48 km

LAGUIOLE   Lou Mazuc

Comfortable restaurant with rooms/Michelin★
Lift   ®

In some ways this is one of the most astonishing restaurants in
France. Laguiole is a dull, small town lost in an area that is hardly
scenically captivating – the Monts d'Aubrac. It's famous for its
cattle – the whole area is a massive pasture, hardly inhabited by
man but certainly dominated by cattle – and also for its cattle
fairs and its cheeses. One cheese is similar to Cantal and the
other is like Tomme de Cantal, one of the prime ingredients of
aligot (see Massif Central regional specialities). Perhaps one can
also now say the town is renowned for its own, 'home-made'
chef, 36 years old Michel Bras. Trained by his parents, this
creative young man is a revelation; he prepares both *nouvelle
cuisine* dishes and many regional recipes, improved no end by
light touches.

It was those two favourite guide book inspectors of mine –
Henri Gault and Christian Millau – who led me to this isolated,
culinary shrine. Don't be surprised when I tell you that Michelin,
yet again, awarded their star well after their rivals had put Michel
and Ginette Bras on the map. Michel's menu is unique in that he
informs you quite clearly what his objectives are; he
acknowledges, too, the debt he owes his mother and he invites
you to share in his research and creative reworking of both old
and new, imaginative specialities.

You will not be disappointed if you accept that unusual
invitation. Menus range from 60 to 200-plus francs and are
studded with delights – witness the following. *assiette de jambon
d'aile de canard, ragoût fin d'artichauts au foie gras de canard
jus à la ciboulette, feuilleté garni d'asperges et de gyromitres
fraîches du pays, blanc de poulet de ferme au vin de noix vertes,
fromages de chez nous* and to cap it all – *assiettes de
gourmandises (sorbets, pâtisseries* and *entremets)* It's
astonishing; Michel would flourish anywhere in France – to do so
at Laguiole is nothing short of a culinary miracle.
menus **A-C** *rooms* 12 **B-D** (a few are excellent and modern)
closed Oct-Mar. 1-8 June. Sun evg/Mon (except July-Aug).
post 12210 Laguiole. Aveyron.
phone (65) 44.32.24 *Mich* 239 Aurillac 82 km

LATRONQUIERE   Tourisme

Very comfortable hotel/Michelin★
Lift

The Bex family continue to break all the rules of hotel finance:
the Tourisme is open for two months each year – July and August
– and only dinner is served. I'm still none the wiser how they can
afford to do it. Be that as it may, Madame Bex continues to entice
back a small, but faithful clientèle – year after year. The
neighbouring hills are unbelievably lovely – pines, oaks,
chestnuts and green pastures beguile you in other ways. It's a
paradise for walkers and fishermen. Delights on the plate? What
about *foie de canard confit à la truffe* and *œufs de ferme pochés
au vin rouge du Lot*. Book ahead.
menus **B** *rooms* 40 **C**
closed Sept-June.
post 46210 Latronquière. Lot.
phone (65) 40.25.11 *Mich* 239 Aurillac 45 km

LE LIORAN   Anglard et du Cerf

Very comfortable hotel/Michelin★
Quiet/Lift

I wouldn't rate the cuisine here as exceptional. The Michelin star
is for honest endeavour – fair reward for doing well what the
owners, Jean-Pierre and Suzanne Anglard, set out to do. That's
common with many a Michelin recommended one-star
restaurant. There are many extra pleasures to add to the
'features' of the hotel: first and foremost its setting, high above
Super Lioran, surrounded by pinewoods and with extensive
views of the Cantal peaks; then there is glorious countryside to
explore – it's in all directions and much of it is deserted. There
are plenty of opportunities to walk and climb; in the evening you
will have the appetite to enjoy a *filet de bœuf mignonnette* (the
beef is from nearby Salers) and *Le Lioran* (a *pâtisserie*).
menus A-C *rooms* 38 B-C
closed Oct-Xmas. Mid Apl-June.
post Super Lioran. 15300 Murat. Cantal.
phone (71) 49.50.26 *Mich* 239 Aurillac 41 km

MONTSALVY   Auberge Fleurie

Simple hotel
Good value

Yvonne Barral – the owner and *cuisinière* – continues to charm
her many friends from Britain, and the odd one or two Americans
enterprising enough to seek out this attractive spot. Some of you
have written to say that the bedrooms in the hotel are noisy –
preferring the annexe and welcoming the relative peace and
quiet there. The Auberge Fleurie is a rustic, creeper-covered
hotel – its name does it justice. Cooking has an equally rustic
touch to it: *chou farci*, *tripoux*, *poulet de fromage* and *clafoutis*
are the sort of things you can expect.
menus A-B *rooms* 18 B
closed Rest: Nov-Feb.
post 15120 Montsalvy. Cantal.
phone (71) 49.20.02 *Mich* 239 Aurillac 35 km

MONTSALVY   Nord

Comfortable hotel
Good value   ®

This modern *Logis de France* has been the cause of many visits
by the postman to Chiltern House – near the beech woods of the
Chiltern Hills. Without exception all your letters have expressed
the pleasure you got from the modern, first-rate hotel run by Jean
Cayron and his wife, Mauricette. Each letter, as it arrived, took
my thoughts back to those high hills that surround Montsalvy –
their woods are as appealing as the Chilterns. Enjoy them and the
honest cuisine of Mauricette Cayron. There are many regional
recipes and a few lighter dishes on offer – and relish, too, the
local wines from the Lot. Both Montsalvy hotels offer quite
exceptional value for money.
menus A-B *rooms* 30 A-C
closed Open all the year.
post 15120 Montsalvy. Cantal.
phone (71) 49.20.03 *Mich* 239 Aurillac 35 km

OBJAT   Pré Fleuri

Comfortable restaurant with rooms/Michelin★
Good value

My readers will know by now that I pay very little attention to the
efforts of decorators in French restaurants – whatever the level
of classification. Like Gault Millau, I take far more notice of what
arrives on the plate and what goes on in the kitchen and dining
room; this restaurant is a perfect example. My notes say nothing
about the interior decoration but they include this caveat: 'easily
missed, behind a ring of small trees.' So it is; a small modern
building on the road to a place you must not miss either – Arnac-
Pompadour.

Jacques and Ingrid Chouzenoux will captivate you in other,
more alluring ways; the fixtures and fittings are not important.
Jacques is yet another chef who successfully manages to
accommodate both the new and the old; the latter being
improved dramatically by light touches. Here is a typical list of
the sort of specialities you'll be offered: *salade 'du Pré' et de la
mer, cuisse de canard confite aux champignons, toast de foie
gras chaud à la crème d'estragon* and *chaud/froid de pêche à la
julienne d'oranges ('confite)*.

menus **B-C** *rooms* 7 **B** *cards* AE DC Visa
closed 1-15 Oct. Mon (out of season).
post route Pompadour, 19130 Objat. Corrèze.
phone (55) 25.83.92 *Mich* 239 Sarlat 71 km

PUYMIROL   L'Aubergade

Very comfortable restaurant/Michelin★★   ®

David Shaw – you were right: Michel Trama is a revelation. This
bearded, extrovert chef 'crackles' with enthusiasm and has had a
rocket-like climb to fame. He and Maryse, his wife, opened their
doors just five years ago: in 1981 he won his first star – in 1983 his
second; a Bocuse-like rise to fame!

Michel, now 37, and Maryse, an attractive blonde, come from
Paris. He was a *maître d'hôtel* – deciding eventually that he could
be a better chef than most. So they made the decision to uproot
the family (they have three children – Muriel, Dominique and
Christophe) and head south to the old perched *bastide* of
Puymirol. As Parisians they met considerable hostility in their
battle to restore the 13th-century house with its lovely beamed
dining room. Both of them are perfectionists – you see endless
examples of that; including the amazing toilets!

But it is the self-taught chef's cuisine that is the real reason for
seeking out this gem of a restaurant. Innovative dishes seduce
you: clever *amuse-bouches*; a light-as-air *flan d'asperges*; a tasty
petit ragoût de langoustines à la ciboulette; an attractive
creation called *'gâteau' de canard*; a *gratin de fruits* and many
more treats. When he started in 1979 he had no help at all in the
kitchen; even now he has only two assistants – one is Solange
Gardillou's son, François. Michel came within an ace of being a
member of my favourite 'team' of XV; let's say he is one of the
reserves on the bench! Use the Résidence Jacobins, in Agen, for
overnight stops.

menus **B-C** *cards* AE DC Visa
closed Feb. Sun evg and Mon (except July-Aug).
post 52 rue Royale, 47270 Puymirol. Lot-et-Garonne.
phone (53) 95.31.46 *Mich* 235 Sarlat 137 km

ST-PARDOUX-LA-CROISILLE   Beau Site

Comfortable hotel
Quiet/Terrace/Gardens/Swimming pool/Tennis   ®

The trouble about this isolated hotel, hidden in the forests of
Corrèze, north of the River Dordogne, is that it already has many
fans; you must book ahead if you are going to share in the utter
perfection of the site and the neighbouring countryside. On top
of all the man-made and Mother Nature's pleasures, you have the
added dividend of really good cooking where both regional
dishes and lighter alternatives fight for space on the menus:
andouille Corrèzienne, escalope de foie d'oie aux myrtilles and
clafoutis are examples of the former. Jacques and Arlette
Tourette have a real jewel of a hotel – share it with them for a day
or two as soon as you can; their prices are not dear.
menus **B-C** *rooms* 37 **B-C**
closed Oct-Apl.
post St-Pardoux. 19320 Marcillac-la-Croisille. Corrèze.
phone (55) 27.85.44 *Mich* 239 Aurillac 81 km

SARLAT-LA-CANEDA   St-Albert

Comfortable hotel
Good value

How this splendid small town has been improved over the last
two decades; many of its treasures in the medieval streets have
been restored. Be sure to see old Sarlat, the Bishop's Palace (a
theatre), the cathedral and the Maison de la Boétie. The Garrigou
family – the longest established hoteliers in town – will offer you
rooms at the St-Albert or the modernised Salamandre (an old
distillery); either way you can eat in the air conditioned
restaurant at St-Albert. Regional cuisine: typical dishes are *cou
d'oie farci* and *truffes sous la cendre*.
menus **A-C** *rooms* 57 **B-C** *cards* AE DC Visa
closed Open all the year.
post place Pasteur, 24200 Sarlat. Dordogne.
phone (53) 59.01.09 *Mich* 239

SAVIGNAC-LES-EGLISES   Parc

Very comfortable hotel/Michelin★★
Secluded/Terrace/Gardens

The Goujons – daughter Georgette is married to the talented chef,
Jean Vessat – have spent 40 years developing their old *relais* into
what is now a modern member of the *Relais et Châteaux* chain.
Don't judge it by a quick glance from the D705; walk round to the
back and enjoy the pretty park – some bedrooms are in a modern
annexe overlooking the verdant picture. Cooking is very much
the *nouvelle cuisine* scene; Jean being inspired by his holiday
visits to his peers in France. He uses regional produce in many
ways; like *magret de canard grillé au coulis de truffes et sa petite
fricassée de cèpes* and *chausson aux truffes*. Other dishes
include delights such as *navarin de coquilles St-Jacques et de
langoustines.*
menus **B-D** *rooms* 14 **D** *cards* AE DC Visa
closed Mid-end Oct. Jan-mid Mar. Tues.
post 24420 Savignac-les-Eglises. Dordogne.
phone (53) 05.08.11 *Mich* 75 Sarlat 84 km

SOUILLAC
Vieille Auberge

Comfortable restaurant with rooms
Swimming pool/Good value

During the last three years this super restaurant has won many more admirers for itself, if the numerous letters I have received are anything to go by. Robert Véril and his family have done *French Leave* readers proud – as not one unfavourable comment has been mentioned. Be certain to ask for rooms in the 'Résidence' – the annexe for the Auberge – and it will be there that you'll find the minuscule pool. Some rooms have *cuisinettes* and the restaurant has air conditioning – welcome on hot evenings. It's regional cooking – with the usual *foie gras chaud*, *magret de canard* and *cassoulet*.
menus A-C *rooms* 20 B-C *cards* Visa
closed Feb. Tues evg/Wed (Nov-Easter).
post place Minoterie, 46200 Souillac. Lot.
phone (65) 32.79.43 *Mich* 239 Sarlat 29 km

SOUSCEYRAC
Au Déjeuner de Sousceyrac

Very simple hotel/Michelin★
Good value

®

If you are more attracted by *objets d'art*, wallpapers, fixtures and fittings and the like, then bypass this decrepit, run-down bistro. If those are the sort of things that please you most in life then it's more than likely you will not be exploring the captivating lanes in the hills surrounding Sousceyrac. Monsieur Espindael makes certain you don't leave hungry – so ensure you arrive with an appetite. Cope with some of these stomach fillers: *omelette de truffes*, *foie de canard aux fruits* and *canette aux navets*. Weightwatchers' torture!
menus A-B *rooms* 15 A-B *cards* AE DC Visa
closed Dec-Easter. Sat (except July-Aug).
post 46190 Sousceyrac. Lot.
phone (65) 33.00.56 *Mich* 239 Aurillac 48 km

VARETZ
Château de Castel Novel

Luxury hotel/Michelin★★
Secluded/Gardens/Swimming pool/Tennis/Lift

Albert and Christine Parveaux – aided and abetted by Jean-Pierre Faucher – run one of the finest châteaux-hotels in France. Both Albert and Jean-Pierre spent some of their training years at the Troisgros Restaurant in Roanne; this reflects in their cooking which is modern and innovative, but neither does it ignore the special pleasures of the table in Périgord. Sadly, one or two letters of criticism have arrived at Amersham – but these have been more than balanced by compliments. The turreted, red sandstone Castel (Colette wrote some of her novels there) has a superb position, on its own small hill, hidden by woods, and overlooking the Vézère Valley. Rooms are clearly expensive, but, considering the luxury of the place, the range of menus on offer are not that shatteringly high.
menus C *rooms* 28 D-D2 *cards* AE DC Visa
closed Mid Oct-mid May.
post Varetz. 19240 Allassac. Corrèze.
phone (55) 85.00.01 *Mich* 239 Sarlat 62 km

HAUTES-ALPES

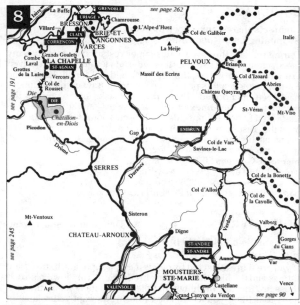

Every letter writer will know of the special joy that comes from addressing some envelopes: it may be to an old friend in Wales or in the Dales – or it could be to a hotel, visited years before, and lost amongst the Alps. The simple writing down of the address brings memories flooding back – images reappear in the mind and one looks forward, with mounting anticipation, to the next visit. All this is true for me when addressing a letter to any favourite hotel in the Hautes-Alpes.

It has been difficult to make it into a region – in the way the others are constructed. For a start, the base hotel method cannot work so well as mountain drives take time; I have given you a couple of ideas for base hotels (a third, *sans restaurant* and not quiet, is the Hotel Edelweiss in **Briançon** – the highest town in Europe, with its triple rows of Vauban fortifications – another, and quieter, is Flots Bleus at **Savines-le-Lac**).

This extensive mountainous region is the least well-known to most travellers in France. Don't you make the same mistake. It is full of treasures; the spectacular sort that make the back of the neck tingle and the heart beat faster.

Where can you begin? To the north are super forests, pastures and mountains. In the **Grenoble** area you can fill your days with pleasure; my favourite bits of country are on your doorstep. The Chartreuse Massif is north of Grenoble; lose yourself in its hidden valleys (see Savoie). A few kilometres to the south-west of Grenoble is the **Vercors** – another great favourite of mine. Make one essential drive in the Vercors: 12 kilometres north-west of Grenoble is Veurey-Voroize – take the safe road up to **La Buffe** and, before you enter the tunnel, stop and enjoy the spectacular views of the **Isère** Valley. Do the same five kilometres due south of that tunnel at La Molière. Under your feet are some of the famous pot-holes of France; the Gouffre Berger is the best known. See Nature's marvels: the **Combe**

124

Laval; the **Grands Goulets**; the Gorges de la Bourne. On no account miss the **Col de Rousset** – the grandfather of hillclimbs.

Drive through the glorious forests above **Uriage** to **Chamrousse** and take the *téléphérique* to the Croix de Chamrousse. Astonishing views will reward you: to the north and east are the Alps and to the far west and south-west are the mountains of the Ardèche and the Cévennes (over 100 kilometres away).

West of Briançon is the majestic **Massif des Ecrins**: the mountains of Barre des Ecrins (the second highest in France), **La Meije** and Mont Pelvoux tower over the surrounding valleys. The whole area is a National Nature Park; it is a happy hunting ground for botanists searching for Alpine flowers.

To the north-east of **Embrun** is one of the best parts of mountain France – seen by just a few fortunate individuals. The imposing **Château-Queyras** is the gateway to the unspoiled Queyras Valley; Hannibal used this route to the Po. But it is the drive southwards to **St-Véran**, the highest *commune* in Europe, which is one of two *déviations* you must make. It is interesting to imagine how this community, now dwindling, flourished years ago. Before you leave this general area follow my second piece of advice to the letter: climb through Aiguilles, Abriès and L'Echalp to the Belvédère du Cirque – you will be quite alone and you will have to yourself the majestic views of **Mont Viso**.

Embrun, an old fortified town, is perched above the Durance; it has the most beautiful church in the Dauphiny Alps. In the forests nearby are conifers, spruce, larch and fine specimens of juniper trees, up to 30 feet in height. To the far south of Embrun the scenic views change to the quite different ones of Provence. The incomparable **Grand Canyon du Verdon** is a must – it has drawn me back time after time over the years.

Mountains intoxicate my spirit and my soul; how can any human being not be stirred by their splendour? For me extra excitement is added in this region by the chance to revel in the best motoring country in Europe: all the high passes and the many narrow valley lanes are known to a past generation of rally drivers and navigators. The **Galibier**, the **Izoard**, the **Vars**, the **Cayolle**, the **Allos** – all are superb *cols*. Try some of the newer ones, too; the **Col de la Bonette** (the highest in Europe) is one example. Don't under any circumstances bypass the **Gorges du Cians**, south of **Valberg**.

Give this fantastic area some of your time.

Michelin *yellow* maps: 244.245.77.81. Green Guide: Alpes
IGN *série verte* maps: 52.54.60.61. *série rouge* maps: 112.115
Airports: Lyon. Nice. Marseille
Distances from: Paris-Grenoble 568 km Calais-Grenoble 860 km

Cheeses

See also the cheeses listed in the Savoie region.

Annot (Tomme d'Annot) a nutty-flavoured, pressed disk; made from ewe's or goat's milk

Picodon is a goat cheese; soft, mellow taste and doughnut size. Various sources – Diois (see map) and Rhône Valley

Regional Specialities

See those listed in the Savoie region.

Wines

Enjoy the light wines from Savoie; see the wines of Provence – **Die** and **Châtillon-en-Diois** varieties are explained there.

Tears of Glory

During 1983 I was sent a small book by one of my readers, Simon Longe, who had read *France à la Carte* and *Hidden France* and knew of my great interest in the French Resistance. The paperback cost a modest £1.25 and I had not seen it before; I read the entire book within hours of receiving it! Like Simon, all my readers will know that I refer often to the heroic struggles of the Resistance; certainly whenever I write about the Vercors (see the north-west corner of the Hautes-Alpes map) I am always reminded of the tragic events that occurred in those wooded mountains during the summer of 1944.

The book – published by Pan Books Ltd., Cavaye Place, London SW10 – is called *Tears of Glory* (hardback by Macmillan); it's by Michael Pearson and tells the true story of 'The Betrayal of Vercors 1944'. It is a riveting, heart-stirring story. When you know the geography of a place like the Vercors as intimately as I do, a book like this becomes a series of visual pictures as you turn each page. An added interest is that Simon's father, Desmond Longe, and his godfather, John Houseman, both played a part in the story of those tragic few months.

The Vercors merits the time and attention of every visitor to France. I implore you – find the time for this natural fortress, full of the majestic handiwork of Mother Nature at her most ferocious and spectacular. Read the splendid story before you go: I think it is the most watertight promise I have made in any of my books when I say that you will be enthralled by both the book and your on-the-spot visit. It will be an important addition to your understanding of people, modern history and geography. There is much to see; read the entries for St-Agnan and Varces for additional information.

I can think of no better way of motivating you to make a personal contribution towards repairing the broken bridges of the *Entente Cordiale*. You will not be disappointed.

> *Thou that comest here*
> *Bring thy soul with thee*

The words on the Grotte de la Luire memorial (photo – opp. page 129)

Base Hotels

CORRENÇON-EN-VERCORS — La Clé des Champs

Simple hotel
Secluded/Gardens/Good value   ®

It's amazing that a 'base' – *sans restaurant* – can flourish in such a glorious, isolated setting; six km to the south of Villard.
No restaurant *rooms* 10 **B**
closed Mid Apl-June. 10 Sept-20 Dec.
post Corrençon-en-Vercors. 38250 Villard-de-Lans. Isère.
phone (76) 95.16.63 *Mich* 244 Grenoble 40 km

ST-ANDRE-LES-ALPES — Monge

Simple hotel
Quiet/Gardens/Good value

Another ideal small base hotel – in majestic country.
No restaurant *rooms* 24 **A-B** *cards* Visa
closed Mid Oct-Mar.
post 04170 St-André-les-Alpes. Alpes-de-Haute-Provence.
phone (92) 89.01.06 *Mich* 245 Grenoble 223 km

Recommendations where cuisine takes second place

CLAIX   Les Oiseaux

Comfortable hotel
Secluded/Terrace/Gardens/Swimming pool

A smart *Relais du Silence* 11 km to the south-west of Grenoble
and it's easily reached if you use the new B48 Autoroute that
avoids Grenoble. Behind the hotel is the eastern wall of the
Vercors – access to the *massif* is simple. Equally easy to find is
the Chartreuse (see Savoie). Modest cooking with dishes like
terrine de grive and *quenelle de brochet*.
menus **A-B** *rooms* 20 **B-C**
closed Nov-Jan. Fri. Sat midday.
post 38640 Claix. Isère.
phone (76) 98.07.74 *Mich* 244 Grenoble 11 km

DIE   La Petite Auberge

Comfortable hotel
Terrace/Good value

An old favourite; it's family owned and that ensures a homely
atmosphere. Cuisine is good – category three standard perhaps.
Order the *demi-sec* and *brut* versions of **Clairette de Die** – a
local sparkling wine. See the Cirque d'Archiane and use the lanes
that head south from Saillans.
menus **A-B** *rooms* 15 **B-C**
closed Dec. Jan. Sun evg and Mon (except July-Aug).
post 26150 Die. Drôme.
phone (75) 22.05.91 *Mich* 244 Grenoble 97 km

EMBRUN   Les Bartavelles

Comfortable hotel
Fairly quiet/Gardens/Swimming pool/Tennis

This modern hotel has a most unusually-shaped roof. Category
two meets the bill perfectly here; ignore the dining room and use
the hotel as a 'base'. An alternative *sans restaurant* hotel is down
the road at Savines-le-Lac – the modern Flots Bleus. The Relais
Fleuri Restaurant and the Hôtel Eden Lac, both at Savines, are
also recommended by *French Leave* readers. All of them give you
the chance to enjoy the Lac de Serre-Ponçon – particularly the D3
on its western bank. Don't miss the Forêt de Boscodon and the
Queyras Valley.
menus **A-B** *rooms* 36 **C-D** *cards* AE DC Visa
closed Rest: Mid Nov-mid Dec.
post Crots. 05200 Embrun. Hautes-Alpes.
phone (92) 43.20.69 *Mich* 245 Grenoble 165 km

GRENOBLE   Novotel

Very comfortable hotel
Quiet/Terrace/Gardens/Swimming pool/Lift

Use as a 'base' – ignore the grill; 12 km north-west of Grenoble
where the autoroute becomes a toll road. (See page 320.)
Ignore restaurant *rooms* 114 **D** *cards* AE DC Visa
closed Open all the year.
post 38340 Voreppe. Isère.
phone (76) 50.81.44 *Mich* 244 Grenoble 12 km

127

ST-AGNAN-EN-VERCORS   Le Veymont

Simple hotel
Quiet/Good value

A modest place – but attractively sited facing a church and
fountain; all of them set around a village square. Four km to the
south are the caves at the Grotte de la Luire – used as a hospital
by the Resistance in 1944. Like La Chapelle-en-Vercors – most of
which was destroyed by the Germans – St-Agnan, too, suffered
badly during that summer. Menus include *truites* in various
forms and *tarte Tatin*.
menus **A-B** *rooms* 19 **B** *cards* AE DC Visa
closed Open all the year.
post St-Agnan. 26420 La Chapelle-en-Vercors. Drôme.
phone (75) 48.20.19 *Mich* 244 Grenoble 66 km

ST-ANDRÉ-LES-ALPES   Grand Hôtel

Simple hotel
Quiet/Terrace/Good value

Please don't get any ideas of grandeur with the impressive-
sounding name. The small hotel lies beside the tiny station on
one of the best privately-owned railway lines in France – the
metric gauge track from Digne to Nice. Food much above
average here – should it be category three?
menus **A-B** *rooms* 24 **A-B**
closed Oct-Easter.
post 04170 St-André-les-Alpes. Alpes-de-Haute-Provence.
phone (92) 89.05.06 *Mich* 245 Grenoble 223 km

URIAGE-LES-BAINS   Mésanges

Simple hotel
Secluded/Gardens

Another ideal candidate for this second category; modest
cooking indeed. Ignore the restaurant but don't ignore the
invigorating forests that stretch away to the east up to the peaks
of the Chamrousse. Uriage is a pretty spa. The Revolution was
said to have started in nearby Vizille in 1788.
menus **A-B** *rooms* 38 **A-C**
closed Oct-Apl.
post 38410 Uriage-les-Bains. Isère.
phone (76) 95.70.69 *Mich* 244 Grenoble 10 km

VALENSOLE   Piès

Comfortable hotel
Quiet/Gardens

I must stress that you should not ignore the cooking here – it's of
a high standard. The hotel is modern, stone-built and on the Riez
road. Valensole is famous for its almonds; the local countryside is
also known for its lavender – you'll see row upon regimented row
of bushes in the fields.
menus **A-B** *rooms* 16 **B** *cards* Visa
closed Jan-mid Feb. Thurs (Oct-Mar).
post 04210 Valensole. Alpes-de-Haute-Provence.
phone (92) 74.83.13 *Mich* 245 Grenoble 197 km

Domme (Dordogne)   Denis Pannett

The memorial at the Grotte de la Luire (Hautes-Alpes)

The market at Grasse (Côte d'Azur)

Recommendations where cuisine takes pride of place

BRESSON
Chavant

Very comfortable restaurant with rooms/Michelin★
Secluded/Terrace/Gardens   ®

Jean-Pierre and Danièle Chavant have taken over both the
kitchen and the running of this fine restaurant south of Grenoble.
Jean-Pierre's father, Emile, put it on the map many decades ago
and the family have continually improved the fabric of the place
as profits materialised – so typical of many family-owned
establishments in France. It looks scruffy as you approach – but
don't let that put you off; it's a charming spot with a shady garden,
hidden from view at the back of the building. Cuisine is classical
and, as a bonus, there's a vast selection of wines and Armagnacs.
Jean-Pierre pays homage to his father with *caille Emile Chavant*
and among other delights are: *saumon mariné aux herbes,
turbot aux morilles, palette de poissons fumés* and *cassolette
d'écrevisses.*
menus **B** *rooms* 8 **D** *cards* AE Visa
closed Last week Dec. Rest: Wed.
post Bresson. 38320 Eybens. Isère.
phone (76) 25.15.14 *Mich* 244 Grenoble 8 km

BRIE-ET-ANGONNES
Auberge des Lombards

Comfortable restaurant
Secluded/Terrace/Gardens

You have to work hard to find this isolated restaurant – the lack
of signs on the D5 would appear to mean that the Charif family
want to keep it unspoilt. Watch for the single sign on the western
side of the D5 just before you reach Brié. Cuisine is classical and
of a better than average standard; things like *gambas grillées,
sole meunière* and *moules farcies*. But the added bonus here that
rewards you well is the wooded setting.
menus **B-C** *cards* AE DC Visa
closed Jan. Aug. Tues.
post Lombards. Brié-et-Angonnes. 38320 Eybens. Isère.
phone (76) 89.63.90 *Mich* 244 Grenoble 10 km

LA CHAPELLE-EN-VERCORS
Bellier

Comfortable hotel/Michelin★
Quiet/Gardens

A guard of honour of green pines welcomes you to this shrine of
Vercors cooking – a modern chalet-style building. I will be the
first to admit this is a place where Michelin are being kind in
continuing to award their star – they do that in many places in
France where older chefs still continue to apply traditional skills
for the benefit of clients. I recognise that and I applaud their
loyalty. When you have read *Tears of Glory* you'll appreciate
better the murderous treatment meted out to La Chapelle and the
part the old Bellier restaurant played. Old-fashioned cuisine?
Yes, nothing changes: *truite, terrine, ballotine* and *poulet aux
écrevisses*. Readers have recommended Le Refuge – a *Logis* at
Echevis, below the Grands Goulets.
menus **B-C** *rooms* 13 **B-C** *cards* AE DC Visa
closed Mid Sept-mid June.
post 26420 La Chapelle-en-Vercors. Drôme.
phone (75) 48.20.03 *Mich* 244 Grenoble 62 km

CHATEAU-ARNOUX   La Bonne Etape

Very comfortable hotel/Michelin★★
Quiet/Gardens/Swimming pool

This entry remains in *French Leave 3* by the skin of its teeth. Like the D'Avaugour at Dinan, La Bonne Etape has a Jekyll and Hyde record with my readers; but what's different here is that most letters have been critical. In one case I received, from a much-travelled reader, an alarming record of his visit. The complaints about the restaurant were so serious that I made an 'incognito' call; and, indeed, all was not well. I am amazed that the Gleize family – having won so many accolades from the major guides – should turn in such poor performances.

What was wrong? Sauces and purées come in for most critical comment; to give you an example let me quote my reader – 'a warm, pink mess with oil separating from the edges.' My visit confirmed that puréed 'blobs' appeared everywhere; as the same reader said 'puréed lettuce (and cabbage?) – an extraordinary and unpleasant addition.' It was *nouvelle cuisine* at its worst: surely these were rare bad days? Were we both just unlucky? My disappointment was not helped by Arlette Gleize – if only she would thaw a bit and try to be a little more friendly; husband Pierre, if you see him, has a smiling personality.

So why is the entry included? I have been very tough on many famous places – as I have here. It's better to discuss disasters openly so that you can then decide for yourself whether to go or not. Pierre (once apparently at the Capital Hotel in London) and son, Jany (he had a stint at the Connaught), are keen Anglophiles; I hope I do not receive many more critical letters from English-speaking clients. In the previous edition I was tough on a much-fancied restaurant at Grimaud in Provence – Les Santons. I waited for your letters defending Claude Girard; none came. Gault Millau have since lowered their rating for Girard; early signs of falling standards can easily be detected. Will any of you jump to the defence of La Bonne Etape – or will we see some of those accolades evaporating here, too?

menus **B-D** *rooms* 18 **C-D2** *cards* AE DC Visa
closed Last week Nov. Jan-mid Feb. Sun evg/Mon (out of season).
post 04160 Château-Arnoux. Alpes-de-Haute-Provence.
phone (92) 64.00.09 *Mich* 245 Grenoble 155 km

MOUSTIERS-STE-MARIE   Les Santons

Comfortable restaurant
Terrace

I have American readers to thank for leading me in the direction of this attractively-sited restaurant with a covered terrace. It was a surprise to come across such enterprise in Moustiers – for so long a gastronomic desert. Messieurs Fichot and Abert will do well; but gentlemen – please keep your prices down a bit! Excellent service, nice touches like warm rolls baked with olives, *œufs brouillés aux truffes* and a fresh lake *truite en croûte farcie à la fleur de thym* with good vegetables were all appreciated. Bravo! This fine town is surrounded by superb local terrain – particularly the spectacular Grand Canyon du Verdon.

alc **B-C** *cards* AE
closed Nov. Tues (Oct-Feb).
post 04360 Moustiers-Ste-Marie. Alpes-de-Haute-Provence.
phone (92) 74.66.48 *Mich* 245 Grenoble 197 km

PELVOUX   Belvédère du Pelvoux

Comfortable hotel/Michelin★
Quiet/Terrace/Gardens

The first things you notice as you drive up the valley are the
majestic high mountains of the Massif des Ecrins – itself part of a
fine National Nature Park. The second things you spot are the
corrugated iron roofs on so many buildings – what eyesores.
Unhappily, the next sad visual impact occurs when you enter this
chalet-style hotel; what a mess they have made of the interior
decorations! I rarely mention such things but sometimes the
French can certainly make a hotchpotch of it. Thankfully,
Jacques and Patricia Sémiond's cooking makes up for all that –
it's good: *trio des torrents (truite, grenouilles* and *écrevisses),
paleron* (shoulder) *d'agneau de lait* and desserts will please. So
will the views.

menus **B-D** *rooms* 30 **B-C** *cards* AE DC
closed Easter-mid May. Mid Sept-20 Dec.
post St-Antoine. 05340 Pelvoux. Hautes-Alpes.
phone (92) 23.31.04 *Mich* 244 Grenoble 149 km

SERRES   Fifi Moulin

Comfortable hotel
Quiet/Gardens/Good value   ®

I first visited this amusingly-named jewel of a hotel 30 years ago.
In those days the Martins owned it – it had been in the family's
hands since 1830. Towards the end of their ownership it became
a sad place to visit – one sensed much bickering in the
background. All that has now changed; many of you have been
delighted by young Philippe Frenoux and his efforts to give
clients real value for money. Simple regional cuisine with
specialities like *lapin à la provençale, carré d'agneau, gratin
Dauphinois* and tasty sweets.

menus **A-B** *rooms* 26 **B-C** *cards* AE DC Visa
closed Mid Nov Feb. Wed (except July-Aug-Sept).
post 05700 Serres. Hautes-Alpes.
phone (92) 67.00.01 *Mich* 244 Grenoble 107 km

VARCES   L'Escale

Very comfortable restaurant with rooms/Michelin★★
Terrace/Gardens

I have to report only negative comments were received from
readers about the home of René and Alyette Brunet. Comments
like 'dreadful desserts' and a 'chalet shared with too many
spiders' were typical of the observations made. Another black
mark, in early 1983, was the sudden change of the weekly closing
day; all the guides got it wrong and in consequence my 'incognito'
visit did not materialise – the doors were shut.

   Don't miss the run through the forests south-west of Villard-de-
Lans – the D215 and D221 roads. You'll pass many monuments to
the memory of dozens who died defending the Vercors in 1944 –
including Chabal who was killed at Valchevrière.

menus **C-D** (almost **D2** – a record?) *rooms* 12 **C-D2** *cards* AE
closed 1-8 May. Mid-end Sept. Jan. Mon evg. Tues.
post 38760 Varces. Isère.
phone (76) 72.80.19 *Mich* 244 Grenoble 13 km

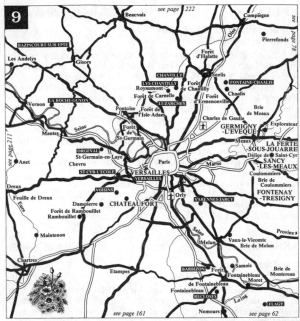

I described the Ile de France in *France à la Carte* as a green, wooded island surrounding **Paris** – full of treasures of both the man-made kind and those legacies endowed by Mother Nature. Full of historical interest, it was the birthplace of the nation and is much the most important region of modern-day France; it is the commercial heart of the country.

What are some of the natural pleasures surrounding Paris? To the north of the busy city are several splendid forests: the **Forêt de Carnelle**; the **Forêt de l'Isle-Adam**; and the forests of **Chantilly**, **Compiègne**, **Halatte** and **Ermenonville**. West of Paris is the forest at **St-Germain-en-Laye** and to the south are the huge tracts of woodland at **Rambouillet** and **Fontainebleau**. The last is my great favourite – at its best when it wears its glowing autumn colours. Oak, beech and Scots pine are the trees that flourish in this vast lung of metropolitan Paris.

Painters have long loved the forest and river country encircling Paris; the rivers include the **Oise** to the north and the **Seine** and **Loing** to the south-east – the latter being favourites of Sisley, Monet and other Impressionists. **Barbizon**, near Fontainebleau, was made famous by the landscape artists of the 19th century; **Samois** and **Moret**, too, were much loved towns of these painters – seek out the views they captured on canvas.

At weekends all the Ile de France is overrun by Parisians fleeing from the crowded, noisy city; it's a nightmare area for any driver – and it's best to ignore it during Saturday and Sunday.

Where are the numerous man-made treasures, mostly similar in type to those found in the Loire Valley? There are several stunning châteaux, abbeys and cathedrals – superb examples of the very best of the last five centuries of French architecture, painting, furnishing and garden design.

The best way of highlighting them all is to describe a clockwise circle round Paris, starting in the south-west corner at **Chartres** (which itself is just outside the true Ile de France). At Chartres is one of the wonders of France – the exquisite cathedral; its great spires, the statuary work and the stained-glass windows are an inspiration. North of the town explore the **Eure** Valley; enjoy the châteaux at **Maintenon** and **Anet** and the old town of **Dreux**. To the east of the latter are two fine châteaux at Rambouillet and **Dampierre**.

The other principal attractions in the south-west segment of the Ile de France are at **Versailles** and St-Germain-en-Laye. The colossal, majestic palace at Versailles is renowned throughout the world. It is not a place to visit just once; you could make several visits and still not absorb all its superb apartments, the vast gardens and the Trianons. The château at St-Germain – in its present form – was the creation of the legendary Henri IV; all manner of things can be seen in the château, the nearby forest and in the old town itself.

To the north of Paris can be found the magnificently-sited château at Chantilly (and its neighbour, the lovely racecourse); the awesome fortress at **Pierrefonds**; the ruins of the 700 years old Abbaye de **Royaumont** and the Abbaye de **Chaalis** – founded in 1136. **Beauvais** is renowned for its cathedral – particularly the fantastic Gothic choir, the double flying buttresses, tapestries and glorious windows. **Senlis** is a splendid town, full of medieval houses and other treasures.

To the east and south-east are two essential sites that must be on your visiting list: the Renaissance-styled château at Fontainebleau – the most secretive and atmospheric of all the châteaux in the Ile de France; nearby, to the north, is the Château de **Vaux-le-Vicomte** – a perfectly balanced structure and the model for what came later at Versailles.

Michelin *yellow* map: 237. Green Guide: Environs de Paris
IGN *série verte* maps: 8.9.20.21. *série rouge* map: 103
Airports: Paris Orly. Paris Charles de Gaulle
Distances from: Paris-Calais 294 km

Cheeses **Cow's milk**

Brie soft, white rind, the size of a long-playing record. It will be frequently described with the addition of the name of the area in which it is made: **Brie de Coulommiers**, **Brie de Meaux**; **Brie de Melun**; and **Brie de Montereau** are the best known. Faint mushroom smell

Chevru similar in size and taste to Brie de Meaux

Coulommiers like Brie, but a smaller, 45 rpm disc. At its best in summer, autumn and winter. Both cheeses are ideal with **Côte de Beaune** reds

Délice de Saint Cyr a soft, triple-cream cheese – nutty-tasting and made in small disks

Explorateur a mild, triple-cream cheese – made in small cylinders

Feuille de Dreux fruity-flavoured, soft disk. Ideal with fruity red wines

Fontainebleau a fresh cream cheese with whipped cream; add a dusting of sugar – and it really is great

Regional Specialities

Refer to the five regional lists elsewhere in *French Leave*: Normandy to the west; the North; Champagne-Ardenne to the east; and Burgundy and the Loire on the southern borders of the Ile de France.

Wines

Refer to the chapters of Champagne-Ardenne – to the east; and Burgundy and the Loire – to the south.

Base Hotels

ST-CYR-L'ECOLE
Aérotel

Comfortable hotel
Quiet

A good *sans restaurant* hotel; modern, away from the main road and just west of magnificent Versailles. The hotel is on the D7 that heads north to Marly-le-Roi – opposite a small aerodrome; the entrance is easily missed.
No restaurant *rooms* 26 **C**
closed Xmas-New Year.
post 88 rue Dr-Vaillant, 78210 St-Cyr-l'Ecole. Yvelines.
phone (3) 045.07.44 *Mich* 237 Paris 27 km

VERSAILLES
St-Louis

Simple hotel
Quiet

Not my cup of tea; but if you must be in Versailles and close to the famous sites this is at least a quiet spot.
No restaurant *rooms* 27 **C**
closed Open all the year.
post 28 rue St-Louis, 78000 Versailles. Yvelines.
phone (3) 950.23.55 *Mich* 237 Paris 23 km

VOISINS-LE-BRETONNEUX
Port Royal

Simple hotel
Quiet/Good value ®

Benefits here are value for money, a quiet site, modern amenities and the chance to try many of the good restaurants in the vicinity. An ideal 'base' of the classic *French Leave* type. There's lots of wooded country to the south-west.
No restaurant *rooms* 20 **B-C** *cards* Visa
closed Open all the year.
post Voisins-le-Bretonneux. 78180 Montigny. Yvelines.
phone (3) 044.16.27 *Mich* 237 Paris 30 km

Recommendations where cuisine takes second place

BARBIZON
Les Alouettes

Comfortable hotel
Quiet/Gardens/Tennis

This *Logis de France* is well away from the main road that runs through the attractive village of Barbizon – made famous by the landscape painters of the 19th century and Robert Louis Stevenson who wrote *Forest's Notes* at the nearby Hôtellerie du Bas-Bréau. Some of the best forest country in France is close at hand; seek out the nearby Gorges d'Apremont and Gorges de Franchard where hundreds of huge rocks combine with the surrounding woods of pine, oak and beech to form an unusual picture. Fairly innocuous dishes here include the following: *terrine de canard* and *poire Belle Hélène*.
alc **B-C** *rooms* 28 **B-C** *cards* AE DC Visa
closed Jan. Sun evg.
post 77630 Barbizon., Seine-et-Marne.
phone (6) 066.41.98 *Mich* 237 Paris 59 km

BAZINCOURT-SUR-EPTE   Château de la Rapée

Comfortable hotel
Secluded/Gardens

This *Relais du Silence* 'château' is in fact a Normandy-styled country house in an isolated site, on the edge of woods and to the north-west of the village. It is reached by a roughish road that requires care – but there is much to compensate you for your navigational efforts: extensive views north; attractive grounds; and all sorts of neat Normandy touches – particularly in the dining rooms. Regional specialities include *tarte soufflée au Livarot, canneton Rouennais*, **Calvados** and cider-based dishes and *douillon Normande* (see Normandy specialities).

menus **B** *rooms* 9 **C-D** *cards* AE DC Visa
closed Feb. Tues evg and Wed (Oct-Feb).
post Bazincourt-sur-Epte. 27140 Gisors. Eure.
phone (32) 55.11.61 *Mich* 237 Paris 76 km

CHANTILLY   Campanile

Simple hotel
Quiet

A modern motel – part of a hotel chain with similar impersonal places dotted throughout France. Hardly an inspiring site – though it is quiet; rooms are basic and small but with the benefit of fully-fitted bathrooms. Ignore the grill and give breakfast a miss, too – a real disaster area. Use it as a 'base'. Be sure, too, to bypass the nearby Relais du Coq Chantant for your evening meal (a place where Gault Millau must have sent a charitable inspector – they 'honour' it with one *toque*). Instead, try other restaurants in Chantilly – and next morning enjoy its many parks and man-made treasures.

Ignore restaurant *rooms* 45 **C** *cards* Visa
closed Open all the year.
post route Creil, 60500 Chantilly. Oise.
phone (4) 457.39.24 *Mich* 237 Paris 49 km

FLAGY   Au Moulin

Very comfortable restaurant with rooms
Secluded/Terrace/Gardens   ®

A magnificently-restored, 13th-century mill with a charming, English-speaking host, Claude Scheidecker, who hails from Alsace. Don't plan an early morning start – you would be sure to regret it because you would miss the chance to enjoy breakfast on the terrace, followed by a leisurely exploration of the gardens and village. A second essential is to ask to be introduced to Pilou! Cuisine is of a sound standard with excellent high-quality local **Brie** and **Coulommiers** cheeses.

Make time, too, to explore the nearby Seine and Loing Valleys near Moret-sur-Loing and downstream on the former river towards Samois. You can sit quietly and watch the barges chugging by – admiring, at the same time, the river country made famous by Sisley, Monet and other Impressionist painters.

menus **B-C** *rooms* 10 **B-C** *cards* DC Visa
closed 10-22 Sept. Mid Dec-end Jan. Sun evg. Mon.
post Flagy. 77156 Thoury-Ferottes. Seine-et-Marne.
phone (6) 096.67.89 *Mich* 237 Paris 100 km

FONTAINE-CHAALIS   Auberge De Fontaine

Comfortable restaurant with rooms
Quiet

A stone building and a good *Logis de France*. Cooking is conventional – with dishes like *terrine de canard, rognons de veau, moules farcies* and *sorbet cassis*. Don't miss the ruins of the Abbaye de Chaalis – one of the many daughters of Cîteaux and founded in 1136; the huge Forêt d'Ermenonville with its strange La Mer de Sable (and also the scene of one of the worst ever air disasters); and the 'empty' island tomb of Jean-Jacques Rousseau in the Ermenonville park.

One *French Leave* reader who has visited this restaurant often warns of an 'arrogant, front-house man' who also apparently whips bottles of wine away before you have finished them! I was lucky – I missed him; he must have been off-duty.

menus **B-C** *rooms* 7 **C**
closed Feb. Rooms: Tues. Rest: Wed.
post Fontaine-Chaalis. 60300 Senlis. Oise.
phone (4) 454.20.22 *Mich* 237 Paris 49 km

LUZARCHES   Château de Chaumontel

Comfortable hotel
Secluded/Gardens

One of northern France's most attractive and alluringly-sited château hotels; a small, perfectly-proportioned, ivy-covered, turreted building – surrounded by trees and flower-filled grounds. A stream and lake add extra interest – indeed you enter the main door by a tiny bridge across the water. Classical cuisine that doesn't quite match the scenic pleasures: *foie gras de canard, caneton au Porto, quenelles* and *salade Niçoise* are some of the choices you'll be offered.

menus **B** *rooms* 19 **B-D**
closed Mid July-end Aug. Mid Dec-mid Jan.
post Chaumontel. 95270 Luzarches. Val-d'Oise.
phone (3) 471.00.30 *Mich* 237 Paris 32 km

LYS-CHANTILLY   Hostellerie du Lys

Comfortable hotel
Secluded/Terrace/Gardens

Lys is south of Chantilly in a mass of forest country, interlaced by roads that have scores of expensive, luxury homes lining their sides; an Ascot-like scene with a world-famous racecourse, at Chantilly, not far away. The Hostellerie is a modern building in wooded grounds. There is a vast choice on the menu – though imagination is hardly the order of the day here. Grills feature strongly; you'll also find a range of other banal dishes like *œuf cocotte à la crème, steak de lotte* and *cuisse de canard*. There are scores of pleasures in the vicinity – both man-made and those designed by Mother Nature: many forests, the château at Chantilly and Royaumont Abbey – all are just a few kilometres away. Book ahead at this hotel.

menus **B** *rooms* 35 **C-D** *cards* AE DC
closed Mid Dec-mid Jan.
post Lys-Chantilly. 60260 Lamorlaye. Oise.
phone (4) 421.26.19 *Mich* 237 Paris 42 km

ORGEVAL
Moulin d'Orgeval

Comfortable hotel
Secluded/Terrace/Gardens/Tennis

Alongside a stream called the Orgeval, this ancient mill has a delectable setting; particularly charming are the gardens, terraces and the fine trees that surround the vine-covered building. Equally you'll enjoy basic cooking with conventional, classical touches – like *caneton à l'orange, pigeon braisé Clamart, tournedos maître d'hôtel* and *meringue Chantilly*.
alc **B-C** *rooms* 12 **B-C** *cards* Visa
closed Mid Dec-mid Feb.
post 78630 Orgeval. Yvelines.
phone (3) 975.95.74 *Mich* 237 Paris 39 km

RECLOSES
Casa Del Sol

Simple hotel
Secluded/Terrace/Gardens   ®

On the edge of the lovely Forêt de Fontainebleau – a pretty place and the perfect example of what one expects a *Logis* and *Relais du Silence* to be. There's marvellous terrain to explore in all directions and simple, satisfactory cooking.
menus **B-C** *rooms* 10 **C-D** *cards* AE DC
closed Dec. Jan. Mon evg. Tues evg.
post Recloses. 77116 Ury. Seine-et-Marne.
phone (6) 424.20.35 *Mich* 237 Paris 72 km

LA ROCHE-GUYON
St-Georges

Simple hotel
Quiet/Terrace/Good value

Well away from the main road and alongside the northern banks of the Seine – a tranquil setting with many interesting sites to see in the village itself. Sound, value for money cooking with a selection of dishes like *ballotine de canard, coq au vin, truite meunière* and *sorbets*. Seek out the Musée Claude Monet at Giverny (where he lived during the last years of his life until his death in 1926); the gardens he created are delightful.
menus **A-B** *rooms* 15 **B-C**
closed Nov 1. Xmas. Wed (Nov-Feb).
post 95780 La Roche-Guyon. Val-d'Oise.
phone (3) 479.70.16 *Mich* 237 Paris 76 km

VARENNES-JARCY
Moulin de Jarcy

Simple restaurant with rooms (no showers or baths)
Secluded/Good value

A handsomely restored small mill – nestling in a wooded site between two arms of the River Yerres. Basic cuisine, guaranteed not to bankrupt you: *saucisson sec, jambon de Bayonne, quenelle de homard* and *onglet* (flank of beef) *à l'échalote* are the sort of choices you'll have at the Moulin.
menus **A-B** *rooms* 5 **A-B**
closed Aug. Mid Dec-mid Jan. Tues. Wed. Thurs.
post Varennes-Jarcy. 91480 Quincy-sous-Sénart. Essonne.
phone (6) 900.89.20 *Mich* 237 Paris 28 km

137

Recommendations where cuisine takes pride of place

CHATEAUFORT   La Belle Epoque
Comfortable restaurant/Michelin★
Terrace   ®

Michel and Josette Peignaud are highly-rated by Gault Millau;
they win the same three *toques* as do many of the more famous
restaurants, including the nearby Trois Marches at Versailles.
Their cuisine is a mixture of classical and innovative dishes but a
three *toques* rating is perhaps overgenerous; GM can be
charitable at times. Warm, turn of the century-furnished dining
rooms welcome you; indeed everything is in the style of *La Belle
Epoque* – including the toilets! There's also a tiny terrace
overlooking the wooded Yvette Valley. Among many specialities
listed I enjoyed *mitonné forestière en feuilleté* (with five types of
fungi – *cèpes, pleurotes, girolles, mousserons* and *trompettes de
la mort*) and *soufflé chaud au 'noyau de Poissy'* (Poissy is
famous for its cherries – *noyau* is a sweet liqueur flavoured with
crushed cherry kernels). Well worth a detour.
alc C *cards* AE DC Visa
closed Mid Aug-mid Sept. Xmas-New Year. Sun evg.
post Châteaufort. 78530 Buc. Yvelines.
phone (3) 956.21.66 *Mich* 237 Paris 27 km

LA FERTE-SOUS-JOUARRE   Auberge de Condé
Luxury restaurant/Michelin★★

Emile Tingaud is approaching 75; he opened his restaurant here
in 1947. If you prefer classical cuisine and want to enjoy it at its
very best – this is the place to which you must then make a
pilgrimage. My preference would lead me elsewhere but I am the
first to acknowledge cooking skills of any sort – and there are
plenty here. From a typical menu that was commonplace two to
three decades ago, I enjoyed a *jambonneau de caneton au Bouzy*
(duck meat shaped to form a 'leg' – cooked in a **Bouzy** red), a
Brie de Meaux and a mouthwatering sweet.
alc **C-D** *cards* AE DC Visa
closed Mid-end Aug. Feb. Mon evg. Tues.
post 1 av. Montmirail, 77260 La Ferté-sous-Jouarre. S.-et-M.
phone (6) 022.00.07 *Mich* 237 Paris 66 km

FONTENAY-TRESIGNY   Le Manoir
Very comfortable hotel
Secluded/Terrace/Gardens/Tennis

This isolated, Normandy-styled mansion – surrounded by woods
and attractive gardens – is to the east of the village and well clear
of the N4. It's expensively furnished and decorated – the
bedroom prices reflect that luxury touch; it's a member of the
Relais et Châteaux chain. Cuisine is as classical as it can get –
innovation is an unknown word in the northern and eastern
corners of the Ile de France: *châteaubriand au beurre
d'échalotes, carré d'agneau* and *tarte Tatin* are hardly inspired
concoctions. Find time to enjoy a real man-made treasure;
Fouquet's château at Vaux-le-Vicomte, just down the road.
alc C *rooms* 11 **D-D2** *cards* AE DC Visa
closed Jan-Mar. Tues.
post 77610 Fontenay-Trésigny. Seine-et-Marne.
phone (6) 425.91.17 *Mich* 237 Paris 56 km

GERMIGNY-L'EVEQUE   Le Gonfalon

Very comfortable restaurant with rooms
Quiet/Terrace

The restaurant is a modern building with the enviable benefit of a quiet setting beside the River Marne – well away from any through traffic. Le Gonfalon has an ever-growing reputation and at lunchtime certainly attracts a full house of local business people – always a good sign. Specialities reflect this quality with offerings like *hure de lotte, mignon de veau au Roquefort, salade de crustacés* and *marmite du chef*. This is **Brie** and **Coulommiers** cheese country – the varieties offered at the end of the meal are excellent.
menus **B-D** *rooms* 10 **C** *cards* AE DC Visa
closed Jan. Rest: Sun evg. Mon.
post Germigny-l'Evêque. 77910 Varreddes. Seine-et-Marne.
phone (6) 025.29.29 *Mich* 237 Paris 61 km

SANCY-LES-MEAUX   La Catounière

Comfortable hotel
Secluded/Gardens/Swimming pool/Tennis   ®

A vine-covered, 18th-century building sitting in the shadow of a village church. A modern extension houses a newly-built, covered swimming pool. Children will be attracted by the neighbouring riding stables at the bottom of the garden. Better than average cuisine with dishes like *filets de sole, magret de canard aux pleurotes, carré d'agneau, sorbets* and – a surprise in **Brie** country – a *crottin de Chavignol chaud* as a first course (see Loire cheeses for an explanation).
alc **B-C** *rooms* 11 **C** *cards* AE DC
closed Mid-end Aug. Nov. Sat and Sun (Dec and Jan). Rest: Sun evg (Feb-Nov)
post Sancy-lès-Meaux. 77580 Crécy-la-Chapelle. Seine-et-Marne.
phone (6) 025.71.74 *Mich* 237 Paris 52 km

VERSAILLES   Trois Marches

Luxury restaurant/Michelin★★   ®

Gérard Vié chose his restaurant site very confidently indeed; many think he may be the 'King' of French cuisine some day in the future. He weaves his magic in his elegant home, just a stone's throw away from the château at Versailles, built by a real, legendary king. Parking is no problem; the huge open space in front of the château is one of the biggest car-parks you will find anywhere. Gérard's cooking is *nouvelle cuisine* at its best; creative and with an artist's touch in the superb presentation of dishes. The highlights of my most recent visit were a delectable *escalope de truite de mer au vin de Bordeaux* (salmon trout in a red wine sauce) and a particularly marvellous 1981 **Pouilly-Fumé**. Unusually, the kitchens are upstairs. Two areas which Vié could improve are his desserts and *petits fours*; but, overall, he must be one of the few *cuisiniers* who could one day win a third Michelin star.
alc **C-D** *cards* AE DC Visa
closed Sun. Mon.
post 3 rue Colbert, 78000 Versailles. Yvelines.
phone (3) 950.13.21 *Mich* 237 Paris 23 km

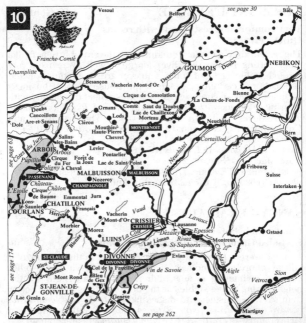

Thank heavens the vast majority of visitors to France ignore most of the Jura's best delights; usually their sights are set on the tourist traps of Paris and the Mediterranean – they are quite oblivious of the huge tracts of gorgeous countryside that stretch across its length and breadth. The quiet hills of the Jura are most certainly one of the more alluring of the regions bypassed by the speeding motorists – hell-bent on using autoroutes as speedtracks and with an insatiable desire to share those ribbons of concrete with their fellow human beings.

The lovely hills of the Jura are thickly wooded with pines, carpeted with green pastures and interlaced with dozens of gurgling streams and rivers. As an extra bonus there are many lakes, ranging in size from the tiniest pool to large, man-made sheets of water. Across the border, in **Switzerland**, is similar hill-country and many additional lakes – some are huge things with all sorts of pleasure steamers plying across their waters; any child will find them fascinating enough.

Most of the sights that I describe are those shaped, fashioned and painted by Mother Nature; this is particularly true of the Jura hills – the highest of them rising to no more than 1700 metres – where seclusion, invigorating air and scenic sights are the main attractions. Local wines and many regional cuisine specialities, relying mainly on the rich produce coming from the hills, and piscatorial pleasures found in the streams and lakes, are other delights to entice and satisfy you.

Let me start in the southern hills and travel northwards – detailing the best man-made sites and the many natural attractions. **St-Claude** would be a fine point to start your exploration; 200 years ago it prospered through its reputation for producing the world's best pipe briars. The town tumbles down from the hills to the floor of the **Bienne** Valley – it was much loved by Nevile Shute. South of St-Claude is one exquisite jewel – tiny **Lac Genin** set amidst tranquil, wooded hills; use the **Valserine** Valley route as you head south to seak it out.

North of St-Claude is another fine valley – the Bienne; be sure to use the minor lanes that run along the western side of the Gorges de la Bienne, northwards to **Morez**. To the east of St-Claude is a ridge of peaks that overlooks Switzerland and **Lac Léman** (Lake Geneva) – on a clear day you'll have magnificent views of the Alps (including Mont Blanc) from the **Col de la Faucille** and the peak called **Mont Rond**. At the foot of those summits is a small pocket of France that contains an attractive, cool spa – **Divonne-les Bains**: a golf course, casino and man-made lake that offers water sports attractions of all kinds, are its main assets – nearby, across the Swiss border, is Lac Léman.

To the east of **Lons-le-Saunier** are some small lakes and the **Hérisson** Valley – the latter is best seen after heavy rain or in the spring, as the river falls over 250 metres in three kilometres and in that short distance there must be two dozen or more cascades; use your legs to see the best of them.

In the hills that form the western edge of the range – between Lons-le-Saunier and **Arbois** – are some of the best examples of the *cirques* (amphitheatres) that abound in the Jura. The **Cirque de Baume** is a classic example; what makes this one so interesting are the 'resurgent' streams that go underground many kilometres away on the cliff tops and then re-emerge at the foot of the rock face – in this case spilling out over a cascade of rocks. Further north a more famous *cirque* is the one called **Cirque du Fer à Cheval**; here the 'resurgent' streams (called Les Reculées) emerge in caves. Be certain to see all the *cirques* from both the valley floors and also from the viewpoints that line their high, rocky walls. Arbois – where Pasteur worked for so long – is well worth exploring; the neighbourhood produces many wines – both sparkling and still, in white and rosé varieties.

North of Arbois is **Salins-les-Bains**, a spa where salt has been mined since pre-Roman times: and the salt town of **Arc-et-Senans**; see the few buildings that remain from what was going to be an 18th-century planned town – La Saline Royale. Southeast of Arbois is the superb pine forest called **Forêt de la Joux** – drive the Route des Sapins from **Champagnole** to **Levier**. Detour to the medieval village of **Nozeroy**.

Further east is the source of the **Doubs** – seek it out and those of the rivers **Lison** and **Loue** (both these rise from the mouths of caves). Explore all the delightful river valleys of the Jura – the three just mentioned and those described earlier. The Doubs rewards you with many attractions: the **Lac de Saint Point**; the **Lac de Chaillexon**; the spectacular **Saut du Doubs**; and many thrilling gorges as it travels northwards. The Loue, too, has the man-made pleasures of small towns like **Mouthier-Haute-Pierre**, **Lods**, **Ornans** and **Cléron**.

Seek out the **Cirque de Consolation** – my favourite; view it from the Roche du Prêtre, high above the valley. Then linger in the abbey park below – a wonderland of springs, streams, trees and woods. Follow the course of the short **Dessoubre** Valley – I can give you no better example of just what satisfaction awaits those enterprising enough to explore the Jura hills.

Michelin *yellow* maps: 243.66.70.74. Green Guide: Jura
IGN *série verte* maps: 37.38.44. *série rouge* map: 109
Airports: Geneva. Bâle/Mulhouse
Distances from: Paris-Besançon 411 km Calais-Besançon 705 km

Cheeses Cow's milk

Cancoillotte very fruity flavour, prepared from **Metton** (an unmoulded, recooked cheese) and looks like a cheese spread. It is available all through the year and is eaten warm in sandwiches or on slices of toast
Comté a hard, cooked cheese, made in great disks. Has holes the size of hazelnuts. Best seasons are summer, autumn and winter
Emmental Français – the French version; another hard, cooked cheese, also made in huge disks but with holes the size of walnuts
Gex (Blue de) a *fromage persillé*, with blue veins, like the pattern of parsley. Made in large disks; at its best in summer and autumn
Morbier strong-flavoured, pressed, uncooked thick disk
Septmoncel (Bleu de) made in thick disks – blue veins, slightly bitter
Vacherin Mont-d'Or soft, mild and creamy; made in cylinders
Goat's milk
Chevret faint goat smell with this small flat disk or square-shaped cheese

Swiss Cheeses

In Switzerland look out for the principal Swiss cheeses: the main types of **Emmental** and **Gruyère** have many varieties – all superb; others are **Vacherin Mont-d'Or**, **Tomme de Valbroye** and **Chèvre de Valois**

Regional Specialities

Brési wafer-thin slices of dried beef
Gougère hot cheese pastry – based on Comté cheese
Jésus de Morteau fat sausage smoked over pine and juniper
Poulet au vin jaune chicken, cream and morilles, cooked in *vin jaune*

Wines

Whites and Rosés
The broadest AC classification is **Côtes du Jura**. Among the best wines are the refreshing rosés from **Arbois**, brownish-pink in colour, and the whites of **Poligny**, fragrant and light. Another AC is **L'Etoile** (just north of Lons), where nice dry and sweet whites are made. There is also an **AC Arbois-Pupillin**, a small village to the south of Arbois.

The brightest star is a *vin jaune*, AC **Château-Châlon**, a rare wine, deep yellow, very dry and made from the Savagnin (Traminer) grape. **L'Etoile** and **Arbois** have their own versions of this *vin jaune*. A *vin de paille* (grapes dried on straw mats) is a very sweet, heady wine; *vin gris* is a pale rosé.
Sparkling wines
Sparkling wines include **L'Etoile mousseux**, the **Côtes du Jura** and **Arbois mousseux** and the *vin fou* (mad wine) from **Arbois**.
Vins de Pays
Jura and **Franche-Comté** labels (**Champlitte** is a village).

Swiss Wines

Swiss wines are known by grape, place and type names. Chasselas is the main white grape: in **Valais** it's used to make **Fendant**; in **Vaud** it's **Dorin**; around Geneva **Perlan**.

Very little red wine is produced: it's made from the Pinot Noir and/or Gamay grape types. The reds of Valais are called **Dôle**; those of Vaud are named **Salvagnin**.

Fine Valais wines come from **Sion**, **Vétroz** and – best of all – the **Domaine du Mont d'Or**. The best Vaud wines are from **Lavaux** (between Lausanne and Montreux) and its principal villages of **Dézaley**, **Rivaz**, **Epesses**, **St-Saphorin** and **Aigle**; **La Côte** (Vaud) is the area south-west of Lausanne. **Neuchâtel** makes reds and whites (best village – **Cortaillod**).

Base Hotels

CHAMPAGNOLE   La Vouivre

Very comfortable hotel
Secluded/Gardens/Tennis

Michelin don't often get their 'direction' information wrong – but
they have in this case. Follow the signs for the hotel near the
level-crossing on the N5, north of the town. A dull-looking
building in extensive grounds.
No restaurant *rooms* 20 **C**
closed Mid Dec-mid Jan. Sat and Sun evg (Nov-Jan).
post 39300 Champagnole. Jura.
phone (84) 52.10.44 *Mich* 243 Besançon 71 km

DIVONNE-LES-BAINS   Coccinelles

Comfortable hotel
Quiet/Gardens/Lift

A modern hotel to the north of the attractive spa of Divonne-les-
Bains. Gabrielle Blanc's base hotel is popular because you have
all the advantages of Switzerland and France on your doorstep –
without paying Swiss prices! So book ahead.
No restaurant *rooms* 18 **B-C**
closed Mid Dec-end Jan.
post route Lausanne, 01220 Divonne-les-Bains. Ain.
phone (50) 20.06.96 *Mich* 243 Besançon 135 km

Recommendations where cuisine takes second place

DIVONNE-LES-BAINS   Mont-Blanc-Favre

Comfortable hotel
Secluded/Gardens/Tennis/Good value   ®

It seems cruel to say ignore the restaurant (only lunches are
available by the way); it's recommended because it makes a
super 'base'. Considering the many benefits on hand, prices are
modest – even charitable when you consider Swiss ones two
miles away. Well-maintained gardens, comfortable rooms and
spectacular views to the east and south-east across Lac Léman
towards the Alps; hope for a haze-free day.
menus **B-C** (lunches only) *rooms* 18 **A-C**
closed Nov-Feb. Rest: Wed.
post route Grilly, 01220 Divonne-les-Bains. Ain.
phone (50) 20.12.54 *Mich* 243 Besançon 135 km

CRISSIER   Novotel

Comfortable hotel
Secluded/Terrace/Gardens/Swimming pool

The postal address is Bussigny; use it as an overnight 'base' for
Girardet's restaurant. Frequently the U.K. and U.S. booking
agencies say 'it's full' – but if you ask Girardet's staff to reserve
rooms they become 'free'! On the west side of the autoroute
(Crissier exit). (See page 320.)
Ignore the restaurant *rooms* 100 **D** (French francs) *cards* AE DC Visa
closed Open all the year.
post rue des Condémines, CH-1030 Bussigny. Switzerland.
phone (21) 89.28.71 (Switzerland) *Mich* 243 Besançon 125 km

MALBUISSON   Les Terrasses

Comfortable hotel
Terrace/Gardens

Owned by the Chauvin family (also see category three entry), this
chalet-style hotel overlooks the Lac de St-Point. Rooms with
views of the garden and lake are the ones to have. Menus make
good use of *morilles* from the hills – with *poulet* and *escalope*;
fresh trout, too, appear in various forms.
menus **B-C** *rooms* 25 **C** *cards* DC Visa
closed Nov-Jan. Mon (out of season).
post 25160 Malbuisson. Doubs.
phone (81) 69.30.24 *Mich* 243 Besançon 74 km

MONTBENOIT   Bon Repos

Simple hotel
Secluded/Terrace/Gardens/Good value   ®

If someone told you there was a railway line outside the hotel,
you may conclude you should bypass the Bon Repos. What a
mistake that would be – it's just a single line with two local trains
each day. Bon Repos is a *Logis* and *Relais du Silence*. Try two
regional specialities: *Jésus de Morteau* and *poulet au vin jaune
aux morilles*. Don't miss the village abbey.
menus **A-C** *rooms* 22 **B-C**
closed Mid Sept-Apl.
post 25650 Montbenoit. Doubs.
phone (81) 38.10.77 *Mich* 243 Besançon 68 km

PASSENANS   Revermont

Comfortable hotel
Secluded/Gardens/Swimming pool/Lift

This hotel would win no prizes for attractive looks. However,
there are large grounds, a swimming pool and lots of fine country
to the east and south. Another bonus – the Revermont is a *Relais
du Silence*. Basic cooking with run of the mill dishes like *truite
au bleu* and *poulet de Bresse à l'Arbois*.
menus **A-C** *rooms* 28 **B-C**
closed Jan. Feb. Sun evg and Mon midday (out of season).
post Passenans. 39230 Sellières. Jura.
phone (84) 44.61.02 *Mich* 243 Besançon 50 km

ST-CLAUDE   Au Retour de la Chasse

Simple hotel
Quiet/Gardens/Tennis/Good value

A chalet-style hotel five kilometres south of St-Claude. Sadly, its
near neighbour – the Hôtel Joly – has been dropped from this
edition after one or two bad reports. Hopefully, this smart,
modern place will not let me down. Jura wines are put to good
use by Gérard Vuillermoz in his specialities: *truite meunière au
Côtes de Jura* is just one example.
menus **A-B** *rooms* 12 **B**
closed Mid-end Apl. Mid Nov-Xmas. Sun evg. Mon.
post Villard-St-Sauveur. 39200 St-Claude. Jura.
phone (84) 45.11.32 *Mich* 243 Besançon 131 km

ARBOIS
de Paris

Comfortable restaurant with rooms/Michelin★
Gathers

I had several letters from readers suggesting it was high time that I paid a call on this long-established shrine of good Jura cooking. I did just that and enjoyed myself considerably. For a start the tiny restaurant – its walls covered with some unusual bric-à-brac – has some character about it; it's an old 17th-century building opposite the town hall, itself a fine sight. But it's André Jeunet who has as much character as the house or town – a huge, jovial individual who continues to make sure that Jura specialities still appear on his menus; *coq au vin jaune et aux morilles* is one. Nowadays son, Jean-Paul, also has a say in things; witness the lighter touches – acquired at the homes of the Troisgros brothers and Chapel. All the sons of 'top' chefs seem to do a stint these days at a 'great' restaurant.

menus **A-C** *rooms* 18 **B-C** *cards* AE DC
closed Mid Nov-mid Mar. Tues.
post rue de l'Hôtel de Ville, 39600 Arbois. Jura.
phone (84) 66.05.67 *Mich* 243 Besançon 49 km

CHATILLON
Chez Yvonne

Simple restaurant with rooms
Secluded/Terrace/Good value ®

An old, old favourite of my family; totally isolated, it snuggles up to the side of the infant River Ain. Would you believe it once had a Michelin star shining overhead in the days of Yvonne Peltier-Perret? Today Madeleine Garnier continues the same tradition of providing regional products at bargain prices: fresh trout, *morilles* from the local forests and *poulet de Bresse*. Chez Yvonne is on the D39 to the east of the village at the point the road crosses the River Ain.

menus **A-B** *rooms* 8 **A**
closed Jan-mid Feb. Mon evg. Tues.
post Châtillon. 39130 Clairvaux-les-Lacs. Jura.
phone (84) 25.70.82 *Mich* 243 Besançon 97 km

COURLANS
Auberge de Chavannes

Comfortable restaurant/Michelin★
Terrace/Gardens

I marvel how Pierre Carpentier and his elegant wife, Monique, manage to make their restaurant pay. For a start, it's six kilometres to the west of Lons-le-Saunier, so there's not much passing trade; then, at best, only about 20 clients can be shoehorned into their tiny dining room. Pierre is a talented chef: I'll forgive him poor *petits fours*; instead I'll praise him for a couple of creations – a *fricassée de langoustines au persil* and a *cassolette des légumes* – both of which were perfection. No mushy purées with the latter either. Good Jura wines – Monique's father is a local grower. Use Motel Solvan in Lons for overnight stays (quiet/*sans restaurant*).

menus **B-C**
closed Mid June-mid July. Dec. Tues. Wed.
post Courlans. 39570 Lons-le-Saunier. Jura.
phone (84) 47.05.52 *Mich* 243 Besançon 94 km

CRISSIER   Girardet

Very comfortable restaurant   ®

The world's greatest 'French' chef is not to be found in France – you must seek him out at Crissier, in Switzerland. Few would dispute that Girardet, a Swiss and a *cuisinier* of genius, is the 'King' of chefs and deserves to wear a crown.

Our first visit to Crissier, many years ago, was an eye-opening revelation (we have Gault Millau to thank for that); since then Anne and I have been back as often as we can. On each visit we expect the 'bubble' to burst and to come down to earth with a bang; we worry that we have put Girardet on an impossible pedestal. But not so; each visit confirms that Frédy operates on a different level from all his peers.

The reason why I am so hard on Bocuse, Vergé, Chapel and others is that when I grudgingly spend money these days to eat at their culinary shrines I inevitably compare them with Girardet and his 'tour de force' restaurant. Reference to those three named entries, as examples, will detail some of the factors where they fall seriously short – and they are reckoned to be great chefs and restaurateurs. Visit after visit to Crissier confirms that this is the only restaurant that I know where it becomes impossible to fault any one of the scores of factors that combine to make the perfect restaurant; I listed many of those factors in previous editions of *French Leave*. More of the great chefs find their way to Crissier than to any of the three-star restaurants listed elsewhere in *French Leave 3*.

How has Frédy Girardet become such a magnificent *cuisinier* and restaurateur? He's 47 – a simple man, but with exquisite taste, a Frenchman's flair for creative brilliance and with a businesslike Swiss brain. His late father owned a humble café in Crissier – an equally modest, small suburb of Lausanne. In his teens Frédy's passion was football – his motivation lay more in playing soccer than working for his father in their bistro. (That love for soccer is still there – watch his face light up when you quiz him about the game; he follows the fortunes of European soccer with great interest.)

His *raison d'être* for life changed in one single day – 16 years ago. His father had sent him on a wine buying trip to Beaujolais country. Frédy had never dined at any of the great French restaurants – on that trip he made his first visit to the Troisgros home at Roanne. For Frédy it was a spiritual moment in time; during one meal his entire concept of what cooking was all about changed out of all recognition. His experience at that time was based solely on his father's tuition and a three year apprenticeship in the Brasserie du Grand Chêne in Lausanne – a modest training, to be sure.

Frédy's development as a chef since that day has been astonishing. He has had no spells at any of the great kitchens and he rarely eats at any of the famous temples of gastronomy; he is very much his own man – a *créateur*. He gives credit to his late father for his basic technique, talent, ideas and principles; what a teacher he must have been. Pierre Troisgros paid Frédy the ultimate compliment – he sent his son, Michel, to Crissier, to serve his apprenticeship. I talked recently to Michel about that spell – he hero worships Frédy and can't praise the talented genius enough. Throughout France, top chef after top chef names Frédy as the chefs' chef!

The family restaurant used to be called the Restaurant de l'Hôtel de Ville; it occupied the corner of the Crissier Town Hall –

and was rented from the local council. When Frédy's father died, he took over the burden of the business and decided to do more ambitious things. It was a hard life in those days – much complicated by the costly financing needed to establish the beginnings of a good cellar. A further burden came at the same time when the town council decided they could not afford to maintain the Hôtel de Ville; the Girardet family agreed to buy it – putting another heavy weight on Frédy's shoulders.

Today, all those tough years are behind the family; the restaurant is now called 'Girardet'. A small sign above the main entrance announces it in a humble way: 'Frédy Girardet – Cuisinier'. There is nothing special about the two small dining rooms; they are ordinary, but comfortable, well-furnished rooms, seating, in total, no more than 60 to 70. (Bookings for any one month must be reserved on the first day of the previous month – by the second day it's too late!) Tiled floors, white walls with modern paintings, lace curtains – it's an unpretentious setting.

There isn't one sign of compromise anywhere. You see perfection in the beautifully designed and printed menu (though Frédy should use a word processor to prepare his continually changing daily menu); you see it in the flowers, the cutlery, the crockery, the mustard-coloured tablecloths and napkins; in the small, silver *cassolettes* – designed by Frédy; in the glassware with their faintly-etched 'fg' symbol; but, above all, on the plates where the real genius of the man and his superb brigade can be shown off so fantastically well.

Girardet has an obsession for fresh produce: a variety of bread – baked twice each day; shellfish from Brittany; poultry from Bresse and the Vendée; salmon from Scotland; a range of perfect Swiss cheeses; vegetables from both local suppliers and from Provence; meat from Rungis (the great Paris market); *foie de canard* from the Landes; the list is endless.

The specialities he has offered his clients over the years must number many hundreds; studded with audacious combinations of tastes and imaginative jewels of creative brilliance. If you want to discover what *nouvelle cuisine* is all about and why classical cuisine is all but dead – this is where you must come. Make certain you go – even at the expense of other pleasures. Frédy's fixed-price menu – £40 ($60) – is expensive (the ultra-strong Swiss franc sees to that), but it provides the perfect way of relishing five superb courses, followed by his glorious Swiss cheeses, fantastic desserts and supreme *petits fours*. Accompany it all by choosing some of his fine Swiss wines.

Girardet has 30 staff – 18 of whom work behind the scenes (ask to see the modern kitchen after your meal). All his staff are young men and women – proud as punch to work for the man; his 'sun' personality brings out the best in all of them.

Last – but not least – Frédy is a loyal family man. Unlike Bocuse, he has no wish to make his fortune away from his home. His wife, Muriel (now recovered from a terrible cycling accident in August 1981 – it's a sport they both love), matches Frédy's humility and grace; his mother, Georgette, still gives a hand in welcoming guests. May all of them – and their talented staff – continue to astonish the favoured few who visit them. Make the financial sacrifice needed to join that fortunate club; you'll have a stunning memory for the rest of your life.

menus **D** (French francs)
closed Mid July–mid Aug. Xmas-New Year. Sun. Mon.
post CH-1023 Crissier. Switzerland.
phone (21) 34.15.14 (Switzerland) *Mich* 243 Besançon 125 km

DIVONNE-LES-BAINS   Bellevue-rest. Marquis

Comfortable restaurant with rooms
Quiet/Terrace/Gardens

The restaurant is south-west of Divonne in an elevated site with
views across Lac Léman to the Alps beyond. Little has changed
here over the last 25 years; classical cuisine remains the order of
the day. At last Michelin have done the charitable thing and taken
away the longstanding star – others, too, need the same
treatment. André Marquis has survived all those years with the
same basic repertoire: *truites*, *écrevisses* and *ris de veau
Périgourdine* – they are not going to change now. Apart from the
Jura hills and Lac Léman, Divonne has a sports complex with a
swimming pool and other facilities.

menus **B-C** *rooms* 17 **B-C** *cards* AE DC Visa
closed Mid Oct-Apl. Rest: Wed.
post av. d'Arbère, 01220 Divonne-les-Bains. Ain.
phone (50) 20.02.16 *Mich* 243 Besançon 135 km

GOUMOIS   Taillard

Comfortable hotel/Michelin★
Secluded/Terrace/Gardens/Good value   ®

There is no other recommendation of mine in France that has
won such unanimous praise from the dozens of readers who
have made the navigational effort needed to seek out this
heavenly spot – 2000 feet above sea-level, overlooking the
glorious wooded valley of the River Doubs, which forms the
frontier with Switzerland. I am happy that so many of you have
fallen in love with the countryside, the hotel and the Taillard
family who have owned this *Logis de France* since 1875. My
family have adored it for the last 20 years. The place is looking
quite smart these days with modern terrace furniture and some
handsome bedrooms. Cuisine remains as appetising and
enjoyable as ever: *jambon de montagne*, *truites* and *caquelon*
(dish in which they are cooked) *de morilles à la crème*. Visit the
nearby *fromagerie* at Charmauvillers to see **Comté** cheese being
made. Ask the Taillards for their booklet – *Guide des
Promenades*; note the entry for *un jour de pluie* – a rainy day!

menus **B-C** *rooms* 16 **B-C** *cards* DC Visa
closed Nov-Feb. Wed (Mar and Oct).
post Goumois. 25470 Trévillers. Doubs.
phone (81) 44.20.75 *Mich* 243 Besançon 95 km

LUINS   Auberge de Luins

Simple restaurant
Terrace   ®

One of four Swiss entries included in this region. Visit this
delectable Swiss bistro, surrounded by the vineyards of **La Côte**.
Relish the Luins wines – the owners, the Marguerats, produce
their own; enjoy the local sausages; but above all, savour a
speciality called *malakoffs* (circular cheese toasts served piping
hot – one at a time as they are cooked).

alc **B** (French francs)
closed Tues.
post CH-1181 Luins. Switzerland.
phone (21) 74.11.59 (Switzerland) *Mich* 243 Besançon 125 km

MALBUISSON   Le Lac

Very comfortable hotel
Gardens/Lift

Fernand Chauvin, like André Jeunet at Arbois, ensured that his
son, Jean-Marie, got a solid basic training; in this case the young
man was despatched to the kitchens of Lasserre in Paris. You will
be offered a range of classical-based dishes: *coquilles St-Jacques
aux petits légumes, coq au vin, gratin de queues d'écrevisses* and
similar fare. The hotel is a big place with a vast dining room –
overlooking the placid waters of the Lac de St-Point. Ideally
placed for Switzerland.
menus **A-C** *rooms* 54 **B-C** *cards* DC
closed 1-15 Jan. Mar.
post 25160 Malbuisson. Doubs.
phone (81) 89.34.80 *Mich* 243 Besançon 74 km

NEBIKON   Adler

Comfortable restaurant with rooms   ®

The Adler is in Switzerland; Nebikon is within a kilometre or two
(on the western side) of the exit serving Willisau/Dagmersellen
on the Basle-Lucerne autoroute. We first discovered Seppi
(Zeppi) Hunkeler some six years ago – and what a revelation he
turned out to be. He is a young, dynamic chef, very much like
Alain Rayé at Albertville; part of his training was at the Savoy in
London but it is his hero, Frédy Girardet, who influences so much
his creative thinking. He's a modern master, full of innovative
ideas; it's no wonder these days that he earns two *toques* from
Gault Millau. His menus and specialities change from day to day
and season to season; you will be offered a *menu surprise* which
comprises several courses, using local products like *sandre*,
truite and *gibiers*.
menus **B-D** (French francs) *rooms* 6 **C-D** (FF) *cards* AE DC
closed Aug. Tues evg. Wed.
post CH-6244 Nebikon. Switzerland.
phone (62) 86.21.22 (Switzerland) *Mich* 21

ST-JEAN-DE-GONVILLE   Demornex

Very comfortable rest. with rooms (no showers or baths)
Quiet/Terrace/Gardens

Eugène Demornex has a picturesque auberge, surrounded by
flowers, nestling in a quiet corner of a tiny hamlet under the
eastern wall of the Jura mountains. Some years ago he fell out of
favour with both Michelin and Gault Millau – but there have been
no complaints from any of my readers. Classical, Bressan and
modern specialities grace his menus: *carré d'agneau, volaille de
Bresse braisée à l'estragon* and *feuilleté de St-Jacques à l'aneth*
are examples. Descriptions like *saucisson de cuisses de
grenouilles à la ciboulette* will amuse you, too. The auberge is 18
km from Geneva – at weekends it's usually full. There's a wide
selection of wines -- I admire his loyalty to the Chardonnay and
Gamay **Bugey** wines (see Lyonnais).
menus **B-C** *rooms* 10 **A-B** *cards* AE DC Visa
closed Jan-mid Feb. Sun evg. Mon.
post St-Jean-de-Gonville. 01630 St-Genis-Pouilly. Ain.
phone (50) 59.35.34 *Mich* 243 Besançon 144 km

LANGUEDOC-ROUSSILLON

What a mixture of delights awaits the traveller prepared to visit this southern area of France. Too many motorists just blast through – right foot hard down on the throttle pedal; all of them blinkered tourists sticking like leeches to the main roads.

They miss all the historical pleasures: the Citadel of **Carcassonne**; the old towns of **Béziers**, **Narbonne** and **Perpignan**; the treasures of **Salses** and **Fontfroide**. They ignore the new resorts; **Port Barcarès** and **St-Cyprien** are examples. I can forgive them the latter – the coast north from Perpignan is not my cup of tea; but why do they speed past the hinterland?

Haut-Languedoc, and the mass of land circling **Albi**, **Castres** and **Cordes** is marvellous, peaceful hill-country. Albi has its fortress-like cathedral, built of red brick, and its Toulouse-Lautrec Museum. Castres is renowned for its Goya Museum. But the attractions that are my cup of tea – and yours if you make the effort to taste them – are the hills of the **Sidobre** and the **Agout** Valley, east of Castres (see the strange rock formation called Peyro-Clabado – like a Centurion tank on top of a Mini); delightful **Najac** overlooking the **Aveyron**; and Cordes, a 700 years old fortified hill-top town, full of old streets with fine Gothic houses – it has become an interesting artistic centre. The minor roads alongside the River Aveyron deserve your time; the wooded hills to the north and south are full of villages, all real gems – the Vère Valley from **Bruniquel** to **Castelnau** is an especially fine example of what I mean. All the recommendations in the northern part of this region will allow you to reach the majestic Lot with its many special pleasures (see the Dordogne region – page 106).

Roussillon, the southern half of the region, rewards richly indeed those drivers who stray off the main roads. The coast south from **Collioure** – a colourful port founded by the Greeks – is renowned for its light; Braque and Matisse painted here. **Céret**, inland, is famous for its Museum of Modern Art; those same two artists, together with Picasso and Chagall, all worked in these luminous hills. **Prades** is known throughout the world by music lovers for its Music Festival founded by the cellist Pablo Casals; it takes place at the nearby Monastery of St-Michel-de-Cuxa. Take the D27 yellow road past the monastery and continue south-west to **Vernet-les-Bains**, in a sheltered valley under the **Pic du Canigou**. South of Vernet is the beautiful 10th-century Abbey of St-Martin-du-Canigou, perched high above the valley; ideal for walkers as it can only be reached on foot. To the north is medieval **Villefranche-de-Conflent** – an intriguing place with its covered ramparts.

Further west is the **Cerdagne**; a verdant, high mountain plateau with scenic aspects quite different from those you will see down on the coast. **Font-Romeu** is a modern winter and summer resort – it is used regularly by athletes for high-altitude training (1800 metres above sea-level). All the neighbouring small towns are a delight. To the north are the exciting **Gorges de l'Aude**, surrounded by forests of pines, beeches and elms.

Study Michelin map 235 carefully: don't miss the ruins of the castles at **Quérigut**, **Montségur** and **Quéribus** – built by the Cathars 700 years ago. From Quérigut go west to **Ax-les-Thermes**; then north to **Foix**, and then via the **Col de Port** to **Massat** and **St-Girons**. Lovely towns, linked by exhilarating mountain roads. Viewpoints, forests, underground grottoes, old villages; there are endless attractions awaiting you. Space, yet again, prevents me from doing justice to it all.

Michelin *yellow* maps: 235.240.79.80.82.83.86

Green Guides: Causses. Pyrénées

IGN *série verte* maps: 57.64.65.71.72. *série rouge* map: 114

Airports: Toulouse. Montpellier

Distances from:

Paris-Albi	704 km	Calais-Albi	998 km
Paris-Perpignan	908 km	Calais-Perpignan	1201 km

Cheeses Cow's milk

Chester Français French Cheshire cheese from Castres and Gaillac
Montségur bland, pressed and uncooked disk
Les Orrys strong-flavoured – big disk; drink with fruity **Corbières**

Goat's milk

Pélardon a *generic* name; small disks, nutty-tasting and soft. **Rogeret des Cévennes** is a related cheese

Regional Specialities

Aïgo Bouido garlic soup. A marvellous, aromatic dish; the garlic is boiled, so its impact is lessened. Served with bread
Boles de picoulat small balls of chopped-up beef and pork, garlic and eggs – served with tomatoes and parsley
Bouillinade a type of *bouillabaisse* – with potatoes, oil, garlic and onions
Boutifare a sausage-shaped pudding of bacon and herbs
Cargolade snails, stewed in wine
Millas cornmeal porridge
Ouillade a heavy soup of bacon, *boutifare*, leeks, carrots and potatoes
Touron a pastry of almonds, green pistachio nuts, hazelnuts and fruit

Wines

This is the land of *Vins de Pays* and *Vin Ordinaire*: the vast majority of table wines which French people drink with their ordinary meals come from this huge area of the Midi.

Reds

Some good, strong reds are made: **Côtes du Roussillon**, **Côtes du Roussillon Villages** (25 villages share this AC – they make wines with a higher alcohol content and yield less wine per acre), **Caramany** and **Latour-de-France** (these two villages also share the general AC but can show their own names) have all recently won AC classifications. Other AC wines are **Fitou** (on the coast and the same AC is shared by the countryside surrounding Tuchan) and **Collioure**. VDQS reds are **Minervois** (dry), **Vin Noble du Minervois**, **Cabardès**, **Côtes du Cabardès et de l'Orbiel**, **Corbières** (soft and fruity), **Corbières Supérieures** (higher alcohol) and **Costières du Gard** (see map on page 244); some whites and rosés are made in all these areas.

A vast VDQS area to the north is the **Coteaux du Languedoc**; scattered throughout it are many individual *communes*, taking either the general classification or their own VDQS. **St-Chinian**, **Montpeyroux**, **Faugères** and **St-Saturnin** are four particularly good wines: other villages are **Cabrières**, **la Clape**, **Pic-Saint-Loup**, **Quatourze**, **St-Drézéry**, **St-Georges-d'Orques** (just west of Montpellier), **La Méjanelle**, **St-Christol** and **Vérargues** (last three have **Coteaux de** with village name).

Whites

A good, inexpensive, sparkling white is **Blanquette de Limoux** (*méthode champenoise)*: **Limoux nature** is still wine. These are AC wines as are **Vin de Blanquette**, **Clairette du Languedoc** and **Clairette de Bellegarde** (east of Nîmes – see map on page 244): the last two get their name from the Clairette grape; this grape is the traditional one for many French vermouths. A VDQS white is **Picpoul de Pinet** (Picpoul is the Armagnac grape). A *vin vert* – from the Roussillon – is a light, refreshing white wine.

Natural Sweet Wines (Vins Doux Naturels) Liqueur Wines Unusual AC wines to look out for are the rich, golden **Muscats** of **Lunel**, **Rivesaltes**, **Frontignan**, **Mireval** and **St-Jean-de-Minervois**; fortified wines, rich in sugar and with added alcohol – they are ideal *apéritifs* (made from Muscat grapes). Similar wines, but darker in colour, like port, and made principally from the Grenache and Malvoisie grapes, are **Banyuls**, **Banyuls Grand Cru**, **Maury**, **Rivesaltes**, **Frontignan** and **Grand Roussillon** (the general AC for the VDN wines of the area). Those kept for a long time are called **Rancio**.

Other wines

Far to the north-west (and certainly not classified as Languedoc wines) are those from the **Gaillac** area – see page 110.

Vins de Pays

Most of it is red and much of it is good wine. If you see it called **Vin de Pays d'Oc** it will have come from any part of the four *départements* that follow. It may on the other hand indicate just the *département* name: **Vin de Pays des Pyrénées-Orientales** or **de l'Aude** or **de l'Hérault** or **du Gard**. Or the label may show a small, specific area within those *départements* (there are more than 50). Space does not provide the chance to list them all but a few are worth a mention: **Coteaux de Peyriac** (from the Minervois); **Haute Vallée de l'Orb** (north of St-Chinian); **Haute Vallée de l'Aude** (Limoux); **Les Sables du Golfe du Lion** (page 244); **Pays Catalan**, **Côte Catalane**, **Val d'Agly** (Roussillon).

COLLIOURE
Casa Païral

Very comfortable hotel
Quiet/Gardens/Swimming pool ®

One of my favourite base hotels – it really is a delectable spot.
The tiny garden is full of firs, palm trees and camellias. Tucked
away in a corner is a minute swimming pool – the surrounding
walls covered in roses and wistaria. Take soap with you.
No restaurant *rooms* 24 **C-D**
closed Nov-Mar.
post 66190 Collioure. Pyrénées-Orientales.
phone (68) 82.05.81 *Mich* 240 Perpignan 27 km

COLLIOURE
Madeloc

Comfortable hotel
Quiet

A good alternative to the Casa Païral; the top two floors have
large balconies – facing the Pyrénées.
No restaurant *rooms* 22 **C-D** *cards* AE DC
closed Mid Oct-mid Apl.
post rue R.-Rolland, 66190 Collioure. Pyrénées-Orientales.
phone (68) 82.07.56 *Mich* 240 Perpignan 27 km

CORDES
Cité

Simple hotel
Quiet

A tiny place in the heart of the perched town. Beware the steep
climb – and be warned that parking can be tricky.
No restaurant *rooms* 9 **B-C**
closed Dec.
post 81170 Cordes. Tarn.
phone (63) 56.03.53 *Mich* 235 Albi 25 km

MOUREZE
Hauts de Mourèze

Comfortable hotel
Secluded/Gardens/Swimming pool/Good value

A modern 'base' lying among the giant rocks of a *cirque*; weird,
fantastically-shaped versions are scattered everywhere.
No restaurant *rooms* 10 **B-C**
closed Nov-Easter.
post Mourèze. 34800 Clermont-L'Hérault. Hérault.
phone (67) 96.04.84 *Mich* 240 Albi 145 km

VERNET-LES-BAINS
Rés. des Baüs et Mas Fleuri

Comfortable hotel
Quiet/Gardens/Swimming pool ®

Vernet is a small spa town – much loved by Rudyard Kipling. A
first-class base hotel with attractive shaded gardens.
No restaurant *rooms* 39 **B-D** *cards* AE DC Visa
closed Nov-Easter.
post bd. Clémenceau, Vernet-les-Bains. 66500 Prades. Pyr.-Or.
phone (68) 05.51.94 *Mich* 235 Perpignan 55 km

ALBI
Host. St-Antoine

Very comfortable hotel
Quiet/Gardens/Lift

This is a place which I suggest you use as a base hotel; the restaurant is disappointing – eat at some of the category three recommendations. Albi is a lovely town, full of interesting sights; the St-Antoine is in a side street and is surprisingly quiet. Parking and garden at the rear. Swimming and tennis are shared with its sister hotel, La Réserve – out of town on the Cordes road.
menus **A-C** *rooms* 56 **C-D** *cards* AE DC Visa
closed Open all the year.
post 17 rue St-Antoine, 81000 Albi. Tarn.
phone (63) 54.04.04 *Mich* 235

AMELIE-LES-BAINS-PALALDA
Castel Emeraude

Comfortable hotel
Secluded/Terrace/Gardens/Lift

This *Relaise du Silence* is to the west of the town, on the north bank of the River Tech, which it overlooks. It has a well-tended garden. Cuisine is of average standard; I would suggest you use it mainly as a base hotel.
closed **A-C** *rooms* 31 **C** *cards* Visa
closed Dec. Jan.
post 66110 Amélie-les-Bains-Palalda. Pyrénées-Orientales.
phone (68) 39.02.83 *Mich* 235 Perpignan 38 km

ARLES-SUR-TECH
Glycines

Comfortable hotel
Terrace/Gardens

A smart *Logis de France* in a relatively quiet site; a small, pretty terrace is a bonus – well shaded by a wistaria and fir tree. There have been complaints about service – and one reader found the long flights of stairs hard work.
menus **A-B** *rooms* 34 **A-C**
closed 1 Dec-Xmas. Jan. Rest: Mon.
post 66150 Arles-sur-Tech. Pyrénées-Orientales.
phone (68) 39.10.09 *Mich* 235 Perpignan 42 km

CARCASSONNE
Domaine d'Auriac

Very comfortable hotel
Secluded/Terrace/Gardens/Swimming pool/Tennis/Lift

You'll not find a more attractive hotel in the region – a wooded park and a secluded site to the south of Carcassonne make it all pretty irresistible; be certain to drive back into the town after dinner to see the famous fortress by floodlight – an astonishing sight. Cooking is not up to much here, despite the Gault Millau *toque*. I feel sorry for local chefs hereabouts; everyone orders *cassoulet* – one of the world's most overrated dishes. **Limoux** sparkling wines are very underrated.
menus **B-C** *rooms* 23 **D** *cards* AE DC Visa
closed Mid-end Jan. Sun evg. Mon midday.
post route St-Hilaire, 11000 Carcassonne. Aude.
phone (68) 25.72.22 *Mich* 235 Perpignan 113 km

LACAUNE
Hôtel Fusiès

Comfortable hotel
Terrace/Good value

A warm, welcoming hotel – you can apply the same description
to the owner, Pierre Fusiès. Lacaune is 800 metres above sea-
level – the countryside reminds me of Wales. Pierre apparently
owns the nearby 'casino' which has swimming and tennis
facilities – you can use them. Enjoy the Lacaune *charcuterie*.
menus A-C *rooms* 65 A-C *cards* AE DC Visa
closed Xmas-end Jan. Sun evg (Dec-Mar).
post 81230 Lacaune. Tarn.
phone (63) 37.02.03 *Mich* 235 Albi 68 km

NAJAC
Belle Rive

Simple hotel
Secluded/Terrace/Gardens/Swimming pool/Good value   ®

What a delectable site the Belle Rive has – alongside the River
Aveyron; towering high above the hotel, on the other bank, is the
majestic ruined fortress of Najac. Eating here is no hardship as it
could just as easily have been a category three entry. Louis
Mazières is a fine cook and a good host – he owns a real charmer
of a hotel. Don't bypass it.
menus A-B *rooms* 34 A-B
closed Mid Oct-Mar.
post 12270 Najac. Aveyron.
phone (65) 65.74.20 *Mich* 235 Albi 54 km

ST-PONS-DE-THOMIERES
Château de Ponderach

Comfortable hotel
Secluded/Terrace/Gardens

As you drive north from Narbonne, across dry, rocky hills, the
17th century château welcomes you like a green oasis of calm
and peace. Cuisine is much above average – a young *cuisinière*
does the cooking and she was trained by Paulette Castaing at
Condrieu. Like most *Relais et Châteaux* hotels it's beautifully
furnished – but expensive. Explore the glorious hill country to
the north – the Monts de l'Espinouse.
menus B-D *rooms* 12 C-D *cards* AE DC
closed Mid Oct-Easter.
post route de Narbonne, 34220 St-Pons-de-Thomières. Hérault.
phone (67) 97.02.57 *Mich* 240 Albi 93 km

ST-SERNIN-SUR-RANCE
France

Simple hotel
Terrace/Good value

Another *Logis de France* where quite honestly it could have been
included in the next category. Surrounded by lovely hill country –
enjoy its delights and the produce that comes from them; *jambon
de pays*, *terrines du Rouergue* and **Roquefort** cheeses.
menus A-B *rooms* 20 A-C *cards* Visa
closed Sun evg and Mon (Nov-Easter).
post 12380 St-Sernin-sur-Rance. Aveyron.
phone (65) 99.60.26 *Mich* 235 Albi 50 km

CASTRES   La Caravelle

Comfortable restaurant
Terrace

Don't be fooled by the thoroughly shabby-looking exterior; at the back there's a terrace overlooking the River Agout. Enjoy many of the treats that come from the nearby hills: the *charcuterie* from Lacaune and *escargots* from the Montagne Noire are examples. Average classical and regional cuisine – but to compensate there's the Goya Museum in Castres and the Sidobre hills; seek out the weird Peyro-Clabado.

menus **A-B** *cards* AE DC Visa
closed Mid Sept-mid June. Sat.
post 150 avenue Roquecourbe, 81100 Castres. Tarn.
phone (63) 59.27.72 *Mich* 235 Albi 42 km

COLLIOURE   La Frégate

Comfortable hotel
Terrace/Lift   ®

Yves Costa is the 'joker in the pack' in my rugby team of XV favourite French chefs. (He's a great rugby fan and will appreciate the pun.) It is a mischievous choice on my part because Yves, more than any other young chef in France, epitomises the differences between the Michelin and Gault Millau approach to awarding 'accolades' for cooking.

Don't go to La Frégate if you put great store on style, polish, and luxurious trappings; but if you judge 'cooking' skills by the chef's efforts alone, then visit this maverick *cuisinier*. Yves breaks most of the rules: he employs unskilled waitresses; his restaurant, part of a busy *pension* hotel, has little character; his barked shouts to his three helpers in the tiny, cauldron-like kitchen can be heard through the communicating door (he's a very hard taskmaster); these are just a few of the rough edges you will find at La Frégate.

But what arrives on the plate more than makes up for those shortcomings. His cuisine is a mixture of light classical and regional specialities and his own creations – witness these examples, some of which were prepared in ways new to me on my most recent visit: *gaspacho en gelée, ratatouille froide aux anchois* and *hure de fruits de mer aux herbes fraîches*. Excellent *pâtisseries* and a range of ice creams are also particularly good. Enjoy, too, his superb **Armagnacs**.

Yves is an enthusiastic, happy family man with a passion for his *pays*. He works like a Trojan: cook, hotel manager, and a jack of all trades. He may be a failed student of politics but he has most certainly applied clear, logical thinking to the use he makes of his small word processor; study his restaurant and *salon de thé* menus and his exceptional, by any standards, wine list – all of which are prepared on his electronic toy. Why don't other chefs in France do the same?

So there you are: to Gault Millau my sincerest thanks for heading me, some years ago, to this young wizard; to Michelin, my regrets that their 'rules' for awarding stars seem to disqualify Yves. Perhaps, soon, I will have to eat my words.

menus **B-C** *rooms* 25 **C-D**
closed Mid Nov-mid Dec. Jan. Rest: Fri (out of season).
post 24 quai Amirauté, 66190 Collioure. Pyr.-Or.
phone (68) 82.06.05 *Mich* 240 Perpignan 27 km

CORDES   Grand Ecuyer

Very comfortable hotel/Michelin★
Quiet   ®

At long last Michelin have taken notice of Yves Thuriès and his remarkable skills – he won his first star in 1983. Yves and his attractive wife, Jacqueline, put on a stunning show at their Gothic home in one of my favourite French towns. For some, eating here is too theatrical; not for me as it reflects Yves' unquenchable extrovert personality. He is one of the greatest *pâtissiers* in France; if, like me, you have a sweet tooth, this is the place for you. Order his *Menu Douceurs* – two starters, followed by five desserts. The presentation is amazing; *sorbets* arrive in duckling-shaped cups, resting on the back of a mother duck! Each course is accompanied by superb figures of people and flowers – made out of ice and sugar.

menus **B-D** *rooms* 16 **B-D** *cards* AE DC
closed Nov-Mar. Rest: Mon (except July-Aug).
post 81170 Cordes. Tarn.
phone (63) 56.01.03 *Mich* 235 Albi 25 km

MARSSAC   Francis Cardaillac

Very comfortable restaurant/Michelin★
Terrace/Gardens/Swimming pool

It's easy to miss the restaurant – it lies well back from the main road, 200 metres after crossing the Tarn as you head west from Albi. It used to be called Tilbury – a rewarding port of call; overlooking the Tarn it has many good features about it. What a pity there are no rooms. Francis Cardaillac is a talented young *nouveau* master – you'll enjoy many light creations of his and a range of fine **Gaillac** wines.

menus **B-C** *cards* AE DC
closed Mid Sept-mid Oct. Jan. Sun evg. Mon.
post 81150 Marssac-sur-Tarn. Tarn.
phone (63) 55.41.90 *Mich* 235 Albi 10 km

MOLITG-LES-BAINS   Château de Riell

Very comfortable hotel/Michelin★
Secluded/Terrace/Gardens/Swimming pools/Tennis/Lift

Can a hotel have any more facilities than that list above? Perhaps not, but what it doesn't tell you is that the hotel is an oasis of green calm – with views south towards Mont Canigou. The château itself is a baroque eyesore – and the modern furnishings don't please all visitors. It's owned by the Barthélémy family (see Eugénie-les-Bains) and one of the daughters runs it. René Sarre, an old student of Guérard, is the chef and he offers his clients a mixture of regional dishes and more modern ones: *grande ouillade* (see the regional list) and the delightfully-named *pets de nonne à la confiture de mûres* are examples (see the *Glossary of Menu Terms*). **Château de Jau** is one of the very best Roussillon wines; another odd-ball feature here is that one of two swimming pools is on the roof!

menus **C** *rooms* 19 **D2** *cards* AE Visa
closed Nov-Mar.
post Molitg-les-Bains. 66500 Prades. Pyrénées-Orientales.
phone (68) 96.20.56 *Mich* 235 Perpignan 50 km

NARBONNE   Réverbère

Very comfortable restaurant/Michelin★   ®

As I type these words I still cannot believe that such value-for-
money cuisine excellence exists. Claude Giraud, a brilliant, 31
years old chef and his attractive, slim wife, Sabine, are heading
for fame. They know what's needed to do it: an air conditioned,
panelled dining room; talented, young waiters (dressed in tails); a
first-class *maître d'hôtel*; Limoges crockery (rather than the
usual German versions); excellent wines; a choice of coffees and
teas; a handsomely-printed menu; and, of course, most
importantly of all, a series of light, creative delights that emerge
from Claude's kitchen. Two of those treasures were jewels: a tiny
jambonneau de poularde and a *soupe légère d'ananas en soufflé*.
As Sabine said: "We like to see our restaurant full – our low-
priced menu ensures that." Use La Résidence or the Regent (both
sans restaurant) for overnight stays. Bravo Claude and Sabine –
and Happiness Tribun as well!
menus B *cards* DC
closed Sun evg. Mon.
post 4 place Jacobins, 11100 Narbonne. Aude.
phone (68) 32.29.18 *Mich* 240 Perpignan 64 km

OUST   Poste

Comfortable hotel/Michelin★
Quiet/Gardens/Swimming pool   ®

The Poste is the most enterprising of the few starred restaurants
in the central Pyrénées. Jean-Pierre Andrieu applies original
touches to many familiar sounding dishes: *pâté chaud de lotte et
saumon, pintadeau au Madiran* (see Southwest wines) *et au
lard fumé* and *soufflé de truite flanqué de langoustines* are
examples. It's no wonder that clients from as far as Toulouse
seek out this family hotel – Jean-Pierre is the fourth-generation
chef/owner. Quiet bedrooms are at the rear – with balconies and
overlooking the pool.
menus B-C *rooms* 30 B-C
closed Nov-mid Mar.
post Oust. 09140 Seix. Ariège.
phone (61) 66.86.33 *Mich* 235 Perpignan 198 km

REALMONT   Noël

Comfortable hotel/Michelin★
Terrace

The major guides have differing opinions about the Noël; both
Michelin and Gault Millau continue with basic accolades – Jean
Didier, on the other hand, doesn't award any star. Jean's probably
right; confirmed by my own visit and several letters from readers
who wrote to say that Noël Galinier is not the cook he used to be.
But consider this; he's a fifth-generation chef who has been
working in kitchens for 50 years – what a record! It's classical
cuisine: enjoy *boudin noir au vinaigre, pascade au Roquefort*
and *gratin de queues d'écrevisses*.
menus B-C *rooms* 14 B-C *cards* AE DC Visa
closed Sun evg and Mon (Oct-May).
post 81120 Réalmont. Tarn.
phone (63) 55.52.80 *Mich* 235 Albi 20 km

ST-GIRONS   Eychenne

Very comfortable hotel/Michelin★
Quiet/Gardens   ®

I have received many letters complimenting Michel and Sylvette
Bordeau on the warm welcome they give to guests and how well
they look after them. I can confirm that: I arrived 'incognito' and
during dinner was asked by Michel (who speaks good English) if
I didn't mind my room being changed. Why? Below the bedroom
was the boiler room – serving as a dog nursery – where their bitch
had just brought a litter of puppies into the world; Michel didn't
want me to be disturbed. If you are a rugby fan you'll know that
he was a great French 'international' – he's also a fine tennis
player. The chef, Maurice Bordes, has been at the stoves for 40
years – his repertoire is a regional and classical one. Nothing
other than honest effort in basic, ordinary dishes like *cassoulet
au confit, saumon grillé sauce Béarnaise* and *poire Belle Hélène.*
There are many fine wines to brighten up the eating scene. See
the 11th-century cathedral at St-Lizier with its frescoes and two-
tier cloisters.
menus A-C *rooms* 48 **B-D** *cards* AE DC Visa
closed Mid Dec-Jan.
post 8 avenue P.-Laffont, 09200 St-Girons. Ariège.
phone (61) 66.20.55 *Mich* 235 Perpignan 181 km

ST-LAURENT-DE-LA-SALANQUE   Auberge du Pin

Simple hotel
Gardens/Good value

The Gots certainly know how not to bankrupt their clients –
straightforward, fresh produce cooked with care and offered at
bargain prices: *gambas grillées mayonnaise, terrine de rouget
and escalope de barbue au pistou* are examples.
menus A-B *rooms* 20 **B**
closed Mid-end Sept. Jan. Feb. Sun evg. Mon.
post 66250 St-Laurent-de-la-Salanque. Pyr.-Or.
phone (68) 28.01.62 *Mich* 240 Perpignan 14 km

UNAC   L'Oustal

Comfortable restaurant with rooms (no showers or baths)
Secluded/Gardens

A rustic auberge perched high above the River Ariège – nine
kilometres north-west of Ax-les-Thermes. Conventional dishes,
sadly not cheap, and much appreciated by locals, who pack the
place at weekends. A few of those offerings are *foie de canard,
matelote anguille, soupe de poisson maison, truite grillée au feu
de bois beurre blanc* and *soupe aux choux.*
  To the north-east of Unac is the village of Montaillou; a book
called *Montaillou* (published by Penguin) tells the story of the
Cathars in this high, remote and tiny mountain village during the
period 1294-1324. I found it compulsive reading; and was even
more fascinated by the modern-day village as a result. Make the
effort to seek out Montaillou.
menus **B** *rooms* 8 **A-B**
closed Jan. Tues/Wed (except rest. July-mid Sept).
post Unac. 09250 Luzenac. Ariège.
phone (61) 64.48.44 *Mich* 235 Perpignan 128 km

LOIRE

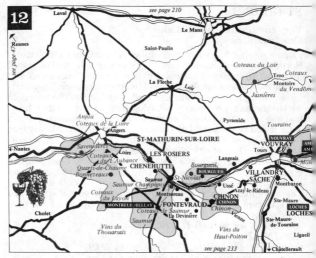

see page 210

This is a region whose charms may not appeal to all my readers; indeed you may have decided already it is not for you. I put it this way because at one time that was my point of view; I was mistaken and you would be, too, if you cut yourself off from this, the most aristocratic part of France. It is a stunning region, filled with treasures created centuries ago, when France was the greatest cultural power in the civilised world. One cannot but feel a sense of awe that such superb skills existed all those hundreds of years ago.

Touraine is the *Garden of France* as far as the French are concerned. It will not be just the châteaux and their magnificent gardens and parks that will delight you. Equally enticing are the rivers and countryside of the region: the **Loire** and its many smaller tributaries – the **Loir**, the **Cosson**, the **Beuvron**, the **Cher**, the **Indre** and the **Vienne**. The country has no hills, but it compensates with magnificent trees, sleepy meadows and many a splendid river view. Spare time for the **Sologne** – a landscape peppered with *étangs* and woods.

There are more than 100 châteaux in the area. You should try to see at least six of the most important ones; to wonder at the skills of our forefathers as they laid some of the essential foundations of our western culture. Once this was the capital of France and to this day Touraine demonstrates why the region had so much influence.

A trip to **Chenonceaux**, which sits astride the Cher, is a first essential. Then **Azay-le-Rideau**, for me the most attractive of them all, should be next on your list. It is small, perfectly proportioned and with a lovely park as a backdrop. Also not to be missed are **Chambord**, **Cheverny** and **Amboise** (many recommendations for hotels and restaurants are close at hand). It was at Chambord that *son et lumière* was born: its creator was Paul-Robert Houdin; now, this summer evening spectacle is common, not just in the Loire Valley, but throughout France. It is imperative you absorb the atmosphere of one of these occasions. Another must, especially for an Anglo-Saxon, is to spend at least half a day in **Chinon**, steeped in history, with its castle

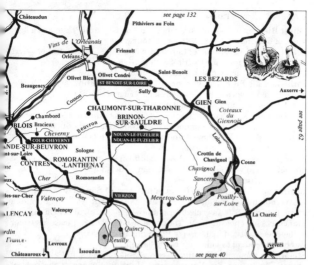

see page 132

see page 62

see page 40

overlooking both the Vienne and the lovely old town below it. My family and I once spent an hour listening to an organist playing in the Church of St-Maurice; we had him to ourselves and the glorious music added rich splendour to ancient Chinon, the town of Richard the Lionheart, Joan of Arc and Richelieu. It was here that *Jeanne d'Arc* first met the Dauphin in 1429. She stayed in the inn at the Grand Carroi.

From Chinon do three things: first, cross the river and admire the view back towards Chinon; then, take the D751 towards **Saumur**, and three kilometres later, turn left on to the D759, signposted Loudun. More or less immediately turn right to **La Devinière**, the birthplace of the great man of the Renaissance, Rabelais. From La Devinière you can continue, via Chavigny, to the nearby Abbey of **Fontevraud** and its important connections with the English Plantagenets; some of them are buried there, not at Westminster Abbey. You will also gasp at its astonishing example of a giant Romanesque kitchen.

Saumur, **Langeais**, **Loches**, **Chaumont** and **Valençay** are all towns in which my wife and I have happily spent time: **Tours**, **Orléans** and **Blois** are much bigger and consequently much more crowded. Equally, we have been more than content to meander slowly through the quieter backwaters, to the gardens of the château at **Villandry**, to the smaller, less-visited châteaux at **Ussé** and **Montsoreau**, to the wine-growing villages of **Vouvray** and **Bourgueil** and to the many caves on the Loire – natural wine cellars. We can remember many tranquil picnics on warm summer days, underneath trees and alongside streams; on one sleepy day, with no pressures on us for time, we watched sand-martins swooping along a river surface catching flies. Be sure to visit this lovely region.

Do also seek out Owen Watson – see page 170.

Michelin *yellow* maps: 232.238.64.68. Green Guide: Châteaux of the Loire (English)

IGN *série verte* maps: 25.26.34. *série rouge* map: 106

Airport: Nantes

Distances from: Paris-Tours 234 km Calais-Tours 526 km

Cheeses Cow's milk

Olivet Bleu small disk, often wrapped in leaves. A fruity taste and a light scent of blue mould. Try it with a red **Bourgueil**

Olivet Cendré savory taste. Cured in wood ashes. Same size as Olivet Bleu. **Chinon** is the wine to drink with it. **Gien** is a related cheese

Frinault a soft, small disk – ideal with light Loire wines

Pithiviers au Foin also known as **Bondaroy au Foin**. A soft cheese, made in thin disks and protected by a covering of bits of hay

Saint-Benoit a fruity, soft, small disk

Saint-Paulin semi-hard, yellow, mild, smooth-textured with a washed, bright orange rind. Made commercially throughout northern France

Vendôme Bleu (**Vendôme Cendré**) related to the Olivet cheeses. Not many seen these days in shops

Make sure you try some of the delightful fresh cream cheeses called **crémets**, eaten with sugar and fresh cream – delicious!

Goat's milk

Crottin de Chavignol from the area just west of **Sancerre**, which, with **Chavignol**, makes the ideal wine to accompany it. It takes the form of a small, flattened ball. In grilled form it now appears regularly throughout France as a hot cheese course. The best season is winter. (Please also refer to the cheeses listed in the Berry-Bourbonnais region)

Levroux identical to Valençay. Nutty flavour

Ste-Maure summer and autumn season. Soft cylinders, full goat flavour cheese. Try it with dry **Vouvray** and **Montlouis** wines or the reds of **Chinon** and **Bourgueil**. **Ligueil** is a similar related cheese

Selles-sur-Cher from the Sologne; also known as **Romorantin**. Dark blue skin, pure white interior with mild, nutty flavour. **Montoire** and **Troo** (the home of Jane Grigson) are related cheeses

Valençay pyramid shaped, usual best seasons for all goat's milk cheeses – summer and autumn. Mild, soft and nutty taste. Often called **Pyramide**

Regional Specialities

Alose à l'oseille grilled shad with a sorrel sauce

Bardette stuffed cabbage

Beuchelle à la Tourangelle kidneys, sweetbreads, morels, truffles, cream

Bourdaines apples stuffed with jam and baked

Crémets fresh cream cheese, eaten with sugar and cream

Sandre freshwater fish, like perch

Truffiat potato cake

Wines

Whites *best years* 47 49 55 59 69 71 75 76 78 81 82

All the Loire wines are charming, light and quite dissimilar in character from each other. The various **Muscadet** wines, which I let Brittany claim as its own, are white, dry and fruity.

White wines from the huge wine-producing areas of **Anjou** and **Touraine** can be sweet, medium-sweet or dry (check wine lists carefully – refer to the terms on page 26). Amongst the many whites worth recording is a personal favourite, **Vouvray**, made just east of Tours from the Chenin Blanc grape, the most important of the Loire white grape types; it is a particularly delicate wine. South of Angers is the **Coteaux du Layon**, with its own very broad AC. Here some fine sweet whites are made: **Quarts-de-Chaume**, **Coteaux du Layon Chaume** and **Bonnezeaux** (all three are sweet) have their own appellations. **Savennières** (dry whites), near Angers, lies on the north bank of the Loire: within that tiny area is **Savennières-Roches-aux-Moines** and **Savennières-Coulée-de-Serrant**, both small vineyards and both making magnificent dry wines.

Look out for the medium-sweet whites of **Jasnières**, from the **Coteaux du Loir**, to the north of Tours; good-value wines of all shades are made here. In the neighbourhood of Tours, the Sauvignon grape is used for a **Sauvignon de Touraine** wine; a much cheaper alternative to Sancerre and nearly equal in quality. A **Touraine Azay-le-Rideau** (Chenin Blanc grape again) is a super dry white. Dry and semi-sweet wines are **Saumur**, **Coteaux de Saumur**, **Coteaux de l'Aubance** and **Anjou Coteaux de la Loire**.

Sparkling Wines *best years* as above

Particularly good are all the dry, sparkling wines; *mousseux* and *pétillant*. The **Vouvray** *sec* and *demi-sec pétillant* whites are superb; others to enjoy are **Montlouis**, just across the river from Vouvray, **Anjou**, **Touraine**, **Saumur** (these, too, are really good) and a delicious **Crémant de Loire**. All these sparkling wines are moreish wines; it is much too easy to empty the bottle.

Other Whites *best years* 73 75 76 78 79 81 82

From the Upper Loire, outside my region and to the east, come some lovely white wines, made from the Sauvignon Blanc grape: **Pouilly-Fumé** and **Sancerre**, both flinty and smoky flavoured. Another white is **Quincy**, from an area south of Vierzon, dryer than Fumé. **Pouilly-sur-Loire** wines are from the same general area, but the wines are inferior, being made from a different grape type, Chasselas. An unknown AC is **Menetou-Salon**, just north of Bourges; it makes dry wines of all shades. **Reuilly**, **Valençay** and **Cheverny** wines are dry and fragrant (they make all shades). The last four named whites, all excellent, are produced from the Sauvignon grape. The same grape is used in the VDQS **Coteaux du Giennois** and **Côtes de Gien** whites.

Rosés *best years* 47 49 55 59 69 71 75 76 78 81 82

There are some notable rosés from **Saumur** and **Anjou** – and their respective **Coteaux** – from **Touraine**, **Touraine Mesland**, **Touraine Amboise** and from the **Coteaux de l'Aubance**, on the south bank of the Loire, opposite Angers. Look out for **Rosé d'Anjou**, **Rosé de Loire** and a rosé made from two different grape types, **Cabernet d'Anjou** (Cabernets Franc and Sauvignon). The **Cabernet de Saumur** is lighter in colour and dryer than the Anjou wine. There is also a sparkling **Rosé d'Anjou pétillant**. From the Sancerre area come good rosés; often described on wine lists as **Rosé de Bué** and **Rosé de Chavignol**. VDQS rosés are the **Coteaux du Vendômois** and **Vins de l'Orléanais** (a *vin gris* – light, pale and fragrant).

Reds *best years* as above

Amongst the good Loire Cabernet reds are **Chinon**, **Bourgueil**, **Saint Nicolas-de-Bourgueil**, **Anjou** and **Saumur-Champigny**. **Sancerre** produces a small amount of excellent red wine, made from the Pinot Noir grape. A **Gamay de Touraine** is a red made from the same grape type used in Beaujolais; other Gamay wines are **Anjou Gamay**, **Cheverny**, **Valençay** and **Coteaux d'Ancenis** (page 49). The VDQS **Vins du Thouarsais** are sound reds; wines of all shades share this classification. Remember Angers is the home of **Cointreau**.

Vins de Pays

These will have labels showing either the *département* or the general area name; examples are **Vin de Pays de Loir-et-Cher** or, in the second case, a **Vin de Pays du Jardin de la France**. Often the labels will also describe the grape type: Sauvignon (Blanc); Chenin Blanc; and Gamay are examples. Some of these Fourth Division wines really do compare well with their First Division brothers. Try them – and surprise yourself.

Base Hotels

AMBOISE
Chanteloup

Comfortable hotel
Fairly quiet/Lift

Most traffic now bypasses Amboise; this is a relatively quiet spot – the bedrooms at the rear are the best 'buy'. Make sure you don't bypass the fine château at Amboise; the Château de Clos-Lucé, where Leonardo Da Vinci spent his last days; and the views from the nearby Chanteloup Pagoda.

No restaurant *rooms* 25 **C-D**
closed Mid Aug-mid Sept. Mid Dec-Mar.
post route de Bléré, 37400 Amboise. Indre-et-Loire.
phone (47) 57.10.90 *Mich* 238 Tours 25 km

BOURGUEIL
Le Thouarsais

Simple hotel
Fairly quiet/Gardens/Good value

Many letters of praise have arrived at Chiltern House for this inexpensive, simple 'base' – with a flower-filled small garden; there is no need to raise a second mortgage here. Bourgueil is another village with a bypass – to the north this time. Enjoy the fine red wines from the local vineyards.

No restaurant *rooms* 30 **A-B**
closed Feb.
post 37140 Bourgueil. Indre-et-Loire.
phone (47) 97.72.05 *Mich* 232 Tours 45 km

CHINON
La Giraudière

Simple hotel
Secluded/Gardens   ®

Compliments have flowed in about this super base hotel from all over the globe. It's a centuries-old converted farmhouse, five kilometres from Chinon towards Bourgueil – lost in the green countryside of the Vienne Valley. One of my favourite base hotels – this one has *cuisinettes* available. There's much in Chinon to fill your days with interest.

No restaurant *rooms* 25 **B-C** *cards* DC Visa
closed Nov-Mar.
post 37420 Avoine. Indre-et-Loire.
phone (47) 58.40.36 *Mich* 232 Tours 49 km

LOCHES
Château

Simple hotel
Quiet

Simple is the right word; and it's well named as it sits in the shadow of the walls of the Cité Médiévale. Explore that fascinating fortress – with towers, keep, museums and church. Then head a few kilometres east to the Chartreuse du Liget (built by Henry II as an act of repentance for the murder of Thomas à Becket) and pretty Montrésor, alongside the Indrois.

No restaurant *rooms* 10 **A-C**
closed Mid Jan-Mar.
post 18 rue Château, 37600 Loches. Indre-et-Loire.
phone (47) 59.07.35 *Mich* 238 Tours 42 km

NOUAN-LE-FUZELIER   Charmilles

Comfortable hotel
Quiet/Gardens

Another gorgeous spot – a candidate for the ideal base hotel
prize; it's in wooded grounds and is surrounded by the Sologne.
The owners are most helpful, willing hosts.
No restaurant *rooms* 14 **B-C** *cards* Visa
closed Mid Jan-mid Mar.
post Nouan-le-Fuzelier. 41600 Lamotte-Beuvron. Loir-et-Cher.
phone (54) 88.73.55 *Mich* 238 Tours 110 km

ONZAIN   Château des Tertres

Simple hotel
Quiet/Gardens

Some *Logis de France*! A château in an elevated position and set
in a large park – to the west of the village (D58).
No restaurant *rooms* 14 **B-C** *cards* Visa
closed Nov-Mar.
post 41150 Onzain. Loir-et-Cher.
phone (54) 79.83.88 *Mich* 238 Tours 43 km

ST-BENOIT-SUR-LOIRE   Labrador

Simple hotel
Quiet

A simple hotel – but from its front door you have a superb view of
the belfry porch of the great abbey at St-Benoit. Be certain to
enjoy the abbey – and the Gregorian chants.
No restaurant *rooms* 16 **B-C**
closed Jan.
post 45730 St-Benoit-sur-Loire. Loiret.
phone (38) 35.74.38 *Mich* 238 Tours 91 km

VIERZON   Le Sologne

Comfortable hotel
Quiet/Gardens

To the south of the town on the way to Châteauroux – and well
back from the main road.
No restaurant *rooms* 24 **C**
closed Open all the year.
post route Châteauroux, 18100 Vierzon. Cher.
phone (48) 75.15.20 *Mich* 238 Tours 116 km

VOUVRAY   Les Fontaines

Comfortable hotel
Fairly quiet/Gardens

On the north bank of the Loire and clear of Tours – a small house
in wooded grounds, on the N152 as it heads east.
No restaurant *rooms* 15 **B-C** *cards* AE DC Visa
closed Open all the year.
post Rochecorbon. 37210 Vouvray. Indre-et-Loire.
phone (47) 52.52.86 *Mich* 238 Tours 4 km

Recommendations where cuisine takes second place

AMBOISE
Novotel

Very comfortable hotel
Secluded/Terrace/Gardens/Swimming pool/Tennis/Lift

One of the newest and most striking of Novotels. It's several storeys high and sits in an elevated, isolated position above Amboise; it offers fine views. To the west of the D81 Chenonceaux road. Ignore the grill. (See page 320.)
Ignore restaurant *rooms* 82 **D** *cards* AE DC Visa
closed Open all the year.
post route de Chenonceaux, 37400 Amboise. Indre-et-Loire.
phone (47) 57.42.07 *Mich* 238 Tours 25 km

COUR-CHEVERNY
Trois Marchands

Comfortable hotel
Good value

Not one of the major guides award this hotel any accolades; that's a surprise as many readers have been very pleased with the efforts of Jean-Jacques Bricault and his chef. Decades ago it had a Michelin star – the same dishes continue to this day: *brochet au beurre blanc, cuisses de grenouilles sautées aux fines herbes* and *matelote d'anguilles*. Standard of cooking is good – perhaps up to category three standards.
menus **B-C** *rooms* 44 **B-C** *cards* Visa
closed Mid Jan-Feb. Tues (Oct-Mar).
post Cour-Cheverny. 41700 Contres. Loir-et-Cher.
phone (54) 79.96.44 *Mich* 238 Tours 71 km

MONTREUIL-BELLAY
Splendid et Relais du Bellay

Comfortable hotel (annexe)
Gardens/Swimming pool

A local *French Leave* reader insisted that I visit this first-class *Logis de France* in a town with a splendid castle. Much above average cuisine with dishes like *terrine de saumon, coq au Champigny* and *saumon* or *brochet beurre blanc*. The modern annexe offers comfortable overnight accommodation.
menus **A-C** *rooms* 35 **B-C**
closed Jan. Sun evg (mid Sept-Easter).
post rue Dr-Gaudrez, 49260 Montreuil-Bellay. Maine-et-Loire.
phone (41) 52.30.21 *Mich* 232 Tours 88 km

NOUAN-LE-FUZELIER
Moulin de Villiers

Simple hotel
Secluded/Terrace/Gardens/Good value

A seductive, heavenly spot – deep in the fascinating Sologne country; the Moulin has its own mini version of the local terrain – extensive, wooded grounds with a small *étang* (pool). Gérard and Gladys Andrieux have made many friends and the most important advice I can give you is to book ahead. Cooking is no more than basic, honest fare.
menus **A-B** *rooms* 20 **B-C**
closed 27 Aug-mid Sept. Jan-mid Mar. Wed (Oct-Dec).
post Nouan-le-Fuzelier. 41600 Lamotte-Beuvron. Loir-et-Cher.
phone (54) 88.72.27 *Mich* 238 Tours 110 km

LES BEZARDS   Auberge des Templiers

Luxury hotel/Michelin★★
Quiet/Terrace/Gardens/Swimming pool/Tennis   Ⓡ

If I had to give an award for the best-run hotel in France – this is
where the accolade would go. Philippe and Françoise Dépée are
second to none in the art of running a luxury *home* – because that
is what it feels like here. Alain, the *maître d'hôtel*, Henri, the
sommelier, and many members of staff speak English and have
the great knack of putting you quite at ease. Jean-Claude Rigollet,
the previous chef, resigned to become a teacher and Stewart
Cunningham left after 13 years – and headed for the South
Pacific. Two shattering blows, but the Dépées have worked hard
to ensure that standards remain consistent. The new chef,
Christian Willer (ex L'Hermitage at La Baule), has settled in well;
it's classical cuisine with a light touch. A superb highlight was
noisettes de marcassin sauce poivrade accompanied by an
orange *confiture* and a chilled **Sancerre rouge** (from a cellar of
60,000 bottles). And at last I have found a top restaurant using
crockery made in France – in this case at nearby Gien; usually it's
made in Germany.
menus **C-D** *rooms* 27 **D-D2** *cards* DC Visa
closed Feb.
post Les Bézards. 45290 Nogent-sur-Vernisson. Loiret.
phone (38) 31.80.01 *Mich* 238 Tours 176 km

BLOIS   La Péniche

Comfortable restaurant

Gérard Bosque won the hearts of many *French Leave* readers at
the Botte d'Asperges in Contrès; now he gives all his time to his
new venture – a 'floating' restaurant in a handsome, renovated
barge, the St-Berthuin. It's on the northern bank of the Loire,
upstream from the main town bridge.
    Classical cuisine is Gérard's forte – at prices that will not break
the bank: enjoy specialities like *terrine de poisson tiède beurre
de corail, gigot de lotte à la crème d'estragon* and *paupiette de
sandre à la mousse de saumon.*
menus **B** *cards* Visa
closed Open all the year.
post prom. du Mail, 41000 Blois. Loir-et-Cher.
phone (54) 74.37.23 *Mich* 238 Tours 63 km

BRINON-SUR-SAULDRE   La Solognote

Comfortable hotel/Michelin★
Quiet/Gardens

It was Jean-Claude Cogny at Mercurey in Burgundy who urged
me to test the skills of Andrée and Dominique Girard. The hotel is
on the eastern edges of the Sologne and is so typical of the local
red-brick buildings you find in the area. I was impressed by the
cooking – luckily I was there in the hunting season when the
game dishes were magnificent. The star was won in 1983.
menus **A-C** *rooms* 10 **C**
closed 1-15 Jun. 1-15 Sept. Feb. Tues evg (Sept-June).
Wed (except evgs July-Aug).
post Brinon-sur-Sauldre. 18410 Argent-sur-Sauldre. Cher.
phone (48) 58.50.29 *Mich* 238 Tours 125 km

CANDE-SUR-BEUVRON   Host. Caillère

Very comfortable restaurant/Michelin★
Quiet/Terrace/Gardens

First-class cooking with the odd liberty taken in describing
specialities; *andouillette de saumon* is one example. It's a pretty
spot; the restaurant is in converted cottages, hidden behind
chestnut trees and lost in the Beuvron Valley. Enjoy local wines:
the **Touraine Mesland** varieties from across the Loire (a 900
years old pedigree); and **Oisly**, a village near Contres.
menus **B-C** *cards* AE Visa
closed Jan. Wed.
post Candé-sur-Beuvron. 41120 Les Montils. Loir-et-Cher.
phone (54) 44.03.08 *Mich* 238 Tours 49 km

CHAUMONT-SUR-THARONNE   Croix Blanche

Very comfortable restaurant with rooms/Michelin★
Quiet (annexe)**/Terrace/Gardens**

After working 40 years in various kitchens, Gisèle Crouzier is
nearing the end of her career and, at last, is beginning to win the
accolades she so richly deserves. She is unique in that she prides
herself on employing only female staff in her kitchens – you can
check that for yourself as you pass through *la cuisine* to the light,
airy dining room. Gisèle is one of a long line of *cuisinières* that
have 'manned' the kitchens here for over 200 years; she is a small,
gentle woman, ably supported by her husband, Pierre. Her menus
are built around the produce of the Sologne and also feature
many old Périgord specialities – she was born there: *mique
royale aux morilles, le vrai cassoulet* and *confit de canard
Sarladais* are typical. Check *l'addition*: our fixed-price menu
courses were charged out at à la carte prices! In my opinion, all
prices here are a bit high. It's a red-brick building with flower-
filled gardens; the annexe bedrooms are quiet.
menus **C-D** *rooms* 15 **B-D** *cards* AE DC Visa
closed 27 June-7 July. Jan. Feb. Wed (except July-Aug).
post Chaumont-sur-Tharonne. 41600 Lamotte-Beuvron. L.-et-C.
phone (54) 88.55.12 *Mich* 238 Tours 109 km

CHENEHUTTE-LES-TUFFEAUX   Le Prieuré

Very comfortable hotel/Michelin★
Secluded/Gardens/Swimming pool/Tennis

The name gives a clue to the site's original use. Centuries later
the setting remains a majestic one; the 16th-century manor is 50
metres or so above the south bank of the Loire – the backdrop is a
large, wooded park with extensive views across the lazy, wide
river. Chefs change regularly here, but the Doumercs take great
care to ensure that standards remain high. Cooking is modern
and light: specialities include *retour de pêche au beurre rouge*
and *confit de lapereau aux pistaches*. Visit the Ackerman cellars at
nearby St-Hilaire (upriver) and the many local caves where
champignons are cultivated. **Brézé** wines – Saumur AC – come
from the village south of that town.
menus **B-D** *rooms* 36 **D-D2** *cards* AE
closed Jan-Feb.
post Chênehutte-les-Tuffeaux. 49350 Gennes. Maine-et-Loire.
phone (41) 50.15.31 *Mich* 232 Tours 74 km

CHINON   Château de Marçay

Very comfortable hotel/Michelin★
Secluded/Terrace/Gardens/Swimming pool/Tennis/Lift

An expensive *Relais et Châteaux* hotel; the splendid château
dates from the 15th-century and, together with its handsome
annexe, Le Pavillon, is lost in the countryside of Rabelais – seven
kilometres south of Chinon, on the D116. Cuisine is a mixture of
classical and modern – but no more than a reasonable standard:
dishes like *coq au vin de Chinon, œufs coque à la purée de
morilles* and *carré d'agneau rôti* are hardly imaginative. But it's
the setting, local countryside and other creature comforts here
that will appeal. Those vines at the gates should remind you this
is red **Chinon** country.

alc **C** *rooms* 26 **D-D3** *cards* Visa
closed Jan. Feb.
post Marçay. 37500 Chinon. Indre-et-Loire.
phone (47) 93.03.47 *Mich* 232 Tours 56 km

CONTRES   Botte d'Asperges

Comfortable restaurant
Good value

'Bundle of Asparagus' is the name of this smashing place;
remarkable quality and value with no need to take out a second
mortgage (a phrase I coined in 1980 and since used by a guide or
two). The Sologne is renowned for its asparagus – during the
season you will see the crop being harvested in the fields with
their long rows of upturned earth. The restaurant is a simple
place – much approved by readers who have appreciated
delights like *œufs pochés meurette, sandre poché au beurre
blanc, andouillette grillée* and, of course, the local asparagus. In
1984 it is likely it will have new owners – Madame Bosque who
continued to run it in 1983 is anxious to join her husband, Gérard,
at their new 'floating home' in Blois (see page 167).

menus **A-B**
closed Jan. Mon. Please check.
post 41700 Contres. Loir-et-Cher.
phone (54) 79.50.49 *Mich* 238 Tours 65 km

FONTEVRAUD-L'ABBAYE   Abbaye

Simple restaurant
Good value

I received many letters from readers appreciating my advice to
explore all the nearby Rabelais country – the area between
Chinon and Fontevraud. Consequently some of them visited this
atmospheric village for the first time – to be bowled over by the
ancient abbey with its important links with the English
Plantagenets and its amazing Romanesque kitchen. I was
recommended to visit some of the village restaurants; this was
the only one I managed to get to – north of the village. André
Côme wins many admirers for his honest cooking at bargain
prices; enjoy basics like *saumon grillé* and *steak au poivre*.

menus **A-B**
closed Oct. Mid-end Feb. Tues evg (winter). Wed.
post 49590 Fontevraud-l'Abbaye. Maine-et-Loire.
phone (41) 51.71.04 *Mich* 232 Tours 72 km

GIEN   Rivage

Comfortable hotel
Good value

More often than not the Michelin 'R' rating is a reliable one –
though it is surprising how many places win it one year and lose it
the next. I have also seen many graduate to one star status:
Philippe at Bas-Rupts (Alsace) and Garrapit at Villeneuve
(Southwest) are examples. Others, like the France at Fayence
(Côte d'Azur), had a star and now do just as well with their 'R'.
The Rivage is a classic example of sound cuisine, requiring you to
part with few francs to savour it. The Gaillards have renovated
their hotel which faces the Loire; menus include *sandre* and
saumon from the river and *coq au vin*.

menus **A-B** *rooms* 29 **B-C** *cards* Visa
closed Rest: 1-15 Aug.
post 1 quai Nice, 45500 Gien. Loiret.
phone (38) 67.20.53 *Mich* 238 Tours 178 km

LOCHES   France

Comfortable hotel
Terrace/Good value

Yet another Michelin 'R' restaurant which does the job it sets out
to do well – yet ignored by other guides. Yves Barrat and his chef
stick with *Bourgeoise* specialities: witness *saumon grillé*,
sandre au beurre blanc and *escalope de veau*.

menus **A** *rooms* **A-B**
closed 1-15 May. Jan-mid Feb. Sun evg and Mon midday (Sept-
June). Fri evg (Oct-Easter).
post 6 rue Picois, 37600 Loches. Indre-et-Loire.
phone (47) 59.00.32 *Mich* 238 Tours 42 km

ONZAIN   Domaine des Hauts de Loire

Very comfortable hotel/Michelin★
Secluded/Terrace/Gardens/Tennis   ®

Gaston and Janine Bonnigal established their famous reputation
at their Host. Château in nearby Chaumont-sur-Loire (it's still
open – but *sans restaurant* and with a swimming pool); for the
last few years all their energies have been devoted to improving
this 18th-century French count's hunting lodge – a creeper-
covered, romantic place surrounded by woods. Today, their son,
Pierre-Alain Bonnigal – who speaks good English – together with
Marie-Noëlle, his wife, manages the Domaine with calm
efficiency. An expensive, excellent hotel.

The new young chef, trained by Marc Demund (an old pupil of
Girardet – Marc was the chef at Chaumont), is establishing
himself well. Certainly his six *sorbets* were as magnificent as
Marc's were; praise, too, for his first-rate appetisers and *petits
fours*. A Brédif **Vouvray** *pétillant* was superb.

Under no circumstances miss the 'Poterie' of Owen Watson (½
km south of Mesland on the D65). A talented, charming
Englishman and a fine potter – full of innovative ideas.

alc **C-D** *rooms* 28 **D2-D3** *cards* AE DC Visa
closed Mid Dec-mid Mar. Rest: Thurs.
post 41150 Onzain. Loir-et-Cher.
phone (54) 79.72.57 *Mich* 238 Tours 44 km

ONZAIN   Pont d'Ouchet

Very simple hotel
Good value   ®

Many of you have taken this very simple auberge to your hearts –
and the Cochets who own it. One of you wrote to say that
Madame Cochet (who speaks English) is a 'real scream'. It really
is at the other end of the hotel spectrum when compared with the
two entries that 'sandwich' it; but it's just as much a favourite of
mine. Specialities include *moules marinière* (Madame claims
them to be the best in the world!) and *poulet à l'estragon*.
Bedrooms are really far too basic – use the Onzain 'base'.
menus **A-B** *rooms* 10 **A-B**
closed Mid Sept-mid Oct. Mid Jan-Feb. Sun evg. Mon.
post Grande Rue, 41150 Onzain. Loir-et-Cher.
phone (54) 79.70.33 *Mich* 238 Tours 44 km

ROMORANTIN-LANTHENAY   Grand Hôtel Lion d'Or

Very comfortable hotel/Michelin★★
Lift   ®

I continue to be seduced by the home of the Barrat family; the
epitome of just how the fabric of a hotel – and indeed the family
itself – can be transformed over the years. Alain and Colette
Barrat – judging from readers' letters Colette is one of the most
popular lady hoteliers in France – have changed and improved
the Grand Hôtel out of all recognition. But it's their welcome and
the treats awaiting you in the dining room that will truly seduce
you. Aided by his chef, young Didier Clément, who is married to
the Barrat's daughter, Marie-Christine, Alain's restaurant wins
my vote as the best in the Loire.

A typical menu could include delights like these: *foie gras frais
de canard au vin de Malvoisie*, *terrine de carpes à la mousse de
cresson*, mouthwatering *crépinette de pigeon au vinaigre de
cidre*, superb cheeses served on five straw 'plates' and a
millefeuille de pommes au lait d'amandes.
menus **C-D** *rooms* 10 **D** *cards* AE DC Visa
closed Jan-mid Feb.
post 41200 Romorantin-Lanthenay. Loir-et-Cher.
phone (54) 76.00.28 *Mich* 238 Tours 93 km

LES ROSIERS   Jeanne de Laval

Very comfortable restaurant with rooms/Michelin★
Quiet (annexe)/**Gardens**

If it's old-fashioned skills and classical cuisine you are seeking
this is the place for you. Albert Augereau (he has a prize-winning
ability for sculpturing blocks of ice and butter), together with his
wife, Marie-Louise, and now aided by his son, Michel, run a
typical French family establishment: honest endeavour and
skilled effort with rough edges here and there – all combining to
create a special sort of charm. Be sure to order fish dishes
accompanied by Albert's remarkable *beurre blanc* sauce; and
reserve rooms in the 17th-century annexe.
menus **C** *rooms* 15 **B-D** *cards* AE DC Visa
closed Mid Nov-Dec. 1-15 Mar. Mon. Tues midday.
post Les Rosiers. 49350 Gennes. Maine-et-Loire.
phone (41) 51.80.17 *Mich* 232 Tours 78 km

SACHE   Auberge du XII siècle

Comfortable restaurant/Michelin★
Terrace/Gardens   Ⓡ

Jean-Louis Niqueux, the chef-owner, first made his name at the
Château d'Artigny at Montbazon; his youthful skills complement
perfectly the remarkably well-preserved, medieval Auberge. As I
said in the last edition, his modern touches seem so much in
keeping with the *Garden of France* at the restaurant's doorstep –
the countryside around is a mass of orchards and many small
vineyards. Relish the dry, crisp **Saché** wines; back home you can
order them from Yapp Brothers of Mere, Wiltshire who import a
wide variety of fine French wines to the U.K. In their delightful,
informative catalogue they write about their Saché supplier –
Gaston Pavy. The dry white wine is labelled **Touraine Blanc** *sec*
but there's also a *moelleux* variety – only made in good years.
They also recommend this restaurant: they call it 'one of the great
undiscovered restaurants of France.' The specialities of Jean-
Louis are numerous – here are a few: *hure de saumon, salade de
lotte, barbue aux huîtres et bigorneaux* and *gigot de poulette au
pot au feu.*

The famous American artist, Alexander Calder, lived part of
each year at Saché until his death in 1976. One of his steel
mobiles sits opposite the Auberge in the village square. You can
see others at the Calder home – on the north bank of the Indre
and high above La Sablonnière. Calder's daughters, Sandra and
Mary, still visit the family home at Saché each summer. My wife,
Anne, together with Joan Kerr, the wife of my American
publisher, had the good fortune to meet Mary at her home in New
York during 1982. Finally, don't miss the Saché Château
associated with Balzac in many ways.

alc **B-C** *cards* AE DC Visa
closed Feb. Tues. Wed.
post Saché. 37190 Azay-le-Rideau. Indre-et-Loire.
phone (47) 26.86.58 *Mich* 232 Tours 25 km

ST-MATHURIN-SUR-LOIRE   La Promenade

Comfortable restaurant
Gardens

Serafina Clarke, a *French Leave* reader, guided me to this first-
class find. Jacques Morisan is the son of ex-hoteliers in Saumur;
he met his English wife, Gillian, when they were both working at
the Plaza-Athénée in Paris. They opened their riverside
restaurant in its attractive setting 20 years ago.

Both are fluent in French and English – both are charming,
friendly hosts. Their menus have a classical base and represent
marvellous value for money. Enjoy pleasures like *pâté chaud de
volaille, sandre beurre blanc, escalope de saumon frais* and
diplomate pudding. They have a fine cellar – particularly
stunning was an *eau-de-vie poire William.*

For those of you who wish to stay overnight and want to be
closer to the restaurant than my Chinon and Bourgueil bases –
Gill recommends Le Castel at Brissac-Quincié (postcode 49320),
a simple *sans restaurant* hotel to the west of the Loire.

menus **B-C** *cards* Visa
closed 1st week Sept. Feb. Mon.
post St-Mathurin-sur-Loire. 49250 Beaufort-en-Vallée. M.-et-L.
phone (41) 80.50.49 *Mich* 232 Tours 88 km

VALENCAY   Espagne
Very comfortable hotel/Michelin★
Terrace/Gardens

Do you want an example of Gault Millau wit? They described the
picturesque courtyard – with its 'finger' trees and creeper-
covered walls – as an 'indoor alley'. No wonder Maurice and
Phillippe Fourré, the fourth generation of a family who have
owned the hotel since 1875, said they didn't much like that
description. Maurice is the chef; trained at the Ritz in both
London and Paris, his classical background shines through his
repertoire – *noisettes d'agneau* and *terrines de gibier* are
examples. Enjoy the local cheese and the dry white **Valençay**
wine. Don't miss the château with its pepper-pot towers,
Talleyrand mementoes and the park with its unusual wildlife.
menus C *rooms* 17 **C-D2** *cards* AE DC Visa
closed Mid Nov-mid Mar.
post 8 rue Château, 36600 Valençay. Indre.
phone (54) 00.00.02 *Mich* 238 Tours 84 km

VILLANDRY   Cheval Rouge
Comfortable hotel/Michelin★

The ugly façade of this oddly-named hotel does not inspire any
confidence – but what goes on behind that unpretentious front
clearly has inspired a lot of you to write and tell me how much
you have enjoyed it all. Monsieur Dudit provides solid classical
fare – with no innovative touches that are likely to offend or
upset you if you seek the old ways. Enjoy *saumon fumé, terrine
de foie gras, magret de canard aux morilles, sandre* and *fraises
en gratin*. There's also a fine selection of Loire wines. To whip up
an appetite for that sort of cooking I implore you to explore the
nearby château and its gardens – formalised, regimented
displays towering acres of ground. Please also see the Saché
entry and the reference to Calder.
menus **B-C** *rooms* 20 C *cards* Visa
closed Jan. Feb. Mon.
post Villandry. 37510 Joué-lès-Tours. Indre-et-Loire.
phone (47) 50.02.07 *Mich* 232 Tours 20 km

VOUVRAY   L'Oubliette
Comfortable restaurant

I am happy to seek out Vouvray at any time – its range of wines is
one of the most captivating in France: still whites, both dry and
fruity, and the great vintages which come just a few times each
century – the golden *moelleux*; then, as a bonus, the seductive,
sparkling varieties – both *sec* and *demi-sec*. Visit the cellars of
Marc Brédif at Rochecorbon, where you will find this restaurant
(on D477 – Michelin site it incorrectly). An American reader
persuaded me to try Carole and Jean-Paul Chevreuil's tiny home,
'*taillé dans le roc*'. They are making a name for themselves: enjoy
panaché de la marée au Vouvray, quiche aux fruits and those
superb **Vouvray** wines.
menus **B** *cards* Visa
closed 1-15 Mar. 25 July-end Aug. Sun evg. Mon.
post Rochecorbon. 37210 Vouvray. Indre-et-Loire.
phone (47) 52.50.49 *Mich* 238 Tours 4 km

LYONNAIS

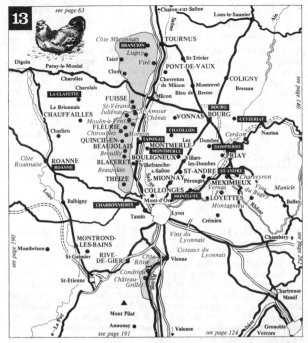

see page 63

I am using the term *Lyonnais* to describe an area which, strictly speaking, covers countryside extending beyond the correct geographical definition. It is one of my favourite French regions.

Ask any 100 travellers, who regularly travel through France, how much they know about this area and probably 99 of them will only remember the difficulty of getting through **Lyon**, on their mad dash south. They are the losers – they have missed so much. Even if you are not able to spend six or seven days based in the area, at least set aside three or four nights sometime in the future to explore its treasures, the minimum time needed to do justice to the region.

West of the River **Saône** are the wooded, rounded hills of Beaujolais country. Explore the lanes lying below the hills; quiet roads taking you through sleepy villages which are a roll call of Beaujolais wines, like **Fleurie**, **Chénas** and **Juliénas**. Drive up to the top of the hills and admire the extensive views. Can you really be so close to that A6 racetrack?

The east bank of the Saône could not be more different – Les Dombes country: hundreds of lakes, peppering the emerald-green, flat countryside – for the ornithologist it is a real paradise. The French equivalent to Slimbridge on the Severn is at **Villars-les-Dombes** – a small, but interesting bird sanctuary. Explore as many of the villages as you can. My wife and I have seen **Châtillon-sur-Chalaronne** change out of all recognition over a period of 20 years; now spotless and a mass of flowers (one of many *villages fleuris* in the area).

Visit the fine abbey at **Cluny** (at the height of its influence it must have been an astonishing sight), the abbey at **Charlieu**,

174

Bourg-en-Bresse and its famous Eglise de Brou, **Crémieu** and especially the old, perched citadel of **Pérouges**. Four centuries ago it was a busy place; three centuries later it had all but disappeared. The last 50 years have seen it completely restored; now it is regularly used for location work in the making of historical films. Seek out the lime tree at its centre that was planted 200 years ago. By all means enjoy the fortified fortress during daylight – no cars are allowed to spoil the pleasure of walking the cobbled streets; but, take my advice, come back in the twilight and see it at its best. North of Bourg are many examples of restored Bressan farmhouses: explore the Ferme de la Forêt at **St-Trivier** and the Ferme du Sougey at **Montrevel**. Their Sarrasine chimneys are particularly interesting. North of Charlieu visit the fine Romanesque churches in an area full of green hills – called **Le Brionnais**.

Le Vieux Lyon (the old part of Lyon) is well worth strolling through, especially the neighbourhood of St-Jean on the west bank of the Saône, with its narrow lanes and dozens of superbly restored old buildings. Above St-Jean is **Tassin La Demi-Lune**, famous for its nurseries and where the wonderful rose *Peace* was first developed.

I would also implore you to put aside at least one day to make any one of these three trips:

1 Explore the area of **Mont Pilat**, a Regional Nature Park, to the east of **St-Etienne** and south to **Annonay**; if time permits, extend your exploration further south into the Ardèche, between Lamastre and Aubenas.
2 Visit the **Vercors** (between **Valence** and **Grenoble**), another Regional Park. The area is a natural fortress and was a citadel of the Resistance during the last war; stop and pay homage at the many roadside monuments where so many were murdered as victims of the Germans. It is known as *Maquis* country; *Mort pour La France* say the carved words on the simple, small monuments. No finer words can be used for any epitaph. Read page 126.
3 Drive up into the **Chartreuse**, that marvellous group of mountains, gorges and valleys between Grenoble and **Chambéry**.

Arguably the Lyonnais has more skilful chefs than any other part of France (though my favourite cuisine region is the Southwest – page 284). The old Lyonnais specialities, born with the many *Les Mères* decades ago, and once exclusive to all the restaurants in the region, are still there, but on a limited scale now: *saucisson en brioche, quenelles, grenouilles, volaille truffée*, as examples, can still be found and eaten in the region. But huge changes have taken place in French cuisine during the last decade. This rejuvenation has confirmed for all the world that the Lyonnais *cuisinier* is amongst the most skilful of all, be it classical or *nouvelle cuisine*. I have devoted several extra pages to the *cuisiniers* of this region; they have an interesting story to tell. Bocuse, the Troisgros brothers, Chapel (just four of Fernand Point's pupils), Georges Blanc, Randoing and many young chefs have led the rest down the new avenues. No one should be surprised these masters have been at the forefront of the transformation. I beg you: explore this lovely region.

Michelin *yellow* maps: 244.70.73.74.77. Green Guide: Vallée du Rhône
IGN *série verte* maps: 43.44.51. *série rouge* maps: 109.112
Airport: Lyon
Distances from: Paris-Lyon 462 km Calais-Lyon 754 km

Cheeses Cow's milk

Bresse (Bleu de) available all the year. A mild, soft, blue cheese, made in small cylinders. Ideal with Beaujolais wines

Mont-d'Or from just north of Lyon. Small disks – delicate, savory taste

Goat's milk

Bressan a small, truncated cone – also known as Petit Bressan

Charolais (Charolles) soft, nutty-flavoured, small cylinder

Chevreton de Mâcon if made of pure goat's milk it is at its best in summer and autumn. A light blue rind and slightly nutty taste

Without fail try fromage blanc; a fresh cream cheese, eaten with sugar and fresh cream – if you've never tried some, you've missed something

Regional Specialities

Bresse (Poulet, Poularde, Volaille de) the best French poultry. Fed on corn and, when killed, bathed in milk. Flesh is white and delicate

Gras-double ox tripe, served with onions

Poulet demi-deuil *half-mourning*; called this because of the thin slices of truffle placed underneath the chicken breast; cooked in a *court-bouillon*

Poulet au vinaigre chicken, shallots, tomatoes, white wine, wine vinegar and a cream sauce

Rosette a large pork sausage

Tablier de sapeur *gras-double* coated with flour, egg-yolk, breadcrumbs

Wines

In Lyon they say there are three rivers: the Rhône, the Saône and the Beaujolais! For my taste some of the most enjoyable red wine comes from this part of France, much of it being inexpensive, even if you choose it at the greatest restaurants. I cannot stress this last piece of information enough; local wines are not prohibitively expensive, even at the region's three star places.

All the reds come from the Gamay grape type. The best wines are from the *communes* of Moulin-à-Vent, Brouilly, Fleurie and Morgon; for some, like myself, the Côte de Brouilly wines are the best of all. Other notable *communes* are Chiroubles, Saint Amour, Chénas and Juliénas. Wines not coming from these nine specific areas are either bottled under the AC Beaujolais, AC Beaujolais Supérieur (not superior in quality, just more alcohol strength) or AC Beaujolais-Villages classifications (see page 186). Near Roanne, look out for a Renaison rosé and Côte Roannaise reds (fine with *Charolais* beef). For details of Côte Mâconnais wines see page 67.

South of Lyon is the start of the Côtes du Rhône. Lyon claims for itself the Côte Rôtie (wines from the northernmost part of the Côtes du Rhône, south of Vienne). Some magnificent reds come from the Rôtie – it means *roasted* – but two world-famous white wines are also made in this narrow part of the Rhône Valley; both come from the rare Viognier grape. Tiny amounts of these expensive wines are produced: Condrieu and Château-Grillet (from a 3½ acre vineyard, one of the smallest French appellations). Vins du Lyonnais and Coteaux du Lyonnais are light reds, made from the Gamay and Syrah grape types.

In the south-east corner of the region you will find some good, inexpensive, and not well-known Bressan wines, Vins du Bugey: these are the whites of Montagnieu and Manicle and the reds of Charveyron and Vernas. Manicle – the name of the grape type – comes from an area 10 km north-west of Belley. Cerdon or Bugey pétillant and mousseux are sparkling wines. Other wines from the Belley area are Roussette de Virieu and Roussette du Bugey. You may also see a Cerdon rosé.

BOURG-EN-BRESSE

Regina

Simple hotel
Quiet/Good value

A quiet spot – off the rue Ch.-Robin. We have used it often in the years gone by; under new owners these days.
No restaurant *rooms* 13 **A-B**
closed Open all the year.
post rue Malivert, 01000 Bourg-en-Bresse. Ain.
phone (74) 23.12.81 *Mich* 244 Lyon 62 km

BRANCION

Montagne de Brancion

Comfortable hotel
Secluded/Gardens
®

High in the hills (480 metres above sea-level), 15 km west of Tournus. A modern base hotel with extensive views.
No restaurant *rooms* 20 **B-C**
closed Open all the year.
post Brancion. 71700 Tournus. Saône-et-Loire.
phone (85) 51.12.40 *Mich* 70 Lyon 117 km

CHARBONNIERES-LES-BAINS

Parc Hôtel

Very comfortable hotel
Quiet/Gardens/Lift

A delightful, small, green spa town. It's in the hills to the west of Lyon and though that bustling city is only eight kilometres away it could just as well be a thousand!
No restaurant *rooms* 48 **C** *cards* AE DC Visa
closed Open all the year.
post 69260 Charbonnières-les-Bains. Rhône.
phone (7) 887.12.33 *Mich* 244 Lyon 8 km

MONTLUEL

Le Petit Casset

Simple hotel
Quiet/Gardens/Swimming pool
®

A super place, well clear of the main N84; a modern building, with nice gardens and a protective border of trees.
No restaurant *rooms* 10 **C**
closed Open all the year.
post La Boisse. 01120 Montluel. Ain.
phone (7) 806.21.33 *Mich* 244 Lyon 20 km

ST-ANDRE-DE-CORCY

Manoir des Dombes

Comfortable hotel
Quiet/Gardens
®

To the north of St-André-de-Corcy – at St-Marcel – on the main N83. It's quieter than you think as all the rooms are at the rear. A favourite – ideal for the many nearby restaurants.
No restaurant *rooms* 16 **C-D** *cards* AE DC
closed Jan. Sun (out of season).
post St-Marcel. 01390 St-André-de-Corcy. Ain.
phone (7) 881.13.37 *Mich* 244 Lyon 27 km

CEYZERIAT   Mont-July

Simple hotel
Quiet/Gardens/Good value

A *Logis de France* with extensive views across Les Dombes to
the Beaujolais hills. You are well placed to explore Bourg-en-
Bresse (eight kilometres to the west), the hills of Bugey, the Jura,
and the pleasures of Les Dombes. Honest classical and regional
cuisine with dishes such as *grenouilles, foie gras en brioche,
fromage blanc à la crème* and *fraises Melba*.
menus A-C *rooms* 19 B-C *cards* AE
closed Mid Oct-Mar. Thurs (Apl-June).
post 01250 Ceyzériat. Ain.
phone (74) 30.00.12 *Mich* 244 Lyon 70 km

CHATILLON-SUR-CHALARONNE Chevalier Norbert

Comfortable hotel

A long-established, smart place in the prettiest town in Les
Dombes. Châtillon is one of many *villages fleuris* in Ain; in
months like June it is an attractive small town and it will
captivate you as it has all my family over the years. Be sure not to
miss the triptych at the nearby Hôtel de Ville. Specialities:
poisson de mer and *poularde de Bresse à la crème*.
menus B-C *rooms* 29 B-D
closed Jan. Rest: Mon.
post 01400 Châtillon-sur-Chalaronne. Ain.
phone (74) 55.02.22. *Mich* 244 Lyon 54 km

CHATILLON-SUR-CHALARONNE   de la Tour

Comfortable restaurant with rooms
Good value

It doesn't look anything like as smart compared with its near
neighbour – but I prefer this *Logis*; it could have perhaps found a
place in category three. No particular originality in the cooking
but plenty of attention to detail, both in the printed menus and
the many dishes on offer: *volaille aux morilles, caille des
Dombes* and *soufflé glacé* are examples.
menus A-C *rooms* 12 A-C
closed Mid Feb-mid Mar. Sun evg. Wed.
post 01400 Châtillon-sur-Chalaronne. Ain.
phone (74) 55.05.12 *Mich* 244 Lyon 54 km

LA CLAYETTE   Poste

Simple hotel
Good value

Yet another modest *Logis de France* in the middle of a small
market town, high in the wooded Beaujolais hills. The famous
white Charolais cattle you will have seen in the local pastures
provide the meat for a speciality or two: *Charolais à la moëlle et
au Fleurie* is just one.
menus A-C *rooms* 15 A-C *cards* AE DC Visa
closed Mid-end Sept. Xmas-mid Jan. Fri evg/Sat (out of season).
post 71800 La Clayette. Saône-et-Loire.
phone (85) 28.02.45 *Mich* 244 Lyon 97 km

DOMPIERRE-SUR-VEYLE
Aubert

Very simple restaurant with rooms (no showers or baths)
Gardens/Good value ®

A *Hidden France* reader wrote to say how much she had enjoyed this modest place. Her meal was a 'delightful occasion' – the restaurant full of 'local people in a festive mood.' I ate there one lunchtime – in the evening I visited Chapel; when you have read my report on the latter you'll not be surprised to hear I enjoyed this humble place more. Specialities: *truite, grenouilles, poulet à la crème* and similar.
menus **A-B** *rooms* 3 **A**
closed Feb. Mon evg. Thurs evg. Fri.
post Dompierre-sur-Veyle. 01240 St-Paul-de-Varax. Ain.
phone (74) 30.31.19 *Mich* 244 Lyon 53 km

MONTMERLE-SUR-SAONE
Rivage

Comfortable hotel
Terrace/Good value

Quite honestly, in any other region, all eight places in the Lyonnais category two section would qualify for category three. The Rivage has an attractive site alongside the Saône – a bonus is the paved, shady terrace. *Petite friture* from the river is on the menu as are *grenouilles fraîches à la crème*.
menus **A-C** *rooms* 16 **A-C** *cards* AE Visa
closed Mid end Sept. Mid Nov-mid Dec. Rest: Wed.
post Montmerle-sur-Saône. 01140 Thoissey. Ain.
phone (74) 69.33.92 *Mich* 244 Lyon 49 km

ROANNE
Le Marcassin

Comfortable restaurant with rooms
Quiet/Terrace/Good value

This modern building is well clear of Roanne, at Riorges, south of the D9 Renaison road. Jean Farge provides good-value cooking in a quiet site. Specialities: *rosette de campagne* (a Lyonnais sausage), *foie gras frais, soufflé de loup* and *omble chevalier* (see the Savoie introduction).
menus **A-C** *rooms* 10 **B** *cards* Visa
closed Aug. Feb. Rest: Sat. Sun (Oct-Apl).
post Riorges. 42300 Roanne. Loire.
phone (77) 71.30.18 *Mich* 73 Lyon 89 km

TAPONAS
Auberge des Sablons

Simple hotel
Quiet/Terrace

Between the autoroute (use Belleville exit) and the Saône, this modern *Logis* and *Relais du Silence* is a smart place with local offerings on its menus: *saucisson cru Lyonnais, fromage blanc à la crème* and *sorbet vigneron*. A *Hidden France* reader wished that Madame would 'thaw out a bit'!
menus **A-B** *rooms* 15 **C** *cards* Visa
closed Rest: Nov. Dec. Tues midday.
post Taponas. 69220 Belleville. Rhône.
phone (74) 66.34.80 *Mich* 244 Lyon 48 km

Recommendations where cuisine takes pride of place

BLACERET   Beaujolais

Comfortable restaurant

Keep your eyes open when looking for this modest,
unpretentious restaurant; it's hard to spot and even when you
find it you will wonder what you are going to discover inside. The
Beaujolais is on the Route du Beaujolais (D43); Jacques
Mayançon has been at his stoves for three decades and he does
what he sets out to do – to provide quality Lyonnais cooking –
really well indeed. Some of his specialities are commonplace in
local restaurants – but here they can be found at their best: *poulet
à la crème*; *crêpes Parmentier* (potato pancakes – Parmentier
was the 18th-century food writer who persuaded the French to
eat the humble potato); and *sorbet vigneron*.
menus **A-B** *cards* AE DC Visa
closed Feb. Mon. Tues.
post Blaceret. 69830 St-Georges-de-Reneins. Rhône.
phone (74) 67.54.75 *Mich* 244 Lyon 42 km

BOULIGNEUX   Auberge des Chasseurs

Comfortable restaurant/Michelin★
Gardens

Yet another restaurant with a shabby-looking exterior which you
would drive past and not give a second glance – something you
will get used to in the Lyonnais area, where outward appearances
count for nothing. Michelin are generous with their stars in this
area; the other guides award no accolades here. Take no notice of
the shabby front – it's at the rear of the building that your spirits
will rise; a tiny garden leads you to an elegant Louis XIII dining
room. Traditional regional fare – rich as anything – with just the
odd modern touch here and there: like *mousse de sandre*,
panaché de poissons and good desserts.
menus **B-C** *cards* Visa
closed Mid-end Aug. Feb. Tues evg. Wed.
post Bouligneux. 01330 Villars-les-Dombes. Ain.
phone (74) 98.10.02 *Mich* 244 Lyon 38 km

BOURG-EN-BRESSE   Auberge Bressane

Luxury restaurant/Michelin★★
Terrace

One or two readers are not in love with Jean-Pierre Vullin's
modern Auberge – 'uninspired cooking' was one comment. Jean-
Pierre and Dominique Vullin became the owners of this famous
restaurant some years ago – prior to that they had worked for the
previous owner, Jacques Férand, for ten years. Regional cuisine
continues to be the order of the day – with the occasional
lightning flash of late 20th-century thinking striking the odd
speciality. If you want to savour Bressan cooking and products
then there's no better place than this: *volailles* in many forms,
grenouilles from Les Dombes and **Bugey** wines. Before or after
lunch on the terrace, be sure to explore the Eglise de Brou and its
adjoining museum – across the road.
menus **B-D** *cards* AE
closed Jun. Mid Nov-mid Dec. Mon evg. Tues.
post 01000 Bourg-en-Bresse. Ain.
phone (74) 22.22.68 *Mich* 244 Lyon 62 km

180

BOURG-EN-BRESSE   Mail
Very comfortable restaurant with rooms/Michelin★

Roger Charolles is not going to make any changes to his own interpretation of what good cooking is about: 'take the local produce, magnificent as it is in Bresse country; hone the regional dishes to perfection; and then stick to the same formula through thick and thin.' It may strike you that this approach leads to boredom and, eventually, to falling standards. True enough; you or I may not choose to do it but Roger, like many other Lyonnais chefs over the decades, is quite happy with his lot. So settle down and relish *pâté de grives, quenelle de brochet, grenouilles sautées aux fines herbes* and *volaille de Bresse*. The Mail is on the busy D936, west of Bourg.
menus **B-C** *rooms* 11 **B-C** *cards* DC
closed 10-end July. Mid Dec-mid Jan. Sun evg. Mon.
post 46 av. Mail, 01000 Bourg-en-Bresse. Ain.
phone (74) 21.00.26 *Mich* 244 Lyon 62 km

CHAUFFAILLES   Paix
Simple hotel/Michelin★

Thankfully, because most of my recommendations are family-owned places, few changes of staff occur between one edition of *French Leave* and the next. I have two changes to report at this hotel – one for the better, one most certainly for the worse. Within three months of the publication of the last *French Leave*, Yves Jury, an exceptional chef, deserted the family home to make his fortune at Dijon. Not a word was said to me in advance – though I had known for years that he felt he would never make his mark in this out-of-the-way spot.

Jean-Pierre, his brother, took over – but pretty obviously, good as he is with *nouvelle cuisine*, he is not as talented as Yves. Many letters during 1982 complained of a glacial atmosphere and ungracious service; old Mama Jury was the unanimous winner of the prize for the most unpopular hostess in France. She has now decided to call it a day and the hotel is run by young Marinette, Jean-Pierre's wife. The couple are going to have to work very hard to re-establish Yves Jury's reputation and win back the three *toques* that he had gained from Gault Millau. The Michelin star has been retained.
menus **B-C** *rooms* 19 **B-C** *cards* DC
closed Nov-Feb. Sun evg/Mon (Mid Sept-June).
post 71170 Chauffailles. Saône-et-Loire.
phone (85) 26.02.60 *Mich* 244 Lyon 88 km

COLIGNY   Le Petit Relais
Comfortable restaurant/Michelin★

As you will have already guessed, the Lyonnais is one region where regional specialities are thriving. Jacques Guy runs a typical Bressan restaurant – his good-value menus bear witness to that: *grenouilles sautées fines herbes, volaille de Bresse* and *fromage blanc*. Some lighter, modern touches are appearing.
menus **A-C** *cards* AE Visa
closed Mid-end June. Mid Feb-mid Mar. Tues evg. Wed.
post 01270 Coligny. Ain.
phone (74) 30.10.07 *Mich* 244 Lyon 83 km

COLLONGES-AU-MONT-D'OR   Paul Bocuse

Luxury restaurant/Michelin★★★

Why is it that during the last two years not one of you has defended Paul Bocuse or admonished me for my earlier criticism of him made in *French Leave* and *The Sunday Times*?

Is it the sheer offensiveness of his ego-dominated operation that sticks in your throat – as it most certainly does in mine? His face and name are everywhere: on his letterhead; the huge sign above his restaurant; the plates; the paper serviette holders; a full-length portrait on the wall; even the foil containers for the *petits fours* have his name embossed on them. Simon Hoggart, writing in *The Observer*, put it like this: 'It was like dining with Lenin.' Others, in a much kinder vein, have called him the 'Emperor of chefs.'

On my last 'incognito' visit I asked for a menu to be signed by the great man – of whom there had been no sign during the meal. Back came a signed menu. I asked to see him. The inevitable reply confirmed that he was away on his travels somewhere far beyond Collonges. He has 'culinary' business interests in many continents – Europe, Asia and the Americas.

These days Bocuse pours scorn on the new culinary trends of today. In his defence it has been suggested that he travels to look for new recipes; perhaps so, but you would hardly guess it when you study his menus! There were no signs of innovative creation when I was there recently. Henri Gault, in an interview with Richard Kann, said: "When a chef ceases to be able to create new dishes he has a tendency to say *nouvelle cuisine* is finished, rather than admit he has reached a deadend." Though you were talking about chefs in general, Henri – and not about Bocuse specifically – don't you think the *toque* fits? An example of Bocuse's present-day 'innovation' is the following; carp and eel in a *meurette* sauce, topped with a poached egg, itself floating on spinach. When I think of the scores of brilliant dishes I have enjoyed at the homes of some of France's young chefs it's no wonder, these days, that I resent spending hard-earned francs at the 'Kremlin'. See the Vergé entry – page 101.

I await your letters telling me how wrong I am.

menus C-D *cards* AE DC
closed Aug.
post 69660 Collonges-au-Mont-d'Or. Rhône.
phone (7) 822.01.40 *Mich* 244 Lyon 12 km

FLEURIE   Auberge du Cep

Comfortable restaurant/Michelin★★   ®

So; you think I have been hard on Bocuse. Well here is one of dozens of places where you'll relish the other end of the French restaurant spectrum. An unpretentious restaurant, anonymous even, opposite the village church. Gérard Cortembert is *in situ* – a talented, brilliant chef (he doesn't need press agents) offering you two alternatives: his regional menu with specialities like *gras-double*, *volaille de Bresse* and so on; or his modern menu with his own light creations such as *étuvée de saumon frais au poivre rose*. Enjoy the Beaujolais wines.

menus C *cards* AE
closed Dec. Sun evg. Mon.
post 69820 Fleurie. Rhône.
phone (74) 04.10.77 *Mich* 244 Lyon 58 km

FUISSE   Pouilly Fuissé
Very simple restaurant
Terrace/Good value

Don't have great expectations of this modest restaurant; it's another perfect example of many places recommended in *French Leave* that win the Michelin 'R' rating – for serving *un repas soigné* (regional cooking at low cost). So the bargain-price menus will be dotted with pleasures such as *rosette de Lyon*, *Charolais* beef, *volaille de Bresse*, *grenouilles*, various fish from the Saône and other fresh, local products. Be sure to enjoy the local vintages; **Pouilly-Fuissé** itself is expensive but **St-Véran** or one of the other **Mâcon-Villages** wines are just as adequate cheaper alternatives.

menus **A-B** *cards* Visa
closed 1-15 Sept. Feb. Tues evg (except July-Aug). Wed.
post Fuissé. 71960 Pierreclos. Saône-et-Loire.
phone (85) 35.60.68 *Mich* 244 Lyon 76 km

LOYETTES   Antonin
Very comfortable restaurant/Michelin★
Gardens   ®

For years we have admired Gérard Antonin's cooking skills; but now, as so often happens, he has improved and polished up his talents – and his restaurant – even more. Inspired by the modern ways of creative cooking, he builds his daily menus around the fresh produce available in the markets: *suprême de volaille de Bresse aux truffes, feuilleté de grenouilles beurre aux herbes* and a *galette d'aubergines* are examples. By far the best way of enjoying Gérard's skills is to have a lunch here; a remarkable 'indoor terrace' – with sliding, glass doors – overlooks the River Rhône. Support his loyalty to Bugey wines by trying the **Montagnieu** vintages – slightly sparkling and still wines; they come from an area upstream on the Rhône – see the map. Explore medieval Crémieu and enjoy the underground caves at La Balme-les-Grottes.

menus **B-C** *cards* Visa
closed 1-15 Sept. Mid Feb-mid Mar. Sun evg. Mon.
post 01980 Loyettes. Ain.
phone (7) 832.70.13 *Mich* 244 Lyon 33 km

MEXIMIEUX   Claude Lutz
Comfortable restaurant with rooms/Michelin★
Gardens

Two readers suggested I visit the Lutz restaurant; apart from the good cooking, they had clearly been appreciative of the warm welcome Mme Lutz had given them. I already knew the town and nearby Pérouges. The call I made confirmed that Claude Lutz, an old student of Bocuse, is a supporter of both regional and classical cuisine. No prizes if you can guess the specialities on his menus. I would suggest you stay overnight at the 'base' down the road (page 177).

menus **B-C** *rooms* 17 **B-C**
closed 17-24 July. Mid Oct-mid Nov. 1-15 Feb. Sun evg. Mon.
post 01800 Meximieux. Ain.
phone (74) 61.06.78 *Mich* 244 Lyon 39 km

MIONNAY Alain Chapel

Luxury restaurant with rooms/Michelin★★★
Terrace/Gardens

My wife and I first visited Chez la Mère Charles nearly 20 years ago, when Roger Chapel ran a typical Lyonnais restaurant. All that changed when son Alain took over the reins; during the last decade or so he has developed his father's old bistro into one of the most famous restaurants in the world. Lavish praise has been heaped on his shoulders by satisfied gourmets from every corner of the globe; there was a time when I, too, agreed with much of that adoration.

But not now. My last 'incognito' visit produced mixed results and left me with equally mixed feelings. The only advantage in eating out on your own is that you see everything that's going on. Let me give you some examples. One of the courses on the menu I ordered was a *feuilleté* with some *grenouilles* in a light garlic sauce; before it ever arrived I wondered why other diners in the room had left the pastry part of it. My serving answered my silent query; the *feuilleté* was as heavy as lead. Cold-bloodedly I left it; but no reaction came from the waiter or the kitchens. It was clear why: the place was packed. I was sitting in a spot where I could see the kitchens: Chapel and his staff were working at top speed; dishes were being prepared and despatched by the score. I sensed there were other diners elsewhere so, at the end of the evening, I nosed around in the hotel section at the rear of the building. Sure enough, I discovered two large groups of diners in private rooms; I would guess over 100 clients were there that night.

Another course was one of the worst dishes I have ever had in France; a catastrophic combination of bits and pieces from a lamb. Tasteless meat itself, sweetbreads, liver and goodness knows what else – all accompanied by the baby-food mush that some chefs serve as vegetables these days. I left most of it – once again there was no reaction. My American neighbours' *rougets* were all but inedible – they, too, were left.

On the credit side I have to say that Chapel does attract a great number of French people – always a good sign. His desserts – which I have criticised before – are still heavy but much improved (what flour does he use?); his *petits fours* are excellent; the atmosphere bubbling; and prices are good value. On the debit side there is much to criticise: with so many guests no wonder standards and service slip so dramatically and, worse still, preparation and cooking suffer badly; only one or two half-bottles of wine are offered on the list; coffee is treated like gold – or are the waiters just too busy; and why such great helpings of everything, Alain?

One of you commented on how 'monastery-like' the place is. Perhaps so – your words have made me realise that Chapel is a purist and, if anything, does apply a clinical approach to his work and environment. It makes me sad to have to say that, during the last three years, my four visits to Bocuse and Chapel have been wretched events; they compared very badly indeed with dozens of lesser-known chefs. Visit them if you must – but, if Chapel's restaurant is packed solid, you may leave, as I did, feeling very disappointed.

menus **D**
closed Jan. Mon. Tues midday.
post Mionnay. 01390 St-André-de-Corcy. Ain.
phone (7) 891.82.02 *Mich* 244 Lyon 20 km

MONTMERLE-SUR-SAONE   Castel de Valrose

Very comfortable restaurant with rooms/Michelin★
Quiet/Gardens   ®

If favourable letters are anything to judge by, this restaurant
must surely win one of the prizes for the most popular spot in
France. Many, many compliments have been paid – praising its
ideal specification for an overnight stop on your way north or
south; it's on the east side of the Saône, away from the autoroute.
A quiet site; light, airy dining rooms; a handful of pleasant
bedrooms; and enjoyable light classical cuisine have all
combined to seduce you. Bernard and Martine Morillon – such a
happy couple – are not likely to let me down in the future.
menus **B-C** *rooms* 5 **C** *cards* AE DC
closed Jan. Sun evg. Mon.
post Montmerle-sur-Saône. 01140 Thoissey. Ain.
phone (74) 69.30.52 *Mich* 244 Lyon 49 km

MONTROND-LES-BAINS   Host. La Poularde

Very comfortable hotel/Michelin★★
Good value   ®

Yes, good value! For the amenities and talented skills offered,
this must be the best value-for-money hotel in France. Joannès
Randoing – 50 years a chef – is taking things easy these days and,
increasingly, is letting his brilliant son-in-law, Gilles Etéocle, and
daughter, Monique, take over; like his father-in-law, Gilles is a
Maître Cuisinier de France and he is also a *Meilleur Ouvrier de
France*. Gilles is the son of Yvonne Randoing (Monique's step-
mother) from her first marriage; he is also Joannès' step-son – an
unusual twist of family relationships! Phew!

    I find the combination of pleasures here most appealing; it's
one of my favourite French hotels and I can't recommend it
enough to you. Gilles Etéocle's cooking is innovative – with many
a speciality paying homage to regional classics. Amongst dozens
of delights there are gems like *feuilleté de homard Breton,
fricassée de St-Pierre en infusion de poivre* and super desserts.
If you are a soccer fan, have a chat with Joannès – a fervent
supporter of the *verts* of St-Etienne.
menus **B-D** *rooms* 15 **B-C** *cards* AE DC Visa
closed Open all the year.
post 42210 Montrond-les-Bains. Loire.
phone (77) 54.40.06 *Mich* 244 Lyon 68 km

PONT-DE-VAUX   Commerce

Comfortable restaurant with rooms/Michelin★

Competition is murderous in this tiny village with a population of
just 2000 people; three first-rate restaurants – two with Michelin
stars and all three have Gault Millau *toques*. According to the
locals, Jean-Claude and Monique Patrone are considered the
best. Bressan products are the order of the day here: *cassolette
d'escargots à la crème, grenouilles fines herbes* and *volaille de
Bresse à la crème*. They like cream in the Lyonnais!
menus **B-C** *rooms* 10 **B**
closed Jun. Mid Nov-Xmas. Feb. Tues. Wed.
post 01190 Pont-de-Vaux. Ain.
phone (85) 37.30.56 *Mich* 70 Lyon 89 km

PONT-DE-VAUX   La Reconnaissance

Comfortable restaurant with rooms

Gilles Germain lost his Michelin star a few years ago; goodness knows why – perhaps they thought it was a bit much having three restaurants with single stars in the village. Try Gilles' seedy-looking restaurant and his first-rate Bressan cooking. I'm not going to bore you with the inevitable specialities.

menus **A-C** *rooms* 12 **A-C** *cards* Visa
closed Mid Nov-mid Dec. Mar. Sun evg/Mon (Sept-June).
post 01190 Pont-de-Vaux. Ain.
phone (85) 37.30.55 *Mich* 70 Lyon 89 km

PRIAY   La Mère Bourgeois

Comfortable restaurant/Michelin★

The incomparable Georges Berger has retired at last. What pleasure that unassuming genius of a chef – and his vivacious, attractive wife – gave us during two decades. I agree with the telling comment, made by Oliver Walston, that for a decade or more, during the sixties and seventies, this simple bistro was indeed 'the greatest restaurant in the world'. Only those fortunate enough to have been will known what we mean.

A new young chef, François Legroz, is in the kitchens – he had a long spell at the side of Georges before he left. Thankfully, the owner, Jacqueline Reydellet – who speaks good English – has allowed François to introduce newer dishes but has retained some old favourites: *pâté chaud*, *haricots verts frais* and *île flottante*. He has made a good start.

menus **B-C** *cards* AE DC Visa
closed Jan-mid Feb. Wed evg. Thurs.
post Priay. 01160 Pont-d'Ain. Ain.
phone (74) 35.61.81 *Mich* 244 Lyon 55 km

QUINCIE-EN-BEAUJOLAIS Aub. du Pont des Samsons

Simple restaurant/Michelin★
Terrace   ®

If I haven't by now made it clear that I am equally happy with the simplest or the greatest of restaurants, you will think I am out of my mind leading you to such a run-down bistro. With a backdrop of **Côte de Brouilly** vineyards, Jean and Dalia Fouillet continue to survive their decision to take the *nouvelle cuisine* road at their simple home. What a pleasure it is to give the regional classics a miss. Fresh produce, bought daily from the markets, is the mainstay of Jean's menus; *lapereau en gelée au lard et vieux Marc* is just one example.

Enjoy the Beaujolais wines – let me explain them in a little more detail. Many **AC Beaujolais Villages** wines will give their village names: **Quincié**, **Lancié**, **St-Etienne-la-Varenne**, **St-Etienne-des-Oullières**, **St-Lager**, **Romanèche-Thorins**, **Beaujeu**, **Vaux**, **Charentay** and **Regnié** are examples. Other villages, in the south of Beaujolais territory, like **Lachassagne** and **Theizé** share the general Beaujolais AC.

menus **A-C** *cards* AE Visa
closed Jan. June. Sun evg. Mon.
post Quincié-en-Beaujolais. 69430 Beaujeu. Rhône.
phone (74) 04.32.09 *Mich* 244 Lyon 56 km

RIVE-DE-GIER   Host. Renaissance

Very comfortable restaurant with rooms/Michelin★★
Terrace/Gardens

The view from the hills surrounding St-Etienne reminds me very
much of the view of the 'Black Country' from the Beacon, south
of Wolverhampton. The holiday visitor would have little reason
to venture below in either case – here there's one good excuse to
descend; to the Laurent family home, an oasis of green in a grim
valley. In his warm dining room Gilbert Laurent will demonstrate
why his skills and reputation continue to grow: light creations
and, as a bonus, one good-value menu.
menus **C-D** *rooms* 10 **C-D** *cards* AE DC Visa
closed Sun evg. Mon (out of season).
post 41 rue A.-Marrel, 42800 Rive-de-Gier. Loire.
phone (77) 75.04.31 *Mich* 244 Lyon 37 km

ROANNE   Hôtel des Frères Troisgros

Luxury hotel/Michelin★★★
Lift   ®

In earlier editions of *French Leave* I explained how my wife and I
first visited the old Hôtel de la Gare; on Sunday, 7th April 1968 –
the day Jim Clark died. Pierre and Jean Troisgros had two weeks
earlier won their third star – the atmosphere was electric and the
talents of the two brothers literally hit you between the eyes – or
was it in the stomach? We have made many visits since and
enjoyed them all.

Imagine my surprise therefore during the last two years when
letters began to arrive expressing disquiet with many aspects of
the place. Specific dishes clearly had not satisfied some of you; a
wine waiter had caused offence to one client; and the ultra-
modern bedrooms were universally disliked. So, off I went to
look for myself; far more critical these days and with the
priceless advantage of comparing one great place with others
over short periods of time.

It was a mixed performance indeed. Many plus points: an easy-
going, unstuffy atmosphere; excellent waiters – some of whom
were there two decades ago; innovative flair in the cooking; and
the bubbling personalities of the brothers and their wives. Sadly,
there were many minus points to be debited against the final
score: it's much too big now; really poor bread; very average
sweets and *petits fours*; a modest choice of cheeses; a much too
strong pepper and ginger sauce with a fillet of *loup*; and no really
outstanding dishes to remember. What I do remember is a visit to
the most spectacular kitchen in France; ask to see it after your
meal – it's an eye-opener.

On balance I would say this is still one of the best of the French
'shrines'. But what's happening in France is that the gulf between
the great *cuisiniers* and the scores of up-and-coming chefs has
all but closed. It is not their fault that the Troisgros brothers – and
the others – have been put on such a high pedestal. They are all
brilliant chefs – but they are not superhuman; they find it tough to
maintain the volcanic talent of their younger days.

Stop Press: Sadly, Jean Troisgros died in August 1983.
menus **C-D** *rooms* 18 **D-D2** *cards* AE DC Visa
closed 1-16 Aug. Jan. Tues. Wed midday.
post place Gare, 42300 Roanne. Loire.
phone (77) 71.66.97 *Mich* 73 Lyon 86 km

ST-ANDRE-DE-CORCY

Bérard

Comfortable restaurant/Michelin★
Gardens   ®

Geneviève and Jean-Louis Paul met each other in London, when
they were both working for Albert Roux at Le Gavroche.
Geneviève is now 35, has two children, 11 and 9, and speaks
excellent English. She will look after you with great charm, while
her husband will weave his marvellous magic in his hot kitchens.
Jean-Louis hails from the Lyon area and the two of them returned
here in 1974 to make their fortune. If you want to discover just
what that means in such a hotly competitive area for restaurants,
ask Geneviève to explain their problems. For a start no
compromises – witness the beautifully-printed menu and the
large cellar. First-class produce is a must; his *goujonettes de
rougets à l'huile d'olive à la crème d'ail doux* put to shame the
rougets served up at Chapel's restaurant the next evening. Lack
of space prevents me from listing the other pleasures I enjoyed;
let me just say that it's at places like this – throughout France –
where you'll enjoy yourself most.
menus **B-D** *cards* AE Visa
closed Wed evg. Thurs.
post 01390 St-André-de-Corcy. Ain
phone (7) 881.10.03 *Mich* 244 Lyon 24 km
Stop Press: the rest. has closed – killed by competition!

THEIZE

Espérance

Simple hotel
Quiet/Good value   ®

No less than three readers sent me postcards from Monsieur
Clavel's small, unpretentious *Logis* with its fine views
overlooking the neighbouring countryside. You loved his hotel;
his honest cooking – *saucisson, coq au vin, haricots verts* and
sorbets; and the surrounding villages like Vaux – the original
Clochemerle. How is it done at such low prices? *Vive La France*!
menus **A-B** *rooms* 9 **A-B**
closed Mid Sept-Oct. Tues evg. Wed.
post Theizé. 69620 Le Bois-d'Oingt. Rhône.
phone (74) 71.22.26 *Mich* 244 Lyon 34 km

TOURNUS

Greuze

Very comfortable restaurant/Michelin★★

There are good reasons for giving Tournus some of your time: the
abbey church of St-Philibert is one of the best examples of the
Romanesque style in France; the narrow streets of the small,
ancient town have many fine, old buildings; and the Greuze
Restaurant – named after Jean Baptiste Greuze, the portrait
painter born in the town – is the home of one of the greatest
classical cuisine supporters in France, Jean Ducloux. These days
he doesn't man the stoves – that's left to others; if you detest the
modern, creative ways of today then here's a place where you
can savour all the old classics: *escargots, quenelles de brochet*
and *grenouilles* are a few of them.
menus **C** *cards* AE Visa
closed 6-17 June. Mid Nov-mid Dec. Thurs.
post 71700 Tournus. Saône-et-Loire.
phone (85) 51.13.52 *Mich* 70 Lyon 102 km

TOURNUS   La Saône

Very simple hotel
Quiet/Good value

La Saône could not be more different from the Greuze. This
scruffy-looking hotel is on the eastern bank of the Saône *(rive
gauche)* – an isolated site, frequently flooded, well away from
noisy traffic. Modest, good-value cuisine (perhaps category
two?) with traditional Burgundian and Lyonnais specialities; an
overall formula which in no way will break the bank.

menus **A-B** *rooms* 12 **A-B**
closed Hotel: Dec. Jan. Rest: Nov-Feb. Thurs.
post 71700 Tournus. Saône-et-Loire.
phone (85) 51.03.38 *Mich* 70 Lyon 102 km

VONNAS   Georges Blanc

Luxury hotel/Michelin★★★
Gardens/Swimming pool/Tennis/Helicopter pad(!)   ®

Arthur Eperon wrote these words in *Encore Travellers' France*:
'among leading chefs it *(nouvelle cuisine)* is already going out of
fashion. It contradicts all classic French cooking.' What
poppycock! I challenge Eperon to say who these 'leading chefs'
are? (Or has he been hoodwinked by Bocuse's utterances on the
subject?) For every 'leading chef' he can name – I'll name ten who
will prove that *nouvelle cuisine* is flourishing. All are in this book
– and here's one of the best.

In the last edition of *French Leave* I deplored the fantastically
expensive rebuilding and refurbishing of the old *Chez* la Mère
Blanc. I still believe that Georges Blanc would have won his third
star without that vast investment in costly fixtures and fittings;
compare Girardet's warm, simple home with Georges' luxury
palace. Great-grandmother Virginie started the family business
in Vonnas; grandmother Elisa won the first star in 1929, the
second in 1931. Georges' mother, Paulette, preserved her
mother-in-law's two stars from 1936 until 1968 – at which time
Georges took over the kitchens. We have known the Blanc home
for nearly 20 years; how the place and the cooking have changed
over that period. But let me put aside all my earlier unhappy
observations about the change of character at La Mère Blanc.

My last visit was a fantastic experience – one of the most
stunning meals I have ever enjoyed in France. Georges, now 40,
has already become a great chef – his best, I think, is yet to come.
A menu of small exquisite creations were a series of jewels: first a
gourmandise Bretonne – a minute cold *gâteau* of lobster, pretty
as a picture; an imaginative *goujonnette de saumon aux
grenouilles au Sauternes et au curry* – tiny bits of salmon and
minuscule frogs' legs in a perfect cream sauce with **Sauternes**
and a pinch of curry; then *St-Jacques et langoustines à la
marinière* – three scallops and three *langoustines* in a
light reduction; *aile et cuisse de pigeonneau* (could they be smaller?)
aux sucs d'aromates petit gâteau de foie blond – with tiny fungi
and a mini *gratin* (no wonder you needed a finger bowl); finally,
superb sweets and *petits fours*. Bravo Georges! No wonder I'm
hard on Bocuse.

meals **C-D** *rooms* 26 **C-D3** *cards* AE DC Visa
closed Jan-mid Feb. Wed. Thurs midday.
post 01540 Vonnas. Ain.
phone (74) 50.00.10 *Mich* 244 Lyon 66 km

MASSIF CENTRAL

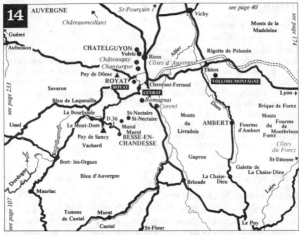

The **Massif Central** – a huge geographical mass of country – is really three separate regions. The map on page 7 showed them as **14 Auvergne**; **15 Ardèche**; and **16 Cévennes**. Study that map to understand the relationship they have to other neighbouring regions. On the pages that follow I have grouped them together under the general heading **Massif Central**; you will see more readily the geographical relationship they have to each other and it also allows me to group together the cheeses, wines and regional specialities that they share.

A few days spent in each of the three magnificent, unspoilt areas will provide you with the ideal method of seeing at least something, in turn, of each part of the Massif Central. Whichever way you select the various options open to you, I can guarantee you one thing; you will receive a dividend every day in peace, pleasure and contentment. The Massif Central requires a leisurely approach in the way you explore it. It is much the quietest part of France – full of wooded mountains, green pastures, river valleys and old historical towns. Here, more than anywhere else in France, is where you must take the advice running through every page of this book: go out and discover for

yourself the hidden corners of the countryside and the unknown inns – they are there in their hundreds. The more you get off the beaten track, the more you will enjoy yourself; this is where a map will repay its small outlay a thousand times.

The maps on these pages and the three pages of text that follow show clearly how the three areas relate to each other and how they can be explored as separate units.

Auvergne (14) is the northern area, based on **Royat** and **Ceyrat** (near **Clermont-Ferrand**): it extends to **St-Flour** in the south (see the Dordogne); to the hills of Limousin in the west – to the towns of **Guéret** and **Aubusson** (see Poitou-Charentes); and to the borders of the Lyonnais in the east.

Ardèche (15) is the lovely countryside to the east of **Le Puy** across to the River Rhône; for the purposes of this book it also includes the attractive terrain on the eastern side of the Rhône

Valley. Sadly, most people ignore its many treasures: have you seen – as examples – the cascade at **Ray Pic**, the crypts at **Cruas**, the attractive village of **Thines**, or travelled on the privately-owned steam railway called the Chemin de Fer du Vivarais that runs from **Tournon** to **Lamastre** – a metre-gauge line that climbs 250 metres in the process?

Cévennes (16) is centred on **Millau**, an ideal base from which you can explore the whole area. Nature has endowed the mountainous area of the Cévennes with a glorious legacy – nowhere else in France do spectacular sights come so thick and fast. Many of them are underground – fantastic caves and grottoes; others are carved, tortuous valleys and gorges; some are rugged mountain cliffs – their summits offer a variety of panoramic views. The whole area is ignored by many visitors to France – don't make that mistake; give it some of your time.

191

Auvergne (14)

The Auvergne is the northern half of the Massif Central and many people consider it the most attractive mountain region in France – much of it is like Scotland. It was once an area of volcanic activity, and the countryside is studded with old volcanoes, now blanketed with green pastures and forests.

Ceyrat and Royat are adjacent to the **Puy de Dôme** and Clermont-Ferrand. Royat, **Le Mont-Dore** (famous for its asthma treatment) and **La Bourboule**, are all spa towns; the Romans favoured them two thousand years ago. One drive you must make is to the summit of the 1465 metres high Puy de Dôme with its breathtaking views. The remains of the temple of Mercury, built by the Romans, are at the top. This is a famous timed stage of the Tour de France; it will require very little of your imagination to feel the agony of the cyclists as they ride up that wall to the summit. One of the finest half-dozen mountain drives in France is on the D36 from **Besse-en-Chandesse** to Le Mont-Dore. On no account should you miss it. Music in many forms will awaken happy memories for me – Canteloube's *Songs of the Auvergne*, sung by that angel amongst singers, Flicka von Stade, always bring back crystal-clear images of this green corner of France (available now as a tape from CBS).

South of Ceyrat and Royat are a whole host of possibilities for half or full-day trips: **Bort-les-Orgues** (with its organ-pipe rock formations) and the upper valley of the Dordogne; the peak of **Puy de Sancy** (the highest peak in the Massif at 1885 metres) and the mass of mountains surrounding it; **St-Nectaire** must not be missed with its superb Romanesque church, one of the wonders of the entire region; **Murol** and its ruined castle, sitting high above the village, is another must.

North of the base hotels is **Vichy**, one of the premier spa towns of France and with its own special place in history. It is an elegant, sophisticated town with several attractive parks, particularly those alongside the River Allier.

West of Royat are the gentler, kinder hills of Limousin. Some 80 kilometres or so away is Aubusson, celebrated for its tapestries and still a centre for the Decorative Arts. The Creuse Valley, and the strangely-named Plateau de Millevaches (a tableland of countless springs – the Vézère, the Vienne and the Creuse all rise there), are well worth visiting.

To the east are the **Monts du Forez. Ambert** is one of my recommendations and certainly you should have an outing to both the town and the surrounding hills; nearby, to the south of the town, is **La Chaise-Dieu**, where a great monastery overshadows the tiny village (the church has a fresco of the *Dance Macabre*). Explore, too, the wooded hills east of Vichy.

All this countryside is at its best in spring or in autumn. In the spring the meadows are full of the yellows and whites of wild flowers: narcissi, celandines, cowslips, wild daffodils, snow-drops and violets; in the autumn it is the turn of the lilac-shaded autumn crocus, tiny dianthus and spiraea. No wonder the coronation dress for Queen Elizabeth II was based on a design of the scores of wild flowers of France; years ago my daughter spent hours, in every part of the huge country, picking and pressing the flowers of the fields and pastures; today, it is against the law.

Michelin *yellow* map: 239.73. Green Guide: Auvergne

IGN *série verte* maps: 49.50. *série rouge* map: 111

Airport: Clermont-Ferrand

Distances from:

Paris-Clermont-Ferrand 389 km Calais-Clermont-Ferrand 681 km

Georges and Jacqueline Blanc – Vonnas (Lyonnais)

The Dourdou Valley – south of Conques (Dordogne)

The Gorges du Tarn from the Point Sublime (Cévennes)

The Tarn – near La Malène (Cévennes)

Ardèche (15)

I have recommended several 'bases' (in all three categories) on the eastern edge of the Massif Central, at **Tain-l'Hermitage**, **Valence** and **Vienne** (in the Rhône Valley). Many benefits accrue from using them; you are ideally placed to do many things. First, you have the chance to explore thoroughly one of my favourite mountain areas of France, from **St-Etienne** in the north and Le Puy in the west, down to **Aubenas** in the south. This is Ardèche country, beguiling at any time but at its best in the grateful, giving month of September. It is full of charming villages and small uncrowded towns.

There is much to do and see. Explore Le Puy, an important historical town and the strangest situated one in France; sharp volcanic hills rise on every side, several of them having chapels and statues (and even a cathedral in one case) on their summits. At nearby **Le Monastier**, Robert Louis Stevenson started his travels south, a journey later made famous in *Travels with a Donkey in the Cévennes*. Beyond **Privas** are some delightful small towns and villages: **Les Vans**, set at the mouth of the beautiful and solitary Chassezac Valley; **Joyeuse**, where, according to legend, Charlemagne buried his sword; the spa of **Vals-les-Bains**; and **Burzet** with its spectacular river scenes.

South-west of Lamastre sits the mountain of **Gerbier de Jonc** (1551 metres high); the **Loire** starts its life from here. All the Ardèche is marvellous motoring country. You will be driving there for different reasons but it will require only a little imagination on your part to understand why the minor roads make such exciting rallying country. The car rallies that use them (particularly the Monte-Carlo Rally) do so at night, when the roads are closed to the public. The bottom right-hand corner of Michelin map 76 will show you a maze of roads; so difficult to navigate at speed in the dark. I always found it an exhilarating sport; when the car was on song, when the driver was on form and his navigator was reading maps without fault – nothing in the world was more thrilling and satisfying. Far more so than racing round the same circuit for hours on end – and a great deal safer as well. One exception to that general rule is the Auvergne Racing Circuit, south of Royat, which uses public roads; drive those roads – it is a sobering experience.

East of the Rhône are the remote **Vercors**, the mountains that were one of the main centres of the French Resistance during the last war. Several parts of the Vercors must be seen; the natural splendours of the **Combe Laval**, the **Grands Goulets** and the Gorges de la Bourne. All these lie in a tight triangle of country and all are connected by safe, spectacular mountain roads. Ensure you use the **Col de Rousset**, the grandfather of all hillclimbs, north of **Die**. From its summit you get one of the best panoramas in the south of France. Please read page 126.

Drôme country, south-east of Valence, is probably known to one in 10,000 of the motorists speeding down the A7. There are several attractive, small towns and villages – **Crest**, Le Poët-Laval, **La Bégude-de-Mazenc** and **Dieulefit** – set in this rocky, wooded country. This is the start of Provence, where the sun shines and where the apple will not flourish. But some of the best fruit in France, including apricots, cherries and peaches, flourishes magnificently well.

Michelin *yellow* maps: 76.77.93. Green Guide: Vallée du Rhône
IGN *série verte* map: 52. *série rouge* map: 112
Airports: Lyon. Marseille
Distances from: Paris-Valence 561 km Calais-Valence 855 km

Cévennes (16)

My 'base' is centred on Millau. This is one of just a few 'bases' I recommend which is set in a town; but do not be put off – it is a small town and you will be surprised how quiet the hotel is. The big extra that Millau offers the visitor is the number of restaurants providing good-value meals. Each one of them is ideal for an evening meal, leaving you free during the day to enjoy the surrounding countryside and a picnic lunch.

To the north of Millau is one of the best single sights in France – the magnificent **Gorges du Tarn**. One whole day must be set aside to drive up the Gorges road to **Florac**, returning via **Meyrueis** to **Le Rozier**. After that trip you will want to return and spend the next one in a boat on the river, enjoying its many calmer stretches. Or, alternatively, you will want to go back again one evening and see some of the illuminated sections.

Make sure you visit some of the exciting caves and grottoes that abound in the Causses – **Aven Armand** (discovered in 1897) is one of the most spectacular with its Forêt Vierge. To the east of Millau is the National Park of the Cévennes, full of wooded hills and gorges and interlaced by deserted, thrilling roads.

It is the Cévennes National Park that helps me to demonstrate – to perfection – just what value a good map can give. Michelin map 240 is the one you need. Maps and mountains, for me, are a mixture of pleasures which do me more good than any stimulant or anti-depressant drug: so beware – I am about to encourage you to do things which, hopefully, will bring you similar pleasures in the future, throughout France and back at home; the more remote the roads, the better.

Allow one long day for this trip. Leave Millau to the east – spectacles come thick and fast. First, the **Canyon de la Dourbie**: then five kilometres before Nant, take the minor road to Trèves; the Gorges de Trevezel come next; then the Abîme (literally – unfathomable depth) du Bramabiau, a subterranean river, small *cirque* and caves – all in one. Continue to the summit of **Mont Aigoual** – from the observatory (1567 metres) you will get glorious and extensive views in all directions. Then choose any of the alternative roads that go south to the **Grotte des Demoiselles** – a dry cavern, with magnificent stalactites. Finally, return to Millau via the Gorges de la Vis and the extraordinary **Cirque de Navacelles** – please don't miss it.

Do the trip over a whole day if you can – or break it into sections: I promise you it will be quite a trip.

All the country to the west and north-west of Millau is almost totally uninhabited. The **Aveyron** and Tarn Valleys will take you down lanes from another world where you may just as well be a thousand kilometres away from civilisation. There are several large lakes and reservoirs in the area.

Visit the town of **Roquefort-sur-Soulzon** where the most famous cheese in the world is produced. Inspect the many caves (said to be the best refrigeration sites in the world) where this exquisite blue cheese, made from ewe's milk, is stored and where it ripens, emerging eventually into that sharp, fine taste enjoyed throughout the world. Over 15,000 tonnes of these cheeses are made every year. All blue cheeses are salty – Roquefort particularly so – as salt is added to slow down the growth of mould on the outside, while the inside matures.

Michelin *yellow* maps: 240.77.80. Green Guide: Causses
IGN *série verte* maps: 58.59. *série rouge* map: 114
Airports: Marseille. Montpellier. Toulouse
Distances from: Paris-Millau 630 km Calais-Millau 924 km

Cheeses Cow's milk

Auvergne (Bleu d') when made on farms at its best in summer and autumn. Strong smell, soft, made in the same way as Roquefort. **Bleu de Laqueuille** is a related cheese

Cantal from the Auvergne. Semi-hard, nutty flavour. Praised by Pliny. Try it with the fruity **Côtes d'Auvergne** reds

Causses (Bleu des) a blue cheese with parsley-like veins, hence the term *persillé*. At its best in summer and autumn

Fourme-d'Ambert has a summer and autumn season. A blue cheese from the Auvergne and in the shape of a tall cylinder

Fourme de Montbrison a bitter blue – as is **Fourme de Pierre-s-Haute Gapron (Gaperon)** a garlic-flavoured, flattened ball

Laguiole related to Cantal. Big cylinders, penetrating bouquet

Loudes (Bleu de) blue-veined and from the hills of Velay, near Le Puy

Murol a semi-hard cheese, like St-Nectaire. Made in small disks, mild

St-Félicien a salty-tasting cheese from the hills west of Tournon

St-Nectaire has a purply-brown skin, made in larger disks than Murol. A semi-hard, mild cheese. **Savaron** and **Vachard** are related

Tomme de Cantal a fresh, softish, cream-coloured, unfermented cheese

Goat's milk

Brique du Forez also known as **Chevreton d'Ambert**. A small loaf with a nutty flavour. **Galette de la Chaise-Dieu** is similar – a flat cake

Rigotte de Condrieu soft, small cylinders with no special flavour; available all the year. **Rigotte de Pelussin** is a related cheese

Ewe's milk

Roquefort read my earlier notes on the previous page. Pliny wrote of it

Regional Specialities

Aligot purée of potatoes with Tomme de Cantal cheese, cream, garlic and butter

Bougnette a stuffing of pork, bread and eggs – wrapped in *crépine* (caul)

Bourriols d'Aurillac sweet pancakes, made from buckwheat flour

Brayaude (gigot) lamb cooked in white wine, onions and herbs

Cadet Mathieu pastry turnover filled with slices of apple

Clafoutis baked pancake batter, poured over fruit, usually cherries

Confidou Rouergat ragout of beef, red wine, tomatoes, garlic and onions

Cousinat (Cousina) chestnut soup (*salée* – salted) with cream, butter and prunes – served with bread

Criques grated potato, mixed with eggs and fried – in the form of pancakes. Related to the *Truffiat* of Berry

Farçon large *galette* of sausage, sorrel, onions, eggs and white wine

Farinette buckwheat flour pancakes – meat and vegetable filling

Friand Sanflorin pork meat and herbs in pastry

Jambon d'Auvergne a lovely mountain ham

Manouls see *Trénels*

Milliard (Millat, Milla) see *Clafoutis*

Mourtayrol a stew with beef, chicken, ham, vegetables and bread

Omelette Brayaude eggs, pork, cheese and potatoes

Perdrix à l'Auvergnate partridge stewed in white wine

Potée Auvergnate stew of vegetables, cabbage, pork and sausage

Pountari a mince of pork fat in cabbage leaves

Pounti small, egg-based savoury soufflé with bacon or prunes

Rouergat(e) Rouergue; the name of the area to the west of Millau

Salmis de colvert Cévenole wild duck, sautéed in red wine, onions, ham and mushrooms

Soupe aux choux soup with cabbage, ham, pork, bacon and turnips

Trénels mutton tripe, white wine and tomatoes

Tripoux stuffed sheep's feet

Truffade a huge *galette* of sautéed potatoes

Wines

For those visitors based in the northern part of the Massif, look out for the really good **St-Pourçain** (near Vichy) reds and a fine, Loire-type white wine. A flourishing VDQS area is **Côtes d'Auvergne**, near Clermont-Ferrand: among the noteworthy reds from here are **Chanturgue** and **Châteaugay** – made from the Gamay grape – and a rosé from **Corent**. From the eastern side of this northern section of the Massif Central come some good, Beaujolais-type reds, the Gamays of the **Côtes du Forez**.

If you are in the Tain area you are in the middle of one of the best wine-producing parts of France. From Tain l'Hermitage (**AC Hermitage**, a wonderful wine and **AC Crozes-Hermitage**, a less-good, junior brother), **Saint Joseph** and **Cornas**, all north of Valence and on both sides of the Rhône, you will find some super, ruby-red wines, dark and powerful. Only the vineyards on the granite hill overlooking Tain have the right to the world-famous Hermitage appellation; the vineyards that lie to the north and east take the Crozes AC.

There are also some good, dry whites from this area: a **Hermitage Blanc** (the best one is **Chante-Alouette**), a **Saint Péray** white and a **Crozes-Hermitage** one. The highlight of the area for me is the **Saint Péray mousseux** – sheer delight! 80 per cent of the vineyard production goes towards the making of this sparkling wine – manufactured in the same way as Champagne – *méthode champenoise*.

South-east of Valence, at **Die**, you will find the lovely *demi-sec* **Clairette de Die** (local, *naturel* method) and a *brut* version (*méthode champenoise*), both **mousseux**. There's a dry still white, too. Near Die are the wines of all shades from **Châtillon-en-Diois**. South of Valence is the **AC Coteaux du Tricastin** with dry rosés and reds. A century ago they were highly thought of; their prestige diminished – but in the last 20 years they have risen from a *Vins de Pays* classification to a full AC.

If you are in Millau, or anywhere in the south, look at my wine notes on pages 110 and 152. You will be offered many of the VDQS Midi wines (from Languedoc to the south): **Saint Chinian**, **Saint Saturnin**, **Montpeyroux** and **Faugères** are among the best. Other wines you will see on wine lists are the **Gaillac** ones – reds, rosés and whites (both still and sparkling). You may also come across the light reds from just west and north of Rodez, the VDQS **Vin de Marcillac**. Try this local wine with a Fourme-d'Ambert cheese.

Vins de Pays
The **Vin de Pays de l'Ardèche** reds (both Gamay and Syrah grapes) are superb examples of how good this classification of wines can be.

Additional comments

Restaurants in the Auvergne
With few exceptions, this area in the north, together with Limousin, is a gastronomic desert when compared with other parts of France and particularly when you compare it with the Lyonnais region sitting to the east of the Auvergne. Do not be put off by this; Auvergne compensates in many other ways.

Restaurants in the Cévennes
This area is particularly recommended for those of you who want to try flourishing regional specialities; at several of the recommended restaurants you will find dishes based on the recipes, produce and wines of the area.

Base Hotels

CEYRAT
La Châtaigneraie

Comfortable hotel
Quiet/Gardens

High above Ceyrat with extensive views to the east – take the D133 from the village to find this modern base hotel.
No restaurant *rooms* 16 **B-C**
closed Sat. Sun.
post Ceyrat. 63110 Beaumont. Puy-de-Dôme.
phone (73) 61.34.66 *Mich* 239 Clermont-Ferrand 6 km

MILLAU
La Capelle

Comfortable hotel
Quiet/Good value ®

In the central part of the town but surprisingly quiet; it has been a great success with readers. Park in the *place* beside the hotel.
No restaurant *rooms* 46 **A-B**
closed Oct-mid May (except 2 weeks at Easter).
post 7 place Fraternité, 12100 Millau. Aveyron.
phone (65) 60.14.72 *Mich* 240

ROYAT
Parc Majestic

Comfortable hotel
Quiet/Gardens

This hotel wins the prize for some of the worst breakfasts in France: remember – and this is true everywhere – you do **not** have to have them; try a local café instead.
No restaurant *rooms* 20 **B-C**
closed Oct-Apl.
post av. Jocelyn-Bargoin, 63130 Royat. Puy-de-Dôme.
phone (73) 35.84.36 *Mich* 239 Clermont-Ferrand 4 km

TAIN-L'HERMITAGE
Deux Côteaux

Simple hotel
Fairly quiet

Alongside the Rhône in a quiet site – with a backdrop, behind the town, of the famous Hermitage vincyards.

Quiet base hotels are hard to find in the northern stretches of the Rhône Valley – further south, in Provence, there are many attractive 'bases'. See the Vienne entry on page 200 for details of two further suggestions and refer also to page 209 for an alternative in the Valence area.

The Tournon 'base' – in previous editions of *French Leave* – has been given the 'boot'. The owners of Le Manoir seem keener these days on developing their camp site facilities at the expense of their hotel guests. The swimming pool is not enough compensation for the awful racket at the site. The owners were guilty, too, of that wretched 'con' trick you must watch out for in France: when you are told that cheaper rooms are taken and only dear ones are free!
No restaurant *rooms* 22 **A-C**
closed Nov. Feb. Sun (Nov-Mar).
post 18 rue J.-Péala, 26600 Tain-l'Hermitage. Drôme.
phone (75) 08.33.01 *Mich* 77 Valence 18 km

Recommendations where cuisine takes second place

LE CHAMBON-SUR-LIGNON   Clair Matin

Simple hotel
Secluded/Gardens/Swimming pool/Tennis

This modern, chalet-style *Logis* is an ideal candidate for category
two with very basic cooking; helpings are far too small – as
Hidden France readers confirm. But all its other benefits will
enchant you; some are listed above – others are the vast forests,
ideal for walking, fishing and riding.

menus **A** *rooms* 31 **C**
closed Mid Nov-Xmas.
post 43400 Le Chambon-sur-Lignon. Haute-Loire.
phone (71) 59.73.03 *Mich* 76 Valence 73 km

MEYRUEIS   Grand Hôtel Europe

Comfortable hotel
Gardens/Swimming pool/Lift/Good value

Remarkable value is what Jean-Paul Roberts provides at his
modern hotel; an annexe is 200 metres up the road – it's there
you'll find the pool. There's fantastic country to all sides: pine
forests to the south – don't miss the Abîme du Bramabiau; and
the caves of Aven Armand and Dargilan.

menus **A** *rooms* 50 **A-B**
closed Oct-Mar.
post 48150 Meyrueis. Lozère.
phone (66) 45.60.05 *Mich* 240 Millau 42 km

MILLAU   Château de Creissels

Comfortable hotel
Secluded/Gardens
                                                          ®

Madame Austruy owns a beguiling hotel – two kilometres from
Millau on the D992 St-Affrique road. It's a modern place with an
extension added to a château – a splendid old tower still stands;
the hotel sits in the shadow of a medieval church. Cuisine is
modest but tasty; specialities include *truite au vert* and *feuilleté
au Roquefort*.

menus **A-B** *rooms* 30 **B-C**
closed Mid Dec-Jan. Wed (out of season).
post 12100 Millau. Aveyron.
phone (65) 60.16.59 *Mich* 240 Millau 2 km

LE ROZIER   Grand Hôtel Muse et Rozier

Very comfortable hotel
Quiet/Terrace/Gardens/Lift

One of the best bits of news in 1982 was to hear that Hugues and
Dominique de Leyssac, together with Marc d'Hamonville – all
charming hosts – had reopened their hotel, totally destroyed by
fire three years earlier. The strikingly-modern structure has a fine
setting, alongside the Tarn. The light cuisine is good – perhaps up
to category three standard.

menus **B-C** *rooms* 38 **C-D2** *cards* AE DC Visa
closed Oct-Mar.
post à la Muse, Le Rozier. 48150 Meyrueis. Lozère.
phone (65) 62.60.01 *Mich* 240 Millau 21 km

ST-AFFRIQUE   Moderne et Gare

Simple hotel
Quiet

What a mixed bag of letters arrived at Chiltern House: first two complaints and, later, two appreciative recommendations from readers. So visit Jean-François and Yves Decuq with no great hopes – and let me know if they are making a continuing effort to restore their good name. Specialities: *confidou Rouergat, soufflé au Roquefort* and *clafoutis*.

menus **A-C** *rooms* 39 **A-C** *cards* Visa
closed Mid Dec-mid Jan.
post 12400 St-Affrique. Aveyron.
phone (65) 49.20.44 *Mich* 240 Millau 31 km

SATILLIEU   Gentilhommière

Comfortable hotel
Quiet/Gardens/Swimming pool/Tennis

A smart, attractive site – on the Lalouvesc road to the south-west of the village. Alongside a small river, the hotel is ideally placed for you to enjoy the pine forests to the south and west and the chestnut woods to the north. The Hôtel du Pont in Satillieu (an annexe) is owned by the same family; it's cheaper – you eat and use the facilities here.

menus **A-C** *rooms* 39 (11 here) **B-D**
closed Nov-Mar.
post 07290 Satillieu. Ardèche.
phone (75) 34.94.31 *Mich* 76 Valence 52 km

SAULCE-SUR-RHONE   La Capitelle

Simple hotel
Quiet   ®

Three kilometres to the east of the N7, this delightful, old hotel, in a tiny picturesque village, has a lovely setting with fine views across a quiet, green valley. Until a year or two ago it was *sans restaurant*; now you can enjoy straightforward meals without paying through the nose for them.

menus **A-B** *rooms* 14 **B-D** *cards* AE
closed Mid Nov-mid Dec. Jan. Tues.
post Mirmande. Saulce-sur-Rhône. 26270 Loriol. Drôme.
phone (75) 61.02.72 *Mich* 77 Valence 33 km

THUEYTS   Nord

Comfortable hotel
Gardens

Nothing marvellous about the cuisine here; enjoy *truite au Champagne* and *tarte aux myrtilles*. But it's the neighbouring countryside that will reward you far more richly: the views of the infant Ardèche from a point just east of the hotel; the village of Burzet; and the Ray-Pic cascade. Dinner only.

menus **A** (dinner only) *rooms* 25 **B-C**
closed Nov-Easter. Tues (out of season).
post 07330 Thueyts. Ardèche.
phone (75) 36.40.38 *Mich* 76 Valence 88 km

VALGORGE   Le Tanargue

Comfortable hotel
Secluded/Gardens/Lift

Amédée Coste owns a modern, ugly-looking *Logis* – away from
the main road and with views across the valley. The menus give
you the chance to try some local products like *jambon cru*,
saucisson, *truites* and *caille Cévenole*. Don't miss the drive to
Joyeuse; enjoy Les Vans; seek out Thines; and include the
magnificent Gorges de l'Ardèche in your travels.
menus **A-B** *rooms* 25 **C**
closed Jan. Feb.
post Valgorge. 07110 Largentière. Ardèche.
phone (75) 35.68.88 *Mich* 80 Valence 96 km

VIENNE   Domaine de Clairefontaine

Simple hotel
Secluded/Gardens/Tennis

At Chonas-l'Amballan, nine km south of Vienne. An old country
house, in extensive grounds, and well clear of both the N7 and A7.
Use it as a 'base' – eating at the nearby good restaurants. Another
good 'base' (*sans restaurant*) is the Midi (secluded/gardens) at
Pont-Evêque, 4 km east of Vienne.
menus **A-B** *rooms* 17 **B-C**
closed Dec. Jan. Sun evg (out of season). Mon midday.
post Chonas-l'Amballan. 38121 Reventin-Vaugris. Isère.
phone (74) 58.81.52 *Mich* 93 Valence 62 km

LE VIGAN   Mas Quayrol

Comfortable hotel
Secluded/Swimming pool

Let me give you careful instructions on how to find this sun trap.
It's up a narrow lane to the north of the village of Aulas, itself
seven km from Le Vigan towards Mont Aigoual. Modern
bedrooms are in a separate building. To the south are orchards –
in spring a stunning sight. Don't miss the Gorges de Navacelles –
one of France's natural wonders. Simple fare: cheeses, meats,
trout and mushrooms. I suggest you use it as a 'base'.
menus **B-C** *rooms* 16 **C** *cards* DC
closed Oct-Apl.
post Aulas. 30120 Le Vigan. Gard.
phone (66) 91.12.38 *Mich* 240 Millau 74 km

VOLLORE-MONTAGNE   Touristes

Very simple hotel
Good value

Marie-Claire Roussel's green-shuttered auberge is a modest,
unpretentious place; 840 metres above sea-level, there are
deserted forests in every direction. Enjoy them and her home-
made *jambon cru*, *tripoux* and *tarte aux myrtilles*.
menus **A-B** *rooms* 17 **A-B** *cards* Visa
closed Nov-mid Dec. Tues evg/Wed (except July-Aug).
post Vollore-Montagne. 63120 Courpière. Puy-de-Dôme.
phone (73) 53.77.50 *Mich* 239 Clermont-Ferrand 63 km

Recommendations where cuisine takes pride of place

AMBERT

Comfortable hotel

Many of you have told me how much you liked this long-established hotel; I understand that old Monsieur Joyeux has handed over his splendid, life-long home to Christian Parrain. He continues the same traditions of classical and regional cuisine – pleasing not just the tourists but the locals, too, in this small, bustling market town. Old treats still dominate the menus: *crêpes au jambon, coquelet au vin d'Auvergne, clafoutis* and *caprice Livradois*. Order the local wines like **Châteaugay** – just north of Clermont-Ferrand – and the varieties from **St-Pourçain**. Relish the blue-veined, tall cylinders of cheese called **Fourme d'Ambert** and then head north-east to the Col des Supeyres; look out for the *jasseries*, the stone-built dairy farms where this famous cheese is made. Seek out also the interesting paper mill, the Moulin Richard-de-Bas, east of Ambert. Finally, be sure not to bypass either La Chaise-Dieu – with its huge church; or Le Puy – a unique town.

menus **B-C** *rooms* 14 **A-C** *cards* AE DC Visa
closed Mid Oct-mid Nov. Jan Sun evg (Nov Easter). Mon.
post 1 place Livradois, 63600 Ambert. Puy-de-Dôme.
phone (73) 82.10.01 *Mich* 239 Clermont-Ferrand 78 km

BESSE-EN-CHANDESSE

Very comfortable hotel/Michelin★
Quiet/Gardens

Les Mouflons means 'wild sheep'. One thing is for sure; this modern, unattractive, chalet-style hotel is certainly sited in wild country. For a start, you are over 1000 metres above sea-level; that should tell you that this is both a summer and winter 'resort' – a generous description – and that Antoine Sachapt has two seasons during each year. Don't miss the D36 run to Le Mont-Dore – a spectacular mountain drive; see Murol – particularly from the D5 to the north; and the magnificent Romanesque church at St-Nectaire. Back at the hotel try the cheeses from the two last-named villages and support Antoine by ordering his Auvergne wines – **Corent** is a good one, **Romagnat** (see map) is another. Cuisine is classical with many an excellent regional speciality – *milliard* is just one example.

menus **A-C** *rooms* 50 **C** *cards* Visa
closed Mid Sept-Xmas. Mid Mar-20 May.
post 63610 Besse-en-Chandesse. Puy-de-Dôme.
phone (73) 79.51.31 *Mich* 239 Clermont-Ferrand 51 km

CHATELGUYON

Comfortable restaurant
Good value

Michelin still place Jacqueline Brandibat's restaurant incorrectly on their town map – it's 100 metres to the east of the spot indicated. Regional menus with *charcuterie d'Auvergne, truite au vin de Chantergue* and *fromages d'Auvergne*.

menus **A-B**
closed Oct-mid May. Tues.
post avenue Baraduc, 63140 Châtelguyon. Puy-de-Dôme.
phone (73) 86.04.17 *Mich* 239 Clermont-Ferrand 21 km

CONDRIEU
Hôt. Beau Rivage

Very comfortable hotel/Michelin★★
Terrace/Gardens

Paulette Castaing – after 40 years at her stoves – continues to organise and run one of the most popular hotels in the Rhône Valley. High above the Beau Rivage are the narrow terraces which produce the wonderful white wines of **Condrieu** and **Château-Grillet** (one of the smallest appellations in France); their output is very limited indeed. I apologise for saying in the last edition that they do not travel well; a reader has put me right – apparently they do.

Paulette is one of a handful of talented *cuisinières* in France who have won the top accolades from both Michelin and Gault Millau. Elsewhere in this book I have written about *Les Mères* (page 23) – Paulette continues those heroic traditions with great stamina, courage and loyalty. Classical cuisine is her forte but with just a few modern touches here and there. Sadly, and inevitably, standards have slipped.

I visited Beau Rivage after a reader wrote suggesting that there was 'an atmosphere of fatigue about the cooking and the hotel.' Alas, he was right. Michelin continue to stay loyal to Paulette – as they do to Madame Point at nearby Vienne; but to be honest her cuisine does not deserve a two-star rating any longer. When you compare her efforts with Michel Chabran's brilliance down the valley you are left wondering why Michelin can be so inconsistent at times.

What a pity, too, that the view south from the hotel terrace has been utterly ruined by a hideous industrial complex. Changing the subject, and ending on a more positive note, I recommend Anthony Hogg's book, *Guide to Visiting Vineyards*; useful in the Rhône, throughout France, and Europe.

menus C *rooms* 22 **C-D** *cards* AE DC Visa
closed Jan-mid Feb.
post 69420 Condrieu. Rhône.
phone (74) 59.52.24 *Mich* 93 Valence 75 km

DIEULEFIT
Les Hospitaliers

Very comfortable hotel/Michelin★
Secluded/Terrace/Gardens/Swimming pool

Five kilometres to the west of Dieulefit is Poët-Laval and high above the latter is Vieux Village. Seek out this remarkable spot; it's one of the most interesting sites in southern France – a marvellous example of how restoration work can bring new life to a community. The splendid hotel is part of that medieval village – a seductive, expensive spot certain to capture any visitor's heart. From the terrace – itself an original and clever creation – there are extensive views of the deserted Drôme hills.

Yvon Morin's son, Bernard, is the chef here – concentrating in the main on classical dishes with some modern interpretations: *terrine de canard au foie gras, fondant de Charolais au vieux vin, sorbets aux fruits* and so on. There is also a range of good wines; try the local **Coteaux du Tricastin** varieties – really first-class examples.

menus **C-D** *rooms* 20 **D-D2** *cards* AE DC Visa
closed Mid Nov-Feb. Rest: Tues (out of season).
post Poët-Laval. 26120 La Bégude-de-Mazenc. Drôme.
phone (75) 46.22.32 *Mich* 93 Valence 67 km

GRANE   Giffon

Very comfortable restaurant with rooms
Terrace/Good value

If the Giffon's menu still persists in using the term 'cherry dry'
will someone put them wise – it's 'dry sherry'. (The words have
been used to describe a *poularde* dish.) It also includes *Maigret
de canard* – the detective was hardly a duck's breast! If Jacques
and his son, Patrick, cannot get their menu descriptions right,
they certainly can do little wrong in their kitchens. Classical and
Lyonnais specialities are the order of the day at their modest inn,
sitting in the shadow of a church steeple. Specialities include
terrine de foie gras maison, poulet de Bresse, truite saumonée
and *loup au fenouil*.
menus **B-C** *rooms* 9 **A-B** *cards* AE DC Visa
closed Mid Nov-mid Dec. Jan. Mon.
post Grane. 26400 Crest. Drôme.
phone (75) 62.60.64 *Mich* 77 Valence 29 km

LAMASTRE   Midi

Comfortable hotel/Michelin★

Elie Perrier and his son, Bernard, like their hotel to be called
Hôtel du Midi – Restaurant Barattéro. No wonder, as this little
town, high in the wooded hills of the Ardèche, was made famous
by their old boss, the legendary, late Madame Barattéro – whom
Elizabeth David admired so much (see her *French Provincial
Cooking*). Nothing changes: the *pains d'écrevisses sauce
cardinal* and *poularde en vessie* are still prepared if you want
them – but, as many of you have rightly said, you are charged a
hefty premium for those two famous delights. An annexe has an
unusual central courtyard. Don't miss the metric-gauge 'steamer'
train – the Chemin de Fer du Vivarais. Lamastre is its terminus –
the track climbs over 250 metres in its 33 kilometres run up the
Doux Valley from Tournon. (If you need a large bath – the Midi
has them. Tell me if you know of others in France.)
menus **B-D** *rooms* 20 **B-C** *cards* Visa
closed Mid Dec-Feb. Sun evg/Mon (except July-Aug).
post place Seignobos, 07270 Lamastre. Ardèche.
phone (75) 06.41.50 *Mich* 76 Valence 40 km

MILLAU   Buffet de France

Comfortable restaurant
Good value   ®

This is the first of four restaurant recommendations in Millau;
together with a 'base' and a category two entry you have a wide
selection of places to choose from. The new name shown above
doesn't impress me; it's still the Buffet Gare as far as I am
concerned – one of the best in France. You'll have to refer
frequently to both the *Glossary of Menu Terms* and the regional
listings in Millau – particularly here: *confidou de bœuf, trénels*
and *jarret de veau* are a few examples. Bravo Albert and Janine
Négron! Be sure to visit them.
menus **A-B** *cards* Visa
closed Feb. Tues.
post 12100 Millau. Aveyron.
phone (65) 60.09.04 *Mich* 240

MILLAU   Capion

Comfortable restaurant
Good value

If you have an appetite at the end of a long day then this is the
place for you; it remains a mystery to me how the owners can
give you so much food at such low prices. Years back Michelin
awarded a star here; ironically, these days, no accolades from the
tyre men but all the other guides give some sort of award to
Blaise Trespaillé-Barrau. No prizes for the décor – but after you
have got over that initial trauma get out your *French Leave* and
do some menu-decoding: *salmis de colvert Cévenole, ris
d'agneau Rouergate, tripoux* and local cheeses. Basic fare –
'hardly subtle' one reader called it.

menus **A-B** *cards* Visa
closed Jan. Mon.
post 3 rue J.-F.-Alméras, 12100 Millau. Aveyron.
phone (65) 60.00.91 *Mich* 240

MILLAU   International

Very comfortable hotel/Michelin★
Lift

Two readers persuaded me to try the Michelin-starred restaurant
of this hotel – a huge 'skyscraper' of a place and quite out of
keeping with the town and the neighbouring hills. Sadly, as you
will also find with the following entry, I was not much impressed
by the cuisine. Do they really deserve stars? (I prefer the station
restaurant – it's cheaper, too.) Here it's classical cooking with
relics of the past like *tournedos Rossini, écrevisses flambées au
whisky* (see next entry) and *médaillon de porc Orloff*. If your
liking is for dishes like that, then the International is for you; but
surely you have not come to the Cévennes to eat the same food
you could be offered back home?

menus **A-C** *rooms* 110 **C-D** *cards* AE DC Visa
closed Rest: Jan. Sun evg/Mon (out of season).
post 1 place Tine, 12100 Millau. Aveyron.
phone (65) 60.20.66 *Mich* 240

MILLAU   La Musardière

Very comfortable hotel/Michelin★
Gardens/Lift

The most charitable thing I can say about my last visit here is
that, when you are the only client in the restaurant, you can
hardly expect the chef – Alain Gestalin – to rise to the heights of
inspired brilliance. Of course, I was travelling 'incognito' – so no
particular efforts were made. Even after making excuses for the
morgue-like atmosphere of the dining room, can Michelin stars
still be won for dull copybook specialities from the days of
Escoffier? Gestalin, once at the stoves of Senderens, a modern
master, can do better than this: *tournedos Rossini* and *écrevisses
flambées au whisky* (do they distil it in Millau?). Order regional
dishes – though they are pricey.

menus **A-C** *rooms* 12 **C-D** *cards* AE DC Visa
closed Nov-mid Mar. Rest: Mon (out of season).
post 34 avenue République, 12100 Millau. Aveyron.
phone (65) 60.20.63 *Mich* 240

PONT-DE-L'ISERE   Chabran

Very comfortable restaurant with rooms/Michelin★
Terrace   ®

One of the reasons why I have omitted two famous restaurants –
the Pyramide at Vienne and the Auberge du Père Bise at Talloires
– from this edition of *French Leave* is because frankly they are
both way past their best. Don't misunderstand me; the quality is
still good – but they are very dear and not really worth visiting.
Tourists from Britain and North America, wanting to get the best
value for their money, should seek out the exciting, younger
masters of French cuisine. You'll find one of them here: the
dynamic Michel Chabran, ably supported by his wife, Rose-
Marie; modern cooking in an ultra-modern setting.

Don't be put off by the fact that Michel's restaurant is on the
N7; his few bedrooms have been well insulated from the road –
many are at the back. (A geographical quirk means that it sits on
the 45th parallel.) Trained by one of the best chefs in France,
Jacques Pic, at Valence, Michel is already showing clear signs
that one day he, too, will become as great a chef as his brilliant
master. I can't pay him a better compliment.

I would have loved to have been a fly on the wall listening to
the Michelin inspectors discussing why they felt they should not
award Michel his second star. What possible reason could you
have Messieurs? Not for the first time you are wrong; your arch-
rivals, Gault Millau, get it right – they rate Chabran as one of
France's best with three *toques*. Make no mistake about it –
Michel is one of the best!

He rates Bocuse as the 'greatest' – he is Michel's 'hero'. My
Bocuse report is likely to upset Michel; I'll shock him further by
saying that, on the evidence of my many visits to their two
restaurants, I would rate Chabran superior to his 'hero' – or
should I say to Roger Jaloux (Bocuse's 'locum'). My evidence? A
superb *petite salade de St-Jacques*; some *rouget et céleri* – a
stunning surprise; a fabulous *ragoût de fins légumes*; and
exquisite sweets and *petits fours*.
menus **B-D** *rooms* 12 **B-C** *cards* Visa
closed Sun evg (out of season). Mon.
post Pont-de-l'Isère. 26600 Tain-l'Hermitage. Drôme.
phone (75) 84.60.09 *Mich* 77 Valence 9 km

PONT-DE-SALARS   Voyageurs

Comfortable hotel
Good value

Henri Guibert's *Logis de France* is about the only smart sight in
drab-looking Pont-de-Salars; the village is set between the two
man-made lakes of the area – terrain similar to parts of Wales.
Henri is another Cévennes chef who believes that his clients
must leave his restaurant weighing a few pounds more than
when they entered; it's all astonishing value for money. You'll
need to refer to the regional specialities list here: *tripoux, cou de
canard farci au foie gras, colvert au sang* and *salmis de colvert*
are a few of the alternatives guaranteed to send any
'weightwatchers' into a guilty sweat.
menus **A-C** *rooms* 36 **A-C** *cards* Visa
closed Oct. Mid Dec-Jan. Sun evg/Mon (out of season).
post 12290 Pont-de-Salars. Aveyron.
phone (65) 46.82.08 *Mich* 240 Millau 46 km

LES ROCHES-DE-CONDRIEU   Bellevue

Comfortable hotel/Michelin★

No other name could describe Jean Bouron's hotel more accurately; it's on the east bank of the Rhône and it overlooks the fast-flowing, wide river. As you would probably expect, Jean has a fine cellar of Rhône Valley wines; the **Côte Rôtie** ones come from the vineyards on the hills you can see from the hotel – on the opposite bank and to the north.

No complaints have arrived from any readers – yet Gault Millau have dropped the hotel completely from their guide. Jean has been joined by his son, Pierre, and their cooking is of a modest standard – with a range of traditional dishes like *turbot braisé au Champagne, poulet aux morilles à la crème, filet de St-Pierre à la moutarde, gratin Dauphinois, pêche Melba* and *œufs à la neige au caramel.*

menus **B-C** *rooms* 20 **B-C** *cards* AE DC Visa
closed 1-15 Aug. Feb. Mon.
post 38370 Les Roches-de-Condrieu. Isère.
phone (74) 56.41.42 *Mich* 93 Valence 62 km

ROYAT   Radio

Very comfortable hotel/Michelin★
Quiet/Gardens/Lift   ®

It gives me great pleasure to see the fortunes of Michel Mioche and his charming wife steam ahead; their first Michelin star came a year or two ago and now they have acquired a second Gault Millau *toque*. Michel is an enthusiastic, passionate man – completely immersed in his craft and determined to polish up his skills at every opportunity. Interestingly, there are many facets to that cuisine skill of his; menus are a combination of classical, *nouveaux* and regional dishes. He is proud of one of his own creations – artichoke hearts with *foie gras* and a truffle sauce; his *assiette de poissons* was good – except there was far too much of it; and his five or six *sorbets* at least retained their flavours – not always the case in France. Admire the magnificent legacy left by Michel's father to the couple – scores of fine paintings, particularly those where the medium used was icing-sugar paste! They certainly brighten up the dull-looking hotel.

menus **C-D** *rooms* 26 **B-C** *cards* AE DC Visa
closed Jan. Feb. Rest: Sun evg. Mon. Hotel: Sun (Nov-Mar).
post av. P.-Curie. Royat. 63400 Chamalières. Puy-de-Dôme.
phone (73) 35.81.32 *Mich* 239 Clermont-Ferrand 4 km

ST-JEAN-DU-BRUEL   Midi

Simple hotel
Good value   ®

A modest *Logis* alongside the Dourbie; explore the gorges of the river and also the Trévezel and Vis Valleys. Back at the Papillon's Midi savour the freshest of local products – put to really effective use in their menus: *truites, champignons des Causses, omelette aux cèpes* and *omelette au Roquefort.*

menus **A-B** *rooms* 20 **A-B**
closed Mid Nov-Mar.
post St-Jean-du-Bruel. 12230 La Cavalerie. Aveyron.
phone (65) 62.26.04 *Mich* 240 Millau 41 km

ST-PERAY   Host. du Château

Very comfortable restaurant/Michelin★
Terrace

I have had a stack of letters from readers who followed my
advice 'to the letter': they thoroughly enjoyed Jean-Marc
Reynaud's light, value-for-money cooking at his picturesque
miniature château – tower and all. It's a few kilometres north of
St-Péray, at Châteaubourg. They were then more than thrilled by
the *déviation* they made up the steep hillsides to the spectacular
viewpoint of St-Romain-de-Lerps. Did they see all of the 38
ceramic tiles which illustrate the fantastic views from the
observation platform? The pleasures of the table include *salade
de canard rosé aux pommes, feuilleté aux asperges* and
aiguillettes de canard au St-Joseph. The headier pleasures from
the bottle include many marvels from the vineyards you can see
from the tower: **Hermitage**, **Cornas** and **St-Péray**. Interestingly
the *sommelière* here is Danièle Reynaud – Jean-Marc's wife.
menus **B-C** *cards* AE DC
closed Mid-end Aug. Jan-mid Feb. Sun. Mon.
post Châteaubourg. 07130 St-Péray. Ardèche.
phone (75) 40.33.28 *Mich* 77 Valence 10 km

ST-ROMAIN-DE-LERPS   Château du Besset

Luxury hotel/Michelin★
Secluded/Terrace/Gardens/Swimming pool/Tennis

My good fortune these days – since I started my 'enterprising'
enterprise – is that, though I pay my own way, all the bills are tax
deductible. But in the case of this luxury, 15th-century, restored
bastide, I am still saving the 1200-plus francs needed to have the
use of one of its six bedrooms – surely the most expensive in
France. Why? Each room is a page from French history; each
bathroom is out of this world. Some of us mortals can at least
afford to eat here; Alain Burnel, trained by Jaloux, Bocuse's
'locum', is a master chef – witness his *civet de canard* and *terrine
de homard aux truffes*. It took the owners, Roger and Suzanne
Gozlan, ten years to restore this man-made wonder; even if you
cannot afford to eat here, navigate down the lanes just to see the
place. No one will mind!
alc **C-D** *rooms* 6 **D4** (also 4 appts; cost?) *cards* AE Visa
closed Oct-Apl.
post St-Romain-de-Lerps. 07130 St-Péray. Ardèche.
phone (75) 44.41.63 *Mich* 77 Valence 13 km

ST-ROMAIN-EN-GAL   Chez René

Comfortable restaurant/Michelin★

St-Romain is on the west bank – *rive droite* – of the Rhône,
opposite Vienne. Henri Schucké's restaurant would win no prizes
for its setting – built, literally, in the middle of a traffic island!
Henri is a classical master: if that's your preference you'll enjoy
*paupiette de sole soufflée Dieppoise, escalope de loup Duglére,
jambonneau à la gelée* and *Marjolaine*.
menus **B-D** *cards* AE DC Visa
closed Mid Aug-mid Sept. Sun evg. Mon.
post St-Romain-en-Gal. 69560 Ste-Colombe-lès-Vienne. Isère.
phone (74) 53.19.72 *Mich* 93 Valence 72 km

ST-VALLIER   Voyageurs

Comfortable restaurant with rooms
Good value

On a hot August evening you will welcome the airconditioned
dining room at the rear of Jean Bouchard's restaurant. Recently
both the Voyageurs and its competitor, the Terminus, have won
Michelin 'R' accolades; and, as I have seen so often in France, that
brings out the best in both places. *French Leave* readers have
clearly benefited because your letters have had nothing
untoward to say about this *Logis*. It's a popular overnight stop for
anyone heading south or north on the autoroute – so book ahead.
Specialities: *gibier (en saison)*, *feuilleté aux truffes* and
aiguillettes de canard aux morilles.
menus A-C *rooms* 9 B *cards* AE DC Visa
closed June. Sun evg. Mon.
post 2 avenue J.-Jaurès, 26240 St-Vallier. Drôme.
phone (75) 23.04.42 *Mich* 77 Valence 33 km

SALLES-CURAN   Host. du Lévézou

Comfortable hotel/Michelin★
Quiet

If it hadn't already struck you by now on your travels across
France, Michelin one-star awards do vary from region to region;
here is another one where, on balance, I think it's an
overgenerous accolade. The cooking is good but not of one-star
quality. David Bouviala's repertoire includes regional specialities
and those from the classical school – like *ris d'agneau sautés
aux morilles*, *steack de canard aux échalottes* and *caille en
cocotte*; but where are the signs of the lighter touches that
surfaced a few years ago? The hotel is a 14th-century house with
an imposing tower and a dominating position, providing fine
views of the surrounding terrain. One thing is for sure; when you
explore that same countryside later, you'll certainly have it all to
yourself. Enjoy the nearby man-made lakes.
menus A-C *rooms* 25 A-C *cards* AE DC
closed Mid Oct-Mar.
post 12410 Salles-Curan. Aveyron.
phone (65) 46.34.16 *Mich* 240 Millau 37 km

TENCE   Le Grand Hôtel

Comfortable hotel/Michelin★
Gardens

What is Jean Placide up to? 'Grand' hotel it's not – it's a pleasant
enough family home in its own *parc*; but 'Grand' hotel-type prices
have caused many of you to shudder. The cost of ordering the
famous *pain d'écrevisses sauce cardinal* (a copy of the one at
Lamastre) has shot up like a rocket! These days the son, Pierre-
Marie, is behind the stoves. His classical menus include *feuilleté
de ris de veau aux gyromitres*, *gratinée de lapereau aux girolles*
and *cuisse de canard à l'Hermitage*. Superb local countryside to
both the east and south.
menus B-D *rooms* 18 C-D
closed Mid Nov-Jan. Mon evg/Tues (out of season).
post 43190 Tence. Haute-Loire.
phone (71) 59.82.76 *Mich* 76 Valence 80 km

VALENCE   Pic

Luxury restaurant with rooms/Michelin★★★
Gardens   Ⓡ

My last visit to Pic was a revelation. I arrived late one spring
evening at the end of the wettest day I had ever known in France,
feeling morose at being on my own. All that changed during the
next three hours; what followed was the best meal I have had in
France during the last few years. It was a magical performance –
each course a miracle of lightness (in the best Japanese style);
accompanied by the most memorable single bottle of white wine
I have ever enjoyed – a 1979 white **Hermitage**.

Why was that meal so superb? It was called a *Menu Rabelais* –
the most famous *menu dégustation* in France. Each course was
a frugal presentation; at the end of the meal you still had an
appetite, albeit small, which is the best compliment you can pay
any chef. I list the dishes as the menu described them: *noix da St-
Jacques au caviar*; *escalope de foie gras aux navets*; *soupe de
rougets aux huîtres*; *sorbet au marc de l'Hermitage*; *couronne de
loup et mousseline de truffes sauce oursin*; *aiguillettes de
canard et ris de veau lié de vin* (a dark red wine sauce);
fromages; *choix de desserts* and *friandises*. Everything was
magnificent – the *friandises* matching Girardet's *petits fours*.
The only debit on the score card had nothing to do with the
cooking – the dining room lacks 'atmosphere'.

For me Jacques Pic has now developed to a point where he
matches Guérard's skill – together with Blanc and Meneau they
are the four best chefs in France. Pic himself is the exact
opposite of Bocuse; quiet, shy and scorning the limelight – you
will not see him but he is there, in his kitchens. It has been a thrill
to see the development that has taken place since my first visit in
1955 when Jacques' father, André – in terrible health – was
fighting a losing battle to keep up standards. (He had his own
three stars in 1939; along with Point and Dumaine, he was one of
only three in provincial France.) It is an equal pleasure, too, to
know that Jacques' son, Alain, now works alongside him. Bypass
all the other three-star places in the Rhône Valley – make Pic
your first port of call.

The restaurant is well clear of Valence – to the south on the N7;
it has only four bedrooms and these are rarely available. Use the
Hôtel 2000; modern and comfortable, it's well clear of Valence on
the Grenoble road – parking is easy.
menus **D** *rooms* 4 **C-D** *cards* AE DC
closed Feb. Aug. Sun evg. Wed.
post 285 avenue Victor-Hugo, 26000 Valence. Drôme.
phone (75) 44.15.32 *Mich* 77

VALS-LES-BAINS   Europe

Comfortable hotel
Lift/Good value   Ⓡ

Albert Mazet was trained by Joannès Randoing at Montrond-les-
Bains; a marvellous pedigree which he puts to such effective use
at his popular *Logis* in this nice spa. Honest, basic dishes like
magret de canard aux cèpes and *truite au St-Péray*.
menus **A-B** *rooms* 36 **B-C** *cards* AE DC Visa
closed Oct-Apl.
post 07600 Vals-les-Bains. Ardèche.
phone (75) 37.43.94 *Mich* 76 Valence 90 km

NORMANDY

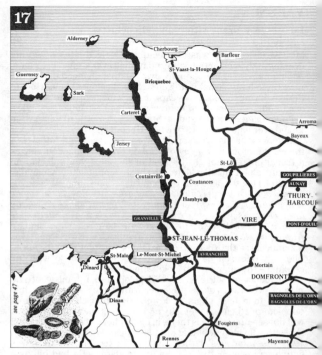

17

Many of my recommendations allow you to explore the entire length of the Normandy coast. Some are inland, ideally placed for enjoying the special pleasures of the surrounding wooded hill and valley country – often called *little Switzerland*.

In May, Normandy is an especially delicious place: its fields are full of wild yellow irises and its great apple orchards laden down with blossom destined to become that strong and fiery apple brandy, **Calvados**; it's all intoxicating country – in more senses than one. It is full of dazzling brown and white timbered cottages, many of them beautifully restored.

The immediate neighbourhood of **Caudebec** rewards you richly: there is the Church of Notre Dame in Caudebec itself and the nearby Abbey of **St-Wandrille**, founded 1300 years ago; on the north bank of the **Seine**, towards **Rouen**, are the ruins of another abbey at **Jumièges**. Two forests border the banks of the Seine – the Forêt du Trait on the northern side and the huge Forêt de Brotonne on the opposite bank. North-east of Rouen is the **Forêt d'Eawy**; to the east is the **Forêt de Lyons**.

Explore Rouen with its many historical sights. Further south lie **Pont-Audemer** and **Orbec**; the latter, luckily untouched by the last War, is a perfect French country town. On your way there make a detour via the Abbey of **Bec-Hellouin**, connected in various ways with William the Conqueror.

There are two coasts to enjoy. First the one running up from **Etretat** to **Dieppe** (the nicest of all the channel ports and a good standard of small resturants) – a magnificent coastline with lovely cliffs and many jewels hidden along it: **Yport**, **Veulettes**-

210

see page 222

VEULES-LES-ROSES

Varengeville-s-Mer — Dieppe

Veulettes-s-Mer

Fécamp

Yport

Bénédictine

Etretat

Caux

LE HODE

CAUDEBEC

CAUDEBEC

Tancarville

Le Havre

Honfleur

CONTEVILLE

BEUZEVILLE

PONT-AUDEMER

DUCL'AIR

Brotonne

Jumièges

St-Wandrille

Trouville

Deauville

Houlgate

OUVILLE

Dives

Pont-l'Evêque

Pont-l'Evêque

Monsieur

Vallée d'Auge

Calvados du Pays d'Auge

d'Auge

Calvados

Lisieux

Livarot

Livarot

Camembert

Mignot

Falaise

Argentan

Le Bec-Hellouin

Bernay

Orbec

Touques

Risle

Le Pin au Haras

L'AIGLE

Château d'O

E-EN-PAIL

Alençon

Sarthe

Mortagne-au-Perche

see page 160

Nogent-le-Rotrou

Forêt d'Eawy

Bondard

Bray

Brillat-Savarin

MONTIGNY

Rouen

La Bouille

Neufchâtel-en-Bray

Forges-les-Eaux

Carré de Bray

Coeur de Bray

Forêt de Lyons

Excelsior

LERY

ST-PIERRE-DU-VAUVRAY

VIRONVAY

Evreux

Seine

LES ANDELYS

Gisors

Eure

Dreux

Chartres

Bondon

Gournay

Beauvais

Mantes

Paris

Rambouillet

Amiens

see page 132

s-Mer, **Veules-les-Roses** and **Varengeville-s-Mer**.

The other coast, a flat one, goes west from **Conteville** across to the D-Day beaches of World War II. 1984 sees the 40th anniversary of D-Day; a new museum is being built at **Caen** and seek out the Merville Battery. The prettiest of all the seaports in Normandy is the one at **Honfleur**. There is sophisticated **Deauville** together with the smaller **Trouville** and **Houlgate**. There are many rivers to search out: **Dives** (the town of **Dives** is where William the Conqueror assembled his invasion fleet), Dorette, **Touques** and **Risle** are some of them. Further west are the towns of **Caen**, now rebuilt and still called the City of Spires, and **Bayeux** with its famous tapestry telling the story of the Norman conquest of England. Further west is **Coutances**, with its remarkable 700 years old cathedral. **St-Lo**, like **Le Pin au Haras**, has its own *haras* (stud farm); don't pass either by. The Cotentin Peninsula is popular with the British – **Carteret** and **Coutainville** will confirm why.

Bagnoles-de-l'Orne is bang in the middle of a Regional Nature Park. No wonder, as it is all marvellous forest country. Our special delight is the **Orne** Valley, between **Thury-Harcourt** and **Argentan**; our children remember to this day a short *séjour* at a farm south of **Pont-d'Ouilly**.

Michelin *yellow* maps: 231.54.55.59.60. Green Guide: Normandy (English)

IGN *série verte* maps: 6.7.16.17.18. *série rouge* map: 102

Airports: Paris. Nantes

Distances from: Paris-Rouen 139 km Calais-Rouen 212 km

211

Cheeses Cow's milk

Bondon (also called **Neufchâtel**) from Pays de Bray (north-east of Rouen). Small cylinder, soft and smooth. **Bondard** is related
La Bouille red-speckled, white rind; strong smell, fruity-tasting small disk
Bricquebec made by monks at the abbey of the same name. A mild-tasting, flat pressed disk. Available all the year
Brillat-Savarin mild, creamy disk – a triple-cream cheese. **Magnum** is the same cheese but much older
Camembert soft, milky flavour with a white rind, made as a small, flat disk. Available all the year and super with a **Beaujolais** wine
Carré de Bray small, square-shaped, mushroom-smelling cheese
Cœur de Bray fruity-tasting, heart-shaped cheese. Best in summer
Demi-sel mild, fresh and salted – made as a small square
Excelsior best in summer and autumn. Small cylinder, mild and soft
Gournay a one inch thick disk – slightly salty, soft and smooth
Livarot best in autumn and winter. Semi-hard, strong and gold. Spicy flavour – try it with a **Riesling**. **Mignot** is similar
Monsieur soft, fruity cylinder – strong smell
Pavé d'Auge (Pavé de Moyaux) spicy-flavoured, soft cheese, made in a yellow square. Try it with full-bodied reds
Petit-Suisse available all the year; a small, round, fresh cream cheese
Pont-l'Evêque rectangular or square shape, strong, soft and gold, at its best in summer, autumn and winter. First made in 13th-century

Regional Specialities

Andouillette de Vire chitterling (tripe) sausage
Barbue au cidre brill cooked in cider and Calvados
Cauchoise (à la) with cream, Calvados and apple
Douillons de pommes à la Normande apples in pastry and baked
Escalope (Vallée d'Auge) veal sautéed, flamed in Calvados and served with cream and apples
Ficelle Normande pancake with ham, mushrooms and cheese
Marmite Dieppoise a fish soup with some, or all of the following: sole, turbot, *rouget*, *moules*, *crevettes*, onions, white wine, butter and cream
Poulet (Vallée d'Auge) chicken cooked in the same way as *escalope Vallée d'Auge*
Tripes à la mode de Caen tripe – stewed, with onions, carrots, leeks, garlic, cider and Calvados
Trou Normand Calvados – a 'dram', drunk in one gulp, between courses; restores the appetite

Wines

There is nothing to say about wines in Normandy but, on the other hand, don't overlook the fact that **Bénédictine** is distilled at Fécamp. And what better compensation could there be than **Calvados**, another *digestive*; distilled apple brandy. There are no less than 10 classified Calvados regions within Normandy but the best is the Appellation Contrôlée **Calvados du Pays d'Auge**. This is a tightly specified area straddling the River Touques – the famous Vallée d'Auge country; see the list of regional specialities. This particular Calvados must be distilled in stills known as *charentais* – there are two production stages. And – last but not least – relish superb **cider**: *cidre bouché* – sparkling cider; *cidre doux* – sweet cider.

Additional comments

I am constantly amazed what poor value Normandy offers visitors on the restaurant front; it has been so richly endowed with the treasures of the earth – yet its chefs let it down badly.

Base Hotels

AVRANCHES   Central

Simple hotel
Quiet

The Central is a tiny hotel in a narrow street; it has a quiet site. My
American readers will want to see the Patton Memorial; it was
from this town that the American 3rd Army made its great
offensive eastwards in August 1944. U.K. readers should seek out
'La Plate-forme' – the spot where Henry II made his public
penance for the murder of Thomas à Becket. All of you should
see the Jardin des Plantes.
No restaurant *rooms* 10 **A-C** *cards* Visa
closed Mid-end Oct. Feb. Sat evg (Nov-Mar).
post 2 rue Jardin des Plantes, 50300 Avranches. Manche.
phone (33) 58.16.59 *Mich* 231 Rouen 225 km

BAGNOLES-DE-L'ORNE   Ermitage

Comfortable hotel
Quiet/Gardens/Good value

With an unusual stone exterior and in a quiet setting, this 'base' is
ideally placed for you to seek out the attractive vistas in the
immaculate spa: streams, a lake and several parks.
No restaurant *rooms* 39 **B-C**
closed Oct-Apl.
post 24 bd. P.-Chalvet, 61140 Bagnoles-de-l'Orne. Orne.
phone (33) 37.96.22 *Mich* 231 Rouen 166 km

CAUDEBEC-EN-CAUX   Manoir de Rétival

Comfortable hotel
Secluded/Gardens   ®

A picturesque spot high above the Seine – extensive views of the
river and, to the east, the unusual and massive harp-like supports
of the Brotonne Bridge. Prices are highish at this turreted,
creeper covered hotel; complaints have been made about the
lack of a relaxing lounge (a very common problem in France) and
lack of heat on coldish days.
No restaurant *rooms* 12 **C-D** *cards* AE DC
closed Nov-mid Mar.
post 76490 Caudebec-en-Caux. Seine-Maritime.
phone (35) 96.11.22 *Mich* 231 Rouen 36 km

GRANVILLE   Michelet

Simple hotel
Quiet/Good value

The Michelet is a severe-looking stone building, ideally placed in
a quiet but steep street not far from a beach and swimming pool.
Be certain to seek out the 12th-century **Hambye** Abbey: the tiny
village is a friendly place and is 'twinned' with a group of villages
near our home in the Chilterns; all of them doing their bit to keep
the *Entente Cordiale* alive.
No restaurant *rooms* 19 **A-C**
closed Mid Nov-Xmas.
post 5 rue J.-Michelet, 50400 Granville. Manche.
phone (33) 50.06.55 *Mich* 231 Rouen 230 km

LES ANDELYS
Chaîne d'Or

Comfortable restaurant with rooms
Quiet

Jean-Claude Foucault owns a 200 years old auberge with a site that must be the envy of many a Normandy restaurateur; sitting in the shadow of the ruins of the fortress built by Richard the Lionheart, it also overlooks the Seine. Possibly a category three entry as cooking is very good: *terrine de saumon, turbot aux aromates* and *filets de sole bonne femme*.
menus **A-B** *(alc* Sun midday **C)** *rooms* 12 **B-C** *cards* Visa
closed Jan. Mon evg. Tues.
post 27 rue Grande, 27700 Les Andelys. Eure.
phone (32) 54.00.31 *Mich* 231 Rouen 39 km

AUNAY-SUR-ODON
St-Michel

Comfortable restaurant with rooms (no showers or baths)
Good value

Another case where this *Logis* – handsome in its light-coloured stone livery – could be a category three entry. Gérard and Liliane Lermenier present classical specialities like *filets de St-Pierre à l'oseille* and *terrine de poissons*. Aunay was one of hundreds of villages devastated in the summer of 1944.
menus **A-B** *rooms* 7 **A**
closed Nov. Sun evg/Mon (except July-Aug).
post 14260 Aunay-sur-Odon. Calvados.
phone (31) 77.63.16 *Mich* 231 Rouen 153 km

BAGNOLES-DE-L'ORNE
Bois Joli

Very comfortable hotel
Quiet/Gardens   ®

A favourite with many of you; no wonder as this Normandy-style house – large, handsome and with a red and white exterior – is surrounded by trees and pretty grounds. No set menus; but a range of rich Normandy specialities. There's plenty of good walking country to keep the weight down.
alc **C** *rooms* 19 **C-D** *cards* AE DC Visa
closed Mid Oct-Easter.
post 61140 Bagnoles-de-l'Orne. Orne.
phone (33) 37.92.77 *Mich* 231 Rouen 166 km

CABOURG
Host. Moulin du Pré

Very comfortable restaurant with rooms
Secluded/Gardens   ®

From the flood of letters I have received from *French Leave* readers I know that many of you love the Moulin with its brown and white annexe and its charming grounds, small lake and stream. Cooking is of a high standard – as many of you appreciated the family efforts. The Moulin is 200 metres from the D513, eight km from Cabourg, towards Caen.
alc **B-C** *rooms* 10 **B-C**
closed Oct. 1-15 Mar. Sun evg/Mon (except July-Aug).
post route de Gonneville, 14860 Ranville. Calvados.
phone (31) 78.83.68 *Mich* 231 Rouen 118 km

214

CAEN
Novotel

Very comfortable hotel
Swimming pool/Lift

Well clear of Caen – on the northern bypass. Ignore the grill; use it as an overnight stop if you want to eat at the nearby Manoir d'Hastings at Bénouville. There's plenty to attract you down the hill at Caen, too. (See page 320.)
Ignore restaurant *rooms* 127 **D** *cards* AE DC Visa
closed Open all the year.
post route de Douvres, 14000 Caen. Calvados.
phone (31) 93.05.88 *Mich* 231 Rouen 124 km

CAUDEBEC-EN-CAUX
Marine

Comfortable hotel
Lift

A new owner is installed here now; Françoise Charlet is determined to restore the reputation the Marine had years ago before Maurice Lalonde, the previous owner-chef, let it slip badly. Mostly complimentary letters arrive at Amersham though there was one serious complaint about service. It overlooks the Seine, and despite rooms insulated against noise some of you have complained about dredgers; when we were there last year there were no signs of those noisy things.
menus **B-C** *rooms* 33 **B-C** *cards* AE DC Visa
closed Mid Dec-Jan.
post 76490 Caudebec-en-Caux. Seine-Maritime.
phone (35) 96.20.11 *Mich* 231 Rouen 36 km

GOUPILLIERES
Auberge du Pont de Bric

Comfortable restaurant with rooms (no showers or baths)
Secluded/Gardens/Good value   Ⓡ

You will not need a second mortgage to enjoy the simple style of this small building in an isolated site on the west bank of the Orne. The only sound you'll hear will be the weir – one of many on the river. Normandy raw materials are to the fore in many dishes – examples are *poulet au cidre, turbot sauce Normande* (cream) and *tarte Normande.*
menus **A-B** *rooms* 6 **A** *cards* Visa
closed 1-15 Oct. Feb. Wed.
post Goupillières. 14210 Evrecy. Calvados.
phone (31) 79.37.84 *Mich* 231 Rouen 144 km

MONTIGNY
Atlas

Comfortable hotel
Quiet/Gardens

Many readers took my advice and used the modern Atlas as a base hotel to explore Rouen – some ignoring its restaurant; no complaints were received about the latter. The village is surrounded by beech forests; it's two km north of the D982.
menus **A-C** *rooms* 22 **C** *cards* AE Visa
closed Rest: Aug. Sun.
post Montigny. 76380 Canteleu. Seine-Maritime.
phone (35) 36.05.97 *Mich* 231 Rouen 8 km

PONT-D'OUILLY
Commerce

Simple hotel
Gardens/Good value

I used this hotel for the first time 20 years ago – and stayed at an annexe called the Clos Fleuri, south of the village and on the other bank of the Orne. Last year I confirmed that the menus still feature regional and classical dishes: *veau Vallée d'Auge* and *tournedos sauce poivre* are examples.

menus **A-B** *rooms* 15 **A-B**
closed Jan. Sun evg/Mon (except June-Sept).
post 14690 Pont-d'Ouilly. Calvados.
phone (31) 69.80.16 *Mich* 231 Rouen 138 km

PUTANGES-PONT-ECREPIN
Lion Verd

Simple hotel
Good value

There's gorgeous country in all directions – it shows off the gentler touches of Mother Nature. Man has contributed some legacies, too: Falaise, Carrouges and Château d'O. It's a smart stone building alongside the Orne. Local products are the mainstay of the menus: ham, trout, pork, cider and cream.

menus **A-B** *rooms* 20 **A-B**
closed Xmas-Jan.
post 61210 Putanges-Pont-Ecrepin. Orne.
phone (33) 35.01.86 *Mich* 231 Rouen 140 km

ST-PIERRE-DU-VAUVRAY
Host. St-Pierre

Very comfortable hotel
Quiet/Gardens/Lift

Some may call this triangular-shaped, Normandy-style building attractive – to me it's a bit of an eyesore. But its site alongside the Seine is pleasant – it merits the *Relais du Silence* label. Cuisine is modest with a vast list of classical specialities: *rable de lapin et sa sauce au cidre* and *pièce de bœuf grillée* are just two typical examples.

menus **B-C** *rooms* 16 **B-D** *cards* DC Visa
closed Rest: Jan. Feb. Tues. Wed midday.
post 27430 St-Pierre-du-Vauvray. Eure.
phone (32) 59.93.29 *Mich* 231 Rouen 33 km

VIRONVAY
Les Saisons

Comfortable hotel
Secluded/Gardens/Tennis

The 'hotel' is in fact a number of black and white cottages that ring a picturesque, flower-filled garden. It's well clear of the nearby autoroute. Though winning no accolades for cuisine, I thought Christian and Françoise Bouchinet put up a fair showing with their cooking; extremely conventional, safe stuff with no modern 'risks' taken whatsoever.

menus **B-C** *rooms* 14 **C-D** *cards* DC Visa
closed Mid-end Aug. Feb. Sun evg. Mon (except hotel).
post Vironvay. 27400 Louviers. Eure.
phone (32) 40.02.56 *Mich* 231 Rouen 31 km

Recommendations where cuisine takes pride of place

L'AIGLE
Dauphin

Very comfortable hotel/Michelin★

Some would call both the old-established hotel – owned by the same Bernard family for over five decades – and the cuisine dull; perhaps, but it's places like this that are the heart and soul of the French hotel and restaurant scene. It's a warm comfortable hotel – with an equally warm welcome from Michel Bernard. If you admire old-fashioned ways you will relish the classical and regional treats from the kitchens – most of them unchanged over the decades: *langouste au porto* and *filets de sole Normande* are just two examples.

menus **B-C** *rooms* 24 **B-D** *cards* AE DC Visa
closed Open all the year.
post 61300 L'Aigle. Orne.
phone (33) 24.43.12 *Mich* 231 Rouen 107 km

BENOUVILLE
Manoir d'Hastings

Very comfortable restaurant/Michelin★★
Gardens

The Manoir is a 17th-century priory – converted with flair and sympathy. A short distance away is Pegasus Bridge – the scene of the British airborne landing on the night of June 5/6 1944. The Café Gondrée there claims to have been the first building to be liberated in France – early on the morning of the 6th. There's also a small museum alongside the bridge.

Claude Scaviner wins an unanimous vote from all the major guides as the best chef in Normandy; by this region's poor standards they are probably right. But he failed to match that reputation on our last visit – a series of miserable disappointments. Why? Two examples: a *filet de sole en sabayon de poireaux et de truffes* – the sole was cold and tasteless and the sauce absurdly rich; a third-rate *le grand dessert* in which the *pâtissier's* attempts at 'decoration' work were banal and corny – I've seen under tens do better in a local cooking competition. Check *l'addition*: our fixed-price menu courses were charged out at à la carte prices! Plus points? No purées in sight and a pot of good coffee left at the table.

menus **B-D** *cards* AE DC Visa
closed 1-15 Oct. 1-15 Feb. Sun evg. Mon.
post 14970 Bénouville. Calvados.
phone (31) 93.30.89 *Mich* 231 Rouen 120 km

BEUZEVILLE
Aub. Cochon d'Or

Comfortable restaurant with rooms
Good value

Long before you arrive at this modern *Logis* you'll be able to guess correctly the sort of choice Charles Folleau will provide: *andouillette grillée, tripes au Calvados, filet de sole Normande* and *poulet Vallée d'Auge*. (The Petit Castel – modernised, gardens and *sans restaurant* – is across the road and is also owned by Monsieur Folleau. A useful 'base'?)

menus **A-B** *rooms* 7 **B** (Pet. Castel 16 **C**) *cards* Visa
closed Mid Dec-mid Jan. Mon.
post 27210 Beuzeville. Eure.
phone (32) 57.70.46 *Mich* 231 Rouen 55 km

CONTEVILLE   Auberge du Vieux Logis

Very comfortable restaurant/Michelin★

Yves Louet is a *Maître Cuisinier de France* – one of over 300 men who have worked hard to win that title. (Incidentally it's a 'closed shop' – because as you flick through the pages of their promotional booklet you will not see a lady's face in it.) Yves is skilled and successful – like his colleagues; but his restaurant has become expensive, trading in on the hordes of tourists who visit Normandy, and the rich citizens of Deauville, keen to spend their francs at the few good restaurants in the neighbourhood. At his Auberge – some delightful brown and white cottages – he still does well with the safe dishes he knows best: *canard au cidre*, *civet de ris de veau* and some real Normandy classics. But, thankfully, many newer, brighter touches have surfaced – like *salade chaude de caille au foie gras* and *terrine aux trois poissons à la crème de ciboulette*.
alc **B-C** *cards* AE DC
closed Jan. Feb. Wed evg. Thurs.
post Conteville. 27210 Beuzeville. Eure.
phone (32) 57.60.16 *Mich* 231 Rouen 60 km

DOMFRONT   Poste

Comfortable hotel

Michelin and Yvette Le Prisé well and truly fell out with each other a year or two ago – her star went up in smoke! There are endless places doing basic things really well – some are worth the accolade, some are not. Michelin can be inconsistent in their standards from region to region. Clearly something upset them; whatever it was my readers have not spotted it. The Poste makes no apologies for being out and out champions of Normandy cooking: *tripes, andouillettes, poulet Vallée d'Auge, caille Normande* and other classics – supported by splendid local cheeses. Domfront itself has a fine site on a rocky hill; explore the ruined keep with its gardens and enjoy the extensive views to the south over the Mayenne Valley.
menus **A-C** *rooms* 28 **A-C** *cards* AE DC
closed Jan. Feb. Sun evg/Mon (Oct-Apl).
post rue Foch, 61700 Domfront. Orne.
phone (33) 38.51.00 *Mich* 231 Rouen 182 km

DUCLAIR   Parc

Comfortable restaurant
Gardens

What a mixed record Pierre Le Patezour's restaurant has had; I have received letters admiring the classical cuisine and I have received some from readers far from happy. As Gault Millau said: 'The cooking comes and goes like the barges on the Seine.' What everyone does like though is the setting – it overlooks the Seine and in the summer the attractive garden is a real bonus. Inevitably – with Rouen so close – ducks feature strongly on the menus! Ideal for a last lunch before you catch the ferry.
menus **A-B** *cards* AE DC Visa
closed Mid Dec-mid Jan. Sun evg. Mon.
post 76480 Duclair. Seine-Maritime.
phone (35) 37.50.31 *Mich* 231 Rouen 20 km

LE HODE   Dubuc

Very comfortable restaurant/Michelin★

Yet another Normandy restaurant where, immediately the first
star arrived, prices were jacked up. Louis-Philippe Dubuc meets
Michelin's Normandy standards spot on: fresh, local produce,
prepared in traditional regional style – copious and perfect for
those with healthy, sizeable appetites. Highlights continue to be
preparations like *salade du Hode*, *cassolette de langoustines* and
two different, magnificent sweets: a *tarte aux pommes chaude*
with fresh cream (worth a star) and an assortment of *petites
tartes tièdes*. The Dubuc is hard to find: if you are coming from
Tancarville, seven km after the bridge follow signs for 'Le Havre
– Port'; keep bearing right, avoiding crossing back over the main
road bridge.

alc C *cards* AE DC Visa
closed Aug. Mid-end Feb. Sun evg. Mon.
post Le Hode. 76430 St-Romain-de-Colbosc. Seine-Maritime.
phone (35) 20.06.97 *Mich* 231 Rouen 68 km

LERY   Beauséjour

Comfortable restaurant
Quiet/Gardens   ®

If you want to enjoy Normandy cooking at its best – in tranquil,
alluring surroundings – head for the Beauséjour, a real favourite
of mine. The anonymous, modern town of Léry makes it difficult
to find – but keep persevering until you come to a stop beside a
small church with a fascinating bell tower. After the war Franz
Nauwelaerts made a real name for himself here; sadly, he died
five years ago and, today, it's his widow, Hélène, who continues
the classical family traditions. You will be given a most gracious
welcome by her attractive daughter-in-law, Annie, and led to a
cosy, comfortable dining room. Two memorable dishes were
outstanding classics: *lotte à l'Armoricaine* – exquisitely sauced;
and an individual-sized *tarte chaude aux pommes* – mouthwatering enough, but accompanied by that lovely, slightly sour-
tasting Normandy cream.

alc B-C *cards* AE DC Visa
closed Nov. Sun evg. Mon.
post 27690 Léry. Eure.
phone (32) 59.05.28 *Mich* 231 Rouen 23 km

PONT-AUDEMER   Auberge du Vieux Puits

Very comfortable restaurant with rooms/Michelin★
Quiet/Gardens

A superb 13th-century Norman house – originally a tannery –
with a marvellous, timbered interior and the bonus of a pretty
garden set around a huge weeping willow. But as time has stood
still at the Auberge so it has with the cooking – 30 years on
Jacques Foltz offers the same dishes his father did before him:
truite Bovary au Champagne, *canard aux cerises* and *tarte*. It's
worth a visit just to see the old tannery.

alc C *rooms* 8 B-C *cards* Visa
closed Mid June-mid July. Mid Dec-mid Jan. Mon evg. Tues.
post 6 rue N.-D.-du-Pré, 27500 Pont-Audemer. Eure.
phone (32) 41.01.48 *Mich* 231 Rouen 52 km

PONT-AUDEMER   Le Petit Coq aux Champs

Very comfortable restaurant with rooms
Secluded/Gardens/Swimming pool

A *Relais et Châteaux* establishment where prices pinch: the Pommiers circumvent the new law which allows guests to eat wherever they want to, by providing both an à la carte meal and breakfast included in the room price. On your own the cost is over **D3** – for two sharing a room it's over **D4**!

Le Petit Coq is ideal for those of you who want luxury, a secluded setting and safe-as-houses classical cooking – at a price which makes this one of the most expensive 'roosts' in France. It's a series of thatched cottages, nicely furnished, set amongst flower-filled gardens; what a pity the interior has quite so many 'artificial' flowers.

Madame Pommier gives you a warm, charming welcome – nothing is too much trouble for either her or her husband, Francis. He is a classical cuisine fan – providing long-established specialities of the *jambon de Parme, coquelet grillé, côtes d'agneau, poire Belle Hélène* and *crêpes aux pommes* variety.
alc **C-D** *rooms* 10 (only ½ *pension* **D3-D4**) *cards* AE DC Visa
closed Thurs (out of season). Rest: Mid Nov-mid Dec.
post 27500 Pont-Audemer. Eure.
phone (32) 41.04.19 *Mich* 231 Rouen 58 km

PRE-EN-PAIL   Bretagne

Simple hotel
Good value

I complained about sky-high costs in the last entry – see above – but here there is no chance whatsoever of prices giving you or your bank manager a heart attack. Octave Lejeune's *Logis de France* must be one of the ugliest in France – and one of the noisiest, sitting at it does alongside the busy N12. You don't have to rest your head here – use the base at Bagnoles; but delight in Octave's amazingly-valued menus – cheaper than the cheapest Chinese or Indian takeaways back home!
menus **A-B** *rooms* 20 **A-C**
closed Mid Dec-Jan. Rest: Mon (Oct-Easter).
post 53140 Pré-en-Pail. Mayenne.
phone (43) 03.00.06 *Mich* 231 Rouen 170 km

ST-JEAN-LE-THOMAS   Bains

Comfortable hotel
Gardens/Swimming pool/Good value

The Bains, a *Logis*, is the epitome of what the Michelin 'R' recommendation means in France; exceptional value-for-money cooking with, in this case, a huge choice of dishes. The endless list of specialities include *soupe de poisson, saumon poché Joinville, coq au vin, jambon au cidre, sole meunière* and *gigot rôti*. From the beach at St-Jean you have fine views across the bay to the superb site of Mont-St-Michel. The Bains is a popular spot with holidaymakers.
menus **A-B** *rooms* 37 **A-C** *cards* AE Visa
closed Oct-Mar. Wed (out of season).
post St-Jean-le-Thomas. 50530 Sartilly. Manche.
phone (33) 48.84.20 *Mich* 231 Rouen 230 km

THURY-HARCOURT   Relais de la Poste

Very comfortable restaurant with rooms
Gardens

Monique Mouge and her daughter, Florence, have at last decided
to throw in the towel after their successful, but tiring fight to
maintain the excellent reputation the late Jean Mouge had
established over the years. 1984 will see the ladies at a *sans
restaurant* hotel in Colmar, Alsace.

    1984 will also see two enthusiastic couples battling away to
make their names at the Poste; let's hope the Fouchers and the
Engrands do well (the latter have returned to France from
Washington) and, along with other local delights, continue to
offer the Poste's memorable *tarte aux pommes chaude*.

menus **B-C** *rooms* 11 **B-C**
closed Jan. Feb. Mon (out of season). Please check.
post 14220 Thury-Harcourt. Calvados.
phone (31) 79.72.12 *Mich* 231 Rouen 150 km

VEULES-LES-ROSES   Les Galets

Very comfortable restaurant/Michelin★   ®

Les Galets is one of very few restaurants in Normandy to which I
would choose to make a *déviation*. Gilbert Plaisance, just 42, is a
fine chef; he and his wife, Nelly, offer remarkable, value-for-
money classical cuisine – full of light touches. On the debit side
there are some unhappy marriages of tastes and some plates
have far too much heaped on them. But even the basic menus
include delights like *saumon rose mariné au poivre doux*, *six
huîtres aux six parfums, feuilleté d'asperges à la crème de
cerfeuil, feuillantines aux fraises* and *gratin de fruits*. An
excellent appetiser, a variety of good *petits fours* and a supply of
plentiful coffee are all plus points at this comfortable and
colourful Normandy restaurant; make the effort to seek it out.
Another ideal place for that last lunch in France.

menus **C**
closed Feb. Tues evg. Wed.
post 76980 Veules-les-Roses. Seine-Maritime.
phone (35) 97.61.33 *Mich* 231 Rouen 57 km

VIRE   Cheval Blanc

Comfortable hotel/Michelin★   ®

What a splendid family enterprise this vine-covered *Logis de
France* is – in the centre of Vire and, sadly, not enjoying the
quietest of situations. Madame Emile Delaunay is still the 'boss';
but her son, Jean-Paul, is clearly the master in the kitchens these
days. He is hardly likely to desert the 'cream with everything'
traditions of Normandy cooking; *filet de sole Carville* is one of
many examples. But, increasingly, more and more newer
creations are springing forth from his imaginative hands – lightly
cooked and based primarily on fish. Remember that some of the
best *andouilles, andouillettes* and butter – salty and sweet –
come from this market town.

menus **A-C** *rooms* 22 **B-C** *cards* AE DC Visa
closed Jan. Fri evg/Sat midday (out of season).
post 2 pl. du 6-Juin-1944, 14500 Vire. Calvados.
phone (31) 68.00.21 *Mich* 231 Rouen 184 km

There is plenty to do, and see, providing you get off the beaten track. There are the magnificent beaches going north from **Le Crotoy** (a small fishing village on the **Somme** estuary) to **Le Touquet**; and also those to the west and east of **Calais**.

Some of the nicest villages lie in the valleys adjacent to that racetrack called the N1. The **Course** Valley runs south from **Desvres** to **Montreuil** and the **Authie** Valley runs roughly east-west (start from the N1, some 10 kilometres south of Montreuil, and aim south-east towards **Douriez**).

There are many towns worth some of your time. Amongst the smaller places are Montreuil (walk the ramparts and don't be faint-hearted about it; do the whole 360 degrees circuit) and **Hesdin** (where many of the *Maigret* episodes were shot). Surprise yourself completely by exploring on foot the delightful streets of **St-Omer**. Between the latter and Dunkirk – **Dunkerque** on the map – is the canal and dyke-lined terrain that helped the retreating British forces so much in 1940.

Further afield is **Arras** and the huge Grand'Place and the smaller Place des Héros, with its restored town hall. Arras is surrounded by many poignant memorials to the dead of World War I – many cemeteries have tens of thousands of graves. Further south are the Somme battlefields: stop and pay silent homage at the memorials of **Thiepval** and **Beaumont-Hamel** and contemplate the sufferings of previous generations.

Amiens is the biggest of the towns with its sublime cathedral, one of the most perfect in France, built 700 years ago. The church of **St-Riquier** (east of **Abbeville** on the D925) will reward a diversion to it a hundred-fold. Spend many hours searching out the battlefields of both **Crécy** (the great victory of 1346) and Agincourt. The latter – **Azincourt** on the map – sits to the east of the D928 between **Fruges** and Hesdin. Crécy is to the west of the same road but south of Hesdin.

Beauvais – its cathedral has the highest Gothic choir in the world – and **Compiègne** – full of treasures and with its history-filled forest – are bypassed by most A1 speeders.

Michelin *yellow* maps: 236.51.53. Green Guide: Nord de la France
IGN *série verte* maps: 1.2.3.4. *série rouge* map: 101
Airports: Paris. Lille
Distances from: Paris–Calais 294 km

Cheeses **Cow's milk**

Boulette de Cambrai a small, ball-shaped, soft, fresh cheese – flavoured with herbs. Available all the year
Edam Français a red ball without holes or with tiny ones
Gouda Français mild, yellow-coloured, small wheel
Gris de Lille a really salty square of cheese with a strong smell
Maroilles soft, slightly salty and gold. Appears in many regional dishes
Mimolette Française orange-coloured, ball-shaped cheese
Rollot spicy tasting, soft, small yellow disk – sometimes heart-shaped
Be certain to visit Phillppe Olivier's La Fromagerie at 43 Rue Thiers in Boulogne; it's one of the best in the North

Regional Specialities

Carbonnade de bœuf à la Flamande braised beef with beer, onions and bacon
Caudière (Chaudière, Caudrée) numerous versions of fish and potato soup served throughout the North
Ficelle Normande pancake with ham, mushrooms and cheese
Flamiche aux Maroilles see *Tarte aux Maroilles*
Flamiche aux poireaux puff-pastry tart with cream and leeks
Gaufres yeast waffles
Goyère see *Tarte aux Maroilles*
Hochepot a *pot-au-feu* of the North (see *Pepperpot*)
Marmite Dieppoise a fish soup with some, or all of the following: sole, turbot, *rouget*, *crevettes*, onions, white wine, butter and cream
Pepperpot stew of mutton, pork, beer and vegetables
Sanguette black pudding, made with rabbit's blood
Soupe courquignoise soup with white wine, fish, *moules*, leeks and Gruyère cheese
Tarte aux Maroilles a tart based on the local cheese (see Cheeses)
Waterzooï a cross between soup and stew, usually of fish or chicken

Wines

Champagne to the east – Calvados to the south-west: there is nothing to talk about in the North other than **Genièvre**, a gin drunk as a liqueur, served chilled, and made from grain and juniper berries; and truly excellent beer.

Additional comments

In previous editions of *French Leave* I wrote that standards of cuisine in the North did not compare too favourably with other parts of France. One of the happier changes in this edition is for me to record that things are looking up on the eating out front in the North – several new young chefs have brought a breath of fresh air to the restaurant scene. Note that there are no base hotels (*sans restaurant*); use the recommendations in the other categories for hotel accommodation.

Recommendations where cuisine takes second place

AIRE
Host. Trois Mousquetaires

Very comfortable restaurant with rooms
Quiet/Gardens

Attractive, wooded grounds and a quiet site are the main benefits of this 19th-century, Normandy-style château – on the outskirts of Aire and on the N43. The son of the owners, Pierre Venet, is the chef; average classical cooking – *magret de canard aux airelles* and *escargots en meurette* are typical.
menus **A-B** *rooms* 8 **B-C**
closed Mid Jan-mid Feb. Sun evg. Mon.
post 62120 Aire. Pas-de-Calais.
phone (21) 39.01.11 *Mich* 236 Calais 58 km

ARRAS
Univers

Very comfortable hotel
Quiet

Use the Univers as a base hotel; it's not far to the recommended category three restaurants. You will be surprised that such a quiet corner existed in Arras. It's a restored, 18th-century monastery with a cloister and tiny 'garden'. Parking is easy; and you are within walking distance of the marvellous Grand'Place and Place des Héros.
menus **A-B** *rooms* 37 **B-D** *cards* AE
closed Open all the year.
post 3 place Croix-Rouge, 62000 Arras. Pas-de-Calais.
phone (21) 21.34.01 *Mich* 236 Calais 117 km

CALAIS
Meurice

Very comfortable hotel
Quiet/Gardens/Lift

These days you don't have to eat at the Meurice; its restaurant, La Diligence, is run as a separate business. Use the Meurice as a 'base' and drive out to the better restaurants at Ardres, Marquise and Wiméreux as examples. Considering the comfortable nature of this quiet place, bedroom prices are modest; compare them with the equivalent scandalous costs across the Channel.
Ignore restaurant *rooms* 40 **C** *cards* AE DC Visa
closed Open all the year.
post 5 rue E.-Roche, 62100 Calais. Pas-de-Calais.
phone (21) 34.57.03 *Mich* 236

DUNKERQUE
Novotel

Comfortable hotel
Quiet/Gardens/Swimming pool

The Novotel is recommended for one reason only – use it as a 'base' and enjoy the superb cuisine of the best chef in the North, at Teteghem. The Novotel is off the N225, on the east side, as you head towards Lille. Use the D252B and D2 to reach Teteghem. Indoor pool. Ignore the grill. (See page 320.)
Ignore restaurant *rooms* 52 **C-D** *cards* AE DC Visa
closed Open all the year.
post Z.I. Petite Synthe, 59380 Bergues. Nord.
phone (28) 65.97.33 *Mich* 236 Calais 50 km

Château d'O (Normandy)

The northern slopes of the Lubéron – near Bonnieux (Provence)

Vieille Ville, Grasse (Côte d'Azur)

Frank Clancy

HESDIN   **Trois Fontaines**

Simple hotel
Quiet/Gardens/Good value

You're not expected to eat at this recently-built, whitewashed hotel – south of the town and well clear of any main road. Use it as a 'base' – it provides inexpensive overnight accommodation allowing you to use the restaurants at Montreuil. I've received complaints that 'service is offhand'. Cooking standards are very modest indeed.

menus **A-B** *rooms* 10 **B-C** *cards* Visa
closed 7-21 Sept. Rest: Sun evg. Fri.
post 16 rte. Abbeville, 62140 Hesdin. Pas-de-Calais.
phone (21) 06.81.65 *Mich* 236 Calais 99 km

TILQUES   **Le Vert Mesnil**

Comfortable hotel
Secluded/Gardens/Tennis

A 19th-century château in extensive grounds; though it's in an isolated position, it's well signposted from the N43. If you cannot book one of the rooms at the Lumbres restaurant – sleep here. If you must eat here expect nothing more than straightforward fare: *tournedos Rossini* and crab cocktails are not normal French 'gastronomic experiences'.

Visit the hideous Blockhaus d'Eperlecques north of Tilques; a ghastly concrete monument to the deadly V2 rockets.
menus **A-B** *rooms* 40 **C-D** *cards* Visa
closed Rest: Sat midday.
post Tilques. 62500 St-Omer. Pas-de-Calais.
phone (21) 98.28.99 *Mich* 236 Calais 37 km

LE TOUQUET-PARIS-PLAGE   **Ibis**

Comfortable hotel
Secluded/Swimming pool

A new hotel overlooking the beach. It's cheaper than the adjoining Novotel; they're connected by a passageway that stretches across a magnificent, indoor, heated, sea-water swimming pool – which they share. Ignore the grill.
Ignore restaurant *rooms* 72 **C-D** *cards* Visa
closed Open all the year.
post 62520 Le Touquet-Paris-Plage. Pas-de-Calais.
phone (21) 05.36.90 *Mich* 236 Calais 66 km

LE TOUQUET-PARIS-PLAGE   **Novotel**

Very comfortable hotel
Secluded/Swimming pool/Lift

All the advantages of the Ibis but just a bit more luxury. It's one of the best of the Novotel chain – but, as always, miss the grill and use the category three restaurants. Book in the U.K. and the U.S.; see page 320 for details.
Ignore restaurant *rooms* 104 **D-D2** *cards* AE DC Visa
closed Open all the year.
post 62520 Le Touquet-Paris-Plage. Pas-de-Calais.
phone (21) 05.24.00. *Mich* 236 Calais 66 km

ARDRES   Grand Hôtel Clément

Comfortable hotel
Quiet/Gardens

I have known this popular, attractive hotel for two decades; I omitted it from the previous editions of *French Leave* because I felt its standards had slipped badly over the years. Now things are looking up just a bit; I suspect the reason is that François, the young son of Paul and Monique Coolen, is bringing his training at Georges Blanc's home at Vonnas (Lyonnais) to bear on the old classical traditions of his father. Like all Flemish cooking there tends to be a 'cream with everything' approach – why not try modern specialities like *pâté chaud de brochet sur lit d'oseille* and *noix de St-Jacques aux dés de tomates*. Perhaps I should have included this hotel in category two? Or should I have left it out all together? Let me know.
menus **B-D** *rooms* 18 **B-C** *cards* Visa
closed Mid Jan-mid Feb. Mon and Tues midday (Oct-Mar).
post 62610 Ardres. Pas-de-Calais.
phone (21) 35.40.66 *Mich* 236 Calais 17 km

ARRAS   Ambassadeur

Very comfortable restaurant/Michelin★

Probably the best of all France's 'Buffets de Gare' restaurants; though my favourite is at Millau (Massif Central). You will find none of the modern trends here towards small helpings; their bread and butter clients are the locals and northern stomachs – particularly in the winter – need filling. If you want to enjoy the specialities of the North this is where you should sit down and tuck in: *tarte aux maroilles, flamiche aux poireaux* (individual size), *ficelles à la Picarde* and many more are on the menu. Otherwise it's mainly fish and grills (in huge quantities); first-class, helpful service.
menus **A-B** *cards* AE DC Visa
closed Sun evg.
post Buffet Gare, 62000 Arras. Pas-de-Calais.
phone (21) 23.29.80 *Mich* 236 Calais 117 km

ARRAS   Chanzy

Comfortable restaurant with rooms

Since Anne and I first tried the Chanzy 20 years ago, little seems to have changed – though Jean de Troy has now joined his father, Robert, at their family restaurant, literally floating on a sea of wine. Can you visualise their cellars with a reputed 100,000 bottles of wine – with 1000 different labels and some dating back over 100 years? To prove it they will give you postcards illustrating the cellars. You have three dining rooms to choose from: a brasserie, a grill and a traditional restaurant. Loosen your belts, don't wear your tight jeans and breathe in: *carbonnade de bœuf Flamande, ragoût de turbot, boudin sucré poêlé aux deux pommes* and a *tarte Flamande* should all help to set you up for a week or longer!
menus **A-B** *rooms* 23 **B-C** *cards* AE DC Visa
closed Open all the year.
post 8 rue Chanzy, 62000 Arras. Pas-de-Calais.
phone (21) 21.02.02 *Mich* 236 Calais 117 km

BOULOGNE-SUR-MER   La Matelote
Very comfortable restaurant/Michelin★   ®

At last some fresh air has blown in from the Atlantic and done wonders for the Boulogne restaurant scene. Young Tony Lestienne, not yet 30, is the revelation that you should seek out and help to encourage. You start by appreciating the light, airy feel of his dining room – various shades of yellow and lemon brighten you up as you study the menu. A clever appetiser encourages you further – a mini, 'folded-napkin' *brioche* with a smoked ham interior. You will wonder if this can be the Pas-de-Calais as your eyes wander down the menu: *fricassée de moules aux pistils de safran, St-Jacques en papillote, nage de turbot au sabayon de fines herbes, gigot de lotte braisé à la fondue de poireaux.* Between the four of us, my family tried those specialities and others; all of them were light, attractive and tasty – modern cooking at its best. Didier Painset, the young *maître d'hôtel*, speaks good English.

alc C *cards* Visa
closed Mid-end June. Xmas-mid Jan. Sun evg. Tues.
post 80 bd. Ste-Beuve, 62200 Boulogne-sur-Mer. P.-de-C.
phone (21) 30.17.97 *Mich* 236 Calais 34 km

ELINCOURT-STE-MARGUERITE   Château de
                                       Bellinglise
Comfortable hotel
Secluded/Gardens/Tennis   ®

In previous editions I suggested you use this handsome, 16th-century château, in its hidden, seductive fold of hills to the north of Compiègne, as a base hotel – eating at nearby Roye. But many of you have fallen in love with the place and have pointed out that the cooking is more than adequate and that the restaurant deserves a mention; well, I agree – though to be honest it only just deserves to squeak into category three. It's classical cuisine and there is no point listing obvious dishes. What is not so obvious is the setting: attractive woods, a pool, a park, peace and quiet – all perfect whether you want to stay put or take a walk. It still makes an ideal 'base' for the super restaurant at Roye.

menus B-C *rooms* 32 C-D *cards* DC Visa
closed Sun evg. Mon.
post 60157 Elincourt-Ste-Marguerite. Oise.
phone (4) 476.04.76 *Mich* 236 Calais 221 km

HAM   France
Comfortable hotel/Michelin★

This is one of those restaurants where you scratch your head and wonder why it wins a Michelin star. You leave convinced that you could do just as well; the French Michelin inspectors certainly have lower standards than their U.K. counterparts – the France would not win any accolades here. A vine-covered hotel, dwarfed by its neighbour, the Hôtel-de-Ville with its high belfry. Dull classical cooking in a dull town, surrounded by vast tracts of consecrated land.

menus A-C *rooms* 16 B-C *cards* AE DC Visa
closed Aug. Feb. Sun evg. Mon.
phone pl. Hôtel-de-Ville, 80400 Ham. Somme.
phone (23) 81.00.22 *Mich* 236 Calais 196 km

HESDIN H. Rôtisserie des Flandres

Comfortable restaurant with rooms
Good value

Not a word of complaint from any readers about this simple
Logis de France. Perhaps it should have been in category two –
but it's here because the fare, though modest, is good value.
Menus include *hors d'œuvre, truite à la crème, sole meunière*
and *coq à la bière.* No prizes for the banal restaurant décor and
the welcome could be warmer, too.
menus **A-B** *rooms* 14 **A-C** *cards* Visa
closed Xmas-mid Jan.
post 22 rue Arras, 62140 Arras. Pas-de-Calais.
phone (21) 06.80.21 *Mich* 236 Calais 99 km

LUMBRES Moulin de Mombreux

Very comfortable restaurant with rooms/Michelin★
Secluded/Gardens

A favourite with many *French Leave* readers; it's the
combination of the verdant setting with a reasonably high
standard of cuisine that attracts many of you. The Moulin is a
converted and restored mill, alongside the River Bléquin,
surrounded by trees and meadows; the restaurant is on the first
floor. What you have complained about are the thin walls
between the six bedrooms – not an uncommon problem in
France! (The weir is noisy, too.) There have also been complaints
that the cheapest menu has not always been presented. Danièle
Gaudry gives you a friendly, smiling welcome – and then her
husband, Jean-Marc, does his part to satisfy you; both of them
hail from the Touraine. Though you can eat more enterprisingly
in many of the region's other restaurants you will not be
disappointed with the fairly light classical dishes. The prices of
wines and liqueurs are scandalous; on behalf of readers I have
asked the Gaudrys to offer one or two cheaper alternatives –
shame on them if they don't. Specialities include *bavarois de
langouste sur un coulis de tomate et basilic, les paupiettes de
bar aux pistils de safran* and *carré d'agneau rôti.*
menus **C** *rooms* 6 **B** *cards* AE DC
closed Mid Dec-Jan. Sun evg. Mon.
post 62380 Lumbres. Pas-de-Calais.
phone (21) 39.62.44 *Mich* 236 Calais 52 km

MARQUISE Grand Cerf

Comfortable restaurant

Young Jean-François Lemercier is a first-class chef; he's highly
thought of by the locals, other chefs in the area, and my readers.
In 1979 he reached the finals of the *Meilleur Ouvrier de France*
competition – a marvellous achievement. Entertaining choices
between modern and traditional: *huîtres chaudes au
Champagne, lotte rôtie à la Waterzooï* and *caudrée de turbot* are
examples. The restaurant has eight basic bedrooms – but I have
no information on them; do let me know if you use them.
alc **B-C**
closed Sun evg. Mon.
post 62250 Marquise. Pas-de-Calais.
phone (21) 92.84.53 *Mich* 236 Calais 21 km

MERLIMONT   Host. Georges

Very comfortable restaurant/Michelin★
Gardens

If you visited Georges Chloupek's restaurant in the dark you
wouldn't be put off by the garish blue tiles on the roof. You would
however still be able to appreciate many other things: his
cheapest menu (not served on Sunday); the attention of both
Georges and his wife, Liliane; the fresh produce – particularly the
fish, and, depending on your taste, his classical-based
specialities. There are several soups, *homard* and *langouste
grillée* and *choucroute aux poissons*.
menus **A-D** *cards* AE Visa
closed Mid Nov-mid Feb. Mon evg/Tues (except July-Aug).
post 62155 Merlimont. Pas-de-Calais.
phone (21) 94.70.87 *Mich* 236 Calais 76 km

MONTREUIL   Auberge La Grenouillère

Comfortable restaurant   Ⓡ

It's quite different from the entry that follows; a series of tiny,
converted cottages, hidden by trees and alongside the River
Canche – all of it in the shadow of the red brick ramparts of
Montreuil. Roland Gauthier, trained at the Crocodile in
Strasbourg, and at Raymond Thuilier's three-star shrine at Les
Baux, is a beguiling *cuisinier*: is it the setting that adds to the
spell? Nothing old fashioned here – witness his *cassolette du
pêcheur aux fonds d'artichauts* and a *feuilleté d'escargots à la
tomate cresson*. First-class cuisine.
alc **B-C** *cards* DC Visa
closed Feb. Wed (out of season).
post à La Madelaine-sous-Montreuil. 62170 Montreuil. P.-de-C.
phone (21) 06.07.22 *Mich* 236 Calais 74 km

MONTREUIL   Château de Montreuil

Very comfortable hotel
Quiet/Terrace/Gardens/Swimming pool   Ⓡ

Since the last edition of *French Leave* appeared, significant
changes have occurred at this old favourite of ours. The previous
owners sold out and March 1982 saw a complete change. What a
rejuvenating shot in the arm Christian and Lindsay Germain have
given this attractive château-hotel. Christian was trained by
Michel Roux at the Waterside in Bray; Michel and Albert Roux
helped to persuade City contacts to finance this brave venture at
Montreuil. Lindsay is English, vivacious and the epitome of the
ideal hostess; she has two children but still supports Christian to
the hilt. Talk to them about their buying problems – and
Christian's weekly Rungis visit; see their modernised kitchen;
enjoy the redecorated bedrooms. Value-for-money lunch menus
– with extras like coffee and wine included. Modern cuisine with
classical touches – very much in the Roux style. Two *toques* from
Gault Millau in their first year was a just reward and an
encouraging start.
menus **C** *rooms* 12 **D-D2** *cards* AE DC Visa
closed Jan-mid Feb.
post 62170 Montreuil. Pas-de-Calais.
phone (21) 81.53.04 *Mich* 236 Calais 72 km

POMMERA   Faisanderie

Very comfortable restaurant
Good value   ®

Just one single complaint was received at Chiltern House about
the Faisanderie; but half a dozen complimentary letters arrived
praising the Dargent family enterprise and expressing thanks
that I had persuaded readers to seek it out. The restaurant is a
converted farm building and is not on one of the normal port
routes; visit it and enjoy the light touches of Jean-Pierre's
cooking – trained at Flavio in Le Touquet. What a refreshing
change his specialities make from those on offer at nearby Arras:
salade d'anguilles fumées de la baie de Somme and *homard
Breton aux petits légumes* are examples. During the week two
good-value menus are available.
menus **A-B** *cards* AE Visa
closed Aug. Feb. Sun evg. Mon.
post Pommera. 62760 Pas en Artois. Pas-de-Calais.
phone (21) 48.20.76 *Mich* 236 Calais 130 km

ROYE   La Flamiche

Very comfortable restaurant/Michelin★   ®

The new young chef, Wilfred Travet, not yet 30, has made a
fantastic start at one of my old favourites. Christine Klopp, the
sympathetic owner, has refurbished the interior of her dull-
looking, café-type restaurant with great style. What arrives on the
plate is anything but dull – attractive creations looking like
pictures: *rémoulade de coquilles St-Jacques au céleri et aux
noix* and *blanc de volaille de Bresse à la vapeur aux radis noirs
et à la mousse d'artichauts* were two examples. Wilfred's sweets
are a dazzling display of his light touch and brilliant talent.
Finally a word of praise for the first-rate, friendly *sommelier*,
Gabriel Laout. Don't rush by Roye on the A1.
menus **B-C** *cards* AE DC Visa
closed Mid Dec-mid Jan. Sun. Mon.
post place Hôtel-de-Ville, 80700 Roye. Somme.
phone (22) 87.00.56 *Mich* 236 Calais 199 km

ST-OMER   Bretagne

Comfortable hotel/Michelin★

It's a pity that more of you do not seek out the Bretagne –
surprisingly quiet, modern and, to be honest, a rather dull place.
But that's not the reason I ask you to go; support the efforts of
young Sylvie Beauvalot – one of the few lady chefs who has
managed to reach the highest levels of French cuisine. Talk to
her about her difficulties; enjoy classical dishes – like *foie gras de
canard* and *turbot aux poireaux*. If you want to save francs try
her husband's inexpensive Grill Maeva. Sadly, one serious
complaint arrived here – an indifferent welcome one evening
from a young male receptionist who then led his guests to a room
with an unmade bed!
alc Rest: **C** Grill: **B** *rooms* 33 **B-D** *cards* AE DC Visa
closed Rest: Mid-end Aug. 1-15 Jan. Sat. Sun/*fêtes* (evg).
       Grill: Xmas-New Year. Sat midday. Mon.
post 2 place Vainquai, 62500 St-Omer. Pas-de-Calais.
phone (21) 38.25.78 *Mich* 236 Calais 40 km

TETEGHEM   La Meunerie

Luxury restaurant/Michelin★   Ⓡ

For me there's no doubt about it; Jean-Pierre Delbé is the best of all the region's chefs. He is 34, self-taught, and a master *cuisinier* and restaurateur. He refuses to compromise in any aspect of his craft: you see it in his appetisers, his *petits fours*, his range of succulent sweets, his excellent choice of cheeses, his wife's fresh flowers and in a host of other ways. His innovative talents and his brilliant touches show best in his *nouvelle cuisine* creations – delectable presentations that would grace any three-star shrine: *terrine de rouget au gingembre, marmite des poissons de la côte au persil, caneton des Marais de Challans aux pommes*, exotic *sorbets* and super-light *millefeuilles*. Use the Novotel for overnight stays. The restaurant is on the D4 – south of the village. Don't miss it – I can't wait to get back there!

alc **C** *cards* AE DC Visa
closed Xmas-Jan. Mon. Sun and *fêtes* evgs.
post 59229 Teteghem. Nord.
phone (28) 61.86.89 *Mich* 236 Calais 49 km

LE TOUQUET-PARIS-PLAGE   Flavio-Club de la Forêt

Very comfortable restaurant/Michelin★

You can be certain of one thing: 'Flavio', who speaks fluent English, would win hands down any prize for the host with the most infectious enthusiasm and personality. This Pas-de-Calais legend reckons his restaurant is the best in the North and one of the best 100 in France. Wrong on both counts: it's expensive, it's good and the kitchens are run by a talented chef – Guy Delmotte. But a second-rate *soupe de poissons*, overcooked vegetables and a *bar* which was much too sweet were all minus points; excellent *sole* and fair sweets (but not the *sorbets* with lumps of ice) were better. The family accompanied me on my last visit – and, a day later, to Teteghem. The vote was unanimous; Delbé was superb – and cheaper!

menus **D** *cards* AE DC Visa
closed Jan. Feb. Wed (Oct-Apl).
post avenue Verger, 62520 Le Touquet-Paris-Plage. P.-de-C.
phone (21) 05.10.22 *Mich* 236 Calais 66 km

WIMEREUX   Atlantic Hôtel

Comfortable restaurant with rooms/Michelin★
Lift

What a mixed letterbag I have had: 'the beach and town are hideous', one reader wrote (I agree); 'too pretentious', 'unfriendly service' and 'exorbitantly expensive wines', were the complaints of three others. Lots of changes here in 1983; Michel Hamiot's son, Claude – aided by two young chefs, one trained by Girardet – now runs the kitchen. Good grills – but with such a fine selection of fresh fish, I suggest you give meat a miss. From mid November to mid December relish their *Kermesse au Poisson* – a fantastic choice of fish is offered on a special menu.

menus **B** *rooms* 10 **B-C**
closed Feb. Sun evg and Mon (Oct-Mar).
post 62930 Wimereux. Pas-de-Calais.
phone (21) 32.41.01 *Mich* 236 Calais 31 km

POITOU-CHARENTES

see page 46

see pages 276/278

There is no better example in this book of a region whose many charms are ignored by most tourists. It offers rewards to all ages; for children, eager to spend time on beaches or in the water – and to grandparents, perhaps just wanting to take things easy. The region divides conveniently into two parts: the coast itself (Charentes) and the area near **Poitiers** (Poitou).

The coast is renowned for its exceptionally clear light. The surest way of understanding why it has this world-wide reputation is to spend some time on the islands of **Oléron** and **Ré**. The former is my favourite; it has fine sandy beaches, quiet villages and, at **La Cotinière**, the biggest shrimp port in France.

Royan is a good resort with beaches to delight children; it was damaged extensively during the last War. Don't miss the new cathedral; one of the best examples of what modern architects can do. **St-Palais** is smaller and has extensive woods to its north-west. **Marennes** and the vast Parcs à Huîtres is famous for its excellent oysters (read the restaurant entry for **Bourcefranc** for a further explanation). To the north is **La Rochelle**, a Protestant stronghold with so many intricate historical links with the past. It is a port of great vitality with its backdrop of massive medieval towers – it will interest every visitor.

Inland from Rochefort is **Saintes**, once the Roman capital of Western Gaul; it is still endowed with some fine remains. Further east along the **Charente** Valley (use the minor roads alongside the river – not the main road) is **Cognac**, a name as well-known as Paris itself. **Niort** and **Angoulême** deserve your time;

see page 160

see page 40

Tours

Vierzon

Loches

Valençay

Vins du
Haut-Poitou

LE GRAND-
PRESSIGNY

Châtellerault

PREUILLY-
S-CLAISE

Issoudun

LA ROCHE-POSAY

Tournon-St-Pierre

Pouligny-St-Pierre

Fontgombault

Châteauroux

CHAUVIGNY

LE BLANC

Poitiers

St-Savin

La Châtre

Ligugé

Nouaillé-Maupertuis

VIVONNE

MONTMORILLON

Lac de Chambon

Pyramide

Lussac

Crozant

Couhé-Vérac

Montluçon

Guéret

Bellac

ST ETIENNE DE FURSAC

Moutier-d'Ahun

Ruffec

Confolens

ST-HILAIRE-
LE-CHATEAU

NIEUIL

PONT-DU-
DOGNON

BOURGANEUF

Aubusson

Limoges

St-Léonard-
de-Noblat

Peyrat-le-Château

Angoulème

NONTRON

Chalusset

Lac de Vassivière

LA ROCHE-L'ABEILLE

Plateau de Millevaches

Brantôme

see page 106

Brive

Signal d'Audouze
Suc-au-May

particularly the old parts within them.

North of La Rochelle is the hidden, unknown fen country of France – Marais Poitevin (*marais* means fen); here, every field is an island, where cows, goats, their milk and their feed and all the crops are moved by punt. You can make trips on these punts from **Coulon**, just west of Niort. Make absolutely sure you don't miss it all: Michelin map 71, for this corner of France, is a strange sight indeed. **Fontenay-le-Comte** is a fine, small town – to the north is the **Forêt de Mervent-Vouvant**.

The other half of the region is centred on Poitiers – a marvellous town and once capital of the Duchy of Aquitaine. But it is the nearby countryside, especially the old towns and sleepy river valleys to the east and south-east, that will enchant you; it is lovely country. South of the town, at **Nouaillé-Maupertuis**, the English archers, led by Sir John Chandos, won the famous battle of Poitiers. Adjacent to this famous battlefield is **Ligugé** with its 1600 years old abbey.

The hotels are ideally placed for you to explore the many treasures near at hand. The church at **St-Savin** is the best example of the Byzantine influence on so many of the Poitevin churches; the decorative murals and paintings are a highlight. Romanesque architecture flourished in the whole region – there are over 700 buildings that demonstrate the point and every village provides an example of these glories of the past.

Chauvigny, **Montmorillon** and **Lussac** are delightful, small towns; between them and St-Savin you can enjoy yourself for hours – a bonus are the valleys of the **Gartempe** and **Vienne**. Both **Châtellerault** to the north and **Limoges** (famous for its intricate porcelain) make worthwhile excursions. The **Creuse** Valley near **Le Blanc** and, to the east, a peppered landscape of *étangs* (small lakes) will give hours of pleasure.

To the north-east, east and south-east of Limoges is the lovely region called Limousin – hardly one of the more popular holiday areas of France, but its countryside is studded with benefits of a less obvious kind: utter peace and quiet; gentle scenic aspects; and hotels and restaurants where good value counts more than exceptional abilities with cuisine.

The Creuse Valley north of **Guéret** has long been adored by both painters and writers; and made famous by Georges Sand, Théodore Rousseau and Claude Monet. Seek out the ruins of what once was a powerful fortress at **Crozant** at the southern end of the **Lac de Chambon**. Further upstream is the man-made abbey church at **Moutier-d'Ahun** – its famous woodwork, carved 300 years ago, is superb. **Aubusson** is world famous for its tapestries and carpets. Three centuries ago over 400,000 Protestants fled from France – Aubusson is just one example of how many skills were lost to the country. Jean Lurçat has done much to restore those old traditions.

To the south and east of Limoges are many man-made attractions, ignored by most on their N20 dash south: the 12th-century abbey church at **Solignac**; the ruins of the equally ancient fortress called the Château de **Chalusset**; the old town of **St-Léonard-de-Noblat**; and, finally, the **Lac de Vassivière** – where every kind of water sport is available. Seek out the **Plateau de Millevaches** – a tableland of countless springs; many rivers rise there. Enjoy the views from the peaks called the **Signal d'Audouze** and **Suc-au-May**.

Michelin *yellow* maps: 233.239.67.68.71.72. Green Guides: Côte de l'Atlantique. Dordogne (English)

IGN *série verte* maps: 33.34.39.40. *série rouge* map: 107

Airport: Bordeaux

Distances from:

Paris-La Rochelle	471 km	Calais-La Rochelle	765 km
Paris-Poitiers	333 km	Calais-Poitiers	627 km

Cheeses Cow's milk

Jonchée from Saintonge area. Fresh cream cheese – served with sugar and cream. **Caillebote** is a similar cheese

Pigouille small, creamy-flavoured disk – served on straw. Can also be made from goat's or ewe's milk

Goat's milk

Chabichou Poitou area cheese: *Laitier* (dairy made) and *Fermier* (farm made) – small, truncated, upright cylinders; soft, sharp-tasting cheese

Couhé-Vérac soft, nutty cheese made in small squares

Jonchée from Niort area. Mild, soft, creamy – best in summer and autumn. A cheese called **Lusignan** is similar, made as a disk

La Mothe-St-Héray best in summer and autumn. A small disk, one inch thick. Try it with the reds of **Haut-Poitou**. **Bougon** is a related cheese

Pouligny-St-Pierre pyramid-shaped; strong smell, soft cheese. A cheese called **Tournon-St-Pierre** is related

Pyramide pyramid-shaped, soft cheese

Ruffec fruity disk, made in a small disk

Taupinière packed and served in chestnut leaves

Ewe's milk

Oléron best in spring; mild, creamy, fresh cheese. Made on Ile d'Oléron; known also as **Jonchée d'Oléron** or **Brebis d'Oléron**

Regional Specialities

Bouilliture (Bouilleture) a type of *matelote d'anguilles* – a freshwater eel stew in red wine, with shallots and prunes

Boulaigou thick sweet or savoury pancake

Bréjaude cabbage, leek and bacon soup

Cagouilles snails from the Charentes

Casserons en matelote squid in red wine sauce with garlic and shallots

Cèpes fine, delicate, flap mushrooms – don't miss them

Chaudrée a ragout of fish cooked in white wine, shallots and butter

Chevrettes local name for *crevettes* (shrimps)

Clafoutis pancake batter, poured over fruit (usually black cherries), and then baked – another treat you must not miss

Embeurré de chou white-heart cabbage, cooked in salted water, crushed and served with butter

Farcidure a dumpling – either poached or sautéed

Farci Poitevin a *pâté* of cabbage, spinach and sorrel, encased by cabbage leaves and cooked in a *bouillon*

Migourée a sort of *chaudrée*

Mique a stew of dumplings

Mogette (Mojette) small pulse beans in butter and cream

Mouclade mussels cooked in wine, egg yolks and cream; can be served with some **Pineau des Charentes**

Oysters for an explanation of *les claires, belons, gravettes, marennes* and other terms see the category three entry for Bourcefranc

Soupe aux fèves des Marais soup of crushed broad beans with bread, sorrel, chevril and butter

Soupe de moules à la Rochelaise soup of various fish, mussels, saffron, garlic, tomatoes, onions and red wine

Sourdons cockles from the Charentes

Tartisseaux fritters

Tourtou thick buckwheat flour pancake

Wines

The countryside of the Charentes offers the world its annual harvest of white grapes – a harvest that eventually matures into **Cognac**; brandy known as the finest on earth. The quality of Cognac varies with the fertility of the soil; this is why there are six districts. The best, **Grande Champagne**, is from the immediate south of Cognac town; the next four districts extend outwards to form a huge circle; the lowest classification is the coastal stretch lying alongside the Atlantic coast. Age is the other vital factor – the maturing process is all important. **Pineau des Charentes** is a liqueur wine (grape juice and Cognac); clear, sweet and heady – drink it cool as an *apéritif*.

Don't miss the chance to try some of the unknown locals of this part of France. The VDQS **Vins du Haut-Poitou** are a revelation: amongst them a **Sauvignon** white – just like its famous big brother from Sancerre; a **Pinot-Chardonnay** – the marvellous white grape of Burgundy; a **Gamay** red – best drunk cool; a dry rosé; and a dry, **Chenin** white. Some wine lists will describe the wines as **Poitou** or **Neuville de Poitou** – the main town of the wine-producing area.

Vins de Pays

Some really obscure wines will be recommended in the La Rochelle area: **Ile de Ré** and **Blanc de Ré** – dry whites from the Ile de Ré. You will also see a **Rosé de Mareuil** (a town in the Vendée); this is one of the wines, made in all shades, called **Vin de Pays de la Vendée** (the *département*) – also referred to by the marvellous name of **Fiefs Vendéens**.

235

Base Hotels

CHALLANS   Antiquité

Comfortable hotel
Quiet/Gardens

All 12 bedrooms overlook a 'garden' – away from the street.
No restaurant *rooms* **B-C** *cards* AE DC Visa
closed Sept. Sun (out of season).
post 14 rue Galliéni, 85300 Challans. Vendée.
phone (51) 68.02.84 *Mich* 67 La Rochelle 123 km

LA COTINIERE   Motel Ile de Lumière

Comfortable hotel
Secluded/Gardens/Swimming pool/Tennis

Don't be put off by the term 'motel'; single storey buildings,
overlooking the sea. Village is famous Ile d'Oléron shrimp port.
No restaurant *rooms* 45 **D**
closed Oct-Mar.
post La Cotinière. 17310 St-Pierre-d'Oléron. Char.-Mar.
phone (46) 47.10.80 *Mich* 233 La Rochelle 77 km

FOURAS   Résidence Le Parc

Comfortable hotel
Secluded/Gardens

Oldish building hidden in a wood – on the road to La Fumée.
No restaurant *rooms* 16 **B-D**
closed Oct-May (except Easter).
post 17450 Fouras. Charente-Maritime.
phone (46) 88.61.26 *Mich* 233 La Rochelle 27 km

NONTRON   Motel la Sapinière

Comfortable hotel
Quiet/Gardens/Swimming pool/Good value

Modern, single storey building – in wooded grounds 9 km north
of Nontron. Useful, too, for northern Dordogne restaurants.
No restaurant *rooms* 10 **B-C** *cards* Visa
closed Nov-Apl. Sat evg.
post Augignac. 24300 Nontron. Dordogne.
phone (53) 56.80.34 *Mich* 233 Poitiers 137 km

LA ROCHELLE   Les Brises

Very comfortable hotel
Secluded/Terrace/Lift   ®

West of the town centre; a classic example of how good a modern
'base' can be. It's five storeys high with a southerly aspect and a
distant glimpse of the Ile d'Oléron (one guide suggests views of
the Ile de Ré – hardly, unless you have a neck a few kilometres
long; it's odd Gault Millau made the same mistake!). Fine terrace
and superb bathrooms.
No restaurant *rooms* 46 **C-D** *cards* Visa
closed Mid Dec-mid Jan.
post digue Richelieu, 17000 La Rochelle. Charente-Maritime.
phone (46) 43.89.37 *Mich* 233

Recommendations where cuisine takes second place

LE BLANC
Domaine de l'Etape

Comfortable hotel
Secluded/Gardens
®

'Gardens' is a word that doesn't do justice to this charming hotel; it's a huge *parc* of over 300 acres. You can fish on the banks of an *étang* in the grounds. If you have children keen on riding, they can enjoy it here. Use the hotel as a 'base'; though inexpensive evening meals – for residents only – are available. South of the River Creuse – 6 km east of Le Blanc.
menus A *rooms* 20 B-C *cards* AE DC
closed Open all the year.
post 36300 Le Blanc. Indre.
phone (54) 37.18.02 *Mich* 233 Poiters 60 km

COULON
Au Marais

Comfortable restaurant with rooms
Quiet

A simple, smart *Logis de France*; it sits alongside the Sèvre Niortaise, the main river that runs through the unusual, but delightful Marais Poitevin. Perhaps this should be a category three entry – it has a Michelin 'R' recommendation; though I had a disappointing meal. Enjoy specialities like *matelote d'anguilles, mouclade Maraîchine* and *fines de claires*.
menus A-B *rooms* 11 C *cards* AE DC Visa
closed Mid Dec-Jan. Sun evg. Mon.
post Coulon. 79270 Frontenay-Rohan-Rohan. Deux-Sèvres.
phone (49) 25.90.43 *Mich* 233 La Rochelle 59 km

LA ROCHE-POSAY
Relais H. Château de Posay

Very comfortable hotel
Secluded/Gardens

In the extensive grounds of a pleasant casino; it's an attractive site and the modern hotel has fine facilities. Use it as a base hotel; dinner is available but you will do far better at the nearby category three recommendations.
menus A-B *rooms* 13 C-D *cards* AE DC
closed Oct. Rest: Tues.
post au Casino, 86270 La Roche-Posay. Vienne.
phone (49) 86.20.10 *Mich* 68 Poitiers 49 km

ST-ETIENNE-DE-FURSAC
Moderne

Simple hotel
Gardens/Good value

A modern, smart-looking building, opposite the church and within 50 metres of the infant River Gartempe. Cuisine is average standard at the Moderne – enjoy specialities like *pâté de canard, magret de canard, cèpes* and *écrevisses*; for a sweet, why not try *crêpes soufflées au Cointreau*?
menus A-C *rooms* 14 A-C *cards* Visa
closed Mid-end Oct. Mid-end Feb. Sun evg and Mon midday (mid Sept-May).
post 23290 St-Etienne-de-Fursac. Creuse.
phone (55) 63.60.56 *Mich* 239 Poitiers 118 km

Recommendations where cuisine takes pride of place

BOURCEFRANC   Les Claires

Comfortable hotel/Michelin★
Quiet/Gardens/Swimming pool/Tennis

Michel Suire was trained by one of the best chefs in France –
Jacques Pic at Valence. His light touch was clearly influenced by
that favourite master of mine; here you see it in the way he
exploits the legacy that his site gives him – fish and oysters play a
vital part in his repertoire. The hotel is a *Relais du Silence*, near
the bridge to the Ile d'Oléron.

Les Claires are the oyster-fattening beds that you see in the
local Marennes country. There are three types of **flat** oysters:
belons (from the River Belon in Brittany) and *gravettes* (from
Arcachon – south-west of Bordeaux) – these two are cultivated
on their home ground; *marennes*, the third type, are transferred
from Brittany and Arcachon to *les claires* where they finish their
growth. **Dished** oysters (sometimes called *portugaises*) breed
mainly in the Charente and Gironde Estuaries; these mature at
Marennes. *Fines de claires* and *spéciales* are the largest – *huîtres
de parc* are standard sized. All this lavish care covers a time span
of between two to four years.
menus **B-C** *rooms* 20 **C-D** *cards* AE DC Visa
closed Open all the year.
post 17560 Bourcefranc-le-Chapus. Charente-Maritime.
phone (46) 85.08.01 *Mich* 233 La Rochelle 54 km

BOURGANEUF   Moulin de Montaletang

Comfortable hotel
Secluded/Terrace/Gardens   ®

Jean-Luc and Nicole Delias own a gorgeous hotel; it's a restored
and secluded mill, alongside a stream, in the forests 13 km south
of the town (follow signs from the Limoges road). Their property
covers acres: *étangs*, streams and woods delight the senses. And
to top all this, Jean-Luc, influenced no doubt by his time at the
Auberge des Templiers at Les Bézards, is a master of the modern
ways: *estouffade de coquilles St-Jacques au gingembre* and
chausson de langouste au bisque are examples.
menus **B-C** *rooms* 14 **B-C** *cards* AE Visa
closed Mid Oct-Mar. Wed (Apl-June: mid Sept-mid Oct).
post 23400 Bourganeuf. Creuse.
phone (55) 64.92.72 *Mich* 239 Poitiers 150 km

CHAUVIGNY   Lion d'Or

Simple hotel
Good value

I'll give you one guarantee here: Monsieur Chartier's prices will
not bankrupt you. Modest cooking and with some enterprising
local produce and recipes appearing on the menus: *farci
Poitevin* and *aiguillette de Marais à l'ail* are typical. This *Logis*
is a fairly noisy spot; readers also recommend the Beauséjour, in
a quieter side street. Be sure to catch a glimpse of the châteaux at
Touffou and Dissay.
menus **A-B** *rooms* 27 **B-C** *cards* Visa
closed Mid Dec-mid Jan. Sun evg (Nov-Mar).
post 8 rue Marché, 86300 Chauvigny. Vienne.
phone (49) 46.30.28 *Mich* 233 Poitiers 23 km

LA FLOTTE
Richelieu

Very comfortable hotel/Michelin★
Quiet/Gardens/Swimming pool/Tennis

If you want to escape traffic, noise and congestion – the Ile de Ré is the place for you. The Richelieu has much the best reputation for cuisine on the island; the chef leans towards the light ways of today, and with such fresh produce available from the ocean each day he has an easy job to make a success of it. Specialities include *millefeuille de turbot, huîtres chaudes aux légumes, langoustines aux herbes rares* and super desserts. Jacqueline and Léon Gendre run a hotel that has style and a fine setting; the main building has the restaurant at the front – overlooking the sea and facing north. Small bungalows have extra bedrooms. Prices pinch hard at the Richelieu.
menus **B-C** *rooms* 24 **D-D2** *cards* Visa
closed Jan-mid Feb.
post 17630 La Flotte. Charente-Maritime.
phone (46) 09.60.70 *Mich* 233 La Rochelle 11 km

LE GRAND-PRESSIGNY
Espérance

Simple restaurant with rooms (no showers or baths)
Good value ®

Bernard and Paulette Torset have pleased so many of you – delighted by low prices, light cooking and the fresh, local produce that this talented chef uses. Only one discordant note was struck by a reader – a case of unnecessary overcharging for a room. Bernard will not be the first chef with a Michelin red 'R' recommendation to one day win a star; enjoy his *loup à la crème de cerfeuil, sandre poché au beurre d'échalotes, cuisses de grenouilles aux herbes du jardin* and good *sorbets*. Don't miss the local castle with its handsome keep.
menus **A-B** *rooms* 10 **B**
closed Jan-mid Feb. Mon.
post 37350 Le Grand-Pressigny. Indre-et-Loire.
phone (47) 94.90.12 *Mich* 68 Poitiers 63 km

MONTMORILLON
France

Comfortable hotel/Michelin★ ®

It's any eye-opener to see how an old family hotel can apply the benefits of modern thinking to their traditional talents. Well done the Merciers; whether you order a classical favourite, a regional dish or some creation of their own, you will be sure of a light touch applied to it with all the benefits that that implies. See what I mean by these examples: *pied de cochon farci, carré d'agneau Poitevine* and *pintadeau poêlé au miel aux airelles*. Those three dishes cover a wide span of type and choice. But please, don't order the *Menu Cru* and then complain that the France is a 'travesty of a restaurant', as Caroline Conran did; *foie gras cru au poivre*, some raw salmon and chopped raw beef is either to your liking or it isn't. 'I could have wept', she wrote. Why, for heaven's sake, did you order it Caroline?
menus **B-C** *rooms* 25 **B-C** *cards* AE DC Visa
closed Jan. Sun evg. Mon.
post 2 bd. Strasbourg, 86500 Montmorillon. Vienne.
phone (49) 91.00.51 *Mich* 233 Poitiers 48 km

MORTAGNE-SUR-SEVRE   France et rest. La Taverne

Comfortable hotel
Gardens/Swimming pool/Lift   Ⓡ

Guy and Marie-Claude Jagueneau are being cheated by Michelin
– they deserve to win their first star. (Gault Millau, already,
reward them with two *toques*.) The Vendée is a gastronomic
desert – Guy is much the most talented chef in the area; he makes
great use of local products in dishes like *foie gras chaud aux
échalotes* – a super success. The marvellous butter of the Vendée
(the best in France comes from nearby Echiré) is served here
from a huge, football-sized, 10 kg sphere: different varieties of
bread are freshly baked by Guy and he offers clients enterprising
appetisers and *petits fours*. They are fantastic supporters of the
local countryside – witness the list of suggested visits they will
give you printed in English. The indoor, heated pool is
magnificent.
menus **A-C** *rooms* 24 **B-C** *cards* AE DC Visa
closed 1-15 Sept. Sat.
post 85290 Mortagne-sur-Sèvre. Vendée.
phone (51) 67.63.37 *Mich* 67 Poitiers 122 km

NIEUIL   Château de Nieuil

Very comfortable hotel
Secluded/Gardens/Swimming pool/Tennis   Ⓡ

The bedrooms may well be expensive at this seductive
Renaissance château, set in a vast, wooded park – but the cost of
eating here is cheap. Luce Bodinaud is a delightful *cuisinière*,
and original thinking applies to much of her work: all her
specialities are divided into two groups – her own light creations
(marked L) and regional treasures (marked T); many visitors
appreciate her home-made soups and her *assiette du végétarien*
– the latter containing not less than eight to ten fresh vegetables.
She was an art teacher before she became a first-class chef; an
exhibition of superb Aubusson tapestries, in modern designs, is
evidence of her continuing interest in her original profession.
Her husband, Michel, is a human dynamo – a charming host for
whom nothing is too much trouble.
menus **B-C** *rooms* 13 **D-D2** *cards* AE Visa
closed Mid Nov-mid Mar. Rest: Wed (except residents).
post Nieuil. 16270 Roumazières-Loubert. Charente.
phone (45) 71.36.38 *Mich* 233 Poitiers 91 km

PONT-DU-DOGNON   Rallye

Comfortable hotel
Secluded/Terrace/Good value

I have known this hotel for years; today it still offers value-for-
money cooking without any fancy touches or pretentious
nonsense. Limousin products feature strongly: *jambon de
campagne*, *omelette aux cèpes* and *truites* – in various forms –
are examples. It's a smart, modern place, facing south and
overlooking the Taurion Valley – at this point a narrow lake.
menus **A-B** *rooms* 20 **B-C**
closed Mid Nov-Feb. Out of season – book ahead.
post Pont-du-Dognon. 87340 La Jonchère-St-Maurice. H.-Vienne.
phone (55) 56.56.11 *Mich* 239 Poitiers 120 km

PREUILLY-SUR-CLAISE   Image

Very simple restaurant
Good value   ®

Another super, small restaurant where you can use the La Roche-
Posay hotel for an overnight stop (the same applies to Espérance
at Le Grand-Pressigny). Camille Boulmier's restaurant has a
décor that takes you back to the turn of the century; his cooking
is straightforward and a real bargain. It costs few francs to test
Camille's skills: perhaps some *rillettes de Preuilly*, a *steck au
poivre flambé* or a *canard à l'orange*, finishing off with a *soufflé
Grand Marnier*?
menus **A-C** *cards* Visa
closed Oct. Mon (except mid July-mid Sept). *Fériés* (holidays).
post 37290 Preuilly-sur-Claise. Indre-et-Loire.
phone (47) 94.50.07 *Mich* 68 Poitiers 61 km

LA REMIGEASSE   Grand Large

Very comfortable hotel/Michelin★
Secluded/Gardens/Swimming pool/Tennis

Like many *Relais et Châteaux* hotels – in magnificent settings –
the Grand Large is an excruciatingly expensive place. The
cooking is good enough; conventional, classic fare with, thank
heaven, many a regional dish and, most certainly, all the best
local produce from the ocean. *Sourdons*, for example, are the
local cockles. But really it's the fabulous site that makes this
hotel such a charmer; a modern building with a superb, covered
swimming pool – all of it overlooking a fine, sandy beach and
protected on three sides by pines.
alc **C-D** *rooms* 26 **D-D2** *cards* Visa
closed Nov-Mar.
post La Remigeasse. 17550 Dolus. Charente-Maritime
phone (46) 76.37.89 *Mich* 233 La Rochelle 71 km

LA ROCHE-L'ABEILLE   Moulin de la Gorce

Comfortable hotel/Michelin★
Secluded/Gardens

First let me list the plus points of this Jekyll and Hyde place: the
Moulin is a magnificent example of how cleverly an old mill can
be restored – in this case a 16th-century building alongside its
own small *étang* and miniature *cascade*; bedrooms are in a
separate building overlooking the waterfall. It really is a super
site. Also on the credit side I would rate the desserts served by
Jean Bertranet and his chef among the best I have seen in France.
But now its debits: it's at places like this that *nouvelle cuisine*
gets a bad name; vast portions with some ghastly combinations –
the plates are huge and it would appear they have to be filled.
Space prevents me listing many examples but consider lobster,
foie gras, vegetables and *fruits de saison* – all served together.
Take my advice: order one speciality and *le grand dessert* – you
get food enough for two.
alc **C** *rooms* 6 **C-D** *cards* AE DC Visa
closed Jan. Mon (out of season). Rest: Sun evg (except mid June-
mid Sept).
post La Roche-l'Abeille. 87800 Nexon. Haute-Vienne.
phone (55) 00.70.66 *Mich* 233 Poitiers 150 km

LA ROCHELLE   Yachtman

Very comfortable hotel/Michelin★★
Quiet/Swimming pool/Lift   ®

I wrote in the last edition of *French Leave*: 'Jacques Le Divellec is
a superb chef – worth far more than his humble one star' and 'he
and his wife, Micheline, will soon be rewarded by the fame they
deserve.' Thankfully, my predictions came right very quickly
indeed because, at the start of 1982, Jacques won his second star.
He is a marvellous, talented chef creating his delights in hot
kitchens below the first-floor restaurant. He's lucky that most of
his raw materials are fresh and varied – bought literally from the
quayside across the road. But innovation and flair can't be bought
– you either have the aptitude or you don't. Specialities include
*rouget braisé, St-Pierre aux pâtes noires, chaudrée Charentaise
à la façon de Le Divellec*. But please Micheline and Jacques – do
you ever smile? Readers have commented on this shortcoming of
yours; go on – try!
menus Rest: **B-C** Grill: *alc* **B** *rooms* 34 **D** *cards* AE DC Visa
closed Rest: Sun evg and Mon (out of season).
post 23 quai Valin, 17000 La Rochelle. Charente-Maritime.
phone (46) 41.20.68 *Mich* 233

LES SABLES-D'OLONNE   Beau Rivage

Comfortable hotel

The Vendée – between Nantes and La Rochelle – is dull, flat
country; for the most part so is the cuisine of the area. Here at the
Beau Rivage, overlooking the beach, Joseph Drapeau shines
forth like a welcoming beacon – about the only good chef
working on the coast itself. The fixtures and fittings need
renovation – hopefully Joseph and his wife will make enough
profits to allow them to do it. His light classical specialities
should ensure success: highlights are fresh fish and shellfish in
splendid sauces, plus a variety of enterprising *sorbets*.
menus **B-C** *rooms* 28 **B-C** *cards* Visa
closed Dec-mid Jan. Sun evg and Mon (mid Sept-mid May)
post 40 prom. G.-Clémenceau, 85100 Les Sables-d'Olonne. Vendée.
phone (51) 32.03.01 *Mich* 233 La Rochelle 100 km

ST-HILAIRE-LE-CHATEAU   du Thaurion

Comfortable hotel
Terrace   ®

Come on Michelin: wake up to the talents of Gérard Fanton who
is making a name for himself in this delightful part of the
unknown *département* of Creuse. Compliments must be paid in
great measure to this clever, enthusiastic chef who takes the
varied products of his *pays* – and applies creative, modern
thinking to them; he noses out old specialities – bringing them up
to date; and then offers his clients a wide spectrum of choice on
his menus. Consider these: *cuisse de poulette à la vapeur de
truffes et de girolles, La Bréjaude (soupe aux choux), lotte au St-
Emilion* and *au concombre* and *clafoutis*.
menus **A-C** *rooms* 10 **C** *cards* AE DC Visa
closed Jan. Feb. Wed (except July-Aug).
post St-Hilaire-le-Château. 23250 Pontarion. Creuse.
phone (55) 64.50.12 *Mich* 239 Poitiers 180 km

STE-MARIE-DE-RE   Atalante

Very comfortable hotel
Secluded/Gardens/Swimming pool/Tennis

To be frank the standard of cooking here made me think twice about including it in category three – it's a border line case, so please do not expect too much of it. What you will enjoy is fresh, cheap, basic produce with no frills – most of the dishes being based on fish and shellfish: things like *lotte*, *sole* and *bar* – all *grillés*, *huîtres fines de claires*(see the Bourcefranc entry – Hôtel Les Claires), *palourdes farcies* and so on. However, other aspects of this dull-looking hotel make it an attractive holiday spot: an isolated, treeless site, a small beach, and the use of an indoor pool make it ideal for energetic types and those wanting to sit quietly and take it easy.

menus **A** *rooms* 65 **C-D** *cards* AE DC
closed Jan.
post 17740 Ste-Marie-de-Ré. Charente-Maritime.
phone (46) 30.22.44 *Mich* 233 La Rochelle 9 km

SOUBISE   Le Soubise

Very comfortable restaurant with rooms
Quiet/Gardens   ®

It was to the credit of Gault Millau that they long ago recognised the talents of Lilyane Benoit – one of the best *cuisinières* in France. Now they have dropped the guillotine – chopping one *toque* off the top of her head; what a pity they don't use that sharp blade on others elsewhere in France. Take no notice – Lilyane still offers an unusual mixture of local, classical and modern dishes: *cotriade*, *soupe d'huîtres* and *daube Saintongeaise* are three of her specialities. Enjoy her cheese dessert – *Jonchée*; a cow's milk cheese served in a most interesting way with an accompanying almond-perfumed sauce. Husband René supports her loyally – he acts as *maître d'hôtel*. Samuel Champlain, the founder of Québec, was born at nearby Brouage – an astonishing place. Built by Richelieu, it was once a port; now the sea is miles away – a *marais* surrounds it.

menus **A-C** *rooms* 22 **C** *cards* AE DC Visa
closed Oct. Sun evg and Mon (except July-Aug).
post 17780 Soubise. Charente-Maritime.
phone (46) 99.31.18 *Mich* 233 La Rochelle 40 km

VIVONNE   La Treille

Very simple restaurant with rooms (no showers or baths)
Terrace/Good value   ®

Have your list of regional specialities and the *Glossary of Menu Terms* at the ready – Jacquelin Monteil is a passionate supporter of old regional delights and he is going to make you work at translating his menus: *mouclade Vendéenne*, *bouilliture d'anguille*, *embeurré de chou* and *potée petit-mousse*. There's much to see and enjoy in the countryside to the east; *France à la Carte* – if you have it – will give you many ideas.

menus **A-B** *rooms* 4 **B** *cards* AE Visa
closed Jan. Wed.
post 86370 Vivonne. Vienne.
phone (49) 43.41.13 *Mich* 233 Poitiers 19 km

PROVENCE

see page 190
see page 191
see page 150

The independent traveller to France is unbelievably spoiled. So many treasures await him throughout the land and here, as if all the others were not enough, is a region offering even more alluring attractions. There is so much to see, assuming you find the inclination to do anything more than shop in the open-air markets, swim, or linger over long midday lunches and picnics, under the cool, shady umbrellas provided by the plane trees. It is a region full of the scent of flowers, lavender and thyme.

There are the many splendours of Ancient Rome to be found in **Arles**, **Nîmes**, **Orange**, **Pont du Gard** (which has the greatest of all Roman aqueducts), **Vaison-la-Romaine** (which has a small scale Pompeii) and **St-Rémy-de-Provence**. The arena at Arles, which seats 25,000 and is older than the Colosseum in Rome, is bordered by the prettiest of small parks; I have spent many happy hours there, sketching in that brilliant light for which Provence is renowned.

Then there are the old, fortified towns: **Avignon**, a papal city within its own walls; **Aigues-Mortes**, with its ramparts and bastions (once a port until the sea receded) sitting at the western edge of the **Camargue** – a vast bird sanctuary and the home of so many wild horses. **Stes-Maries-de-la-Mer**, further along the coast, is on the seaward side of the stark Etang de Vaccarès. Legend has it that the first Christians landed here: Mary of Bethany, Mary Magdalene, Mary, mother of James, Lazarus and Sarah. It is here the gypsies come, once each year on May 24/25, to pay homage to Sarah, their patron Saint.

South of Avignon is the **Chaîne des Alpilles**, the strangest outcrop of rocky hills in France. Amongst those rocks is the ghostly village of **Les Baux**. To the south-east of the region lies aristocratic **Aix-en-Provence**, the city of fountains, surrounded

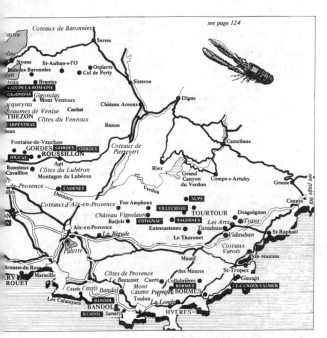

see page 124

by the beautiful countryside of Cézanne. Beyond Aix are **Cassis**, **Bandol** and the rocky coast known as **Les Calanques**.

East of Avignon is the mysterious, lonely **Lubéron** mountain – see **Gordes** and the attractive red and ochre village of **Roussillon**. Just north of these villages is **Fontaine de Vaucluse** – famous for its 'resurgent' spring – and the extinct volcano of **Mont Ventoux** – 1909 metres high. Drive to the top and recall, as you get near the summit, the tragic death in 1967 of Tommy Simpson, the greatest of British road cyclists, on those hot, steep slopes. Wonder too, how in 1966, the Mini-Coopers of BMC were faster up the climb than the powerful Porsches from Germany. The organisers of the Monte-Carlo Rally couldn't believe it either; they stripped the cars down completely, eventually disqualifying them through a technicality on lighting!

Two mountain areas merit some of your time: one is to the north-east of Vaison-la-Romaine; the other is the inland part of the *département* of Var. Ancient villages and splendid hills are the attractions north-east of Vaison: **Brantes**, in the shadow of Mont Ventoux; **Buis-les-Baronnies**, famous for its herb market; and medieval **St-Auban-s-l'O** and **Orpierre** – at either end of the **Col de Perty**. Var hides many jewels: the abbey at **Le Thoronet**; the villages of **Entrecasteaux**, **Cotignac** and **Barjols**; **Tourtour** – 'the village in the sky'; **Fox-Amphoux** – tiny, but a real gem. See Var in May or June – it's at its best then.

Hyères was the home of R. L. Stevenson – he called it the loveliest spot in the Universe. Further east are some fine resorts – **St-Tropez** needs no introduction. To the north are the pine and cork forests of the **Massif des Maures** – at their best in May. Don't miss **Collobrières** and the forest tracks surrounding it.

Another exhilarating mountain drive (a good deal easier than the Ventoux climb) is on the new road built along the north side of the **Gorges de l'Ardèche**. This is the D290 from **Vallon Pont d'Arc**, running south-east to **Pont-St-Esprit**, north of Orange and on the **Rhône**. It is a drive with magnificent views, a close rival of the **Grand Canyon du Verdon**(see pages 124/125).

There is so much to see one could devote pages to it. Remember this is the area that supplies so much of the lovely fruit and vegetables that fill the markets throughout France and especially here in Provence. There is no other area in France where shopping in the open-air markets is such a pleasure; markets where you can buy local produce with the Provençal smell, texture and freshness. The rows of cypresses you see everywhere are there to protect the crops from the dreaded *Mistral* that roars down the Rhône from the north. Note, too, how the northern walls of the farmhouses have no windows and the flat roofs are weighed down with stones.

This is Provence, a land you cannot bring yourself to imagine even existing during the cold, winter months back home in North America or Northern Europe; but it does. See it for yourself.

Michelin *yellow* maps: 240.245.80.81.83.84.93

Green Guide: Provence (English)

IGN *série verte* maps: 66.67. *série rouge* map: 115

Airports: Marseille. Montpellier

Distances from: Paris-Avignon 687 km Calais-Avignon 981 km

Cheeses Goat's milk

See the cheeses listed in the neighbouring regions: Côte d'Azur; Hautes-Alpes; and Languedoc-Roussillon

Picodon de Valréas soft, nutty-tasting, small disk

Ewe's milk

Brousse du Rove a creamy, mild-flavoured cheese. At its best in the winter. **Palette** is an ideal wine to drink with it

Cachat also known as **Tomme du Mont Ventoux**. A summer season; very soft, sweet and creamy flavour. Drink **Côtes du Ventoux** wines with it

Regional Specialities

See the specialities listed in the Côte d'Azur (page 93)

Côtes du Rhône Wines best years 67 70 72 76 78 80 82

At the northern end of the Rhône Valley, near Vienne, is the **Côte Rôtie**. Some of the oldest and most distinguished of red wines, fine and heady, come from here. So do two marvellous white wines, **Condrieu** and **Château-Grillet** (see page 176).

Futher south, from Tain l'Hermitage (**AC Hermitage**, a wonderful wine and **AC Crozes-Hermitage**, a less-good, junior brother), **Saint Joseph** and **Cornas**, all north of Valence, you will find some super, ruby-red wines, dark and powerful. The best of the Rhône reds are made from the Syrah grape. There are also some good dry whites from the same area: a **Hermitage Blanc** (the best is **Chante-Alouette**), a **Saint Péray** white and a **Saint Péray mousseux**. Some whites take the **Crozes-Hermitage** AC (refer to the map and notes on pages 191 and 196).

South-east of Valence, at **Die**, you'll find the lovely **Clairette de Die mousseux**; Clairette grapes for the *brut* version – mainly Muscat for the *demi-sec*. Near Die are the wines of all shades from **Châtillon-en-Diois** (see the map on page 124). To the south of Valence is the **AC Coteaux du Tricastin** and its dry rosés and reds (see the map on page 191).

From the southern end of the Rhône Valley come some of the best wines in the region, particularly at **Châteauneuf-du-Pape** (with its own AC), a strong, full-bodied red. **Gigondas** (with its own AC) and **Vacqueyras** are both red and very similar to Châteauneuf-du-Pape; the **Lirac** red is now considered important – keep your eyes open for the very rare white Lirac.

Tavel was the pioneer among rosés and nearby Lirac makes another famous one – both are among the best. The Tavel rosé, slightly orange in colour, is made from the Grenache grape.

A fine wine from the lovely area just west of Mont Ventoux is **Muscat de Beaumes de Venise**, a delicious, sweet dessert wine. Another one comes from nearby **Rasteau**; both are made from the Muscat grape.

Many cheaper wines, mainly reds, come from the fringe areas on both the eastern and western edges of the Rhône Valley: amongst them the **AC Côtes du Ventoux**, the VDQS **Côtes du Lubéron**, **Côtes du Vivarais** and the **Coteaux de Pierrevert**. Another small VDQS area is **Coteaux des Baux-de-Provence** – wines of all shades but rarely seen other than locally.

The *generic* AC classifications for the whole Rhône area are **Côtes du Rhône** and **Côtes du Rhône-Villages**. 14 villages qualify for the tougher controls of the latter AC: **Chusclan** and **Laudun** in the *département* of Gard; **Cairanne**, **Vacqueyras**, **Rasteau**, **Valréas**, **Visan**, **Roaix** and **Séguret** in Vaucluse;**St-Maurice-sur-Aygues**, **Rousset**, **Rochegude**, **St-Pantaléon-les-Vignes** and **Vinsorbes** in Drôme. One of these controls requires the **Villages** wines to have at least 12.5 per cent alcohol as against the 11 per cent for the former AC. The main grape type for all these southern reds is the Grenache.

Provence Wines

Fresh, fragrant whites and rosés are made at **Palette** (east of Aix – look out for **Château Simone**, a property within this AC area), **Cassis**, **Bandol**, **Coteaux d'Aix-en-Provence**, **Côtes de Provence** and **Bellet**, in the Var Valley (see page 93).

Many good reds appear throughout those areas – **Château Vignelaure**, near Rians, is really good, as are the **Bandol** wines.

Languedoc Wines

At the northern end of this vast wine-producing mass of country (see page 152) are some interesting areas. One is the general **Costières du Gard** – mainly reds and rosés are made here; between Nîmes and Arles is Bellegarde – it has a sound reputation for its dry, white **Clairette de Bellegarde**. Some of the **Coteaux du Languedoc** and **Muscat** wines may appear on wine lists – see page 152 again.

Vins de Pays

You will come across many really sound wines, of all shades. **Vin de Pays des Sables du Golfe du Lion** (around Aigues-Mortes) is especially good; so is the **Vin de Pays du Vaucluse** (the *département* name). Further east are the Var locals or sometimes called **Coteaux Varois** (really good bargains). Two other area classifications are **Les Maures** (near St-Tropez) and **Mont Caume** (Bandol area).

If you see the label **Vin de Pays d'Oc** this will mean the wine can have originated in any of these five *départements* – **Ardèche**, **Drôme**, **Var**, **Bouches-du-Rhône** or **Vaucluse** (or four *départements* to the south-west – see page 152). Labels may give just the *département* name or, in the case of **Gard**, it may be identified by one of no less than 11 small area names – **Coteaux du Salavès** is just one. **Vin de Pays des Coteaux de Baronnies** (Drôme) borders some of the best Rhône areas.

Base Hotels

ARLES
D'Arlatan

Very comfortable hotel
Quiet/Gardens
®

A magnificent 'base': a 15th-century delight tucked away in a tiny street in glorious Arles – full of ancient treasures.
No restaurant *rooms* 46 **C-D** *cards* AE DC
closed Open all the year.
post 26 rue Sauvage, 13200 Arles. Bouches-du-Rhône.
phone (90) 93.56.66 *Mich* 245 Avignon 37 km

ARLES
La Roseraie

Simple hotel
Quiet/Gardens

A modest, small base hotel – away from the busy N453 and two kilometres to the south-east of Arles.
No restaurant *rooms* 11 **B-C**
closed Mid Oct-mid Mar.
post Pont-de-Crau. 13200 Arles. Bouches-du-Rhône.
phone (90) 96.06.58 *Mich* 245 Avignon 39 km

BANDOL
Golf Hôtel

Comfortable hotel
Quiet

This 'base' has three advantages: it's away from the centre of Bandol; it has a super site – overlooking the Plage Rènecros, a beach; and there's no road in front of the hotel.
No restaurant *rooms* 19 **C-D**
closed Mid Oct-Easter.
post 83150 Bandol. Var.
phone (94) 29.45.83 *Mich* 245 Avignon 147 km

LA CROIX-VALMER
Parc

Comfortable hotel
Quiet/Gardens/Lift

East of the main N559 to St-Tropez; on the D93 that heads towards Cap Camarat. The Parc is a huge, old mansion, built originally as a school. Garden has magnificent palm trees.
No restaurant *rooms* 33 **C-D** *cards* DC Visa
closed Oct-Mar
post 83420 La Croix-Valmer. Var.
phone (94) 79.64.04 *Mich* 245 Avignon 197 km

FONTVIEILLE
Valmajour

Comfortable hotel
Quiet/Gardens/Swimming pool/Tennis

Well clear of the small town of Fontvieille – on the road to Arles; attractive, large grounds.
No restaurant *rooms* 32 **B-D**
closed Nov-Feb
post 13990 Fontvieille. Bouches-du-Rhône.
phone (90) 97.70.37 *Mich* 245 Avignon 30 km

GORDES   Le Gordos

Comfortable hotel
Quiet/Gardens

A modern, stone building on the southern approach to the village:
conveniently located for you to explore the many local *bories* –
Stone Age, beehive-shaped, stone dwellings. Seek out the ancient
Abbaye de Sénanque – it has an interesting museum.
No restaurant *rooms* 15 **C**
closed Dec-Feb.
post route Cavaillon, 84220 Gordes. Vaucluse.
phone (90) 72.00.75 *Mich* 245 Avignon 38 km

MAUSSANE-LES-ALPILLES   Touret

Comfortable hotel
Quiet/Swimming pool

A newly-built, Provençal-style 'base' – nearer Paradou, west of
Maussane. To the south you get extensive views and to the north
the craggy Chaîne des Alpilles provides a dramatic backdrop. An
old rallying friend of mine, John Brown, suggests you visit the
'fantastic stone quarries' about two kilometres north of Les Baux
– great square chambers cut out of solid rock; 'you can even drive
into some of them – one after another, like the inside of a palace,
cool and shadowy!'
No restaurant *rooms* 16 **C**
closed Feb.
post 13520 Maussane-les-Alpilles. Bouches-du-Rhône.
phone (90) 97.31.93 *Mich* 245 Avignon 30 km

ST-REMY-DE-PROVENCE   Château de Roussan

Comfortable hotel
Secluded/Gardens

Two kilometres from St-Rémy – on the Tarascon road; the
approach to this secluded, 18th-century 'château' is up an avenue
of fine trees – three centuries old. It's a much more expensive
base than the other two St-Rémy hotels; but if it's character, style
and a family atmosphere that you want – all of it surrounded by
an unformalised *parc* – then head here.
No restaurant *rooms* 12 **D**
closed Mid Oct-Mar.
post 13210 St-Rémy-de-Provence. Bouches-du-Rhône.
phone (90) 92.11.63 *Mich* 245 Avignon 23 km

ST-REMY-DE-PROVENCE   Soleil

Comfortable hotel
Quiet/Gardens/Swimming pool/Good value

Many of you have written saying how much you have enjoyed
this base hotel; it's an older building, on the road south from the
centre of St-Rémy, towards the Roman treasures of Les Antiques
– once the prosperous town of Glanum.
No restaurant *rooms* 15 **C** *cards* Visa
closed Mid Nov-Jan.
post avenue Pasteur, 13210 St-Rémy-de-Provence. B.-du-R.
phone (90) 92.00.63 *Mich* 245 Avignon 21 km

249

ST-REMY-DE-PROVENCE   Van Gogh

Comfortable hotel
Quiet/Gardens/Swimming pool/Good value   ®

A more modern hotel than the Soleil; it's on the eastern exit of the
town – just 300 metres or so from the centre of St-Rémy. It's an
old favourite of ours and has become popular with *French Leave*
readers – be sure to book ahead.
No restaurant *rooms* 18 **B-C**
closed Mid Nov-mid Feb.
post avenue J.-Moulin, 13210 St-Rémy-de-Provence. B.-du-R.
phone (90) 92.14.02 *Mich* 245 Avignon 21 km

SALON-DE-PROVENCE   Sélect-Hôtel

Simple hotel
Quiet/Good value

It's a simple place, in a quiet side street. Parking is easy in the
nearby place du Général-de-Gaulle. My main purpose in
suggesting it is to provide you with a convenient overnight 'base',
allowing you the chance to try the Robin Restaurant – a 200
metres walk away from the Sélect.
No restaurant *rooms* 19 **B**
closed Open all the year.
post 35 rue Suffren, 13300 Salon-de-Provence. B.-du-R.
phone (90) 56.07.17 *Mich* 245 Avignon 46 km

VILLECROZE   Le Vieux Moulin

Simple hotel
Quiet/Gardens/Good value

Once more the reason for listing this modest 'base' is to give you
an ideal spot to stay overnight if you decide to try Paul Bajade's
super little restaurant – Chênes Verts – at nearby Tourtour.
Madame Gillin will look after you well at her old, restored
moulin à huile – on the outskirts of the village. Don't miss the
interesting Villecroze caves.
No restaurant *rooms* 10 **B-C**
closed Oct-Mar.
post Villecroze. 83690 Salernes. Var.
phone (94) 70.63.35 *Mich* 245 Avignon 150 km

VILLENEUVE-LES-AVIGNON   Résid. Les Cèdres

Simple hotel
Quiet/Terrace/Gardens/Swimming pool   ®

Nothing has pleased me more than to hear how much this lovely
base hotel has delighted so many of you. The hotel is an old
building, set in its own grounds with cedar trees, a swimming
pool and a 'folly'. But it is the way eight bedrooms – in two
bungalows – have been built amongst the trees that is so
interesting; reserve one of these. I understand light meals are
available; but I suggest you use Les Cèdres as a 'base'.
No restaurant *rooms* 25 **C** *cards* Visa
closed Open all the year.
post 39 bd. Pasteur, 30400 Villeneuve-lès-Avignon. Gard.
phone (90) 25.43.92 *Mich* 245 Avignon 3 km

Recommendations where cuisine takes second place

AUPS
Auberge de la Tour

Comfortable hotel
Quiet/Good value

A 13th-century house, the Auberge de la Tour sits in the northern shadow of the village church, hidden behind two huge trees and looking smart in its whitewashed coat. Conventional cooking with no fancy touches; menus include *crudités, salade verte aux pignons* and, popular in the Var hills, *gigot de pays grillé aux herbes de Provence*.
menus **A-B** *rooms* 24 **B-C**
closed Open all the year.
post 83630 Aups. Var.
phone (94) 70.00.30 *Mich* 245 Avignon 168 km

BANDOL
Réserve

Very comfortable restaurant with rooms
Terrace

Between the main road and the Mediterranean, the Réserve has one of the most unusual sites on the coast. The odd-looking restaurant juts out into the sea; one of the pleasures here is the shady terrace – another benefit is the direct access it provides to a beach. Cooking is not as good as it was; but apart from one complaint about an undercooked *rouget*, nothing untoward has been heard from readers.
menus **B** *rooms* 16 **B-D** *cards* DC Visa
closed Dec. Jan. Mid-end May. Sun evg. Mon.
post route de Sanary, 83150 Bandol. Var.
phone (94) 29.42.71 *Mich* 245 Avignon 147 km

BORMES-LES-MIMOSAS
Safari Hôtel

Comfortable hotel
Secluded/Gardens/Swimming pool/Tennis

Clear of the picturesque hill-top village of Bormes. Modern hotel with many facilities and spectacular views; sadly, it's dear. Use the Safari as a 'base' – bypass the grill.
menu **A-B** (dinner only) *rooms* 33 **C-D** *cards* DC Visa
closed Mid Oct-Mar.
post route Stade, 83230 Bormes-les-Mimosas. Var.
phone (94) 71.09.83 *Mich* 245 Avignon 196 km

CADENET
Aux Ombrelles

Comfortable restaurant with rooms
Gardens

The Drabins' *Logis* is a modern establishment, hiding behind a willow tree; don't be put off by the railway – it's a single rusty line and is hardly likely to worry you. Dishes take advantage of local products: witness the *coq aux Côtes du Lubéron, crudités, asperges du pays* and *civet de porcelet. Soupe de poisson* is an added pleasure.
menus **A-C** *rooms* 11 **B-C**
closed Dec. Jan. Mon (out of season).
post 84160 Cadenet. Vaucluse.
phone (90) 68.02.40 *Mich* 245 Avignon 60 km

CARPENTRAS   La Genestière

Comfortable hotel
Quiet/Terrace/Gardens/Swimming pool/Tennis

I am happy to be able to reintroduce this lovely hotel to *French Leave* readers again; after several complaints about the cooking I left it out of the second edition. There have been problems with changes of chefs – but now that I have my new second category I suggest you enjoy the facilities here and don't expect too much of the cooking. The hotel is four kilometres after leaving Carpentras, on the Avignon road, before you reach Monteux; my wife and I can still remember the rose-perfumed gardens from our first visit. Dishes include *coquilles St-Jacques au coulis de tomates, terrine de saumon au poivre vert* and others that make good use of the vegetables and fruit from the local fields.
menus **B** *rooms* 20 **C** *cards* DC Visa
closed Rest: Xmas-New Year. Sun evg and Mon (out of season).
post 84170 Monteux. Vaucluse.
phone (90) 62.27.04 *Mich* 245 Avignon 20 km

COTIGNAC   Auberge du Vieux Fox

Comfortable restaurant with rooms
Secluded/Terrace   ®

The Auberge is at Fox-Amphoux, 11 kilometres north of Cotignac. The hamlet is no more than a tiny collection of houses on a hill-top; its main attraction is an old Eglise Templière – the adjoining 16th-century presbytery is the Auberge du Vieux Fox. The original owners, Pierre and Martine Phillipe, worked wonders here, converting the Auberge into a delectable home. The new owners have continued to improve the facilities – it's now in the capable hands of Mme Martha Paule. Honest cooking in the style of *cuisine Bourgeoise* – using fresh local products. Combine the ingredients of a lovely setting, views, simple cooking – and you have a perfect recipe. No wonder so many of you have fallen in love with Fox-Amphoux.
menus **B** *rooms* 10 **C**
closed Oct-Easter. Please check weekly closing dates.
post Fox-Amphoux. 83670 Barjols. Var.
phone (94) 80.71.69 *Mich* 245 Avignon 145 km

COTIGNAC   Lou Calen

Comfortable hotel
Quiet/Terrace/Gardens/Swimming pool   ®

Another favourite of *French Leave* readers; several letters have arrived at Chiltern House praising Huguette Caren's garden, the fine cooking – up to category three standards – and the particularly charming bedrooms. Cuisine relies primarily on classical and regional recipes – using the raw materials of Provence: *terrine de grives* and *soupe au pistou* are examples. Some of you have recommended Le Matécalou – *sans restaurant*, gardens, pool and tennis; sounds like a good secluded 'base'.
menus **B-C** *rooms* 16 **C-D**
closed Oct-Mar. Rest: Thurs (except July-Aug).
post Cotignac. 83570 Carcès. Var.
phone (94) 04.60.40 *Mich* 245 Avignon 148 km

GIGONDAS
                                                                    Les Florets
Comfortable hotel
Secluded/Terrace   ®

An isolated, captivating spot – hidden in the amusingly-named
hills called the Dentelles de Montmirail. The most attractive
feature of the hotel must be its large, shaded terrace – ideal for
outdoor meals. Cooking is traditional with a fair number of
Provençal treats: things like *tian d'aubergines, pieds et paquets
maison* and *lapin au vinaigre*. Just to the west are the vineyards
of Gigondas; needless to say the owners offer a wide selection of
vintages from those world-famous vines. Mont Ventoux must be
included on your list of excursions – try the drive late at night
when the view of the lights is amazing; find time, too, to visit the
villages to the north of the mountain, Brantes and Buis-les-
Baronnies – the latter is famous for its herb market.
menus **B** *rooms* 15 **B-C**
closed Jan-mid Feb. Wed.
post Gigondas. 84190 Beaumes-de-Venise. Vaucluse.
phone (90) 65.85.01 *Mich* 245 Avignon 40 km

GORDES
                                                                   La Mayenelle
Comfortable hotel
Quiet

An exceedingly dismal exterior does no justice at all to the real
interior charm of this lovely, small hotel – without any shadow of
doubt one of the least expensive members of the *Relais et
Châteaux* chain. Once inside you will find it handsomely
furnished and, to the south, you'll have fabulous views of the
huge Lubéron. You go 'down' a flight of stairs to the dining room.
The Maynard's cuisine is traditional fare (dare I say dull?) – with
dishes like *terrine aux herbes, canard aux olives* and *pâté de
grives*. Anything but dull is the neighbouring Musée Vasarely
and, to the north of the village, the isolated, 12th-century
Cistercian Abbey of Sénanque.
alc **B-C** *rooms* 10 **B-C** *cards* AE DC Visa
closed Jan. Feb. Rest: Tues.
post 84220 Gordes. Vaucluse.
phone (90) 72.00.28 *Mich* 245 Avignon 38 km

JOUCAS
                                                          Host. des Commandeurs
Simple hotel
Good value

A small *Logis de France*; it's at the foot of the village and it
rewards visitors – just as La Mayenelle does at Gordes – with
extensive and commanding views of the vast wall of the
Montagne du Lubéron, 15 kilometres to the south. Later you can
enjoy many of the villages that sit in the northern shadow of that
sulking mass of mountain; here you will relish basic cooking with
specialities like *daube Provençale, poulet Vauclusienne, jambon
cru, cuisses de grenouilles à la Provençale, selle d'agneau
grillée, pâtisserie* and *pêche Melba*.
menus **A-B** *rooms* 12 **B** *cards* Visa
closed Jan. Feb. Rest: Wed.
post Joucas. 84220 Gordes. Vaucluse.
phone (90) 72.00.05 *Mich* 245 Avignon 42 km

ST-REMY-DE-PROVENCE   Auberge de la Graïo

Comfortable restaurant with rooms
Terrace/Gardens/Good value   ®

Jean-Luc Perrin, a Swiss, has won many hearts at his 18th-century home – much modernised and furnished with style and character. Most of the bedrooms have a fairly quiet location and one of the most pleasing aspects of this delightful Auberge is its shaded patio. Menus include specialities of the region and Jean-Luc's own creations, some of which have a lighter, more modern touch about them: *calamars a la Provençale, feuilleté de brandade de morue, terrine de loup aux concombres, loup en papillotte* and *daurade de la Graïo* are a representative selection of the wide choice available.

menus **A-B** *rooms* 10 **B-C** *cards* AE DC Visa
closed Jan. Mid Nov-mid Dec.
post 12 bd. Mirabeau, 13210 St-Rémy-de-Provence. B.-du-R.
phone (90) 92.15.33 *Mich* 245 Avignon 21 km

SALERNES   Host. Allègre

Simple hotel
Gardens/Good value

Don't expect miracles at this modest place – once called the 'Grand Hôtel' would you believe! Menus are very basic and in no way will they break the bank; conventional offerings with little inspiration such as *pâté de grives* and *figues au sirop*. However, compensating for these modest pleasures of the table are a string of man-made sights that you should most certainly seek out – two lie to the immediate south of Salernes. The first is the château at Entrecasteaux; owned by the McGarvie-Munn family, it was reconstructed by the late Ian McGarvie-Munn and is full of the most unusual, even weird, collections of paintings and other items. The second is further south – the 12th-century abbey at Le Thoronet; it's one of three Cistercian abbeys worth visiting in this region.

menus **A-B** *rooms* 26 **A-C**
closed Mid Jan-mid Feb. Mon.
post 83690 Salernes. Var.
phone (94) 70.60.30 *Mich* 245 Avignon 168 km

VAISON-LA-ROMAINE   Le Beffroi

Comfortable hotel
Quiet/Terrace/Gardens   ®

Chefs come and go at this 16th-century hotel, lost in the narrow lanes of the medieval Haute Ville; consequently I have to say cuisine must take second place. In the past it has been of a high standard with enterprising choices such as *feuilleté de moules au pastis, escalope de haddock à la crème de basilic* and *saumon mariné à l'huile d'olive et au romarin*. Vaison is my favourite small town in Provence – a small-scale Pompeii; magnificent finds have been made over the years. To the south-east is the sinister bulk of Mont Ventoux.

menus **B** *rooms* 19 **B-C** *cards* AE DC Visa
closed Nov-mid Mar. Rest: Mon. Tues midday.
post 84110 Vaison-la-Romaine. Vaucluse.
phone (90) 36.04.71 *Mich* 245 Avignon 47 km

LES ANGLES   Ermitage-Meissonnier

Very comfortable restaurant with rooms/Michelin★★
Terrace/Gardens   ®

Sadly, I have to report that standards have slipped backwards
here; it hurts to say that because in the last edition of *French
Leave* I wrote that Paul Meissonnier, the 'father' of the house,
'puts to shame some of his more famous Rhône Valley
neighbours.' I felt sure that Paul was moving forward to a
possible third star – but not now. How has this come about?

Paul-Louis Meissonnier is now 62; it would appear that he has
made the decision to let his son, Michel, take over completely the
stoves at their family restaurant. Father and son combinations at
this *haute cuisine* level are not unique to the Meissonniers; you
see it at Lameloise in Chagny, at Boyer in Reims and with the
Rostangs at La Brague and in Paris. Paul, unlike the others, has
obviously decided to stop chasing star three – 'Papa' Rostang and
Lameloise won their third stars in their sixties! Unlike the sons of
the others – Jacques Lameloise, Gérard Boyer and Michel
Rostang – Michel Meissonnier has to develop quite a bit before he
can be said to be on equal terms with them. It is not for me to
reason why, but it is a pity that Paul has backed off from total
involvement. You will still have some contact with him and you
will enjoy his marvellous temperament and personality. He is one
of the top chefs who acknowledges his debt to Escoffier – though
these days the cuisine of the Ermitage follows the modern road
with light touches everywhere. Michel continues those traditions
and still finds room to include many interesting old regional
specialities – he's happy to give you the recipes.

What are some of those delights? There is a host of them: *pâté
d'aubergines menthe sauvage, selle d'agneau de lait barigoule,
crème de baudroie ciboulette, petites pattes rouges façon mon
père* and the famous *bisquebouille d'Avignon*. The latter is a sort
of *bouillabaisse* – including fish like *grondin, lotte, brochet* and
anguille in its ingredients. Overall I would still suggest you visit
this fine restaurant with its attractive gardens – in summer the
terrace is perfect for a meal. It offers great value for money.
Please Michel, throw those plastic flowers away! Please Paul, get
involved again!

menus C-D *rooms* 16 C-D *cards* AE DC
closed Rest: Mar. Sun evg (Nov-Mar). Mon. Hotel: Jan. Feb.
post Bellevue (D900). 30400 Villeneuve-lès-Avignon. Gard.
phone (90) 25.41.68 Hotel: (90) 25.41.02 *Mich* 245 Avignon 4 km

BANDOL   Grotte Provençale

Simple restaurant
Good value   ®

A tiny place, tucked away in the narrow street that runs parallel
with the promenade in Bandol. An enjoyable meal for the price of
two or three gallons of petrol – what value! Tuck in to honest
fare: *soupe de poissons, salade Niçoise, friture du Golfe,
brochette de moules* or *brochettes de gambas*. You can't grumble
with bargains like that, can you? Seek out the Ile de Bendor;
owned by the Ricard family – of *pastis apéritifs* fame.
menus A *cards* Visa
closed Tues evg. Wed (except July-Aug).
post 21 rue Dr-L.-Marçon, 83150 Bandol. Var.
phone (94) 29.41.52 *Mich* 245 Avignon 147 km

LES BAUX-DE-PROVENCE   Oustaù de Baumanière

Luxury restaurant with rooms/Michelin★★★
Secluded/Terrace/Gardens/Swimming pool/Tennis

I made the tough decision to omit two world-famous restaurants from this edition of *French Leave*: the Pyramide at Vienne and the Auberge du Père Bise at Talloires. Neither of them can now be compared with some of the other great shrines of *haute cuisine*. Indeed there are many younger chefs listed in this third edition who put them to shame; it was that fact alone that made me decide to drop them completely.

The Oustaù was another likely candidate – but I decided to let it stand as it still represents excellent value for money if you eat here; staying overnight is anything but cheap (use the 'bases'). On top of that it has a magnificent setting and a special charm about it that is unique in France; it's an exquisite building with flowers and shrubs everywhere. The cooking on the other hand is good – but not great. It's a place where it seems Michelin cannot bring themselves to take away star three (though they did at Talloires last year); I understand why, and I can see that they want to stay loyal to Raymond Thuilier, who for so long has reigned supreme at his old *mas*.

What will you expect to see on the menus? *Terrine d'anguille aux pistaches*, *gigot d'agneau en croûte* and *soufflé à l'orange* are representative of the sort of uninspiring dishes that still make up the repertoire of the Oustaù.

alc **C-D** *rooms* 15 **D2** *cards* AE DC Visa
closed Mid Jan-Feb. Rest: Wed/Thurs midday (mid Oct-Mar).
post Les Baux. 13520 Maussane-les-Alpilles. B.-du-R.
phone (90) 97.33.07 *Mich* 245 Avignon 30 km

LES BAUX-DE-PROVENCE   La Riboto de Taven

Very comfortable restaurant/Michelin★
Terrace/Gardens   ®

French Leave readers have certainly appreciated La Riboto; I have received many letters singing its praises. It's another handsomely restored old *mas* with gorgeous terraces and gardens – where any outdoor meal is perfection. Cuisine is based on classical traditions with some modern influences appearing here and there on the menus: *agneau des Alpilles* (a renowned local speciality) is a must; lighter alternatives would include *assiette du pêcheur* or a *salade de poissons crus à la mousse d'avocat*. Whatever you order be sure to accompany it with these wines: **Château d'Estoublon** is a local property – as are the **Coteaux des Baux-de-Provence** varieties; or better still **Château Fonsalette** which is the best of all the **Côtes du Rhône** vintages. Before or after your meal explore the ghost-ridden, Renaissance village of Les Baux – it's perched on the rocky hill-top above you. The village was completely destroyed in 1632 on the orders of Louis XIII, when its population was some 6,000 people. If you visit the area in the evening you may be fortunate enough to witness a spectacular sunset; to this day my wife and I can recall one such sunset some years ago when three-quarters of the sky glowed like a red fire.

alc **C** *cards* AE Visa
closed Jan. Feb. Sun evg (out of season). Mon.
post Les Baux. 13520 Maussane-les-Alpilles. B.-du-R.
phone (90) 97.34.23 *Mich* 245 Avignon 30 km

Alain and Nicole Rayé – Albertville (Savoie)

'The one that got away' – at Alain Rayé's restaurant

Beaufort (Savoie)

The abbey at Tamié (Savoie)

BORMES-LES-MIMOSAS   Tonnelle des Délices

Comfortable restaurant
Terrace

What on earth possessed Gault Millau to give André and Guy
Gedda a *toque*? The day following our visit here my wife and I
were stunned by the efforts of Francis Robin at Salon – he, too,
gets a single *toque* from GM; it's this sort of example that shows
up the variances that you can find from one inspector to
another. A *French Leave* reader has described the cooking here
as 'gimmicky'. It is. There's a terrace where you can tuck into a
range of supposedly authentic Provençal specialities (so say
GM): *brouillade Provençale* and a couple of dishes incorporating
Marc de Provence or various herbs are the only offerings that
resemble anything like my definition of regional specialities. Two
readers have recommended the Belle-Vue in Bormes; one wrote
to say it provided 'simple, honest fare'. Trusted friends have
spoken highly of the excellent Pergola at Cavalaire-sur-Mer –
'light, value-for-money cuisine'.
menus **B-C** *cards* DC
closed Oct-Mar. Each midday (except Sat and Sun).
post 83230 Bormes-les-Mimosas. Var.
phone (94) 71.34.84 *Mich* 245 Avignon 196 km

CARRY-LE-ROUET   L'Escale

Very comfortable restaurant/Michelin★
Terrace

Dany and Gérard Clor's restaurant has one of the best settings on
the coast. A series of terraces overlook the port and vast views
stretch as far as Cap Croisette, beyond Marseille. Fish dishes are
good: *soupe de poissons* is fresh and authentic; a *feuillatine de
rougets* has the pastry shaped like a fish; and, to end your meal,
some of the best *sorbets* you'll find anywhere. I visited L'Escale
on my own; I had a good opportunity to watch a group of
businessmen tuck into one of the biggest meals I have ever seen
consumed in France. I guessed fat expense accounts ensured
that nothing else needed to be eaten for the rest of the week – by
any of them!
alc **C-D** *cards* Visa
closed Nov-Feb. Mon (except evg-July and Aug).
post 13620 Carry-le-Rouet. Bouches-du-Rhône.
phone (42) 45.00.47 *Mich* 245 Avignon 97 km

CHATEAUNEUF-DU-PAPE   Mule-du-Pape

Very comfortable restaurant
Good value

La Mule has a first-floor Provençal dining room; its name came
from the humble mules that carried the Avignon popes on their
journeys here while building the Château des Papes. Young
Dominique Olive uses local produce in his classical and regional
dishes like *estouffade, caille Vauclusienne aux herbes* and *pâté
de rouget en croûte sauce pastis*.
menus **A-B** *cards* Visa
closed Mon evg. Tues.
post 84230 Châteauneuf-du-Pape. Vaucluse.
phone (90) 39.73.30 *Mich* 245 Avignon 18 km

COURTHEZON
Porte des Princes

Very simple restaurant with rooms
Terrace/Good value

You'll not find a more modest restaurant in Provence than this one; its main attraction is a shaded terrace, under some huge plane trees and across the road from a fountain. We have known it for many years and it continues to offer excellent value for money. Specialities: *soupe de poissons* (evenings only), *mousseline de turbot* and *caille en gelée*.

menus A-B *rooms* 9 A-B
closed Mid Nov-mid Dec. Wed (except hotel; Apl-Sept).
post 84350 Courthézon. Vaucluse.
phone (90) 70.70.26 *Mich* 245 Avignon 21 km

GORDES
Les Bories

Very comfortable restaurant/Michelin★
Quiet/Terrace/Gardens
®

Gabriel Rousselet continues to make progress; it was no surprise to me, or to the many readers who have visited his unique restaurant, to see that Gault Millau awarded him a second *toque* in 1983. Gabriel is over 60; he served his apprenticeship in Gordes itself in 1938 – after the war he spent some time in London working in the Howard kitchens. 1966 saw him open Les Bories – more about that later.

His cooking covers the whole spectrum of old and new traditions; but whatever he does, he applies a light touch to his creations. His menus are built around his purchases each day from the markets – and, of course, they vary from season to season. October to February sees him working wonders with *sangliers, chevreuils, faisans, perdreaux* and so on – it's the season for *la chasse* (the hunt). Other delights include *cassolette de truffes aux cèpes feuilletée, bourride de baudroie au safran* and *omelette aux truffes*. Only lunches are served.

Bories are beehive-shaped, stone dwellings that date back to the Stone Age. Made of dry-stone slabs, they sit very low on the ground – a village of them can be seen near Gordes. Here, at the restaurant, Gabriel makes clever use of them.

alc C Note: Lunches only.
closed Dec. Wed.
post 84220 Gordes. Vaucluse.
phone (90) 72.00.51 *Mich* 245 Avignon 40 km

HYERES
Le Tison d'Or

Comfortable restaurant
Good value

If you want a change from Provençal specialities, give Philippe Delsarte a call – his restaurant is a little bit of Morvan (Burgundy) here on the south coast. You'll need to look up the Burgundian regional specialities: *jambon persillé, œufs pochés en meurette, délice de volaille Chablisienne, jambonnette de caneton au Vieux Bourgogne* and others.

menus B *cards* AE DC Visa
closed Sun evg (Nov-Feb). Mon.
post 1 rue Galliéni, 83400 Hyères. Var.
phone (94) 65.01.37 *Mich* 245 Avignon 174 km

NOVES   Auberge de Noves

Luxury hotel/Michelin★★
Secluded/Terrace/Gardens/Swimming pool/Tennis

For the benefit of several English-language guides, the family
name here is *Lalleman* – not Lallemand! In 1956 they moved lock,
stock and barrel – and their staff – from Sauveterre, midway
between Avignon and Orange, to this ravishing, Provençal
country house, standing in its own large, wooded grounds. The
gardens and the rooms are full of flowers and even if you have to
be inside you feel no hardship – it's light and airy and fitted out in
very expensive style.

   Three Michelin stars once shone overhead at Noves – but in
1968 that all important third one was extinguished by Michelin.
Standards remain high but not up to the level of the real 'greats';
it's modern cuisine in the hands of Jean-Claude Aubertin.
Specialities include *caneton en papillote, huîtres gratinées,
terrine aux trois chocolats* and *tarte au citron*. If you want
luxury rooms you pay a high price for them here; if you want to
save francs use my 'bases'.

menus **C-D** *rooms* 20 **D-D3** *cards* Visa
closed Jan-mid Feb. Rest: Wed midday.
post 13550 Noves. Bouches-du-Rhône.
phone (90) 94.19.21 *Mich* 245 Avignon 13 km

ROUSSILLON   David

Comfortable restaurant

The restaurant sits on top of one of the remarkable red and ochre
cliffs that make Roussillon so famous. Seek out the village – you
will enjoy the unusual spectacle. If classical cuisine is your
preference seek out, too, this long established restaurant – you
will be in your element with *truite pochée Dugleré, coq au vin*
and similar dishes. You'll enjoy, too, the fine views to the north.
The nearby Résidence des Ocres (*sans restaurant*/quiet) makes
a good 'base'.

menus **B-C** *cards* DC Visa
closed 1-15 July. Feb. Mon. Tues (mid Sept-June).
post Roussillon. 84220 Gordes. Vaucluse.
phone (90) 75.60.13 *Mich* 245 Avignon 48 km

ST-MARTIN-DE-LONDRES   La Crèche

Comfortable restaurant with rooms
Secluded/Terrace/Gardens/Swimming pool/Tennis   ®

No accolades from Michelin yet but, as usual, Gault Millau are
one step ahead; quite rightly Georges Rousset deserves their
plaudits. Light cooking with many delightful specialities:
asperges des sables vinaigrette, huîtres from the Thau lagoon,
aiguillette de canard au poivre vert and a *pélardon chaud*. The
setting is superb; isolated 15th-century *bergeries* (sheepfolds)
surrounded by vineyards and with extensive views. Comfortable
bedrooms, named after colours. Cosy, comfortable dining room –
matched by an equally warm welcome.

menus **C** *rooms* 6 **C** *cards* AE DC
closed Mon (Oct-Easter).
post 34380 St-Martin-de-Londres. Hérault.
phone (67) 55.00.04 *Mich* 240 Avignon 102 km

SALON-DE-PROVENCE   Robin

Very comfortable restaurant/Michelin★   ®

An English guide – available in both the U.K. and North America –
suggested that 'the new proprietor of this restaurant, previously
called Boissin, has given it a well-needed boost.' How wrong can
you be? Francis Robin has indeed now dropped the old name
Boissin – but for the record he has been here for over 11 years!
And what progress this marvellous 36 years old chef continues to
make; it has been a delight to see his talent develop over nearly a
decade – the time span of my visits.

Anne was with me on my last call; during the previous week we
had eaten at both simple and great restaurants on the coast.
Francis put to shame some of the so-called 'greats' – and when
you consider the miserly number of francs he demanded from us
at the end of the meal, it emphasised the point even more. He
hails from the Bordeaux area; both he and his wife, Christiane,
are quiet, charming folk. They will offer you a range of menus –
one is inexpensive. But choose from the others and marvel at
some of the skilled pleasures that will be put in front of you:
*saumon cru à l'aneth avec les concombres à la crème, salade
d'avocats aux poissons fumés, poissons du jour* and *noisette
d'agneau et rognons 'Nostradamus'* (one of his predictions?) are
the sort of things to expect. You will be offered a cheese trolley
with a choice of over 30 fresh, appetising varieties – of all kinds;
among the 20 or so desserts, savour the smooth melon, fig and
guava *sorbets*.

You will be pleased, too, by some of the best Provençal wines –
of all shades: **Château Simone**, **Château de la Bégude** and
Château de Selle. Not surprisingly, considering where Francis
used to live, there is a good selection of **Médoc** reds to choose
from on his wine list. If you want to stay overnight use the nearby
Sélect-Hôtel (quiet – no restaurant). Francis is one of the
reserves for my favourite team of XV chefs.
menus **B-C** *cards* AE DC
closed Feb. Sun evg. Mon.
post 1 bd. G.-Clémenceau, 13300 Salon-de-Provence. B.-du-R.
phone (90) 56.06.53 *Mich* 245 Avignon 46 km

SEGURET   La Table du Comtat

Comfortable restaurant with rooms/Michelin★
Secluded/Terrace/Swimming pool

Personally I think both the star and the Gault Millau *toque* are
hardly merited. I suspect that inspectors are sometimes carried
away by 'features' like views – which are marvellous here,
stretching away into the distance to the other side of the Rhône;
or by a seductive setting – that applies here, too. Mind you, I have
no sympathy with visitors to starred restaurants who choose the
cheapest menus and expect 'gastronomic experiences'. The
cooking here will not be spectacular – but the setting and views
are; well worth the very steep climb up a narrow, pot-holed track.
Dishes are classical with the odd lighter creation: *feuilleté de
saumon à l'oseille* is one and a more filling *gigot d'agneau* are
typical. Good local wines.
menus **B** *rooms* 8 **C-D**
closed Mid Jan-Feb. Tues evg. Wed (except July-mid Sept).
post Séguret. 84110 Vaison-la-Romaine. Vaucluse.
phone (90) 36.91.49 *Mich* 245 Avignon 44 km

TAVEL
Host. du Seigneur

Comfortable restaurant with rooms (no showers or baths)
Good value   ®

I have not attempted to count the exact number of reports I have received about my recommendations – over three thousand I should think, because often one reader comments on several places. The most remarkable report I received was from a couple at Chalfont-St-Peter, five miles from my home; they sent me an amazingly-detailed series of records. Let me quote their comments about this simple place: 'outstanding in every respect'; 'outstanding again (our second visit) – deserves a Michelin rosette.' Ange and Juliette Bodo have delighted so many of you at their medieval, vine-covered home. Delights like *agneau grillé aux herbes*, *caneton aux olives*, *jambon braisé* and super cheeses will seduce you, too.

menus **A-B** *rooms* 7 **A-B**
closed Mid Dec-mid Jan. Thurs (out of season).
post 30126 Tavel. Gard.
phone (66) 50.04.26 *Mich* 245 Avignon 14 km

TOURTOUR
Chênes Verts

Comfortable restaurant/Michelin★   ®

Paul Bajade, now 40, has survived the most amazing gamble; even now, as I write these words, I marvel how he has managed to put nearly nine years under his belt at this minuscule home of his – two kilometres to the west of Tourtour. About 20 people or so must be the maximum number he can sit down in his restaurant at any one time; on my evening visit I was his sole client! Not for the first time, Gault Millau recognised his talents long before Michelin grasped the nettle. Innovative, light creations are what Paul specialises in: a delectable *terrine de homard et la salade de champignons* (cream, mayonnaise and the lightest taste of orange), *émincée de saumon sauvage à la crème de safran* and a mouthwatering *parfait glacé au miel du pays et la sauce de chocolat* – all seduced me on that cool evening. Use the 'base' at Villecroze – just down the road.

menus **C-D**
closed Jan-mid Feb. Sun evg (out of season). Wed.
post Tourtour. 83690 Salernes. Var.
phone (94) 70.55.06 *Mich* 245 Avignon 156 km

TOURTOUR
La Bastide de Tourtour

Luxury hotel/Michelin★
Secluded/Terrace/Gardens/Swimming pool/Tennis/Lift

Tourtour – 'the village in the sky'; you will believe it when you gaze southwards with a vast area of Var beneath your feet. You may have already seen this hotel – in the film version of Frederick Forsyth's *The Day of the Jackal*. It was here the *Jackal* met Colette (in the book it was the du Cerf in Gap). Luxury in every respect but average, modest cooking – hardly meriting a star. Enjoy the local **Villecroze** wines.

menus **C** *rooms* 26 **D-D3** *cards* AE DC Visa
closed Nov-Feb. Mon (out of season). Tues midday.
post Tourtour. 83690 Salernes. Var.
phone (94) 70.57.30 *Mich* 245 Avignon 156 km

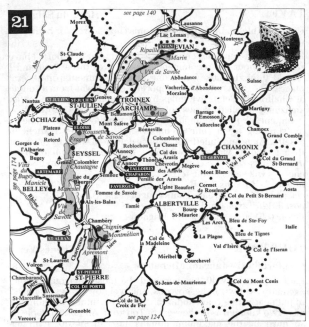

For me this is a very special region of France, one where I have
that natural instinct of being at home. My love for mountains was
nurtured in the first ten years of my life, spent high in the
Himalayas. Both my father and uncle had known F. S. Smythe and
I recall hearing much about his climbing exploits in the
Himalayas during my early days. Consequently, I have since read
many of his books and particularly those describing the British
pioneers who did so many of the first climbs in the French and
Swiss Alps: men like Wills, Smith, Hudson, Whymper and Forbes,
just a few of the brave individuals who started Alpine
mountaineering in the 19th century.

As a result of this the French and Swiss Alps have always been
like a magnet for me; many happy days have been spent in the
glorious, invigorating and inspiring countryside of **Chamonix**
and its high mountains. It was only 100 years ago that many of the
spectacular needles were first climbed. It is worth making as many
of the cable-car, rack-railway and chair-lift trips as you can
afford, but for the best free views of the whole Mont Blanc range
use your own car, cross the Swiss border at **Vallorcine** (15
kilometres north of Chamonix) and immediately follow signs for
Finhaut and the new **Barrage** (Dam) **d'Emosson**. You will climb
to just under 2000 metres, on a well-engineered road, and if the
day is clear you will be rewarded richly. To the north-east are the
Bernese Oberland peaks, to the east is **Grand Combin** and the
mountains towards Zermatt and to the south is the whole Chaîne
du **Mont Blanc**.

Different mountains, but equally appealing, are the secret,
hidden peaks, valleys and gorges of the **Chartreuse** country – the
area between **Grenoble** and **Chambéry**. Resolve now to spend
some time there, even if you are in transit to another part of

France. This resolve should also apply to the **Vercors** Regional Park, south-west of Grenoble. At any time the Chartreuse is a special place, but in the autumn it betters anything Walt Disney could produce; the tints and shades of all the dying leaves are indescribably lovely and, what is more, you have the countryside to yourself. Desert your car and use your legs!

Apart from the attractions of all this scenery it is also great motoring country. You will be taking it quietly and safely, stopping frequently to admire a view or village aspect. But use your imagination: think of the roads in mid-winter, covered in ice, with banks of snow lining the sides and rally cars covering the ground at average speeds well in excess of the speed you are travelling – they have the benefit of studded tyres.

The other splendours of the region are the lakes; especially beautiful is **Annecy** and its lovely eastern shore, with its own jewel of **Talloires**. **Lac du Bourget** and **Lac Léman** (Lake Geneva) are not so attractive but both provide the opportunity for many boating trips. All the lakes yield piscatorial treasures unknown anywhere else in France. The menus of many restaurants in the region are built around these superb fish: salmon trout, some a metre long and weighing 15 kilograms; *omble chevalier*, the most subtle and finest tasting of all freshwater fish (a char – it looks like a large salmon trout); *féra*; *lavaret*; *brochet* and *lotte* (a burbot, not unlike an eel).

If you stay at Chamonix, I recommend you to make two trips: a short one into Switzerland to marvel at one of the most beautiful of the small lakes in the Alps, at **Champex**, south of **Martigny** and high in the wooded mountains; the other trip is a drive through the Mont Blanc tunnel and, on leaving it, turn left up into **Val Ferret**, a hidden, dead-end valley, with spectacular views of the other side of Mont Blanc and the Grandes Jorasses. This is one of the best, unspoilt valleys in the high Alps. Use your legs.

Old Annecy deserves hours of your time to roam its narrow streets, filled with flowers and shops (many streets are pedestrian-only ways and many have covered arcades). Chambéry is another town with a central, pedestrian-only area and it, too, has fine arcades with lovely shops. **Evian** is a spa town on the southern shores of Lake Geneva; millions of bottles of its spring water are sold throughout France each year. **Aix-les-Bains** has many lakeside attractions and quiet gardens. **Megève** and **St-Gervais** are both winter and summer resorts with marvellous, wooded country surrounding them both.

There are several other drives you should make. One is from Annecy, east to **La Clusaz** and then south, climbing up to the summit of the **Col des Aravis** and descending again to Flumet and **Ugine**. Return via Talloires on Lake Annecy. Another drive starting from Annecy takes the minor road, the D41, climbing up to the Crét de Châtillon on the **Semnoz** mountain. If you have a clear day – try to leave it until late afternoon, when the sun is in the west – you will get an exceptional view of Mont Blanc. A drive well worth doing is to climb the lanes to the west of St-Gervais-les-Bains, up to Le Bettex. Mont Blanc lies majestically across the valley; hope for a clear day.

Due west from Annecy and across on the other side of the River **Rhône**, lies an area of hill-country virtually ignored by tourists in France; it's the countryside of **Bugey** – which is part of the *département* of Ain. Bugey is an enclave of wooded hills and hidden within it are several spots you should seek out: **Belley** – the birthplace of Brillat-Savarin; the peak called the **Grand Colombier** – you get a vast panorama from its summit; the

Gorges de l'Albarine; and the **Plateau de Retord** – another citadel of the Resistance during the last War.

In the south-east corner of my map you'll find a mass of super mountain country – packed with visitors during the winter months, enjoying some of the very best ski resorts in France – examples being **La Plagne**, **Val d'Isère**, **Les Arcs**, **Courchevel** and **Méribel**. In the summer the area is ignored by most tourists in Savoie; this is a shame as there are many magnificent, high mountain drives worth your attention – don't miss them.

The first one is the new road that strikes east from **Albertville**, passes through **Beaufort** – famous for its cheese – and climbs the **Cormet de Roselend**. At **Bourg-St-Maurice** make a short detour and climb the series of zigzag bends to the summit of the **Col du Petit St-Bernard** (spectacular views of the southern side of Mont Blanc); then descend again to the **Isère** Valley and climb the **Col de l'Iseran** – at 2770 metres one of the highest of all Alpine passes. If you have the stamina – or should I say if your car has – climb the **Col du Mont Cenis**, world famous for its mountain views. Use the N6 and skirt the southern slopes of the Massif de la Vanoise – a National Park – and then choose between two high passes: the **Col de la Madeleine** that climbs north, back to Albertville; or the **Col de la Croix de Fer** that takes you west towards Grenoble. Both passes usually form part of the Tour de France cycle race – marvel at those brave men.
Michelin *yellow* maps: 244.74.77. Green Guide: Alpes
IGN *série verte* maps: 44.45.51.53. *série rouge* map: 112
Airports: Geneva. Lyon
Distances from: Paris-Geneva 546 km Calais-Geneva 839 km

Cheeses Cow's milk

Abondance from the hills and valleys encircling the town of the same name. Best in summer and autumn – small, firm wheel

Beaufort at its best in winter, spring and summer. A hard, cooked cheese, equivalent to Gruyère, but with no holes. Try it with **Savoie** wines

Beaumont mild, creamy, hard disk. Related to Tamié

Chambarand made by monks near Roybon. A mild, creamy-tasting, small disk. Ideal with the light wines of **Savoie**

Colombière from the Aravis area; mild-flavoured, flat disk

Fondu aux Raisins (**Fondu au Marc**) big disk of processed cheese and covered in grape pips

Reblochon best in summer and autumn. Semi-hard, gold colour with a mild and creamy flavour. Made in flat, small disks. A local term – *reblocher* – means 'to milk the cow for the second time'. Try **Crépy** or **Abymes** wines with it or the red from **Chautagne**

St-Marcellin available all the year. Small, mild-flavoured disks

Ste-Foy (**Bleu de**) a blue-veined cheese, made in a flat cylinder. Best in summer and autumn. **Bleu de Tignes** is a related cheese

Sassenage a summer and autumn season. A soft, spicy-flavoured, blue-vein cheese, related to Bleu de Gex – see Jura region

Tamié made by monks at the monastery of the same name, south of Lake Annecy; a light rind and a pressed, uncooked disk

Tomme de Savoie a semi-hard, flat cylinder, with a slight nutty smell. A summer and autumn season. Has many relations – all called Tomme

Vacherin d'Abondance mild, soft and the size of a thick pancake. At its best in winter. Ideal with **Crépy** or a **Chautagne** wine

Goat's milk

Chevrotin des Aravis a small, flat cylinder with a summer and autumn season. Mild, with no particular smell

Persillé des Aravis blue-veined, sharp-tasting, tall cylinder. Also known as **Persillé de Thônes** and **Persillé du Grand-Bornand**

Regional Specialities

Féra a freshwater lake fish
Fondue hot melted cheese and wine
Gratin Dauphinois a classic potato dish with cream, cheese and garlic
Gratin Savoyard another classic potato dish with cheese and butter
Lavaret a freshwater lake fish, like salmon
Longeole a country sausage
Lotte a burbot, not unlike an eel
Omble chevalier a char, it looks like a large salmon trout

Savoie Wines

Whites and Rosés

There are many good whites and rosés. The whites from **Seyssel** are delicate and flinty (**Clos de la Peclette** is the best). Another fine white is **Crépy**, made from the Swiss Chasselas grape type; this is an AC wine, from the general area south of Lake Geneva. The **AC Vin de Savoie** applies to white wines: of these, **Chignin**, **Apremont** and its close neighbour **Abymes** – Abîmes on the maps – (both on the northern slopes of the glorious Chartreuse Massif) are fresh, light and dry; so is the wine called **AC Roussette de Savoie**. **Roussette de Fragny**, north-east of Seyssel, is a pleasant, subtle wine, as is **Marestel**. These last three are made from the Altesse grape type.

Reds

Montmélian and the neighbouring **Chignin** – both south of Chambéry – are good reds and are made from the Mondeuse grape. Another red is **Chautagne**, made from the Gamay grape, from the vineyards south of Seyssel. These three share the AC **Vin de Savoie**. Often reds will be listed on menus as **Mondeuse** or **Gamay** – their *varietal* names.

Sparkling wines

Look out for the **Seyssel mousseux, Vin de Savoie mousseux**, **Vin de Savoie pétillant, Mousseux de Savoie** and **Pétillant de Savoie**. Other sparklers are the rare **Vin de Savoie Ayze mousseux and pétillant** (Ayse on the maps). Remember you are in **Chartreuse** country; don't miss those lovely green and yellow liqueurs. Also see page 305 – Chambéry *vermouths*.

Vin de Pays

These will be labelled by *département* names: **Haute-Savoie**, **Savoie** and **Isère**.

Additional comments

I would imagine I know the Alps better than any other region of France: the high mountains bordering Switzerland and Italy, the glorious Chartreuse and the inspiring Vercors (see Hautes-Alpes) are all areas I know so well that I rarely need to use even large-scale maps. The region is studded with hotels of all kinds – providing easy access to the myriad delights that Mother Nature has created in this wonderland.

On the cuisine front the picture is not so attractive – with the exception of three top-class *cuisiniers*. You will notice that the category two section has 12 entries – no less than four of them are at Talloires, and three of those are prestige hotels. You may think I have been hard on those three 'top' hotels. Well, I have been even harder on yet another: the world-famous and most expensive restaurant in France – the Auberge du Père Bise; I have dropped that 'shrine' completely from this edition. I have not been hard on those 'top' three; their standards of cooking are really very modest indeed.

EVIAN-LES-BAINS

Florida

Simple hotel
Quiet/Gardens/Good value ®

The great pity with this modest but charming base hotel is that it has such a terribly short season – just three months long. It's high above Evian-les-Bains on the route d'Abondance. Apart from the extensive views northwards over Lac Léman, it's also at the door of lovely country to the immediate south; the plateau above Evian is particularly nice.

No restaurant *rooms* 25 **B-C**
closed Mid Sept-mid June.
post Milly. 74500 Evian-les-Bains. Haute-Savoie.
phone (50) 75.00.44 *Mich* 244 Geneva 44 km

ST-ALBAN-DE-MONTBEL

St-Alban-Plage

Comfortable hotel
Quiet/Gardens ®

A new find for me; it has a magnificent position on the western edge of the Lac d'Aiguebelette – between the road and the lake itself. It's a modern hotel and is just a few kilometres from a convenient autoroute exit – the last one before you enter the long tunnel that takes you under the Mont du Chat and on to Chambéry. One day do the trip over the Mont du Chat.

No restaurant *rooms* 16 **B-D**
closed Nov-Apl.
post St-Alban-de-Montbel. 73610 Lépin-le-Lac. Savoie.
phone (79) 36.02.05 *Mich* 244 Geneva 95 km

ST-GERVAIS-LES-BAINS

L'Adret

Comfortable hotel
Quiet

A chalet-style hotel built on the inside of a hairpin bend. It's on the western side of the spa, so the views you get are the ones across the valley to Mont d'Arbois. There's never a dull moment: tramway rides to Le Nid d'Aigle; cable-cars; the Val Montjoie; walking, climbing, swimming and much more.

No restaurant *rooms* 15 **B-C**
closed Mid Sept-Xmas. 3-19 Jan. Easter-May.
post chemin La Mollaz, 74170 St-Gervais. Haute-Savoie.
phone (50) 93.50.60 *Mich* 244 Geneva 68 km

ST-JULIEN-EN-GENEVOIS

Le Soli

Simple hotel
Quiet/Lift/Good value

A modern, small place, well away from the main Geneva–Annecy road. It's about 100 metres behind the Diligence restaurant. This 'base' – like the hotels at Divonne (see Jura) – is well placed for you to enjoy the pleasures of Switzerland, too, but at more modest cost than staying in Swiss hotels.

No restaurant *rooms* 22 **B-C**
closed Open all the year.
post rue Mgr. Paget, 74160 St-Julien-en-Genevois. H.-Savoie.
phone (50) 49.11.31 *Mich* 244 Geneva 9 km

Recommendations where cuisine takes second place

ARTEMARE
Vieux Tilleul

Simple hotel
Quiet/Terrace/Good value ®

I can only repeat what I said in *Hidden France*: this modest hotel
has a delectable situation – eight km to the north of Artemare, at
Luthézieu. You can enjoy local delights like *jambon cru, lavaret*
and *gratin Dauphinois* on a shaded terrace or in an attractive
dining room. Order **Bugey** wines.
menus **A-C** *rooms* 11 **B**
closed Jan-mid Feb. Wed (except in summer).
post Luthézieu. 01260 Champagne. Ain.
phone (79) 87.64.51 *Mich* 244 Geneva 64 km

CHAPARON
Châtaigneraie

Simple hotel
Secluded/Gardens ®

One of many hotels in category two which fit the bill perfectly if
all you want is peace and quiet. The Châtaigneraie is a *Logis* with
a large, shaded garden (in reality a small, green 'field'). It's south
of Brédannaz and is a kilometre or so from the lake. Fish features
strongly on the menus: *petite friture, truites* (in various ways)
and *omble chevalier*.
menus **A-C** *rooms* 21 **C** *cards* Visa
closed Nov-Jan. Mon (Oct and Feb-May).
post Chaparon. 74210 Faverges. Haute-Savoie.
phone (50) 44.30.67 *Mich* 244 Geneva 51 km

COL DE PORTE
Chalet Hôtel Rogier

Simple hotel
Secluded/Good value

High in the Chartreuse Massif – 1350 metres above sea-level. It's
in an isolated spot on the dead-end track that leads from the Col
de Porte towards the Charmant Som, in magnificent wooded
country. Andrée Bouquin's cooking is modest – but more than
compensated for by the inspiring mountains.
menus **A-C** *rooms* 17 **B-C**
closed Nov-Xmas. Tues (except Feb, July and Aug).
post Col de Porte. 38700 Le Tronche. Isère.
phone (76) 08.82.04 *Mich* 244 Geneva 122 km

ELOISE
Le Fartoret

Comfortable hotel
Secluded/Gardens/Swimming pool/Tennis/Lift ®

What a list of features this hotel has: apart from those shown
above, it's also a *Logis de France*, a *Relais du Silence*, on a dead-
end road, and within a few kilometres of an exit on the newly-
completed autoroute. Extensive views and handy for the Jura.
Many specialities – two examples are *jambon cru* and *crêpe
fourrée Savoyarde*. A useful 'base'.
menus **A-B** *rooms* 40 **C** *cards* Visa
closed Xmas-New Year.
post Eloise. 01200 Bellegarde-sur-Valserine. Ain.
phone (50) 48.07.18 *Mich* 244 Geneva 44 km

267

FAVERGES
Gay Séjour

Simple hotel
Secluded/Terrace/Good value ®

A *French Leave* reader from Bingley in West Yorkshire led me to this small, chalet-style *Logis de France* – owned by the same family (Gay) for three generations. Of the scores of recommendations I have received from readers, this one is perhaps the most likely to please you as it did me.

The Gay Séjour is situated in the glorious, wooded hills south of Faverges – at Tertenoz. All of you who know my books will already realise how much I love the surrounding countryside. Let me list some of the pleasures that are on hand to please and inspire you, too. But first let me give credit to the Grimwoods who gave me an immense amount of detailed information – what follows is just a tiny sample.

There are countless walks in the pastures and fields – in May and June the Grimwoods have counted over 150 species of wild flowers. Further south at Tamié is a Cistercian abbey, famous for its cheese and the Gregorian chants of its monks – to which the public are welcome. Let me quote the Grimwoods: 'no visitor of whatever faith, or none, should miss attending one of the 5/6 daily offices at the abbey. It is an unforgettable religious and musical experience.' (See the photograph opposite page 257.) Climb the glorious Combe d'Ire, south of Doussard. From Ugine take the 'Route Forestière' (macadam surface) to the Signal de Bisanne – views of Mont Blanc (*Hidden France* readers will already know of the delights of the Col des Saisies and Beaufort). And, before I forget, enjoy the good cooking at the Gay Séjour – perhaps even up to category three standards: dishes like *truite grillée*, *pâté deux poissons*, *gougère au fromage* and excellent cheeses. The cuisine complements the superb, secluded site.

Let me end with a caveat which in no way concerns the Gay Séjour. On the strength of a good meal – confirmed by a Michelin 'R' recommendation – I included the Alpes at Faverges in *Hidden France*. The Alpes, a *Logis de France*, had a dark, dismal, uninviting interior, but I felt the cooking made up for its other shortcomings. Sadly, I have to report I have received several complaints. Bypass the Alpes, because the owners – the Guobots – have won no friends at all among my readers. Will Michelin drop that 'R' recommendation next year, too?

menus A-C *rooms* 14 B-C *cards* AE Visa
closed Mid Dec-Jan. Sun evg/Mon (except school holidays).
post Tertenoz. 74210 Faverges. Haute-Savoie.
phone (50) 44.52.52 *Mich* 244 Geneva 64 km

ST-JULIEN-EN-GENEVOIS
Hôtel Rey

Comfortable hotel
Fairly quiet/Gardens/Swimming pool/Tennis/Lift

Another perfect example of a category two entry – use it as a 'base' and eat elsewhere; the restaurant is a separate business and is in another building. At the summit of the Col du Mont-Sion on the Geneva-Annecy road. The owners are extremely warm, friendly people. Ask for a quiet room.

menus A-B *rooms* 31 C
closed Jan.
post 74350 Cruseilles. Haute-Savoie.
phone (50) 44.13.29 *Mich* 244 Geneva 18 km

ST-PIERRE-DE-CHARTREUSE

H. du Cucheron

Simple restaurant with rooms
Secluded/Terrace/Good value   ®

André Mahaut and his wife have been here nine years; the full name of their restaurant is Chalet Hôtel du Cucheron – and they continue to win the hearts of all their clients. They start with a fantastic advantage – their simple chalet sits on the summit of the Col du Cucheron, 1140 metres above sea-level. There are splendid views to the north and even better ones to the south – Charmant Som standing like a sentinel on the horizon; you are surrounded by dense forests and plenty of fine walking country. Whether you have a single lunch or stay overnight and enjoy a dinner, you will be able to choose simple, modest fare that seems so appropriate to the mountain setting: *jambon cru de montagne, truite saumonée meunière, gratin Dauphinois, fromage blanc à la crème* and *tarte maison.* Try the **Apremont** white or **Mondeuse** red wines.

menus **A-B** *rooms* 8 **A-B**
closed Mid Oct-mid Dec. Tues.
post St-Pierre-de-Chartreuse. 38380 St-Laurent-du-Pont. Isère.
phone (76) 08.62.06 *Mich* 244 Geneva 130 km

ST-PIERRE-DE-CHARTREUSE

Beau Site

Comfortable hotel
Swimming pool

The Beau Site is quite different from the simple auberge to the north at the Col du Cucheron; it's a smart, modernised building in the higher part of St-Pierre. Though the facilities are a great deal better, the cuisine is still nothing more than basic fare. But what are superb are the many walks and drives in the area: be sure to explore the whole length of the strangely-named Guiers Mort – from its source down to St-Laurent-du-Pont; and on your way there visit La Correrie – a museum showing the way of life of the Carthusian monks who live in seclusion at the Couvent de la Grande Chartreuse.

menus **A-C** *rooms* 34 **B-C** *cards* AE
closed Mid Oct-mid Dec. Wed (out of season).
post St-Pierre-de-Chartreuse. 38380 St-Laurent-du-Pont. Isère.
phone (76) 08.61.34 *Mich* 244 Geneva 134 km

TALLOIRES

Abbaye

Very comfortable hotel
Secluded/Terrace/Gardens

The Tiffenat family own a superb hotel. No, I'm not out of my mind – it is a category two entry; Talloires no longer offers flair, or value, at any of its restaurants. This 11th-century monastery, founded by St-Germain, a *Bénédictin,* was restored in the 17th century. Its setting is incomparably beautiful and, of course, you pay for all the luxury. Classical cuisine with no inspirations likely to surprise you: *noisettes d'agneau, omble chevalier* and other lake fish.

menus **C** *rooms* 34 **D-D2** *cards* AE DC Visa
closed Mid Oct-Apl. Rest: Apl. Mid Oct-Nov. Tues. Wed.
post Talloires. 74290 Veyrier-du-Lac. Haute-Savoie.
phone (50) 67.40.88 *Mich* 244 Geneva 58 km

TALLOIRES   Le Cottage

Very comfortable hotel
Quiet/Terrace/Lift

Long before I knew that Le Cottage had lost its Michelin star in
1983, I had decided to include it in category two. My visits, and
your many letters, had already confirmed my view that the best
thing about the hotel is its fabulous site – luckily, these days, you
do not have to eat here. (Indeed, I came close to dropping it all
together – like its grossly overrated, excruciatingly expensive
neighbour, the Père Bise; no wonder the latter lost its third star –
that was long overdue.) Another caveat: avoid *demi-pension*
terms; you get little choice in the menu offered. One complaint
mentioned 'poor service.'

So I suggest you use it as a 'base' and marvel instead at the
talent and exciting, innovative cooking skills of Alain Rayé at
Albertville. Enjoy the lovely garden, shady terrace and lakeside
setting back at this comfortable 'base'.
menus **B-D** *rooms* 36 **C-D2** *cards* AE DC
closed Mid Oct-mid Mar.
post Talloires. 74290 Veyrier-du-Lac. Haute-Savoie.
phone (50) 60.71.10 *Mich* 244 Geneva 58 km

TALLOIRES   Les Grillons

Comfortable hotel
Quiet/Terrace/Gardens/Good value

Les Grillons is at Angon, two km south of Talloires. Though it
does not have a lakeside position, this large, modern *Logis* offers
better value-for-money bedrooms than its expensive neighbours
at Talloires. It was recommended to me by a reader who lives just
100 metres away from our home! Other readers have spoken very
highly of the Beau Site in Talloires.
menus **B** *rooms* 30 **B-C** *cards* AE
closed Nov-Mar.
post Angon. 74290 Veyrier-du-Lac. Haute-Savoie.
phone (50) 60.70.31 *Mich* 244 Geneva 60 km

TALLOIRES   Hermitage

Very comfortable hotel
Secluded/Gardens/Swimming pool/Tennis/Lift   ®

On behalf of several readers I have a bone to pick with the
Chappaz family. For some years now Michelin have indicated
that eating is not compulsory at their hotel; yet in July and August
last year the owners bent the rules and insisted clients used their
restaurant. Which is a pity, because the cooking at this
magnificently-sited hotel is mediocre to say the least. I would
suggest you use it as a base hotel (the new French law allows you
to sleep here and eat elsewhere). It's a *Logis* and *Relais du
Silence*, in an isolated spot high above the village; there are
glorious views of the lake. When it's dark, drive up to the
Ermitage St-Germain (see the Abbaye entry); the lights
encircling the lake are a glittering spectacle.
menus **B-C** *rooms* 37 **C-D** *cards* AE
closed Nov-Feb.
post Talloires. 74290 Veyrier-du-Lac. Haute-Savoie.
phone (50) 60.71.17 *Mich* 244 Geneva 58 km

Recommendations where cuisine takes pride of place

ALBERTVILLE
Alain Rayé

Very comfortable restaurant/Michelin★
Terrace ®

Alain Rayé, 32 in October 1983, has the talent to become one of
the 'great' French chefs. He is a dark, small, dynamo of a man and
his creative skills generate dozens of beguiling dishes. Coupled
to his innovative flair are other priceless talents: he has an eye for
detail and he's not afraid of putting in long hours to ensure that
nothing is compromised. He's a great fan of Girardet – and it's not
lost on him that 'real' success in the world of cooking means
everything must be perfect.

Perfection? You see it in the six different types of bread you are
offered – all baked in his kitchen (shame on you Vergé); you
respect it in the wide selection of cheeses served – both local
ones and those from other parts of France (some will be new to
you); you admire it in his succulent *petits fours* – they put many
of the super stars' efforts to shame; you welcome it in his long list
of wines – with over 50 half-bottles on offer (Bocuse cannot
manage 10!). The specialities that Alain beguiles you with are
numerous – light, modern, magnificent dishes: a soup of salmon,
oysters and leeks; some *bar* with red peppers and carrots; *foie
d'oie* in a cabbage leaf; a ginger *sorbet*; a fantastic dish of 12 tiny
bits of lamb – in a circle interspaced with minuscule *navets*,
courgettes and sliced truffle. You'll relish his *raviolis aux
mangues* – minute *crêpes* with mango – and his six smooth-as-
silk *sorbets*.

Nicole, his wife, is a vivacious, charming girl; she spent some
years in Canada and consequently speaks fluent English. She and
Alain have two boys, aged six and three. Four restaurant staff
assist Nicole with ordering and serving food – Alain has five or
six helpers in his kitchens. (Use the Million bedrooms.)
menus **B-C** *cards* **AE DC** Visa
closed Last week June. 1st week July. Mid-end Nov. Tues.
post Pont des Adoubes, 73200 Albertville. Savoie.
phone (79) 32.00.50 *Mich* 244 Geneva 89 km

ALBERTVILLE
Million

Very comfortable hotel/Michelin★★
Terrace/Gardens/Lift

What a coincidence that two of the best chefs in the French Alps
should both be based at Albertville. One is Alain Rayé; the other
is Philippe Million, the seventh generation to continue the
tradition at this hotel – owned by the family for nearly 200 years.
Philippe is an excellent chef but Rayé is better; if you think I'm
hard on the Talloires *cuisiniers* come to Albertville and then
compare them. Million has moved slowly but surely from a
classical base to a cuisine that is light and modern in outlook.
You'll like this unattractive hotel in a busy corner of the town –
the nice interior more than compensates. Here are some most likely
specialities that will please: *escalope de truite saumonée au vin
rouge et son feuilleté, mignon de veau aux raviolis* and a huge
range of mouthwatering desserts.
menus **B-D** *rooms* 29 **B-D** *cards* **AE DC** Visa
closed Mid Apl-mid May. 1-15 July. Mid Sept-mid Oct.
Rest: Sun evg. Mon (except evgs mid July-Aug).
post 8 place Liberté, 73200 Albertville. Savoie.
phone (79) 32.25.15 *Mich* 244 Geneva 89 km

ARCHAMPS
Auberge de Vovray

Simple restaurant
Terrace/Good value
®

In describing the setting of this tiny bistro you will appreciate that it's unlikely to be overcrowded. Archamps sits in the shadow of Mont Salève – just south of the autoroute that acts as a bypass to Geneva; the Auberge is a kilometre or so to the east of the village. Annick and Jean-Claude Gouin offer clients inexpensive fare: *andouillette poêlée au vin blanc, longeole, grillades aux herbes, gratin Dauphinois* and simple sweets. One *French Leave* reader – an expert wine shipper – wrote to say that: 'Gouin's own bottled wines need careful selection – the **St-Véran** was undrinkable and it had obviously been untreated after their supplier had handed over the goods.' Make a trip to the summit of Mont Salève, high above you.

menus A
closed Mid Feb-Mar. Xmas-New Year. Sun evg. Mon.
post Archamps. 74160 St-Julien-en-Genevois. Haute-Savoie.
phone (50) 43.60.07 *Mich* 244 Geneva 9 km

BELLEY
Chabert

Comfortable restaurant with rooms/Michelin★

Like its neighbour, the Pernollet, this drab-looking restaurant is an excellent example of local Bugey cooking. You will see it in these dishes: *gratin d'écrevisses Nantua* (the town that gave its name to the sauce of cream and puréed crayfish), *filet aux morilles* (the latter from the hills to the north), *jambon cru* and many fish specialities like *lavaret, truite* and so on. Order the various wines of Bugey (see Lyonnais): **Manicle**, **Montagnieu** and the Chardonnay, Pinot and Gamay grape type varieties are examples. There have been some complaints about the traffic noise and, overall, I must say that, though the cooking is good, it hardly merits a Michelin star.

menus A-C *rooms* 16 A-C *cards* Visa
closed Mid-end June. Mid-end Oct. Sun evg/Mon (not Aug).
post 2 bd. Mail, 01300 Belley. Ain.
phone (79) 81.01.56 *Mich* 244 Geneva 78 km

BELLEY
Pernollet

Comfortable hotel/Michelin★

Brillat-Savarin was born in Belley in 1775 (see *Pen Pictures*); you can visit his birthplace in the Grande Rue (behind the Chabert Restaurant). He died in 1826 at Belley, five years after this family-owned hotel was opened. Five generations later Ernest Pernollet is at the stoves – continuing the same traditions of classical and Bugey cooking. At the vine-covered hotel you'll see provincial France at its strongest – solid values, where the family count most and where cuisine depends entirely on local products. Witness these examples: *lavaret glacé au vin blanc*, magnificent *cèpes* and *morilles* from the Bugey hills and *quenelle de brochet*. Excellent **Bugey** wines here, too.

menus B-C *rooms* 20 C *cards* AE DC Visa
closed Mid Nov-mid Dec. Rest: Wed.
post 9 place Victoire, 01300 Belley. Ain.
phone (79) 81.06.18 *Mich* 244 Geneva 78 km

CHAMONIX   Albert 1er et Milan

Very comfortable hotel/Michelin★
Gardens/Swimming pool/Tennis/Lift   ®

This remains one of my family's favourite hotels; we have known it for nearly two decades and it gives us great pleasure to see that the next generation of Carriers are slowly but surely taking over from their parents. Our old friends, father and mother Carrier, still help for part of the day – but their efforts are now directed towards the other smaller and newer enterprise across the valley (see the next entry). Son Denis looks after the restaurant and his brother, Pierre, is the chef. The hotel is a large, chalet-styled, warm place with its own facilities; the sports centre at Chamonix is across the road – there you will find an all-seasons ice rink. Surrounding you are the high peaks of the Mont Blanc range – and there's many a trip that takes you up to those icy heights. Cuisine is classical and specialities include *filet mignon de veau au Madère et foie gras* and *Mont Blanc glacé* (with chestnut purée). Enjoy the **Ripaille** wines from the southern shores of Lake Geneva (see map).

menus **B-C** *rooms* 32 **C-D** *cards* AE DC Visa
closed Mid Apl-mid May, Oct-mid Nov
post 74400 Chamonix-Mont-Blanc. Haute-Savoie.
phone (50) 53.05.09 *Mich* 244 Geneva 83 km

CHAMONIX   Auberge du Bois Prin

Very comfortable hotel
Secluded/Gardens/Lift   ®

A small, luxury chalet, owned by the Carrier family – mother and father Carrier run it. Marcel's cooking is based on classical traditions and is similar to that of the Albert 1er. Only dinner is served; you also have the use of the facilities at the other hotel. Apart from the comfortable bedrooms, the other bonus here is the magnificent panorama you have of Mont Blanc, high above you on the other side of the valley. One trip you should not miss is to the church of Notre-Dame-de-Toute Grâce at Assy (north of St-Gervais): full of the works of Léger, Lurçat, Matisse, Chagall, Braque and others. Include the tiny Lac Vert on the trip – study Michelin map 244 carefully.

menus (dinner only) **B** *rooms* 11 **D-D2** *cards* AE DC Visa
closed Oct-mid Dec. May-mid June.
post Moussoux. 74400 Chamonix-Mont-Blanc. Haute-Savoie.
phone (50) 53.33.51 *Mich* 244 Geneva 83 km

EVIAN-LES-BAINS   Bourgogne

Comfortable restaurant with rooms/Michelin★

An attractive, vine-covered building in the centre of Evian – and certainly not quiet. Claude Riga is devoted to his classical cuisine – which probably suits the majority of visitors taking the waters at this handsome spa. Specialities include *foie gras d'oie, filet de truite du lac au Champagne, omble chevalier* and *carré d'agneau.*

alc **B-C** *rooms* 10 **C** *cards* AE DC Visa
closed Nov-mid Dec. Rest: Tues evg/Wed (except July-Aug).
post 73 rue Nationale, 74500 Evian-les-Bains. Haute-Savoie.
phone (50) 75.01.05 *Mich* 244 Geneva 42 km

EVIAN-LES-BAINS   La Verniaz et ses Chalets

Luxury hotel/Michelin★
Secluded/Terrace/Gardens/Swimming pool/Tennis/Lift

Arguably one of the best hotels in the French Alps. The Verdier
family have a collection of charms to bewitch you: there's a
virginia-creepered, turreted building at the centre of the complex
and separate chalet-style houses that contain the bedrooms;
there are a whole range of facilities to attract you – see the list
above; and there's the gorgeous countryside surrounding the spa
of Evian, alongside Lac Léman, and some hundreds of metres
below you. It's all very luxurious and very stylish – the list of
famous guests over the years bears witness to that. Prices are of
Mont-Blanc steepness. *Nouvelle cuisine* has not reached Evian
yet; what you will enjoy are classics such as *omble chevalier*,
andouillette (a 'cheat' word) *de truite saumonée Sylvette* and
filet de Charolais à la broche. **Marin** is a local wine from
vineyards west of Evian.
menus **B-C** *rooms* 35 **D-D2** *cards* AE DC Visa
closed Dec. Jan. Sun evg and Mon (out of season).
post route Abondance, 74500 Evian-les-Bains. Haute-Savoie.
phone (50) 75.04.90 *Mich* 244 Geneva 42 km

OCHIAZ   Auberge de la Fontaine

Comfortable restaurant with rooms
Quiet/Terrace/Gardens

Claude and Colette Ripert own a charming, rustic Auberge; it's
five kilometres to the west of Bellegarde – and, rising further to
the west, behind the restaurant, are the high, wooded hills of
Bugey. You are ideally placed to see plenty of the southern end of
the Jura, too. Conventional, classical cooking with both Savoie
and Lyonnais treats: *volaille de Bresse au vinaigre, omble
meunière, pâté chaud de canard, pintadeau garni, escargots de
Bourgogne* and *marjolaine Cointreau.*
menus **A-C** *rooms* 7 **B** *cards* AE DC Visa
closed Jan. Sun evg. Mon.
post Ochiaz. 01200 Bellegarde-sur-Valserine. Ain.
phone (50) 48.00.66 *Mich* 244 Geneva 46 km

ST-JULIEN-EN-GENEVOIS   Diligence et Taverne

Very comfortable restaurant/Michelin★

What makes this restaurant unusual is that it's in the basement of
a modern building, alongside the main Geneva-Annecy road.
Though it has a warm, cosy atmosphere, it really is ideal only for
an evening meal – perhaps at the end of a wet day. Robert and
Christine Favre – now joined by their son, Christophe, who has
completed the obligatory training 'tour' – clearly depend on
business from Geneva. On my last 'incognito' visit a huge party of
UN staff were winning all their time and attention; I may just as
well have been invisible. There were few signs of any modern
ways on that visit: *omble du lac, pigeonneau 'juste rose'* and good
sorbets were adequate enough.
menus (Taverne) **B-C** *cards* AE DC
closed 1-15 July. 10-end Jan. Sun evg. Mon.
post avenue Genève, 74160 St-Julien-en-Genevois. H.-Savoie.
phone (50) 49.07.55 *Mich* 244 Geneva 9 km

ST-PIERRE-DE-CHARTREUSE   Aub. Atre Fleuri

Comfortable restaurant with rooms
Quiet/Terrace/Gardens/Good value

A modest Auberge complemented by equally simple, straightforward fare from the kitchens of André Revest. It's on the D512, three kilometres from St-Pierre-de-Chartreuse as you head south towards Grenoble. André's a good chef – his repertoire includes *jambon cru de montagne, truites* (in various forms), *grillades, gigot des Alpilles* and *pieds et paquets* (see Côte d'Azur) and *neige à la liqueur de Chartreuse*, which seems an appropriate way to end any meal hereabouts.

menus **A-B** *rooms* 8 **B**
closed Nov-Xmas. Tues evg and Wed (out of season).
post St-Pierre-de-Chartreuse. 38380 St-Laurent-du-Pont. Isère.
phone (76) 08.60.21 *Mich* 244 Geneva 137 km

SEYSSEL   Rhône

Comfortable hotel/Michelin★
Terrace

A typical Michelin one-star establishment where you wonder why on earth the star is awarded; it's good, average cuisine – no more. Robert Herbelot's forte is regional and classical fare: dishes make use of fish from the lakes and Rhône (the nice terrace overlooks the west bank of the river) – *lavaret Robert's* is one; *poularde de Bresse aux morilles* is good. **Peclette** is one of the best of all the Savoie wines – the vineyards are to the north. Any reports on the nearby Rôt. du Fier restaurant?

menus **A-C** *rooms* 17 **A-C** *cards* AE DC Visa
closed Mid Nov-Jan. Sun evg/Mon midday (out of season).
post 01420 Seyssel. Ain.
phone (50) 59.20.30 *Mich* 244 Geneva 49 km

TROINEX   Vieux Moulin

Very comfortable restaurant/Michelin★★   ®

Gérard Bouilloux, celebrating his 36th birthday on the day we visited the Vieux Moulin (in Switzerland), is a Frenchman from Mâcon – making a name for himself as the best chef in the Geneva area. Eliane, his wife, is Swiss; together they form the typical young husband and wife team that I admire so much.

Their restaurant is five kilometres to the south of Geneva – at Troinex. It's very easy to reach from either the 'base' or the category two entry at nearby St-Julien (both are in France and much cheaper than hotels in Geneva). The old mill is a small place, with two attractive dining rooms; the kitchen is even smaller – you pass it on your way in.

Gérard is an imaginative *créateur* – deserving of his increasing reputation. One dish was amazingly good – *langoustines à l'anis*; two huge *langoustines* in a piquant sauce with a tomato-based reduction. A white chocolate *mousse* was a tasty delight. His single appetiser was a shocker – defeating accurate analysis; his *petits fours*, too, were of a poor standard.

menus **C-D** (French francs) *cards* AE Visa
closed 1-15 Apl. 1-15 Sept. Sun evg. Mon.
post 89 route Drize, CH-1256 Troinex. Switzerland.
phone (22) 42.29.56 (Switzerland) *Mich* 244 Geneva 5 km

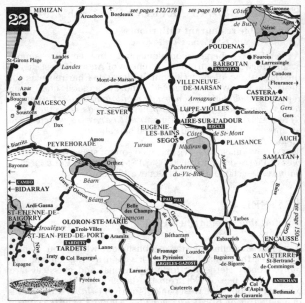

A region of France endowed with every type of scenery: a glorious coastline from **Biarritz** to **Arcachon**; a high range of mountains in the **Pyrénées**; the lush, green and gently-rolling hills and valleys of **Gers**; the vast pine forests of the **Landes**; and a variety of different streams and rivers throughout the area. No other region offers you such a wide choice.

Pau makes the ideal starting-point for exploring the Southwest. It is a town with exquisite grace, an air of Edwardian elegance, attractive and quiet parks, and above all, the unique Boulevard des Pyrénées, from where the view of the mountain range, particularly on a crisp winter or early spring day, is breathtaking. My wife and I have seen the countryside in early April, fruit blossom everywhere and snow still on the peaks; something July and August cannot emulate.

A visit to **Lourdes** is always memorable, particularly if it includes participating in one of the outdoor processions and services. It is one of the most important pilgrimage centres in the world, because of a vision seen by Bernadette Soubirous on 11th February 1858. Of the smaller towns, **Dax**, with fountains bubbling forth hot spring waters, **Condom**, and the fortified towns like **Plaisance** and **Fleurance** are all worth a visit. Be sure to see **Fourcès** and **Larressingle** – both gems (see page 286).

Make one trip to the magnificent coastline, to spots like **Mimizan**, **Vieux-Boucau** or **St-Girons-Plage**. The sight and sound of the Atlantic hurling itself against the long, sandy beaches is unforgettable. Explore the hills and valleys to the north of Pau. It is lovely countryside; ideal for easy, relaxed driving in the lanes, which, at anytime, you will find deserted. Explore, too, the hills surrounding **St-Jean-Pied-de-Port**.

At least one drive into the Pyrénées is a must. For many people the range is not as attractive as the Alps, but it does have its own stark beauty. The passes are severe and are not the best engineered of roads, but they are safe enough and uncrowded. When you see them, think of the annual Tour de France and those brave cyclists ascending the steep passes and then descending, at two to three times the speed you will come down them.

The **Cirque de Gavarnie** is an unforgettable sight; savage mountains at their best. Vertical rockfaces rise in several tiers – to a total height in excess of 3000 metres. In spring cascades of melting snow add extra interest. The **Adour** and Adour de Gripp Valleys – south of **Bagnères-de-Bigorre** (sometimes called the Campan Valley) – are considered by many to be among the finest in the Pyrénées. West of **Sauveterre** is **St-Bertrand-de-Comminges**; in Roman days it boasted a population of 50,000. The Avignon popes built the huge cathedral. **Bétharram**, near Lourdes, has underground caves and lakes on several levels. The **Col d'Aspin** is a must – the best of the passes.

Without any doubt this region offers the visitor the highest quality of cuisine, at the lowest cost, in France. My recommendations demonstrate the remarkable mixture of regional, classical and *nouveaux* skills to be found in the Southwest. See page 284.

Michelin *yellow* maps: 234.79.82.85.86. Green Guide: Pyrénées
IGN *série verte* maps: 62.63.69.70. *série rouge* map: 113
Airports: Biarritz. Bordeaux. Pau. Toulouse
Distances from: Paris-Pau 750 km Calais-Pau 1042 km

Cheeses Cow's milk

Belle des Champs from Jurançon, white, mild and an aerated texture
Bethmale a hard cylinder from the valleys south of St-Gaudens
Fromage des Pyrénées a mild, semi-hard, large disk with a hard rind
Goat's milk
Cabécous small, flat cheese. Mild, nutty flavour. At its best in winter
Ewe's milk
Esbareich in the form of a big, flat loaf. A summer and autumn season; ideal with **Madiran**. Related cheeses: **Laruns, Amou** and **Ardi-Gasna**
Iraty a strong-flavoured, pressed loaf. Contains some cow's milk

Regional Specialities

Besugo *daurade* – sea-bream
Chorizos spicy sausages
Confit de canard (d'oie) preserved duck meat (goose)
Cousinette (Cousinat) vegetable soup
Echassier a wading bird of the Landes
Garbure (Garbue) vegetable soup with cabbage and ham bone
Gâteau Basque a shallow, custard pastry – often with fruit fillings
Grattons (Graisserons) a *mélange* of small pieces of rendered down pork fat (duck and goose), served as an appetiser – very filling
Hachua beef stew
Jambon de Bayonne raw ham, cured in salt. Served as paper-thin slices
Lamproie eel-like fish, with leeks, onions and red Bordeaux wine sauce
Lou-kenkas small, spicy sausages
Loubine (Louvine) grey mullet (like a sea-bass)
Magret (de canard) breast (of duck)
Ortolan a small bird (wheatear) of the Landes
Ouillat (Ouliat) Pyrénées soup; onions, tomatoes, goose fat, garlic
Palombes (Salmis de) wild doves and wood pigeons from the Landes and Béarn, sautéed in red wine, ham and mushrooms
Pastiza see *Gâteau Basque*
Ramereaux ring doves
Salda a thick cabbage and bean soup
Tourin (Tourain) see *Ouillat*: *Touron* – see page 151
Ttoro (Ttorro) a Basque fish stew

Southwest Wines

In the countryside near **Jurançon** (south-west of Pau), you will find both sweet and dry (*sec*) whites; other whites (of both tastes) to look out for are the strangely-named **Pacherenc du Vic-Bilh** and **Tursan**. From **Madiran** come some excellent reds, which I strongly recommend: **Tursan** (VDQS) also produces some reds. Tursan wines come from the area to the south and west of Eugénie-les-Bains; Vic-Bilh and Madiran wines are made in the country to the east of Eugénie, in the hills before reaching the Adour. North of Condom are the **Côtes de Buzet** – mainly reds, and some whites, are made there. North-west of Plaisance is the newly-promoted VDQS **Côtes de St-Mont** – its reds are good.

Further south try **Irouléguy** wines: red, white and rosé. From the Orthez area come **Béarn** wines, again of all shades. **Armagnac**, France's oldest brandy, is one marvel of the region; many of the restaurants lie in the heart of Armagnac country. The Basques make a liqueur called **Izarra**, meaning *star*; there are two varieties, yellow and green. Enjoy a **Floc** (Armagnac and grape juice) – the Gascon *apéritif*.

Vins de Pays

In the Southwest these will be classified by the names of *départements*: **Landes**, **Gers** or **Pyrénées-Atlantiques**. Alternatively, in the Gers area you will see **Vin de Pays des Côtes du Condomois** (from the hills surrounding Condom); **Côtes de Montestruc** and **Côtes de Gascogne** (red and rosé).

Bordeaux Wines

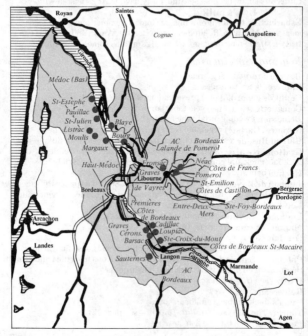

These are outside the geographical limits of the Southwest region but I am including them here for all those travellers in France who love the superb harvests from the vineyards surrounding Bordeaux. This is another area where some of the local wines are beyond the means of most of us. A classic red Bordeaux (called *claret* in the U.K.) is dryer than a Burgundy, less heavy in alcohol, and is really only drinkable when accompanied by food. It has a longer life than a Burgundy red wine.

There are five great wine areas, the first four listed producing reds:

> **Médoc**, the largest area and divided into Bas-Médoc and Haut-Médoc. In **Haut-Médoc** is the very famous village of **Pauillac**, from where three of the five great red châteaux wines come.
>
> **Graves** (which means gravelly soil), the second largest area. Whites also are made here.
>
> **St-Emilion** and **Pomerol**, much smaller areas and both on the banks of the Dordogne.
>
> **Sauternes** is the fifth area, famous for its white wines.

Some of the best-known wines in the world come from the vineyards of Bordeaux: amongst the reds are **Château Lafite**, **Château Latour** and **Château Mouton-Rothschild** (all three in the village of Pauillac); **Château Margaux**, also in the Haut-Médoc; and **Château Haut-Brion** from Graves. These five reds are at the top of the pyramid, the *Premiers Crus* (first growths). It is a white from Sauternes, **Château d'Yquem**, that has a special rank above even those five, *Premier Grand Cru*. Dozens and dozens of other châteaux follow, split into various levels of prestige, rather than excellence of quality – see the lists that follow on page 281. Thankfully, there are many clarets towards the bottom of the pyramid (see *Crus Bourgeois*) which are sensibly priced; the Bordeaux area producing a high proportion of quality wine for all of us, whatever the size of our pockets.

We need to understand how the Appellation Contrôlée system works in Bordeaux. Think of a pyramid: the wines from a specific vineyard, perhaps just as big as a football field, sit at the top and are the most expensive. The bottom of the pyramid represents those wines from any part of the whole region, the ones that do not have a pedigree in the form of their own individual AC status. In Bordeaux, unlike Burgundy, an individual château does not have its own AC; it will share the *commune*, or even the region's, AC classification. Do not imagine the term *château* always means a fine, imposing building; more often than not it refers to vineyards making up an estate, the only building perhaps being a humble shed, half-buried, where the wine is stored. How does the system work?

1 A bottle label with **AC Bordeaux** or **AC Bordeaux-Supérieur** (this means higher alcohol strength, not superior quality) is wine that has come from anywhere in the entire region; it will certainly be from the fringe areas and it will be the cheapest wine.

2 A label with **AC Médoc** indicates it comes from that general area to the north-west of Bordeaux, on the west bank of the Gironde. This will be both dearer and better wine. It is likely it will be from the Bas-Médoc, considered inferior to Haut-Médoc.

3 A label with **AC Haut-Médoc** will signify it was produced in that specific part of the Médoc considered superior for vineyard quality. These wines will be further up the quality and price scale.

All three examples are *generic* wines, those carrying the name of a geographical area, though many of them, even some in example 1, may still carry a château name.

    4 A label with **AC Pauillac** means the wine was made in that *commune* within the Haut-Médoc. It will be getting expensive and will be an excellent claret. Most labels will be carrying a château name as well, from the humble to a few like **AC Pauillac Château Lafite**; this label would indicate that not only have you a specific vineyard in Pauillac but also one of the top five reds in Bordeaux.

Reds *best years* 45 47 49 53 55 61 62 64 66 70 75 78 79 81 82

There are dozens of good clarets available at relatively modest cost. Clearly the first three examples I have mentioned qualify and some from the fourth example. So do wines from other Haut-Médoc *communes*: from north to south, **Saint Estèphe, Saint Julien, Listrac, Moulis** and **Margaux**; all have their own AC.

Wines from the other great red areas qualify: **Graves, Pomerol** (**Château Pétrus** is thought by many to be amongst the best of all Bordeaux wines) and **Saint Emilion**. Saint Emilion has three extra AC levels: its best châteaux are classified as **Saint Emilion Premier Grand Cru Classé** and some 70 others as **Saint Emilion Grand Cru Classé**. A lower rating is **Saint Emilion Grand Cru**. Saint Emilion is bordered by five smaller *communes*, all having their own AC with the addition of the word **Saint Emilion: Lussac, Montagne, Parsac, Puissegiun** and **Saint Georges**. Other reds from lesser-known areas are (from north to south): **Premières Côtes de Blaye, Bourg, Cotes de Bourg** (considered better), **Côtes de Fronsac, Fronsac, Côtes Canon Fronsac, Lalande de Pomerol, Néac, Bordeaux Côtes de Francs** and **Bordeaux (Supérieur) Côtes de Castillon**, these last two being just east of Saint Emilion.

Other areas are the **Premières Côtes de Bordeaux**, on the east bank of the Garonne; **Graves de Vayres**; **Bordeaux Haut Benauge** (part of the Entre-Deux-Mers territory). **AC Bordeaux** or **AC Bordeaux Supérieur** are the most common reds.

Rosés

Rarely seen are the **Bordeaux Clairet** and **Bordeaux Supérieur Clairet** – wines with a shorter fermentation period and thus dark rosé in colour; equally rare are the **AC Bordeaux Rosé** and the **AC Bordeaux Supérieur Rosé**.

Whites *best years* 45 47 49 53 55 61 62 67 70 75 78 79 81 82

The white wines of Bordeaux have gone through a significant transition during recent years. Because of both the increasing demand for dry wines and the crippling costs of producing sweet, dessert wines, growers have responded by making crisp, light whites – lovely wines and cheap, too. Dry white wines will normally be in green bottles – sweet ones in clear glass.

Of the various whites made from the Sauvignon Blanc grape, look out for the crisp drys of **Entre-Deux-Mers, Entre-Deux-Mers-Haut Benauge** and **Graves de Vayres**. A white **AC Bordeaux** will be a dry alternative as will **Blaye, Côtes de Blaye, Côtes de Bourg** and **Graves**. From **Côtes de Bordeaux Saint Macaire**, north of Langon, **Premières Côtes de Bordeaux** and **Ste-Foy-Bordeaux** come both dry and sweet wines.

For those of you with a sweet tooth the golden **Sauternes, Barsac, Cérons, Loupiac, Sainte Croix-du-Mont** and **Cadillac** will be the answer (the Sémillon grape is the most common – ideal with its high sugar content). **AC Bordeaux Supérieur** and **Graves Supérieur** will be medium-sweet, golden white alternatives. An AC is also given to a **Bordeaux mousseux**.

Great Growths (Grands Crus) of the Médoc – 1855 list

Château	AC taken	Château	AC taken
First Growths (Premiers Crus)		**Third Growths** (Troisièmes Crus)	
Lafite	Pauillac	Marquis d'Alesme-Becker	Margaux
Latour	Pauillac	Palmer	Margaux
Margaux	Margaux	**Fourth Growths** (Quatrièmes Crus)	
Haut-Brion (not in Médoc)	Graves	Beychevelle	St-Julien
Mouton-Rothschild (1973)	Pauillac	Branaire-Ducru	St-Julien
Second Growths (Seconds Crus)		Duhart-Milon	Pauillac
Brane-Cantenac	Margaux	Lafon-Rochet	St-Estèphe
Cos d'Estournel	St-Estèphe	La Tour-Carnet	Haut-Médoc
Ducru-Beaucaillou	St-Julien	Marquis-de-Terme	Margaux
Durfort-Vivens	Margaux	Pouget	Margaux
Gruaud-Larose	St-Julien	Prieuré-Lichine	Margaux
Lascombes	Margaux	St-Pierre-Bontemps	St-Julien
Léoville-Barton	St-Julien	St-Pierre-Sevaistre	St-Julien
Léoville-Las-Cases	St-Julien	Talbot	St-Julien
Léoville-Poyferré	St-Julien	**Fifth Growths** (Cinquièmes Crus)	
Montrose	St-Estèphe	Batailley	Pauillac
Pichon-Longueville and Pichon-		Belgrave	Haut-Médoc
Longueville-Lalande	Pauillac	Camensac	Haut-Médoc
Rauzan-Gassies	Margaux	Cantemerle	Haut-Médoc
Rausan-Ségla	Margaux	Clerc-Milon	Pauillac
Third Growths (Troisièmes Crus)		Cos Labory	St-Estèphe
Boyd-Cantenac	Margaux	Croizet-Bages	Pauillac
Calon Ségur	St-Estèphe	Dauzac	Margaux
Cantenac-Brown	Margaux	du Tertre	Margaux
Desmirail	Margaux	Grand-Puy-Ducasse	Pauillac
Ferrière	Margaux	Grand-Puy-Lacoste	Pauillac
Giscours	Margaux	Haut-Bages-Libéral	Pauillac
d'Issan	Margaux	Haut-Batailley	Pauillac
Kirwan	Margaux	Lynch-Bages	Pauillac
Lagrange	St-Julien	Lynch Moussas	Pauillac
Langoa	St-Julien	Mouton-Baronne Philippe	Pauillac
La Lagune	Haut-Médoc	Pédesclaux	Pauillac
Malescot-St-Exupéry	Margaux	Pontel-Canet	Pauillac

Then follow about 160 *Crus Bourgeois* properties – making quality wines at lower prices than the classified growths listed above. Until recently there were two additional classifications – *Cru Grand Bourgeois* and *Cru Bourgeois Exceptionnel*: the EEC objected to these terms and now all of them are called *Crus Bourgeois*.

First Great Growths (Premiers Grands Crus) of St-Emilion

12 châteaux share this 1955 classification:
Ausone, Cheval-Blanc, Beauséjour-Duffau-Lagarrosse, Beauséjour-Becot, Bel-Air, Canon, Figeac, Clos Fourtet, La Gaffelière, La Magdelaine, Pavie, Trottevieille.

Classified Growths of the Graves: the best châteaux

Red wines: Bouscaut, Haut-Bailly, Carbonnieux, Domaine de Chevalier, Fieuzal, Olivier, Malartic-Lagravière, La Tour-Martillac, Smith-Haut-Lafitte, Haut-Brion (see *Médoc* list) – and its excellent white wine as well, La Mission-Haut-Brion, Pape Clément, Latour-Haut-Brion.

White wines: Bouscaut, Carbonnieux, Domaine de Chevalier, Olivier, Malartic-Lagravière, La Tour-Martillac, Laville-Haut-Brion, Couhins.

1855 Classification of Sauternes and Barsac châteaux

Premier Grand Cru – the only one in Bordeaux: d'Yquem.

Premiers Crus: Climens, Coutet, de Rayne-Vigneau, de Suduiraut, Guiraud, Haut-Peyraguey, Lafaurie-Peyraguey, La Tour-Blanche, Rabaud-Promis, Rieussec, Sigalas-Rebaud.

Seconds Crus: Broustet, Caillou, d'Arche, de Malle, de Myrat, Doisy-Daëne, Doisy-Védrines, Filhot, Lamothe, Nairac, Romer, Suau.

CAMBO-LES-BAINS

Errobia

Comfortable hotel
Secluded/Gardens/Good value

I was taken to task by an American reader over my description of this 'base' in the last edition of *French Leave*. I will be careful with my words this time: the 'setting' for this old Basque house is superb. Overlooking the Nive, its grounds, in May, are 'perfection'; the camellias and rhododendrons a delight. Rooms seedy? Perhaps – but Nature counts more here. The spa is full of handsome trees; how just it would be if the folk who planted them all those years ago could see them now.

No restaurant rooms 15 **B-C** *cards* Visa

closed Nov-Apl (except Easter).

post 64250 Cambo-les-Bains. Pyrénées-Atlantiques.

phone (59) 29.71.26 *Mich* 234 Pau 113 km

PAU

Bilaa

Comfortable hotel
Secluded/Lift

®

The Bilaa is a modern, ugly-looking, concrete box-type hotel. But don't be put off by that; it's in a secluded site some six km to the west of Pau. It has 80 bedrooms with all modern facilities – and it's not too expensive. Don't use the Novotel at Pau!

No restaurant rooms 80 **C** *cards* AE Visa

closed Open all the year.

post 64230 Lescar. Pyrénées-Atlantiques.

phone (59) 32.63.00 *Mich* 234 Pau 6 km

Recommendations where cuisine takes second place

ANTICHAN

Host. Ourse

Simple hotel (no showers or baths)
Quiet/Gardens/Good value

What a pretty setting for this hotel, sitting as it does on the east bank of the River Ourse. Like so many hotels in the Southwest, it has the compulsory red and white shutters. Basic cuisine with dishes using local trout and rabbit.

menus **A-B** *rooms* 10 **A-B**

closed Sept-Easter. Fri (out of season).

post Antichan. 65370 Loures-Barousse. Hautes-Pyrénées.

phone (62) 99.25.02 *Mich* 85 Pau 110 km

ARGELES-GAZOST

Miramont

Comfortable hotel
Terrace/Gardens/Good value

An unusually-styled, smart hotel; apart from its own garden it's close to a circular-shaped park. Could well be in category three; classical cuisine is good – things like *jambon du pays* and *saumon frais au beurre blanc*.

menus **A-B** *rooms* 29 **B-C**

closed Mid Oct-Xmas. Rest: Mon (Mid Jan-Apl).

post rue Pasteur, 65400 Argelès-Gazost. Hautes-Pyrénées.

phone (62) 97.01.26 *Mich* 234 Pau 53 km

ARGELES-GAZOST   Thermal

Simple hotel
Secluded/Terrace/Gardens/Good value   ®

You'll be delighted by the attractive setting; the small, fort-like
hotel is in fact the thermal 'resort' of Beaucens (the spring is
under the building). The term 'gardens' doesn't do it justice – it's
a *parc* surrounded by trees and with fine views of the nearby hills
from the terrace. Cooking is modest – but other benefits more
than compensate; the *cirques* at Gavarnie and Troumouse are
just two. Beaucens is five km south-east of Argelès, on the
eastern side of the Gave.
menus **A-B** *rooms* 28 **B-C**
closed 10 Oct-10 May.
post Beaucens. 65400 Argelès-Gazost. Hautes-Pyrénées.
phone (62) 97.04.21 *Mich* 234 Pau 58 km

BARBOTAN-LES-THERMES   Château Bellevue

Very comfortable hotel
Secluded/Gardens/Swimming pool/Lift

At Cazaubon, just south of the spa town. The hotel is more of a
small 'mansion' than a 'château'. Cooking is above average,
though Francis Latreille seems to depend a lot on local ducks:
pâté chaud de canard, *aiguillettes de canard*, *confit de canard*
and *magret de canard* all appear on his menus.
menus **B-C** *rooms* 27 **B-D** *cards* AE
closed Jan. Feb. Tues (Dec and Mar).
post 32150 Cazaubon. Gers.
phone (62) 09.51.95 *Mich* 234 Pau 81 km

BARBOTAN-LES-THERMES   Château de Bégué

Comfortable hotel
Secluded/Gardens/Swimming pool

Use this fort-like hotel as a 'base' – bypass the restaurant.
Delightful setting and a park with fine trees. On clear days the
Pyrénées can be seen from the southern entrance.
menus **B** *rooms* 25 **B-D**
closed Nov-Apl.
post 32150 Cazaubon. Gers.
phone (62) 09.50.08 *Mich* 234 Pau 82 km

PAU   Domaine du Beau Manoir

Comfortable hotel
Secluded/Terrace/Gardens/Swimming pool   ®

Many of you have written to say how much you appreciated this
isolated, modern hotel – in a gorgeous spot in the hills to the
south-east of Pau (use D209). The bonus here is the superb view
of the Pyrénées mountain wall – stretching right across the
southern horizon. I'm told there are new owners and that
cooking standards should be better. Do let me know please.
menus **A-B** *rooms* 32 **B-D** *cards* Visa
closed Feb. Rest: Sun evg. Mon midday.
post route N.-D. de Piétat, 64110 Jurançon. Pyr.-Atl.
phone (59) 06.17.30 *Mich* 234 Pau 6 km

RISCLE

Paix

Simple hotel
Good value

Typical of the value for money you get at even the simplest of places; in no way can it compare, in cuisine terms, with the category three entries, yet it has a sound local reputation. The produce of Gers takes pride of place: *foie gras, canard, saumon* from the nearby Adour, and the **Côtes de St-Mont** wines from the hills to the west.

menus A-B *rooms* 17 A-B
closed 1st 3 weeks Sept.
post 32400 Riscle. Gers.
phone (62) 69.70.14 *Mich* 234 Pau 55 km

TARDETS-SORHOLUS

Gave

Simple hotel
Gardens/Good value

Mme Etcheverry owns a modest hotel with a riverside setting; 'gardens' don't mean much here – it's just a bit of natural grass alongside the River Saison. *Cuisinettes* available. Enjoy local dishes like *œuf piperade, omelette Basquaise* and trout from the Saison. Super country to the south.

menus A-B *rooms* 12 B-C *cards* Visa
closed Mid Nov-Feb. Mon (out of season).
post 64470 Tardets-Sorholus. Pyrénées-Atlantiques.
phone (59) 28.53.67. *Mich* 234 Pau 60 km

My favourite 'cuisine' region

I am frequently asked what region of France I like best; I cannot give an answer if geography is the only consideration. I would not want to take sides in debating whether, for example, the quiet charms of the Jura, the majestic peaks of Savoie, the colourful coast of the Côte d'Azur or the river valleys of the Dordogne should be considered the 'best'. Each region will mean more to one visitor than it does to another; it is quite impossible to give a simple answer.

However, when it comes to giving an objective reply to the same question if it concerns 'cuisine', I'll get off the fence and plump for one region – the Southwest. For many years my vote would have gone to the Lyonnais; certainly it has more good chefs in its tiny area than any other region. But for a combination of skill, variety of cuisine and exceptional value for money you cannot beat the fantastic Southwest – confirmed by the numerous ℝ symbols.

In the nine pages that follow I list 22 recommendations (a 23rd – Puymirol – is included in the Dordogne region); they range from the very simplest of restaurants to arguably one of the world's greatest. Some of the chefs I write about are young men; others are in their fifties and sixties; one is a lady. Some *cuisiniers* will offer you their regional specialities; a few stick with the classics; others with *Bourgeoise* delights; and many have turned to the modern-day ways. All of them are proud of their *pays* and make great use of the bountiful regional produce; all of them – Guérard, too, in his own way – offer really remarkable value for money. *Bon appétit!*

284

Recommendations where cuisine takes pride of place

AIRE-SUR-L'ADOUR

Commerce

Comfortable restaurant with rooms
Gardens/Good value

Be certain to do one thing if you stay overnight; ask for a quiet room at the back, as André Labadie's restaurant is alongside the N134, as it winds its way through Aire-sur-l'Adour. The last word of the town's name should remind you that, in the season, you will be offered salmon; at other times the products of Landes and Gers will predominate. It's all rich stuff: *foie gras au confit, civet de canard au Madiran, cœurs d'oie* and *omelette aux cèpes*. In addition there are many classical treats, too.

menus **A-B** *rooms* 22 **A-B**
closed Jan. Hotel: Sun. Rest: Mon.
post 3 rue Labeyrie, 40800 Aire-sur-l'Adour. Landes.
phone (58) 76.60.06 *Mich* 234 Pau 49 km

AUCH

France

Very comfortable hotel/Michelin★★
Lift

®

Still on the right side of 50, André Daguin wins all the top prizes for the most extrovert, handsome chef in France; passionate in his love for his country, for Gascony and cooking in all its forms – in that order. (Secretly, I think I may be wrong – rugby must sneak a place in there somewhere; he was a great player in his younger days.) Fluent in his command of English, witty, and with a great sense of humour, I know of no other *cuisinier* in France who can hold your attention so easily: he promotes Gascony and its superb products here at Auch and in every corner of the globe – on his annual one-month vacation; his repertoire combines in innovative ways old regional delights with the simple, light pleasures of today.

I have received letters commenting that André is living on his reputation – I don't agree with that observation in any way. No chef works harder creating new dishes – inevitably with many a mistake made; and no other chef provides better value for money. I have been lucky enough to see his team at work at their hot stoves on a busy day – it was a revelation.

André's grandfather, grandmother, father and mother were cooks. His wife, Jocelyne, was trained as a *cuisinière*; and now their oldest son, Arnaud, has joined them in their family kitchens. The hotel is a large building with a dining room that is anything but intimate. (Across the road, on the other side of a splendid fountain, is the magnificent Auch Cathedral – don't miss seeing the superb choir stalls, among the best in Europe.) Eating here offers value for money; bedrooms are expensive – though the breakfasts are perfection.

What specialities are available? I can only give a small sample of the possibilities: his *grandes soupes, magret poêlé sur sa rissole, foies gras crus ou cuits, pintade à l'ail confit* and a dish of several chocolate desserts – surprisingly light. And last – but not least – try his majestic **Armagnacs** and order the local wines: **Pacherenc** and **Madiran**.

menus **B-D** (Le Neuvième: *alc* B) *rooms* 30 **C-D2** *cards* AE DC Visa
closed Rest: Jan. Sun evg and Mon (out of season).
post place Libération, 32000 Auch. Gers.
phone (62) 05.00.44 *Mich* 82 Pau 104 km

BARBOTAN-LES-THERMES   La Bastide Gasconne

Very comfortable hotel
Quiet/Terrace/Gardens/Swimming pool/Tennis

Chefs come and go each year at this seductive hotel in a small spa; but you can be certain of one thing – they are all students of Michel Guérard. Why? Well, the 18th-century La Bastide (in the south it means both a 'fortified town' and a 'small country house or farm') is part of the Barthélémy chain of spa hotels; it, too, like its famous sister at Eugénie-les-Bains, was furnished with exquisite taste by Christine Guérard. As is Michel's way these days, menus offer you the choice of light, easy-to-digest dishes and also interpretations of many hearty Gascony classics. On one hand: *feuilleté léger de saison* and *gâteau soufflé de langoustines et son coulis*. On the other: *filets de mignons d'oie grillés aux cèpes* and *meurette de dorade au vin de Graves*. It's expensive – though not so dear as Eugénie.

Don't miss Fourcès (English-built, circular *bastide*) and Larressingle (restored, fortified village – the size of two tennis courts) – both to the east; 30 km to the south-east is Castelmore, the home of the real *d'Artagnan* (see Tardets entry on page 293) – hidden in the best **Armagnac** country.
menus **B-C** *rooms* 47 **D** *cards* AE
closed Nov-Mar.
post Barbotan-les-Thermes. 32150 Cazaubon. Gers.
phone (62) 09.52.09 *Mich* 234 Pau 84 km

BIDARRAY   Pont d'Enfer

Comfortable hotel
Quiet/Terrace/Gardens/Good value

A *Logis* with the standard red and white livery of the area; it's on the west bank of the Nive, well away from the main road through the village. Extra pleasure comes in the form of a tiny terrace alongside the river; that would complement an outdoor meal made up of local Basque specialities: *poulet Basquaise, piperade au jambon, jambon Bayonne* and – last but not least – a mouthwatering *gâteau Basque*.
menus **A-B** *rooms* 18 **A-C**
closed Nov-Feb.
post Bidarray. 64780 Osses. Pyrénées-Atlantiques.
phone (59) 37.09.67 *Mich* 234 Pau 122 km

CASTERA-VERDUZAN   Florida-Besant

Simple restaurant with rooms
Terrace/Good value

Castéra is a minute thermal resort; cooking here is in the hands of Paulette Abadie and her son, Bernard Ramouneda. The latter is a member of Daguin's band of 'musketeers'. Gascony cooking – examples are *foie gras, magret de canard* and *confit de canard*. Tiny terrace shaded by a chestnut tree. Rooms are at the Besant part of the establishment.
menus **A-C** *rooms* 23 **B** *cards* Visa
closed Rest: Nov. Mar. Sun evg and Mon (Oct-May). Hotel: Nov-Mar. Mon.
post 32410 Castéra-Verduzan. Gers.
phone (62) 68.13.22 Hotel: (62) 68.10.22 *Mich* 82 Pau 114 km

ENCAUSSE-LES-THERMES   Marronniers

Simple restaurant with rooms (no showers or baths)
Quiet/Terrace/Good value   Ⓡ

I smile when I see this modest auberge sharing the same page
with the most luxurious hotel in France. A chestnut-shaded
terrace alongside a stream provides a tranquil spot for a lunch of
jambon, some *cèpes* and a *gâteau des prélats*.
menus **A-B** *rooms* 10 **A**
closed Oct. Mon (Nov-Feb).
post Encausse-les-Thermes. 31160 Aspet. Haute-Garonne.
phone (61) 89.17.12 *Mich* 86 Pau 116 km

EUGENIE-LES-BAINS   Les Prés d'Eugénie

Luxury hotel/Michelin★★★
Secluded/Gardens/Swimming pool/Tennis/Lift   Ⓡ

Michel and Christine Guérard continue to weave their carpet of
magic in this verdant corner of France – hidden in one of the
alluring valleys of the Chalosse, on the borders of the
départements called Landes and Gers. The combination of
Michel's brilliant, imaginative cuisine; Christine's exquisite eye
and talent for style and moods – demonstrated to perfection in
this luxury home of hers; and Nature's bewitching handiwork is
unique. After many visits I still find it difficult to describe it all in
words and I have given up trying to work out how the whole
operation can pay for itself. The Barthélémys must have sunk
many millions of francs into backing their daughter and son-in-
law – the mind boggles at what it has all cost! New in 1982 was
another floor added to the hotel section; done so cleverly that
even a regular visitor like myself didn't notice it until it was
pointed out. The 30 or so bedrooms have been restyled and
refitted – they're expensive. The place is shut for five months of
the year and Michel works hard during that time earning extra
income around the world. He needs it! However, to his credit, he
stays at home throughout the season – unlike some others I can
name elsewhere in France.
  Eating at Eugénie is expensive – but not cruelly so when you
consider what skill and luxury are provided. For example a
recent menu I relished cost a little over £25 ($40) – service and
tax included. This is what I enjoyed: *foie gras en gelée de poivre
mignonnette et le mesclum de printemps* – a famous innovation
of his; *raviole de truffe à la crème de mousserons et de morilles* –
tiny bits of truffle inside ravioli cases; *fine rouelle de bar sauce
simple*; *noisettes d'agneau poêlées au thym*; and finally a
millefeuille d'Impératrice. The latter took ages to arrive – I
imagine a disaster, or two, must have taken place in the kitchen
as even the final offering was badly burnt. Eating on my own it
was noticeable what a sepulchral silence there was in those
pretty dining rooms. Out of character features of the furnishings
are two hideous *paintings* on the dining room walls; where, in
one example, fruit emerges, in a 3-D effect, from the surface.
Ignore those unimportant points – make whatever financial
sacrifice is needed to visit Eugénie, the glittering 'crown' of
France. (Use the Pau 'base' for inexpensive bedrooms.)
menus **D** *rooms* 35 **D2-D3** *cards* AE
closed Nov-Mar.
post Eugénie-les-Bains. 40320 Geaune. Landes.
phone (58) 58.19.01 *Mich* 234 Pau 53 km

LUPPE-VIOLLES   Relais de l'Armagnac

Comfortable restaurant with rooms
Gardens   ®

Roger Duffour, now 60, is approaching the time when most
people think about retiring – yet he is putting up performances
which are as stunning as ever. Decades ago he had a Michelin
star; these days Roger's most loyal supporters are Gault Millau.
Michelin should give him back that star: why do they ignore this
talented, third-generation chef?

My last visit was an eye-opener – coming 24 hours after a visit
to the great Guérard. Frankly, I enjoyed my meal here just as
much. And, as a bonus, Roger's prices were half those I had paid
at Eugénie-les-Bains. A successsion of light dishes, using local
produce, were delicious: a *salade de Luppé*, salmon from the
nearby Adour, a *feuilleté chaud aux asperges nouvelles*, a
brochette de cœurs d'oie sur la braise, 18 sweets to choose from
plus a most unusual and delectable *fromage blanc à l'Armagnac
blanc*. Save your francs, too, for the last treat – one of Roger's
superb **Bas Armagnacs**.

These days the Relais is looking smarter than ever – the view at
the rear of the dining room does wonders for your appetite.
Elisabeth Daro, Roger's daughter, is a delightful girl and has an
excellent command of English – she puts you at ease and looks
after you well. Roger is one of the *Mousquetaires* (Musketeers)
de la cuisine de Gascogne (Daguin and Coscuella are others); he
certainly does them proud.

Luppé-Violles is on the N124 from Aire-sur-l'Adour to Nogaro;
the latter has a small motor racing circuit. It's used frequently by
the Renault Formula One Team; you may be lucky and have a
chance to see them testing cars on the circuit – or, better still, to
meet them, Alain Prost included, at the Relais.

menus A-C *rooms* 10 B-C *cards* DC Visa
closed Jan. Mon (except July-Aug).
post Luppé-Violles. 32110 Nogaro. Gers.
phone (62) 09.04.54 *Mich* 234 Pau 62 km

MAGESCQ   Relais de la Poste

Very comfortable hotel/Michelin★★
Quiet/Gardens/Swimming pool/Tennis

These days the vastly-improved, dual-carriageway N10 takes the
busy traffic away from the village and, more importantly, has
turned this Basque-style Relais into a quiet spot. Spacious,
wooded grounds include both swimming pool and tennis court.
What have not changed are the old regional classics – a way of
life with Bernard Coussau and his son. So if you have a healthy
appetite and a desire to tuck into hearty, stomach-filling fare,
choose from the likes of *foie gras de canard aux raisins*, *magret
de canard* and *omelette aux truffes*.

In previous editions of *French Leave* I recommended you to
enjoy the run through the woods from Azur, along the western
edge of the Etang de Soustons, to Soustons. I now discover that
President Mitterrand's summer home is on that road; if he's there
you'll not fail to see it – surrounded by *gendarmes*!

menus C *rooms* 15 B-D *cards* AE DC
closed Mid Nov-Xmas. Mon evg and Tues (except July-Aug).
post Magescq. 40140 Soustons. Landes.
phone (58) 57.70.25 *Mich* 234 Pau 95 km

The Chaîne du Mont Blanc – from Mont Salève (Savoie)

Near St-Alban – north-west of the Chartreuse Massif (Savoie)

The abbey park at the Cirque de Consolation (Jura)

Anne, Sally-Anne, Andrew, 'Rusty' and 'Dusty' – at Chiltern House

MIMIZAN   Au Bon Coin

Comfortable restaurant with rooms/Michelin★
Quiet/Terrace   ®

Jean-Pierre Caule continues to thrive at this prettily-situated,
well-named spot; his restaurant lies among the pine forests of the
Landes and alongside a quiet lake, the Etang d'Aureilhan – a
kilometre or so north of Mimizan. The most significant change in
his outlook comes from a positive decision to concentrate on
nouvelle methods – you see it in many of his specialities: *ragoût
fin de homard, rougets de roche farcis à la mousse* and in a first-
class dessert – *grand dessert Folie*. However, just to make
certain you refer to your list of regional specialities, you can also
choose *salade de l'échassier Landais* or *loubine de Mimizan
aux truffes*. Try a **Madiran** red instead of a claret – you'll not be
disappointed.
menus **B-C** *rooms* 12 **B-C** *cards* Visa
closed Feb. Sun evg and Mon (out of season).
post 40200 Mimizan. Landes.
phone (58) 09.01.55 *Mich* 234 Pau 150 km

OLORON-STE-MARIE   Béarn

Comfortable hotel
Lift   ®

A big effort is being made by Guy Darroze and his wife (who
speaks English) to restore the hotel to its previous peak – years
ago it had a Michelin star. It's in a relatively quiet spot alongside
the *mairie*, but away from the main road through this bustling,
pleasant town. The Gave d'Oloron is famous for its salmon; the
Gave d'Oussau and Gave d'Aspe – which join at Oloron to form
the Gave d'Oloron – are renowned for their trout. Enjoy those
fish, *salmis de palombes, magret de canard* and the wines from
the hills at **Jurançon**, just up the road outside Pau. Don't miss the
Eglise Ste-Marie, in Oloron, with its splendid portal. For keen
walkers I recommend *Long Walks in France* (Weidenfeld).
menus **B-C** *rooms* 32 **B-D** *cards* AE DC Visa
closed Feb. Fri evg and Sat (out of season).
post 4 pl. Clémenceau, 64400 Oloron-Ste-Marie. Pay.-Atl.
phone (59) 39.00.99 *Mich* 234 Pau 33 km

PEYREHORADE   Central

Comfortable restaurant with rooms/Michelin★
Good value   ®

A favourite of ours; François Barrat is the brother of Alain Barrat
who runs the best hotel/restaurant in the Loire – at Romorantin-
Lanthenay. The cooking here is at the other end of the cuisine
spectrum; primarily regional with the odd modern touch. So
piperade and *foie de canard aux raisins* are there to be ordered
– and, for a change, *pigeon grillé à la crème d'ail* or *bar en
papillote*. One caveat: the church clock is a near neighbour of the
Central – it strikes twice on the hour and every half-hour. Take
some earplugs if you stay overnight!
menus **A-B** *rooms* 10 **A** *cards* Visa
closed Mid Nov-Dec. Sun evg and Mon (except July-Aug).
post place A.-Briand, 40300 Peyrehorade. Landes.
phone (58) 73.03.22 *Mich* 234 Pau 71 km

PLAISANCE   La Ripa Alta

Simple hotel/Michelin★
Good value   ®

Three cheers! Maurice Coscuella has won his star back from
Michelin. I would like to think that *French Leave* and *Sunday
Times* readers wrote many letters to Paris badgering Michelin to
see justice done – because, believe me, they take great notice of
your letters, rating them as very important.

Maurice Coscuella is now in his fifties; he was trained 30 years
ago by the legendary Point at Vienne. Among his fellow
apprentices were Bocuse, Jean Troisgros and many more of
today's legends. After a spell as a chef on ocean liners he opened
his own hotel 20 years ago. It took him ten years to win his first
star and another ten to lose it – at a time when his wife, Irène, was
very seriously ill; happily, she has recovered. Maurice is a
bubbling extrovert – though hampered by a stutter, he speaks
English well. Always experimenting, always creating, I can still
savour the aroma of a *consommé de saumon au beurre de truffes*
– characteristic of his work.

His new word processor is his greatest joy; for me it was an
eye-opener to see how he used it (after 20 years in computers I
thought I had seen it all). His menus change daily – both à la carte
and his fixed-price ones; he can buy fresh produce every day to
his heart's content, knowing that all he has to do is press a button
and out come as many copies of his menus as he wants. His
creations number hundreds: *civet de lotte, gratin d'orties, figue
au whisky, saumon mariné, mousse de palombes, poulet sauté
Armagnac* – the list is endless.

What else can I do to entice you here? Maurice is the champion
of the Southwest chefs when it comes to judging the birthplace
and age of **Armagnacs**; no wonder when you gasp at his fantastic
selection. Just go!
menus **A-C** *rooms* 15 **A-C** *cards* AE Visa
closed Nov. Mon (except June, July, Aug and *fêtes*).
post 32160 Plaisance. Gers.
phone (62) 69.30.43 *Mich* 234 Pau 65 km

POUDENAS   La Belle Gasconne

Comfortable restaurant/Michelin★   ®

Fate struck a cruel blow to Marie Claude Gracia in 1983. This
delightful, 47 years old *cuisinière* – a fifth-generation chef and
the only lady culinary 'musketeer' – won her first star; sadly,
Michelin forgot to place Poudenas on their map of starred
restaurants. Many tourists must have therefore missed this
talented chef – so loyal to the culinary delights of Gascony.

Make sure you don't pass her by. She was trained by Jo
Rostang at Sassenage (now at La Brague – Côte d'Azur), 25 years
ago. Since then she has managed to bring up five children and
establish herself as a leading chef; husband Richard has played
his part in supporting and encouraging her. Let's hope it will not
be long before they can afford to complete the conversion of
their old *moulin* across the road. Regional specialities at bargain
prices. Book ahead.
menus **B-C**
closed Jan. Sun evg. Mon.
post Poudenas. 47170 Mézin. Lot-et-Garonne.
phone (53) 65.71.58 *Mich* 234 Pau 112 km

ST-ETIENNE-DE-BAIGORRY   Arcé

Comfortable hotel/Michelin★
Secluded/Terrace/Gardens   ®

This is one of those delectable spots universally loved by all
those who make the effort to seek it out – to find it head your car
up the Vallée des Aldudes. The Arcé takes its name from the
owners; Emile, the current *cuisinier* and *patron* is the fourth-
generation of the family – Pascal, his son, is now back from his
training and is helping his parents. The hotel sits beside the fast-
flowing Nive des Aldudes; nothing could be more perfect than a
lunch on the terrace beside the swirling torrent. Classical and
regional specialities will be the order of the day: *truite* (from the
Nive) *au beurre blanc, foie de canard, saumon de l'Adour* and
gâteau Basque. Order **Irouléguy** wines – you'll see the vineyards
on your way to St-Jean.
menus **B** *rooms* 24 **C-D**
closed Nov-Feb.
post 64430 St-Etienne-de-Baïgorry. Pyrénées-Atlantiques.
phone (59) 37.40.14 *Mich* 234 Pau 114 km

ST-JEAN-PIED-DE-PORT   Pyrénées

Comfortable hotel/Michelin★
Terrace/Lift   ®

My enthusiasm for the skills of Firmin Arrambide remain as great
as ever but, sadly, I have to report blemishes in other areas –
more about that later. Firmin is still well on the right side of 40
and I continue to be convinced that he will become a better chef
still as the years go by. One thing I can guarantee is that you will
not find anywhere else in France such fine skills at such
remarkably low prices – as I said in the last edition, Paris ones
seem like blackmail.
    Firmin is self-taught; his annual holiday each year – in
November and December – is a series of visits to the restaurants
of the great chefs. He takes note of what he sees and back home
he experiments with his own ideas – the outcome is a personal
style that covers the whole spectrum of cuisine possibilities.
Primarily he is an advocate of the new freedom young chefs have
these days – you see it in many of his specialities: *soupe aux
écrevisses, ragoût de sole et de homard, saumon frais à la
fondue de poireaux, feuilleté aux poires caramélisées* and *soupe
de pêches blanches*. But his light touch also influences regional
classics: *garbue aux choux, piperade du jambon, salmis de
palombes, confit de canard* and *foie gras grillé*. Whatever you
choose, you'll see the good use he makes of *cèpes, truffes,
morilles* and local vegetables.
    As much as I regret turning to the debit side of things, I feel I am
honour bound to do so. Too many letters have complained about
'very slow' and 'very poor service'. (St-Jean these days can at
times be like a tourist trap: is business coming too easily?) Worse
still are the many complaints about the 'surly' and 'unhelpful'
attitude of Raymonde, Firmin's mother. Thank heavens that
Anne-Marie, his pretty wife, has not attracted any negative
comments from readers.
menus **B-C** *rooms* 31 **B-C**
closed Mid Nov-Xmas. Tues.
post pl. Gén.-de-Gaulle, 64220 St-Jean-Pied-de-Port. Pyr.-Atl.
phone (59) 37.01.01 *Mich* 234 Pau 103 km

ST-SEVER   Relais du Pavillon

Comfortable hotel/Michelin★
Gardens   ®

The Relais is two kilometres to the north of St-Sever – on the
other side of the River Adour; it's an ugly, modern box of a hotel.
Fortunately it's all much better looking at the back – the
bedrooms are at the rear. The architecture may be dismal – but
you will get a super welcome from the owners and staff. Many of
you have mentioned the happy atmosphere at the Relais. René
Dumas is a supporter of regional classics, honest cooking, honest
effort and honest prices. What will some of those treats be?
Choose from *foie de canard frais en terrine, jambon des Landes,
cèpes à la Landaise, escalope de louvine au Madiran* and
brochette de cœurs d'oies.
menus **B** *rooms* 14 **B-C** *cards* AE DC Visa
closed Sun evg (Nov-Mar).
post 40500 St-Sever. Landes.
phone (58) 76.20.22 *Mich* 234 Pau 71 km

SAMATAN   Maigné

Simple hotel
Good value   ®

I received two letters of commendation for this humble place
from *French Leave* readers; both of them thought it deserved a
Michelin star. Though I cannot agree with that proposal, what is
certain is that here is a classic example of a good Michelin 'R'
recommendation – 'good food at moderate prices'. Who knows,
Louis Maigné may just one day win that proud accolade, but
meanwhile he provides rich, regional cuisine at prices that will
not mean taking out a second mortgage. Tuck in and enjoy *foie
gras, confit de canard* and other dishes like *soupe de fèves* and
gratin d'endives. This simple hotel has an unusually-styled, vine-
covered façade.
menus **A-C** *rooms* 15 **A-B**
closed Mid Sept-Oct.
post 32130 Samatan. Gers.
phone (62) 62.30.24 *Mich* 82 Pau 140 km

SAUVETERRE-DE-COMMINGES   Sept-Molles

Very comfortable hotel/Michelin★
Secluded/Gardens/Swimming pool/Tennis/Lift   ®

As much as I love this super country hotel and admire the honest,
fresh and copious cooking, it's at places like this that I think
Michelin are really excessively charitable – particularly when
you consider that they give the thumbs-down sign to talented
chefs like Roger Duffour at Luppé-Violles.

No matter, because Raymond Ferran, his son, Gilles, and the
rest of the family, though sticking to simple, basic things, offer
good menus: a huge *hors d'œuvre, truites, charcuterie maison,*
grills and *confit de canard aux cèpes.* Nothing changes – nor does
the glorious, local countryside.
menus **B-C** *rooms* 23 **C-D** *cards* AE DC
closed Nov-mid Mar.
post Sauveterre-de-Comminges. 31510 Barbazan. H.-Garonne.
phone (61) 88.30.87 *Mich* 86 Pau 108 km

SEGOS   Domaine du Bassibé

Very comfortable hotel/Michelin★
Secluded/Terrace/Gardens/Swimming pool   Ⓡ

Jean-Pierre and Mayi Capelle are near neighbours of Guérard;
Segos is on the eastern side of the N134, about nine kilometres
south of Aire-sur-l'Adour. A recommendation from *French Leave*
readers who live just a few miles away – they know all the best
Southwest chefs – brought me to this attractive corner of Gers,
with its ravishing views eastwards across the Larcis Valley. The
Capelles have a reputation for looking after their clients. Jean-
Pierre is a self-taught chef; he spent many years in the States, and
as a consequence, he speaks excellent English. Very much a
modern chef, his specialities have a light touch – particularly
enjoyable on my visit were a *consommé de St-Jacques aux
asperges et aux truffes* and an individual-sized *tarte au citron
vert*. There are good-value menus available – but make
absolutely certain you ask for them.
menus **B-C** *rooms* 6 **D-D2** *cards* AE DC Visa
closed Nov-Mar. Sun evg and Mon midday (out of season).
post Segos. 32400 Riscle. Gers.
phone (62) 09.46.71 *Mich* 234 Pau 40 km

TARDETS-SORHOLUS   Pont d'Abense

Simple restaurant with rooms (no showers or baths)
Quiet/Terrace/Gardens/Good value   Ⓡ

A small, whitewashed building with red shutters; it's on the
western side of the River Saison and its terrace is particularly
inviting. Simple fare at value-for-money prices: *truite meunière*,
asperges vinaigrette and *gâteau Basque*. This is *The Three
Musketeers* country: Aramits (*Aramis*) and Lanne (the home of
M. de Porthau – *Porthos*) are to the east; Trois-Villes (*Tréville*) is
to the north (also see page 286). Don't miss the Col Bagargui
drive to St-Jean. Keen walkers – read the Oloron entry.
menus **A-B** *rooms* 12 **B-C**
closed Mid Nov-Dec. Fri (out of season).
post Abense de Haut. 64470 Tardets-Sorholus. Pyr.-Atl.
phone (59) 28.54.60 *Mich* 234 Pau 60 km

VILLENEUVE-DE-MARSAN   Europe

Simple hotel/Michelin★
Swimming pool/Good value   Ⓡ

It's fitting that the last entry in *French Leave* should be for a chef
who is representative of so much that I find exciting on the
cooking scene in France. Robert Garrapit is a young man who
won his first star two years ago – prior to that he had earned the
'R' accolade; ages ago it was easy to spot he would take that step
up. He's loyal to the produce and recipes of the Southwest:
salmis de palombes, poule farcie Henri IV and much else. But
he's also a convert to the *cuisine libre* of today – *gambas
cuisinées au vin de Tursan* and *rouget rôti à l'huile d'olive* are
just two of his value-for-money creations.
menus **A-C** *rooms* 18 **A-C** *cards* Visa
closed Jan.
post 40190 Villeneuve-de-Marsan. Landes.
phone (58) 58.20.08 *Mich* 234 Pau 70 km

Abatis (Abattis) poultry giblets

Abats offal

Ablette freshwater fish

Abricots apricots

Acarne sea-bream

Acidulé(e) acid

Affiné(e) refined

Africaine (à l') African style: with aubergines, tomatoes, *cèpes*

Agneau lamb

Agneau de pré-salé lamb fed on salt marshes

Agnelet young lamb

Agnès Sorel thin strips of mushroom, chicken and tongue

Aiglefin haddock

Aigre-doux sweet-sour

Aiguillettes thin slices

Ail garlic

Aile wing

Aileron winglet

Aïoli mayonnaise, garlic, olive oil

Airelles cranberries

Albert white cream sauce, mustard, vinegar

Albuféra *béchamel* sauce, sweet peppers

Alénois watercress-flavoured

Algues seaweed

Aligot purée of potatoes, *Tomme* cheese, cream, garlic, butter

Allemande *velouté* sauce with egg yolks

Allemande (à l') German style: with sauerkraut and sausages

Allumettes puff pastry strips

Alose shad

Alouette lark

Alouette de mer sandpiper

Aloyau sirloin of beef

Alsacienne (à l') Alsace style: with sauerkraut, sausage and sometimes *foie gras*

Amandes almonds

Amandine almond-flavoured

Amer bitter

Américaine (à l') Armoricaine (à la) sauce with dry white wine, cognac, tomatoes, shallots

Amourettes ox or calf marrow

Amusettes appetisers

Ananas pineapple

Anchoïade anchovy crusts

Anchois anchovy

Ancienne (à l') in the 'old style'

Andalouse (à l') Andalusian style: tomatoes, sweet red peppers, rice

Andouille cold smoked sausage

Andouillette chitterling (tripe) sausage

Aneth dill

Ange angel

Angevine (à l') Anjou style: with dry white wine, cream, mushrooms, onions

Anglaise (à l') plain boiled

Anguilles eels

Anis aniseed

Arachides peanuts

Araignée de mer spider crab

Ardennaise (à l') Ardenne style: with juniper berries

Argenteuil asparagus flavoured (usually soup)

Arlésienne stuffed tomatoes *à la provençale*, eggplant, rice

Armoricaine see *Américaine*

Aromates aromatic – either spicy or fragrant

Artichaut artichoke

Asperges asparagus

Assiette (de) plate (of)

Aubergine aubergine, eggplant

Aulx (plural of *ail*) garlic

Aumônière pancake

Aurore (à l') pink sauce, tomato flavoured

Auvergnate (à l') Auvergne style: with cabbage, sausage and bacon

Avelines hazelnuts

Avocat avocado pear

Baba au rhum sponge with rum syrup

Baguette long bread loaf

Baies berries

Baigné bathed or lying in

Ballotine boned and stuffed poultry or meat in a roll

Banane banana

Bar sea-bass

Barbarie Barbary duck

Barbeau barbel

Barbue brill

Barigoule (à la) brown sauce with artichokes and mushrooms

Baron de lapereau baron of young rabbit

Barquette boat-shaped pastry

Basilic basil

Basquaise (à la) Basque style: Bayonne ham, rice and peppers

Bâtarde butter sauce, egg yolks

Baudroie monkfish, anglerfish

Bavaroise bavarois mould, usually of custard, flavoured with fruit or chocolate. Can describe other dishes – particularly shellfish

Bavette skirt of beef

Béarnaise thick sauce with egg yolks, shallots, butter, white wine

Béatilles (Malin de) sweetbreads, livers, kidneys, cocks' combs

Beaugency *Béarnaise* sauce, artichokes, tomatoes, marrow

Bécasse woodcock

Bécassine snipe

Béchamel creamy white sauce

Beignets fritters

Belons flat-shelled oysters

Bercy sauce with white wine and shallots

Berrichone *Bordelaise* sauce

Betterave beetroot

Beuchelle à la Tourangelle kidneys, sweetbreads, morels, truffles, cream

Beurre butter

Beurre blanc sauce with butter, shallots, wine vinegar and sometimes dry white wine

Beurre noir sauce with browned butter, vinegar, parsley

Bifteck steak

Bigarade (à la) orange sauce

Bigarreau type of cherry

Bigorneaux winkles

Billy By mussel soup

Biscuit à la cuiller sponge finger

Bisque shellfish soup

Blanc (de volaille) white breast (of chicken): can describe white fish fillet or white vegetables

Blanchailles whitebait

Blanquette white stew

Blettes Swiss chard

Blinis small, thick pancakes

Bœuf à la mode beef braised in red wine

Bœuf Stroganoff beef, sour cream, onions, mushrooms

Bombe ice cream

Bonne femme (à la) white wine sauce, mushrooms

Bonne femme (à la) potato, leek, carrot soup

Bordelais(e) (à la) Bordeaux style: brown sauce with shallots, red wine and beef bone marrow

Bouchée mouthful size (either a tart or *vol-au-vent*)

Boudin sausage-shaped pudding

Boudin blanc white coloured – pork and sometimes chicken

Boudin noir black pudding

Bouillabaisse Mediterranean fish stew and soup – see Côte d'Azur

Bouillon broth, light consommé

Boulangère sauce of onions, potatoes

Boulette small ball of fish or meat

Bouquet prawn

Bourdaloue hot poached fruit

Bourdelot whole apple pastry

Bourgeoise (à la) sauce of carrots, onions, diced bacon

Bourguignonne (à la) Burgundy style: red wine, onions, bacon, mushrooms

Bourride creamy fish soup with *aïoli*

Braisé braised

Brandade de morue salt cod

Bréjaude cabbage and bacon soup

Brème bream

Brési thin slices dried beef

Bretonne sauce with celery, leeks, beans, mushrooms

Brioche sweet yeast bread roll

Broche (à la) spit roasted

Brochet pike

Brochette (de) meat or fish on a skewer

Brouet broth

Brouillade stewed in oil

Brouillés scrambled

Broutard young goat

Brugnon nectarine

Brûlé toasted

Brunoise diced vegetables

Bruxelloise sauce with asparagus, butter, eggs

Bugnes sweet pastry fritters

Cabillaud cod

Caen (à la mode de) cooked in Calvados and white wine

Café coffee

Cagouilles snails

Caille (Caillette) quail

Calmars inkfish, squid

Campagne country style

Canapé a base, usually bread

Canard duck

Canard à la presse (Rouennaise) duck breast cooked in blood of carcass, red wine and brandy

Canard sauvage wild duck

Caneton (canette) duckling

Cannelle cinnamon

Capilotade small bits or pieces

Capoum scorpion fish

Caprice *whim* (desserts)

Capucine nasturtium

Carbonnade braised beef in beer, onions and bacon

Cardinal *béchamel* sauce, lobster, cream, red peppers

Cardons large celery-like vegetable

Caroline chicken consommé

Carpe carp

Carré d'agneau lamb chops from best end of neck

Carré de porc pork cutlets from best end of neck

Carré de veau veal chops from best end of neck

Carrelet flounder, plaice

Carvi caraway seeds

Casse-croûte snack

Cassis blackcurrants

Cassolette small pan

Cassoulet casserole of beans, pork or goose or duck

Céleri celery

Céleri-rave celeriac

Cèpes fine, delicate mushrooms

Cerfeuil chervil

Cerises (noires) cherries (black)

Cerneaux walnuts

Cervelas pork garlic sausage

Cervelle brains

Champignons (des bois) mushrooms (from the woods)

Chanterelles apricot-coloured mushrooms

Chantilly whipped cream, sugar

Chapon capon

Chapon de mer *rascasse* or scorpion fish

Charcuterie cold cut meats

Charcutière sauce with onions, white wine, gherkins

Charlotte sweet of sponge fingers, cream, etc.

Charolais (Charollais) beef

Chartreuse a mould form

Chasse hunting (season)

Chasseur sauce with white wine, mushrooms, shallots

Châtaignes chestnuts

Châteaubriand thick fillet steak

Châtelaine garnish with artichoke hearts, tomatoes, potatoes

Chaud(e) hot

Chaudrée fish stew

Chausson pastry turnover with various fillings

Chemise (en) pastry covering

Chevreuil roe-deer

Chicon chicory

Chicorée curly endive

Chiffonnade thinly-cut

Chinoise (à la) Chinese style: with bean sprouts and soy sauce

Chiperones see *calmars*

Choisy braised lettuce, sautéed potatoes

Choron *Béarnaise* sauce with tomato

Chou (vert) cabbage

Choucroute sauerkraut, peppercorns, boiled ham, potatoes, Strasbourg sausages

Chou-fleur cauliflower

Chou-pommé white-heart cabbage

Chou rouge red cabbage

Choux (au fromage) puffs (cheese)

Choux de Bruxelles Brussels sprouts

Ciboules spring onions

Ciboulettes chives

Cidre cider

Citron lemon

Citron vert lime

Civet stew

Civet de lièvre jugged hare

Clafoutis tart (usually cherries)

Claires oysters (see page 238)

Clamart with petits pois

Clouté (de) studded with

Cochon pig

Cochonnailles pork products

Cocotte (en) cooking pot

Cœur (de) heart (of)

Coffret (en) in a *small box*

Coing quince

Colbert (à la) fish, dipped in milk, egg and breadcrumbs

Colin hake

Colvert wild duck

Compote stewed or preserved fruit

Concassée coarsely chopped

Concombres cucumbers

Condé creamed rice and fruit

Confit(e) preserved or candied

Confiture jam

Confiture d'oranges marmalade

Congre conger eel

Consommé clear soup

Contrefilet sirloin, usually tied for roasting

Copeaux literally *shavings*

Coq (au vin) chicken in red wine sauce (or name of wine)

Coque (à la) soft-boiled – or served in shell

Coquelet young cockerel

Coques cockles

Coquillages shellfish

Coquilles St-Jacques scallops

Corail (de) coral (of)

Coriandre coriander

Cornichons gherkins

Côte d'agneau lamb chop

Côte de bœuf side of beef

Côte de veau veal chop

Côtelette chop
Cou (d'oie) neck (of goose)
Coulibiac hot salmon *tourte*
Coulis (de) thick sauce (of)
Coupe ice cream dessert
Courge pumpkin
Courgettes baby marrows
Couronne circle or ring
Court-bouillon aromatic poaching liquid
Crabe crab
Crapaudine (à la) grilled game bird with backbone removed
Crécy with carrots and rice
Crème cream
Crème (à la) served with cream or cooked in cream sauce
Crème à l'anglaise light custard sauce
Crème brûlée same, less sugar and cream and with praline
Crème pâtissière custard filling
Crème plombières custard filling: egg whites, fresh fruit flavouring
Crêpe thin pancake
Crêpes Suzette sweet pancakes with orange liqueur sauce
Crépinette (de) wrapping (of)
Cresson watercress
Cressonière purée of potatoes, watercress
Crêtes cockscombs
Creuse long, thick-shelled oyster
Crevettes grises shrimps
Crevettes roses prawns
Cromesquis croquettes
Croque Monsieur toasted cheese or ham sandwich
Croquette see *boulette*
Croustade small pastry mould with various fillings
Croûte (en) pastry crust (in a)
Croûtons bread (toast or fried)
Cru raw
Crudités raw vegetables
Crustacés shellfish
Cuillère soft (cut with spoon)
Cuisses (de) legs (of)
Cuissot (de) haunch (of)
Cuit cooked
Cul haunch or rear
Culotte rump (usually steak)
Cultivateur soup of chopped vegetables
Dariole basket-shaped pastry
Darne slice or steak
Dattes dates
Daube stew (various types)
Daurade sea-bream
Dégustation tasting

Délice delight
Demi-glace basic brown sauce
Demi-sel lightly salted
Diable seasoned with mustard
Diane (à la) peppered cream sauce
Dieppoise (à la) Dieppe style: white wine, cream, mussels, shrimps
Dijonnaise (à la) with mustard sauce
Dijonnaise (à la belle) blackcurrant sauce
Dinde young hen turkey
Dindon turkey
Dindonneau young turkey
Dodine (de canard) cold stuffed duck
Dorade dorado
Doria with cucumbers
Douceurs desserts
Doux (douce) sweet
Du Barry cauliflower soup
Duxelles chopped mushrooms, shallots and cream
Echalotes shallots
Echine spare ribs
Echiquier *checkered* fashion
Ecrevisses freshwater crayfish
Ecuelle bowl or basin
Effiloché(e) frayed, thinly sliced
Emincé thinly sliced
Encornets cuttlefish
Endive chicory
Entrecôte entrecôte, rib steak
Entremets sweets
Epaule shoulder
Eperlan smelt
Epices spices
Epinards spinach
Epis de maïs sweetcorn
Escabèche fish (or poultry) marinated in *court-bouillon* – cold
Escalope thinly cut (meat or fish)
Escargots snails
Espadon swordfish
Estouffade stew with onions, herbs, mushrooms, red or white wine (perhaps garlic)
Estragon tarragon flavoured
Etrilles crabs
Etuvé(e) cooked in little water or in ingredient's own juice
Exocet flying fish
Façon cooked in a described way
Faisan(e) pheasant
Farci(e) stuffed
Farine flour
Faux-filet sirloin steak
Favorite garnish *foie gras*, truffles

297

Favouilles spider crabs
Fenouil fennel
Féra freshwater lake fish
Ferme (fermier) farm (farmer)
Fermière mixture of onions, carrots, turnips, celery, etc.
Feuille de vigne vine leaf
Feuilleté light flaky pastry
Fèves broad beans
Ficelle (à la) tied in a string
Ficelles thin loaves of bread
Figues figs
Filet fillet
Financière (à la) Madeira sauce with truffles
Fines herbes mixture of parsley, chives, tarragon, etc.
Flageolets kidney beans
Flamande (à la) Flemish style
Flambé flamed
Flamiche puff pastry tart
Flan tart
Flétan halibut
Fleur flower
Fleurons puff pastry crescents
Florentine with spinach
Foie liver
Foie gras goose liver
Foies blonds de volaille chicken liver mousse
Foin (dans le) cooked in hay
Fond (base) basic stock
Fondant see *boulette*: a *bon-bon*
Fonds d'artichauts artichoke hearts
Fondue (de fromage) melted (cheese with wine)
Forestière with bacon and mushrooms
Four (au) baked in oven
Fourré stuffed
Frais, fraîche fresh or cool
Fraises strawberries
Fraises des bois wild strawberries
Framboises raspberries
Française (à la) mashed potato filled with mixed vegetables
Frangipane almond custard filling
Frappé frozen or ice cold
Friandises sweets – *petits fours*
Fricadelles minced meat balls
Fricandeau slice topside veal
Fricassée braised in sauce or butter, egg yolks and cream
Frisé(e) curly
Frit fried
Frites chips
Fritot fritter
Frittons see *grattons*
Friture small fried fish
Frivolles fritters

Froid cold
Fromage cheese
Fromage de tête brawn
Fruit de la passion passion fruit
Fruits confits crystallised fruit
Fruits de mer seafood
Fumé smoked
Fumet fish stock
Galantine cooked meat, fish or vegetables in jelly – served cold
Galette pastry, pancake or cake
Galimafrée (de) stew (of)
Gambas big prawns
Garbure (Garbue) vegetable soup
Gardons small roach
Garni(e) with vegetables
Garniture garnish
Gâteau cake
Gâtinaise (à la) with honey
Gaufre waffle
Gayettes faggots
Gelée aspic jelly
Géline chicken
Genièvre juniper
Génoise rich sponge cake
Germiny sorrel and cream soup
Gésier gizzard
Gibelotte see *fricassée*
Gibier game
Gigot (de) leg (of lamb) – can describe other things
Gigue (de) shank (of)
Gingembre ginger
Girofle clove
Girolles apricot-coloured fungi
Glacé iced. Crystallised. Glazed
Glace ice cream
Godard see *financière (à la)*
Gougère round-shaped, egg and cheese *chou* pastry
Goujonnettes (de) small fried pieces (of)
Goujons gudgeon
Gourmandises sweetmeats – can describe *fruits de mer*
Gousse (de) pod or husk (of)
Graine (de capucine) seed (nasturtium)
Graisse fat
Graisserons duck and goose fat scratchings
Grand Veneur sauce with vegetables, wine vinegar, redcurrant jelly and cream
Granité water ice
Gratin browned
Gratin Dauphinois potato dish with cream, cheese, garlic
Gratin Savoyard potato dish with cheese and butter

Gratiné top of sauced dish browned with butter, cheese, etc.

Grattons pork scratchings

Gravettes oysters

Grecque (à la) cooked vegetables served cold

Grenade pomegranate

Grenadin thick veal escalope

Grenouilles frogs

Grillade grilled meat

Grillé(e) grilled

Griottes bitter red cherries

Grisets mushrooms

Grive thrush

Grondin gurnard, red gurnet

Gros sel coarse rock or sea salt

Groseilles gooseberries

Groseilles noires blackcurrants

Groseilles rouges redcurrants

Gruyère hard, mild cheese

Gyromitres fungi

Habit vert *dressed* in green

Hachis minced or chopped-up

Hareng herring

Hareng fumé kippered

Hareng salé bloater

Haricot (de) stew (of)

Haricots beans

Haricots blancs white beans (dried)

Haricots rouges kidney beans

Haricots verts green beans or French beans

Hochepot thick stew

Hollandaise sauce with butter, egg yolk, lemon juice

Homard lobster

Hongroise (à la) Hungarian style: sauce with tomato, paprika

Hors d'œuvre appetisers

Huile oil

Huîtres oysters (see page 238)

Hure (de) head (of). Brawn. Jellied

Ile flottante unmoulded soufflé of beaten egg white and sugar

Imam bayeldi aubergine with rice, onions and sautéed tomatoes

Impératrice (à la) desserts with candied fruits soaked in *kirsch*

Indienne (à l') Indian style: with curry powder

Italienne (à l') Italian style: artichokes, mushrooms, pasta

Jambon ham

Jambonneau knuckle of pork

Jambonnette (de) boned and stuffed (knuckle of ham or poultry)

Jardinière diced fresh vegetables

Jarret de veau stew of shin of veal

Jarretons cooked pork knuckles

Jésus de Morteau – smoked Jura pork sausage

Joinville *velouté* sauce with cream, crayfish tails, truffles

Joue (de) cheek (of)

Judru cured pork sausage

Julienne thinly-cut vegetables. See *lingue*

Jus juice

Lait milk

Laitance soft roe

Laitue lettuce

Lamproie eel-like fish

Langouste spiny lobster or crawfish

Langoustines Dublin Bay prawns

Langue tongue

Languedocienne (à la) mushrooms, tomatoes, parsley garnish

Lapereau young rabbit

Lapin rabbit

Lapin de garenne wild rabbit

Lard bacon

Lard de poitrine fat belly of pork

Lardons strips of bacon

Lavaret freshwater lake fish

Lèche thin slice

Léger(ère) light

Légumes vegetables

Lieu fish – like cod

Lièvre hare

Limande lemon sole

Limon lime

Lingue ling – cod family

Lit bed

Livèche lovage (like celery)

Longe loin

Lotte (barbot) burbot – like eel

Lotte de mer monkfish, anglerfish

Lou magret see *magret*

Loup de mer sea-bass

Lyonnaise (à la) Lyonnais style: sauce with wine, onions, vinegar

Macédoine diced fruit or veg'

Madeleines tiny sponge cakes

Madère sauce *demi-glace*, Madeira

Magret (de canard) breast (of duck)

Maigre fish – like sea-bass

Maillot carrots, turnips, onions, peas and beans

Maïs maize flour

Maison (de) of the restaurant

Maître d'hôtel sauce with butter, parsley, lemon

Maltaise (sauce) orange-flavoured hollandaise sauce

Manchons see *goujonnettes*

Mandarine tangerine

Mangetout peas and pods
Mangues mangoes
Manière (de) style (of)
Maquereaux mackerel
Maraîchère (à la) market-gardener style: *velouté* sauce with vegetables
Marais marsh or market-garden
Marbré(e) marbled
Marc pure spirit
Marcassin young wild boar
Marché market
Marchand de vin sauce with red wine, chopped shallots
Marée fresh seafood
Marengo tomatoes, mushrooms, olive oil, white wine, garlic, herbs
Marennes (blanches) oysters, flat shelled
Marennes (vertes) green shells
Mareyeur fishmonger
Marinade – mariné(e) pickled
Marinière see *moules*
Marjolaine marjoram
Marjolaine almond and hazelnut meringue with chocolate cream and praline
Marmite stewpot
Marquise (de) water ice (of)
Marrons chestnuts
Matelote (d'anguilles) fresh-water fish stew (or of eels)
Mauviette lark
Médaillon (de) round piece (of)
Mélange mixture or blend
Melba (à la) poached peach, with vanilla ice cream, raspberry sauce
Ménagère (à la) housewife style: onions, potatoes, peas, turnips, carrots
Menthe mint
Mer sea
Merlan whiting (in Provence – hake)
Merle blackbird
Mérou grouper (sea fish)
Merveilles hot, sugared fritters
Mesclum mixture of salad leaves
Meunière (à la) sauce with butter, parsley, lemon (sometimes oil)
Meurette red wine sauce
Miel honey
Mignardises *petits fours*
Mignon (de) small round piece
Mignonette coarsely ground white pepper
Mijoté(e) cooked slowly in water
Milanaise (à la) Milan style: dipped in breadcrumbs, egg, cheese
Millassou sweet maize flour flan

Mille-feuilles *1001* thin layers of pastry
Mimosa chopped hard-boiled egg
Mique stew of dumplings
Mirabeau anchovies, olives
Mirabelles golden plums
Mirepoix cubes of carrots, onion, ham
Miroton (de) slices (of)
Mitonée (de) soup (of)
Mode (à la) in the manner of
Moelle beef marrow
Mojettes see Poitou-Charentes
Moka coffee
Montagne (de) from mountains
Montmorency with cherries
Morilles edible, dark brown, *honeycombed* fungi
Mornay cheese sauce
Morue cod
Mostèle (Gâteau de) cod mousse
Mouclade mussel stew
Moules mussels
Moules marinière mussels cooked in white wine and shallots
Mousse cold, light, finely-minced ingredients with cream and egg whites
Mousseline hollandaise sauce with whipped cream
Mousserons edible fungi
Moutarde mustard
Mouton mutton
Mulet grey mullet
Mûres mulberries
Muscade nutmeg
Museau muzzle
Myrtilles bilberries. Blueberries
Nage (à la) *court-bouillon*: aromatic poaching liquid
Nantua sauce for fish with crayfish, white wine, tomatoes
Nature plain
Navarin stew, usually lamb
Navets turnips
Nègre literally *negro*
Newburg sauce with lobster, brandy, cream and Madeira
Nid nest
Nivernaise (à la) Nevers style: carrots and onions
Noisette sauce of lightly browned butter
Noisettes (de) round pieces (of)
Noix nuts
Noix (de veau) topside of leg (veal)
Normande (à la) Normandy style: fish sauce with mussels, shrimps, mushrooms, eggs and cream

Nouilles noodles
Nouveau (nouvelle) new or young
Noyau sweet liqueur from crushed stones (usually cherries)
Œufs à la coque soft-boiled eggs
Œufs à la neige see *île flottante*
Œufs à la poêle fried eggs
Œufs brouillés scrambled eggs
Œufs durs hard-boiled eggs
Œufs moulés poached eggs
Oie goose
Oignon onion
Oison rôti roast gosling
Omble chevalier freshwater char: looks like large salmon trout
Ombre grayling
Ombrine see *maigre* – fish
Onglet flank of beef
Oreilles (de porc) ears (pigs')
Orléannaise (à l') Orléans style: chicory and potatoes
Orly dipped in batter, fried and served with tomato sauce
Orties nettles
Ortolan wheatear (thrush family)
Os bone
Oseille sorrel
Ouillat see Southwest
Oursins sea-urchins
Pailleté (de) spangled (with)
Paillettes pastry straws
Pain bread
Pain doré bread soaked in milk and eggs and fried
Paleron shoulder
Palmier (cœurs de) palm hearts
Palombe wood pigeon
Palomète see *maigre* – fish
Palourdes clams
Pamplemousse grapefruit
Panaché mixed
Panade flour or bread paste
Panais parsnip
Pané(e) breadcrumbed
Panier basket
Pannequets like *crêpes*, smaller and thicker
Paon peacock
Papillote (en) cooked in oiled paper (or foil)
Paquets (en) in parcels
Parfait (de) *perfect*
Parisienne (à la) leeks, potatoes
Parmentier potatoes
Pascade sweet or savoury pancake
Pascaline (de) *quenelle (of)*
Passe-pierres seaweed
Pastèque watermelon
Pastis (sauce au) aniseed based

Pâté minced meats (of various types) baked. Usually served cold
Pâte pastry, dough or batter
Pâte à choux cream puff pastry
Pâte brisée short crust pastry
Pâté en croûte baked in pastry crust
Pâtes (fraîches) fresh pasta
Pâtés (petits) à la Provençale anchovy and ham turnovers
Pâtisserie pastry
Pâtisson custard marrow
Patte claw, foot, leg
Paupiettes thin slices of meat or fish – used to wrap fillings
Pavé (de) thick slice (of)
Paysan(ne) (à la) country style
Peau (de) skin (of)
Pêche peach
Pêcheur *fisherman*
Perche perch
Perdreau partridge
Périgourdine (à la) sauce *Périgueux* and goose liver
Périgueux sauce with truffles, Madeira
Persil parsley
Persillade mixture chopped parsley, garlic
Petite marmite strong consommé with toast and cheese
Petits fours miniature cakes, biscuits, sweets
Petits gris small snails
Petits pois tiny peas
Pétoncle small scallop
Pets de nonne small soufflé fritters
Pieds de porc pig trotters
Pigeonneau young pigeon
Pignons pine nuts
Pilau rice dish
Pilou drumstick
Piments doux sweet peppers
Pintade (pintadeau) guinea-fowl (young guinea-fowl)
Piperade omelette or scrambled eggs with tomatoes, peppers, onions, sometimes ham
Piquante (sauce) sharp-tasting sauce with shallots, capers, wine
Piqué larded
Pissenlits dandelion leaves
Pistaches green pistachio nuts
Pistil de safran saffron (*pistil* from autumn-flowering crocus)
Pistou see Côte d'Azur
Plateau (de) plate (of)
Pleurotes mushrooms
Plie franche plaice

301

Plombières sweet with vanilla ice cream, *kirsch*, candied fruit and *crème chantilly*

Pluches sprigs

Pluvier plover

Poché(e)-Pochade poached

Pochouse freshwater fish stew with white wine

Poêlé fried

Poire pear

Poireaux leeks

Pois peas

Poisson fish

Poitrine breast

Poitrine fumée smoked bacon

Poitrine salée unsmoked bacon

Poivrade a peppery sauce with wine vinegar, cooked vegetables

Poivre noir black pepper

Poivre rose red pepper

Poivre vert green peppercorns

Poivrons sweet peppers

Pojarsky minced meat or fish – cutlet shaped and fried

Polenta boiled maize flour

Polonaise Polish style: with buttered breadcrumbs, parsley, hard-boiled eggs

Pommade thick, smooth paste

Pommes apples

Pommes de terre potatoes
    à l'anglaise boiled
    allumettes thin and fried
    boulangère sliced with onions
    château roast
    dauphine croquettes
    duchesse mashed with egg yolk
    en l'air hollow potato puffs
    frites fried chips
    gratinées browned with cheese
    Lyonnaise sautéed with onions
    vapeur boiled

Pomponnette savoury pastry

Porc (carré de) loin of pork

Porc (côte de) pork chop

Porcelet suckling pig

Porto (au) port

Portugaise (à la) Portuguese style: fried onions and tomatoes

Portugaises oysters with long, deep shells

Potage thick soup

Pot-au-crème dessert – usually chocolate or coffee

Pot-au-feu clear meat broth served with the meat

Potée heavy soup of cabbage, beans, etc.

Pouchouse see *pochouse*

Poularde large hen

Poulet chicken

Poulet à la broche spit-roasted chicken

Poulet Basquaise chicken with tomatoes and peppers

Poulet de Bresse corn-fed, white flesh chicken

Poulet de grain grain-fed chicken

Poulette young chicken

Poulpe octopus

Pounti small, egg-based, savoury soufflé with bacon or prunes

Poussin small baby chicken

Poutargue grey mullet roe

Praires small clams

Pralines caramelised almonds

Praslin caramelised

Primeurs young vegetables

Princesse *velouté* sauce, asparagus tips and truffles

Printanièr(e) (à la) garnish of diced vegetables

Produits (de) products (of)

Profiteroles choux pastry, custard filled puffs

Provençale (à la) Provençal style: with tomatoes, garlic, olive oil, etc.

Pruneaux prunes

Prunes plums

Purée mashed

Quenelles light dumplings of fish or poultry

Quetsches small, purple plums

Queue de bœuf oxtail

Queues tails

Quiche (Lorraine) open flan of cheese, ham or bacon

Râble de lièvre (lapin) saddle of hare (rabbit)

Raclette scrapings from specially-made and heated cheese

Radis radish

Ragoût stew, usually meat, but can describe other ingredients

Raie (bouclée) skate (type of)

Raifort horseradish

Raisins grapes

Ramequin see *cocotte (en)*

Ramier wood pigeon

Rapé(e) grated or shredded

Rascasse scorpion fish

Ratafia brandy and unfermented Champagne. Almond biscuits

Ratatouille aubergines, onions, courgettes, garlic, red peppers and tomatoes in olive oil

Raves (root) turnips, radishes, etc.

Ravigote sauce with onions, herbs, mushrooms, wine vinegar

Ravioles ravioli

Régence sauce with wine, truffles, mushrooms

Reine chicken and cream

Reines-Claude greengages

Reinette type of apple

Réjane chicken consommé with shredded eggs

Rémoulade sauce of mayonnaise, mustard, capers, herbs, anchovy

Rillettes (d'oie) potted pork (goose)

Rillons small cubes of fat pork

Ris d'agneau lamb sweetbreads

Ris de veau veal sweetbreads

Rissettes small sweetbreads

Rivière river

Riz rice

Riz a l'impératrice cold rice pudding

Robert sauce *demi-glace*, white wine, onions, vinegar, mustard

Rocambole like a shallot

Rognonnade veal and kidneys

Rognons kidneys

Romarin rosemary

Rossini see *tournedos*

Rôti roast

Rouelle (de) round piece or slice

Rouget red mullet

Rouget barbet red mullet

Rouille orange-coloured sauce with peppers, garlic and saffron

Roulade (de) roll (of)

Roulée(s) rolled (usually *crêpes*)

Roux flour, butter base for sauces

Royans fresh sardines

Rutabaga swede

Sabayon sauce of egg yolks, wine

Sablés shortbread

Safran saffron (see *pistil de*)

Sagou sago

St-Germain with peas

St-Hubert sauce *poivrade*, bacon and cooked chestnuts

St-Jacques (coquilles) scallops

St-Pierre John Dory

Saisons (suivant) depending on the season of the year

Salade Niçoise tomatoes, beans, potatoes, black olives, anchovy, lettuce, olive oil, perhaps tuna

Salade panachée mixed salad

Salade verte green salad

Salé salted

Salicornes marsh samphire

Salmigondis hotchpotch

Salmis red wine sauce

Salpicon meat or fish and diced vegetables in sauce

Salsifis salsify

Sanciau thick sweet or savoury pancake

Sandre freshwater fish, like perch

Sang blood

Sanglier wild boar

Santé potatoes and sorrel

Sarcelle teal

Sarriette (poivre d'âne) savory, bitter herb

Saucisse freshly-made sausage

Saucisson large, dry sausage

Saucissons cervelas saveloys

Sauge sage

Saumon salmon

Saumon blanc hake

Saumon fumé smoked salmon

Sauté browned in butter, oil or fat

Sauvage wild

Savarin see *baba au rhum*

Savoyarde with Gruyère cheese

Scarole *endive*

Scipion cuttlefish

Seiches squid

Sel salt (see *gros sel*)

Selle saddle

Selon grosseur (S.G.) according to size

Serpolet wild thyme

Sévigné garnished with mushrooms, roast potatoes, lettuce

Smitane sauce with sour cream, onions, white wine

Soissons with white beans

Sole à la Dieppoise sole fillets, mussels, shrimps, cream

Sole Cardinale poached fillets of sole, cream sauce

Sole Dugléré sole with tomatoes, onions, shallots, butter

Sole Marguery sole with mussels, prawns, white wine

Sole Walewska *mornay* sauce, truffles and prawns

Sorbet water ice

Soubise onion sauce

Soufflé(e) beaten egg whites, baked (with sweet or savoury ingredients)

Soupière soup tureen

Soupion small inkfish

Sourdons cockles

Souvaroff a game bird with *foie gras* and truffles

Spaghettis (de) thin strips (of)

Spoom frothy water ice

Strasbourgeoise (à la) Strasbourg style: *foie gras, choucroute*, bacon

Sucre sugar

Suppions small cuttlefish

Suprême sweet white sauce

303

Suprême boneless breast of poultry – can also describe a fillet of fish

Talleyrand truffles, cheese, *foie gras*

Tanche tench

Tapé(e) dried

Tartare raw minced beef

Tartare (sauce) sauce with mayonnaise, onions, capers, herbs

Tarte open flan

Tarte Tatin *upside down* apple tart

Terrine baked minced meat or fish, served cold

Tête de veau vinaigrette calf's head *vinaigrette*

Thé tea

Thermidor grilled lobster with browned *béchamel* sauce

Thon tunny fish

Thym thyme

Tiède mild or lukewarm

Tilleul lime blossom

Timbale mould in which contents are steamed

Tomates tomatoes

Topinambours Jerusalem artichokes

Torte sweet-filled flan

Tortue turtle

Tortue sauce with various herbs, tomatoes, Madeira

Toulousaine (à la) Toulouse style: truffles, *foie gras*, sweetbreads, kidneys

Tournedos fillet steak (small end)

Tournedos chasseur with shallots, mushrooms, tomatoes

Tournedos Dauphinoise with creamed mushrooms, *croûtons*

Tournedos Rossini with goose liver, truffles, port, *croûtons*

Tourte (Tourtière) covered savoury tart

Tourteaux large crabs

Tranche slice

Tranches de bœuf steaks

Tripes à la mode de Caen tripe stew

Tripettes small tripe

Trompettes de la mort fungi

Trou water ice

Truffée with truffles

Truffes truffles – black, exotic tubers

Truite trout

Truite (au bleu) trout poached in water and vinegar – turns blue!

Truite saumonée salmon trout

Tuiles tiles (thin almond slices)

Turbot (turbotin) turbot

Vacherin ice cream, meringue, cream

Valenciennes (à la) rice, red peppers, onions, tomatoes, white wine

Vallée d'Auge sauce with Calvados and cream

Vapeur (à la) steamed

Veau veal

Veau à la Viennoise (escalope de) slice of veal with chopped egg

Veau Milanaise (escalope de) with macaroni, tomatoes, ham, mushrooms

Veau pané (escalope de) thin slice of veal in flour, eggs and breadcrumbs

Velouté white sauce with *bouillon* and white *roux*

Velouté de volaille thick chicken soup

Venaison venison

Ventre belly or breast

Vernis clams

Véronique grapes, wine, cream

Verte green mayonnaise with chervil, spinach, tarragon

Vert-pré thinly-sliced chips, *maître d'hôtel* butter, watercress

Verveine verbena

Vessie (en) cooked in a pig's bladder – usually chicken

Viande meat

Vichy glazed carrots

Vichyssoise creamy potato, leek soup – served cold

Vierge (sauce) olive oil sauce

Vierge literally *virgin*

Vigneron wine-grower

Vinaigre (de) wine vinegar or vinegar of named fruit

Vinaigre de Jerez sherry vinegar

Vinaigrette (à la) French dressing with wine vinegar, oil, etc.

Volaille poultry

Vol au vent puff pastry case

Xérès (vinaigre de) sherry (vinegar)

Yaourt yoghourt

Zeste (d'orange) rubbing from (orange skin)

If you come across any terms not in the glossary ask for the constituent parts to be written down; translate them using these pages.

Example: **sauce gribiche** *three of the ingredients you'll recognise – mayonnaise, capers and herbs. The other ingredients of œufs durs* **(hachis)** *and* **cornichons** *can be translated easily.*

French Leave *Cocktails*

Apéritifs of France you can enjoy three main types

Alcohol-based most common are the *aniseed* ones: **Berger Blanc** and **Pernod 45** (coloured) – these contain no liquorice. The *pastis apéritifs* do have it: **Berger Pastis**, **Pernod Pastis 51**, **Ricard 45**. Drink them with cool water (not ice) – one part to five parts water; initial alcohol content of 45 per cent is then reduced to safe levels.

Other alcohol-based drinks are the *amers*, *bitters* and *gentians* – 20 per cent. Extracts of various plants are used: **Picon** and **Mandarin** are *amers* – long drinks, one part to two parts water. *Bitters* are extra-bitter: **St-Raphaël Bitter** is one. **Suze** and **Aveze** are *gentian* based.

Wine-based *(aromatised wines)* some are *quinquinas* (tropical tree bark); usually red, drunk straight or as a long drink with soda. Main ones are based on Roussillon wines: **Ambassadeur**, **Byrrh**, **Dubonnet**, **St-Raphaël**. Alcohol content 16–18 per cent.

Others are *vermouths*; usually white, dry and *aromatised* by bitter substances – reds are white wine coloured with caramel. Main centres are Chambéry (page 262) and Languedoc: examples **Noilly-Prat**, **Clarac**, **Valtoni**, **Cazapra**, **Chambérizette** – Chambéry *vermouth* with strawberry juice.

Natural sweet wines *(vins doux naturels)* – **Liqueur wines**

See regions: Languedoc-Roussillon, Poitou-Charentes, Provence.

The types and shades of wines

White wine is made from white or red grapes – the skins are removed at the start of the wine-making process.

Rosé is wine from red grapes – juice is separated from skins after a brief period – fermentation is completed without them: *vin gris* (grey) is pale pink – skins and juice kept apart at pressing.

Red end product of red grape juice and skins which ferment together.

Dry wine is the end product of allowing fermentation to run its whole course – all sugar converts to alcohol.

Sweet wine results when fermentation is prematurely stopped – while sugar remains; this done by filtration or adding sulphur dioxide.

Sparkling wine results when juice is bottled before fermentation is complete; it finishes in bottle – hence the carbon dioxide bubbles.

Méthode champenoise is difficult, lengthy process; fermentation is helped by adding yeast and sugar. Dom Pérignon invented the process. Madame Clicquot developed the technique of keeping it clear and sparkling. To compensate dryness, a *dosage* (sweetening) is added.

Brandies Cognac is the end product of distilled white wine; first heated, the vapour is collected and condensed – process is repeated. Armagnac is distilled once. **Fines** – brandies from wine-making areas.

Marc is pure spirit, distilled from grape pulp after pressing.

Eaux-de-vie read notes in Alsace region (page 32).

Still and sparkling waters of France

Perrier a sparkling water. From a spring at Vergèze, between Lunel and Nîmes (page 244); gases of volcanic origin mix with spring waters. Distinctive, green club-shaped bottle.

Vichy another sparkling spring water. From Vichy (page 190).

Evian a pure, still water. From Evian on Lake Geneva (page 262).

Vittel a still water from the spa, south of Nancy (page 79).

Badoit a sparkling water from St-Galmier, west of Lyon (page 174).

Volvic a still water from the Auvergne (page 190).

Vins de Corse

Not one of my regions – yet. Its fine AC wines are:

Vin de Corse – followed perhaps by a local name: **Coteaux du Cap Corse**, **Patrimonio** (both near Bastia), **Coteaux d'Ajaccio**, **Sartène**, **Figari**, **Porto Vecchio** (all in the south) and **Calvi**.

Dry whites, fruity rosés and strong reds are all there. Look out for the sweet Muscat and Malvoisie (Malmsey) grape type wines. *Vins de Pays* are called **L'Ile de Beauté**.

Don't take wines too seriously – enjoy them. **Don't** be dogmatic about combinations – experiment with local wines and surprise yourself. **Don't** drink good, expensive wines with acid foods, highly-spiced foods, with eggs or salads with sharp dressings.

	Shellfish – Fish Charcuterie	Fish (Sauced)	White Meats Mild Cheeses	Red Meats Strong Cheeses	Game	Desserts
Alsace (page 32)						
Dry whites: **Riesling, Sylvaner, Pinot Blanc, Tokay, Traminer**	•	•	•			
Medium-sweet whites: **Tokay, Traminer**		•				•
Light red: **Pinot Noir**	•	•	•	•	•	
Sparkling *brut* or *sec*	•		•			
demi-sec						•
Dessert wine: **Muscat** (*sec*)						•
Berry-Bourbonnais (page 41)						
Whites: **St-Pourçain, Reuilly, Quincy**	•	•	•			
Reds: **St-Pourçain, Châteaumeillant**	•	•	•	•		
Brittany (page 49)						
Dry whites: **Muscadet, Gros Plant du Pays Nantais, Vins de Pays**	•	•	•			
Reds: **Coteaux d'Ancenis, Vins de Pays**	•	•	•			
Burgundy (page 65)						
Dry whites: **Chablis, Meursault, Viré, Pouilly-Fuissé, St-Véran, Mâcon** and many more; great and humble	•	•	•			
Rosés: **Marsannay, Irancy**	•		•			
Light reds: some **Côte de Beaune** wines, **Mercurey, Givry, Mâcon Supérieur, Gd-Ordinaire, Passetoutgrains,** etc.	•	•	•	•		
Full-bodied reds: some **Côte de Beaune** (like **Pommard**) and any **Côte de Nuits** wines…				•	•	
Sparkling *brut* or *sec*	•		•			
demi-sec						•
Champagne-Ardenne (page 81)						
Champagne *brut* or *sec*	•	•	•	•	•	•
demi-sec						•
Still whites: **Cramant, Chouilly**	•		•			
Rosés: **Rosé des Riceys, Côtes de Toul**	•		•			
Reds: **Bouzy, Vertus, Damery**			•	•	•	
Côte d'Azur (page 93)						
Whites: **Côtes de Provence, Cassis**	•	•	•			
Rosés: **Côtes de Provence, Cassis**	•		•			
Reds: **Bandol, Ch. Vignelaure**				•	•	
Dordogne (page 110)						
Dry whites: **Bergerac, Côtes de Duras**	•	•	•			
Sweet whites: **Monbazillac**		•				•
Rosés: **Gaillac**	•		•			
Light reds: **Bergerac, Frontonnais, Marmandais, Lavilledieu, Gaillac**			•	•		
Full-bodied reds: **Cahors**				•	•	
Sparkling: **Gaillac** – *brut* or *sec*	•					
demi-sec						•
Hautes-Alpes (page 125) see region						
Ile de France (page 133) see region						
Jura (page 142)						
Dry whites: **Arbois, Côtes du Jura, Château-Châlon**	•	•	•			

If a dish is prepared with a specific wine (including fish in a red wine sauce) **do** order a similar wine to accompany it. **Do** ask questions and **do** drink local wines with local cheeses. **Do** please treat these two pages as guidelines . . . **Santé!**

	Shellfish – Fish / Charcuterie	Fish (Sauced)	White Meats / Mild Cheeses	Red Meats / Strong Cheeses	Game	Desserts
Jura (continued)						
Rosés: **Arbois**	•		•			
Sparkling: **L'Etoile, Arbois**	•		•			
Languedoc-Roussillon (page 152)						
Dry whites: **Clairette du Languedoc** and **Bellegarde, Vins de Pays**	•	•	•			
Light/medium reds: **Costières du Gard, Coteaux du Languedoc** (all villages), **Minervois, Corbières, Vins de Pays**	•	•	•	•	•	
Full-bodied reds: **Fitou, Roussillon**				•	•	
Sparkling: **Blanquette de Limoux**	•		•			
Dessert wines: **Banyuls, Maury, Rivesaltes, Frontignan**						•
Loire (page 162)						
Dry whites: **Sancerre, Fumé, Reuilly, Quincy, Vouvray, Savennières**	•	•	•			
Sweet whites: **Vouvray, Bonnezeaux**		•				•
Rosés *sec:* **Touraine, Rosé de Loire**	•		•			
demi-sec: **Rosé/Cabernet d'Anjou**	•					•
Reds: **Chinon, Bourgueil, Gamay**	•		•	•		
Sparkling *brut* or *sec*	•		•			
demi-sec						•
Lyonnais (page 176)						
Whites: **Vins du Bugey**	•	•	•			
Reds: **Beaujolais, Côte Roannaise**	•	•	•	•		
Massif Central (page 196)						
Reds: **Côtes d'Auvergne, Côtes du Forez, Vin de Pays de l'Ardèche**	•	•	•	•		
See Provence for **Côtes du Rhône** wines						
Normandy (page 212) see region						
North (page 223) see region						
Poitou-Charentes (page 235)						
Dry whites: **Ile de Ré, Haut-Poitou**	•	•	•			
Reds: **Vins du Haut-Poitou**	•	•	•	•		
Dessert wine: **Pineau des Charentes**						•
Provence (page 246)						
Whites: **Cassis, Côtes de Provence**	•	•	•			
Rosés: **Lirac, Tavel**	•		•			
Full-bodied reds: **Côtes du Rhône, Côte Rôtie, Hermitage, Cornas**				•	•	
Sparkling *brut:* **Die, St-Péray**	•		•			
demi-sec: **Die**						•
Dessert wines: **Beaumes de Venise**						•
Savoie (page 265)						
Dry whites: **Seyssel, Crépy**	•	•	•			
Rosés: **Savoie**	•		•			
Reds: **Mondeuse, Chautagne, Gamay**	•	•	•	•	•	
Sparkling: **Seyssel**	•	•	•			
Southwest (page 278)						
Dry whites: **Graves, Tursan, E-D-Mers**	•	•	•			
Sweet whites: **Sauternes, Jurançon**		•				•
Medium reds: **Graves, Médoc**, others	•	•	•	•	•	
Full-bodied reds: **St-Emilion, Madiran**				•	•	

Index of Wines

313

This Index does not pretend to be a definitive list of French cheeses; many others are very rarely seen and some are very closely related to the list above. Do take all the advice given on page 22 – try as many of the different varieties as you can. Make waiters identify all the cheeses offered at restaurants – and ask for **une bouchée** *(a mouthful) of as many types as possible; don't be prejudiced about any of them – many taste better than they look.*

So you think you know that road sign?

(Compiled by Shirley Clancy)

Absence d'accotements no verges

Absence de glissières latérales no protective barriers

Absence de marquage no road markings

Absence de signalement horizontal no road markings

Absence de signalement vertical no road signs

Accotement étroit narrow verge

Accotement non stabilisé soft verges

Affaissement subsidence

Aire parking area

Allumez vos feux switch on lights

Arbres inclinés trees leaning over the road

Arrosage et boue watering – mud on the road

Atelier d'entretien maintenance workshop

Attachez vos ceintures fasten your seat belts

Attente de marquage no road markings

Attention (!) look out (!)

Attention aux travaux danger – road works

Autoroute péage toll motorway

Autres directions other directions

Bande d'arrêt d'urgence emergency hard shoulder

Bande d'arrêt d'urgence déformée emergency hard shoulder – bad surface

Betteraves beet harvesting – mud on road

Bifurcation road divides

Bouchon bottleneck – traffic jam

Boue mud

Brouillard fog or mist

Carrefour crossroads

Cédez le passage give way

Centre d'entretien maintenance centre

Centre ville town centre

Chantier roadworks

Chantier mobile 'mobile' roadworks

Chaussée deformée bad road surface

Chaussée inondable road liable to flooding

Chute de pierres danger – falling rocks or stones

Circulation alternée single line traffic – alternately

Convoi exceptionnel large load

Dans l'agglomération built-up area

Déviation diversion

Eboulements landslides

En cas de pluie when raining

Enquête de circulation traffic census

Essence petrol – gasoline (2 star)

Eteignez voz phares switch off headlights

Fauchage mowing

Feux traffic lights

Feux clignotants flashing lights

Fin de . . . . end of . . . .

Flèches vertes green arrows (secondary route)

Gendarmerie traffic and local police

Gravillons loose chippings

Hauteur limitée height limited

Hors des cases (accompanied by sign) no parking outside bays

Interdiction de stationner parking prohibited

Interdit prohibited

  aux piétons no entry to pedestrians

  du 1er au 15 du mois no parking from 1st to 15th of month

  du 16 à fin de mois no parking from 16th to end of month

  sauf aux livraisons no entry except for deliveries

  sauf aux riverains no entry except for residents

  sauf services no entry except for service vehicles

  sur accotement no stopping on verges

Itinéraire bis secondary route

Itinéraire conseillé recommended route

Itinéraire obligatoire compulsory route

Laissez libre la bande d'arrêt d'urgence do not obstruct hard shoulder

Libre service self-service

Mairie town hall

Mouvements de chars heavy vehicles

Nappe d'eau puddles on road

Nappe de fumée smoke patches

Ni vitesse ni bruit drive slowly and quietly

Nids de poules pot holes

P parking

P.T.T. (P et T) post office and telephone

Par temps de pluie during rain

Passage à niveau level crossing

Passage protégé you have right of way

Péage toll

Piétons pedestrians

Pique-nique picnic area

Pique-nique jeux d'enfants picnic area with children's playground

Piste cyclable cycle track

Poids lourds heavy vehicles

Priorité à droite give way to traffic coming from your right

Prochaine sortie next exit

Prudence take care

Rainurage grooves in road

Ralentir slow down

Rappel reminder (accompanied by instruction: e.g. speed limit)

Renseignements information

Respectez les feux obey traffic lights

Risque de brouillard possible fog

Risque d'inondation flooding risk

Risque de verglas possible risk of ice (usually 'black ice') on road

Route barrée road closed

Route bombée badly cambered road (usually bumps in road)

Route glissante slippery road

Sens interdit no entry

Sens unique one-way street

Serrez à droite keep to the right

Servez-vous help-yourself (petrol – gasoline)

Signal automatique automatic signal

Sortie exit

    de camions lorries emerging

    de carrière quarry exit

    d'engins machinery or plant emerging

    de secours emergency exit

    d'usine factory exit

    de véhicules traffic exit

Stationnement alterné semi-mensuel parking alternates half-monthly

Stationnement génant park 'tidily' – do not obstruct

Stationnement interdit no parking

Super petrol – gasoline (4 star)

Toutes directions all directions

Travaux roadworks

Travaux cachent les hommes roadworks obscuring men

Traversée de véhicules vehicles crossing the road

Trou hole in the road

Troupeaux cattle

Trous en formation holes developing

Un train peut en cacher au autre (seen at level crossings) one train may be concealing another coming in the opposite direction

Véhicules lents slow vehicles

Véhicules lents serrez à droite slow vehicles keep to the right

Véhicules lents voie de droite slow vehicles use right hand lane

Vendange grape harvesting

Vent latéral cross wind

Vent violent strong cross winds

Verglas fréquent often icy

Virages bends

Virages en épingle à cheveux hairpin bends

Virages en d'envers bends with opposite or reverse camber

Virages sur (km) bends for (km)

Voie sans issue no through road

Zône bleue parking for permit (disc) holders only in a 'blue zone' (you need a 'disc' obtained locally from newsagents)

Do

drive on the right

wear seat belts and put under-tens in the back seat

take a red warning triangle for emergency breakdowns

adjust your headlights for right-hand driving

take a complete set of spare bulbs for your car

give priority to vehicles coming from the right – especially at roundabouts – unless road markings or signs indicate otherwise

observe speed limits:

    built-up areas 60 kmh – 37 mph

    ordinary roads 90 kmh – 56 mph (if **wet** 80 kmh – 50 mph)

    dual carriageways and toll-free motorways 110 kmh – 68 mph (if **wet** 80 kmh – 50 mph)

    all motorways 130 kmh – 81 mph (if **wet** 110 kmh – 68 mph)

Do not

stop on *any* road unless you can pull right off the carriageway

drive with a provisional licence – or if under 18 years old

General Notes

Telephone
Making phone calls within France
If you ring ahead to any hotel or restaurant, always remember to dial **16** (the French internal code) before you continue with the area code (shown in brackets in *French Leave*) and the establishment number.
Making phone calls to other countries
If you ring abroad, dial **19** to first obtain an overseas line but then **wait** until you hear a continuous tone before dialling the country code you need. (For U.K. calls: always drop the 0 from the STD code you are ringing.)

Maps
I recommend you use the Michelin yellow maps of France (scale 1 cm for 2 km) – particularly the new '200' numbered series – or the Institut Géographique National (IGN) *série verte* maps (scale 1 cm for 1 km) or the *série rouge* maps (scale 1 cm for 2.5 km) for the regions you are touring. Each regional introduction in this guide indicates which maps are needed. Each hotel and restaurant entry also indicates on which Michelin yellow map it is sited – usually the '200' series number, where applicable.

Guides
Michelin Green Guides provide invaluable information on the various regions covered by this book. I tell you which Green Guides apply to each of the *French Leave* regions; there are 19 in total, though only seven are in English. I also recommend the annual *Logis de France* Guide (contact the French Tourist Offices – details below – for information on this publication). Also use the annual *Bison Futé* (Clever Buffalo) map – published, in May, by the French Ministry of Transport. It shows traffic-free, bypass routes throughout France and is available, free of charge, from large garages in France or from AA port offices in the U.K. The Tourist Offices will also supply further detailed literature on all the regions of France. In France, get used to asking for advice on local touring matters at the *Syndicat d'Initiative* (Tourist Office) in each town.

Novotels
Over the years I have used many of the hotels owned by Novotel; some of them are in this edition of *French Leave*. Others are worth bringing to your attention – all are modern, outside large towns and are easy to find; but please note I **do not** recommend their simple restaurants – usually grills. Here are eight additional Novotels: Chamonix; Dijon (at Marsannay-la-Côte, south of the town); Ferney-Voltaire (in France and alongside Geneva Airport); Lille (at Lomme on the autoroute to Dunkerque); Lyon Nord (at Dardilly, west of the A6); Narbonne; Ile d'Oléron (at St-Trojan-les-Bains); and at Toulouse (west of the town, near the airport).
Novotel reservations
These can be made in the U.K. by phoning 01-724-1000 or 01-499-0734; in the U.S. by phoning Los Angeles (213) 649-2121 or New York (212) 354-3722.

Other Chiltern House publications
France à la Carte
is an unusual guide that brings together, under themed headings, the many treasures of France. 66 pages of maps help you identify over 1200 separate locations. The guide is still available.
Hidden France
was published as a limited edition in 1983. You may still find a copy or two in bookshops.

List of French Tourist Offices
London W1V 0AL, 178 Piccadilly
New York (N.Y. 10020), 610 Fifth Avenue
Chicago (Illinois 60611), 645 North Michigan Av – Suite 430
Dallas (Texas 75258), World Trade Center 103, 2050 Stemmons Freeway, P.O. Box 58610
Beverly Hills (Cal. 90212), 9401 Wilshire Boul
Montréal (P.Q. H3H 1E 4), 1840 Ouest, Rue Sherbrooke
Toronto (M5H 2W9 Ont.) 372 Bay St – Suite 610